OVERCOMING DYSLEXIA

OVERCOMING DYSLEXIA

A New and Complete
Science-Based Program for
Reading Problems at Any Level

Sally Shaywitz, M.D.

Alfred A. Knopf New York 2003

THIS IS A BORZOI BOOK
PUBLISHED BY ALFRED A. KNOPF

Copyright © 2003 by Sally Shaywitz, M.D.

All rights reserved under International and Pan-American Copyright
Conventions. Published in the United States by Alfred A. Knopf,
a division of Random House, Inc., New York, and simultaneously
in Canada by Random House of Canada Limited, Toronto.
Distributed by Random House, Inc., New York.
www.aaknopf.com

Knopf, Borzoi Books, and the colophon
are registered trademarks of Random House, Inc.

Owing to limitations of space, all acknowledgments for permission to
reprint previously published material may be found following the index.

Library of Congress Cataloging-in-Publication Data
Shaywitz, Sally E.
Overcoming dyslexia : a new and complete science-based program
for reading problems at any level / Sally Shaywitz. — 1st ed.
p.   cm.
Includes bibliographical references and index.
ISBN 0-375-40012-5 (alk. paper)
1. Reading disability.   2. Dyslexia.   3. Reading—Remedial teaching.
4. Dyslexic children—Education.   I. Title.
LB1050.5 .S42 2003
371.91'44—dc21   2002040621

Manufactured in the United States of America
First Edition

For my children, Adam, Jonathan, Diana, and David,
who give so much to me,

and

for Bennett, who is my life

Contents

Note to the Reader   *ix*

Part I   The Nature of Reading and Dyslexia

1	The Power of Knowing	3
2	The Historical Roots of Dyslexia	13
3	The Big Picture: Who Is Affected and What Happens over Time	25
4	Why Some Smart People Can't Read	36
5	Everyone Speaks, but Not Everyone Reads	45
6	Reading the Brain	59
7	The Working Brain Reads	71

Part II   Diagnosing Dyslexia

8	Early Clues to Dyslexia	93
9	Later Clues to Dyslexia	102
10	Should My Child Be Evaluated for Dyslexia?	120
11	Diagnosing Dyslexia in the School-Age Child	131
12	Identifying the At-Risk Child	142
13	Diagnosing Bright Young Adults	150

Part III   Helping Your Child Become a Reader

14	All Children *Can* Be Taught to Read	169
15	Helping Your Child Break the Reading Code	176

Contents

16 Helping Your Child Become a Reader   198

17 Helping Your Child Become a Skilled Reader   230

Part IV   Overcoming Dyslexia:
Turning Struggling Readers into Proficient Readers

18 Sam's Program: A Model That Works   251

19 Teaching the Dyslexic Child to Read   261

20 Helping Adults Become Better Readers   288

21 Choosing a School   294

22 Protecting and Nourishing Your Child's Soul   309

23 Accommodations: Building a Bridge to Success   314

Epilogue: A Person Like *That* . . .   345

Notes   367

Acknowledgments   395

Index   399

Note to the Reader

This book is for anyone who cares about reading and wants to understand and help those with reading difficulties. In the course of giving lectures, publishing scientific articles, and appearing on radio and television, I have heard countless stories about children who struggle to read, bright adolescents who read slowly and avoid the printed page, and accomplished adults for whom reading remains an elusive goal. I am repeatedly asked, "Can you help me?" Happily, the answer is a resounding yes! As a result of extraordinary scientific progress, reading and dyslexia are no longer a mystery; we now know what to do to ensure that each child becomes a good reader and how to help readers of all ages and at all levels.

I see *Overcoming Dyslexia* as a trusted source to which you can turn for information, for advice, for guidance, and for explanation. Here I have tried to bring together and synthesize all the relevant elements that can help solve the dyslexia puzzle—science, education, and public policy. In part, I hope to enrich the reader's perspective by placing dyslexia and the advances in brain science within a historical context, sharing with the reader the centuries-old quest for the location of the mind that has now culminated in our ability to "see" reading in the brain itself.

At last we know the specific steps a child or adult must take to build and then reinforce the neural pathways deep within the brain for skilled reading. For both younger and older adults who are dyslexic, I offer here a means of learning not only what science teaches us about their needs, but how to access their strengths as well.

If you care about reading and dyslexia, it is important for you to know that we have entered a new era in which there is now a science of reading. It is an era of enormous hope.

Sally Shaywitz, M.D., October 2002

Part I

The Nature of Reading
and Dyslexia

1

The Power of Knowing

This book is about reading—an extraordinary ability, peculiarly human and yet distinctly unnatural. It is acquired in childhood, forms an intrinsic part of our existence as civilized beings, and is taken for granted by most of us. The unspoken belief is that if, as a child, you are sufficiently motivated and come from a home in which reading is valued, you will learn to read with ease. But as with many other assumptions that appear to make intuitive sense, the assumption that reading comes naturally and easily to all children is simply not true. A substantial number of well-intentioned boys and girls—including very bright ones—experience significant difficulty in learning to read, through no fault of their own. This frustrating and persistent problem in learning to read is called *dyslexia*.

Most children look forward to learning to read and, in fact, do so quickly. For dyslexic children, however, the experience is very different: For them, reading, which seems to come effortlessly for everyone else, appears to be beyond their grasp. These children, who understand the spoken word and love to listen to stories, cannot decipher the same words when they are written on a page. They grow frustrated and disappointed. Teachers wonder what they or the child might be doing wrong, often misdiagnosing the problem or getting bad advice. Parents question themselves, feeling alternately guilty and angry.

It is for these parents, teachers, and children that I have written this book. Exhilarated by new scientific discoveries about reading and

3

dyslexia, and frustrated by the relative lack of dissemination and practical application of these remarkable advances, I want to share with you all that I know about the science of reading. I want to make it very clear that it is now possible with a high degree of accuracy to identify children who have dyslexia early on and then treat and remediate their difficulties, helping them learn to read. We can also do more than ever before for teenagers, young adults, and older adults.

As virulent as any virus that courses through tissues and organs, dyslexia can infiltrate every aspect of a person's life. It is often described as a *hidden* disability because it was thought to lack visible signs, but dyslexia is hidden only from those who do not have to live with it and suffer its effects. If you have a broken arm, an X ray provides visible evidence; if you are diabetic, a blood glucose measurement confirms it. Heretofore, reading difficulties could be explained away in any number of ways. Now, however, men and women with dyslexia can point to an image of the brain's internal workings, made possible by new brain imaging technology, and say, "Here. Look at this. This is the root cause of my problem." We now know exactly where and how dyslexia manifests itself in the brain.

The harsh realities of the day in and day out experience of living with dyslexia can often clash dramatically with the perceptions of those teachers, administrators, acquaintances, and self-appointed opinion makers who question the very existence of the disorder that holds so many captive. Some still claim that dyslexia doesn't exist. They ascribe children's reading problems entirely to sociological or educational factors and totally deny the biology. Those who question the validity of dyslexia declare that there is no scientific evidence that supports either a biological or a cognitive basis for the disorder and contend that students with dyslexia reap the benefits of special treatment associated with their misdiagnosis.

George,* a student at the University of Colorado, described dyslexia as "the beast," an unknown predator that silently stalks him, continually disrupting his life. Not knowing why causes him great pain, including grades on examinations that do not reflect the hours he spends studying or his considerable fund of knowledge or his high level of intelligence.

---

* Throughout this book I have changed the names and some identifying characteristics of many individuals in order to maintain their confidentiality. All those who are well known to the public are identified by their real names.

George wants to see "the face of the beast," to understand why this is happening to him. In addition to this deep desire to comprehend the nature of the mysterious problem enveloping him, he harbors the fear of being found out and being severely embarrassed as a dyslexic. The hidden nature of dyslexia—not knowing what to expect or when the difficulty will manifest itself—fills George with apprehension: "It's as if it is lying there, waiting for me to make a wrong move, and then all of a sudden it's there, taunting me again."

This all-too-common state of affairs is now unnecessary. We know why dyslexics, no matter how bright and motivated, experience reading difficulties. Dyslexia is a complex problem that has its roots in the very basic brain systems that allow man to understand and express language. By discovering how a disruption in these fundamental neural circuits for coding language gives rise to a reading impairment, we have been able to understand how the tentacles of the disorder reach out from deep within the brain and affect not only how a person reads but surprisingly, a range of other important functions as well, including the ability to spell words, to retrieve words, to articulate words, and to remember certain facts. For the first time since dyslexia was initially described more than a century ago, scientists can see the "face of the beast," and we are now well on our way to taming and taking command of it.

I remember spending hours trying to convince Charlotte, a first-year law student who is dyslexic, to seek accommodations for her upcoming final exams. Charlotte is brilliant but is an incredibly slow reader who needed more than the allotted time. Her professors respected her, and she was sure to make Law Review—unless, she thought, it become known that she was dyslexic. With all the stereotypical views of dyslexia, she reasoned, her professors would have second thoughts about her abilities. Charlotte anguished over the decision: "If I take extra time, they'll all think I don't deserve my grade and that I'm really not so smart. If I don't take the extra time, I'll never finish." For Charlotte and others like her, so-called special treatment is a cruel irony.

I am often asked to lecture about dyslexia, and each time I speak I am asked: Where can I read about what you have just said? Where can I get this information? Have you a book to recommend?

I have written this book in response to these questions and all the other questions I never had time to answer. I want to lift the barrier of ignorance surrounding dyslexia and replace it with the wonderful comfort of knowledge. I want to empower each and every parent to know, first, what is best for your child and, second, what you can do to ensure that he or she becomes a reader.

With this book I want to bridge the enormous chasm that exists between what we are learning in the laboratory and what is being applied in the classroom. The field of neuroscience is exploding. Recent advances in our understanding of the brain mechanisms underlying reading are nothing short of revolutionary. Alas, much of the time this new information appears to be a well-kept secret. In an era when we can image the brain as an individual reads and literally see the brain at work, it is unacceptable to have children and adults struggling to read when they could benefit from what modern neuroscience has taught us about reading and dyslexia.

As a working scientist who has wrestled with the conundrum of dyslexia for more than two decades, I want to see this explosion of knowledge put to use. As a physician specializing in learning disorders, I have cared for dyslexic children for more than two decades, and it is these boys and girls and their parents who have served as the inspiration for all my work. In science there is often interest in the theoretical questions surrounding a disorder but far less interest in the clinical entity itself. Similarly, there are often insightful physicians who understand the clinical disorder and its effect on the human condition but who are far less familiar with the latest scientific developments. As a physician-scientist I know that in order to help children and adults with dyslexia most effectively, we need the contributions of both of these often disparate worlds of knowledge. So another of my goals in writing this book is to bring to the reader a new level of scientific understanding of dyslexia and to demonstrate how this new knowledge can be applied to help those with the disorder. Once you understand dyslexia, its symptoms and treatment will make sense to you. There will be no mystery, and you will be in charge. You will be able to determine what is best for you, your child, or your student. I have helped many parents understand, clearly and logically, what a reading disability is, how to identify it, what causes it, and, most critically, what can be done to help.

We now know that dyslexia affects one out of every five children—ten million in America alone. In every neighborhood and in every classroom worldwide there are children struggling to read. For many affected children dyslexia has extinguished the joys of childhood.

Caitlyn was almost one of these children. I received a call from her grandfather, Adam, a college friend of mine and now a pediatrician in northern California, asking if I could see his grandchild. Caitlyn, seven years old and just completing first grade, couldn't seem to catch on to reading. As Adam told me, "I always thought she was as smart as a whip. It just doesn't make any sense. Her mother, Peggy, is beside herself. She would do anything for Caitlyn, but neither she nor anyone else seems to know what to do."

Once I met Caitlyn, it became apparent why her mother was so upset. Caitlyn, after two full years of formal schooling, had not yet mastered beginning reading. She had memorized a few words that she could read by rote, but if shown a new word, she could barely begin to sound it out. Instead, she would call out words she knew, which generally had no relation to the word on the page. Sometimes she knew the first letter; for example, when shown the word *boy,* Caitlyn blurted out *bat.* Overall, out of twenty-four words that a first grader should have mastered, Caitlyn knew four. Perhaps most frustrating to Peggy was the attitude of the school. The principal acted as if Peggy had some unspecified emotional problems; the school guidance counselor suggested that she was an overly anxious mother. But no one at the school seemed to be doing anything to address Caitlyn's lack of progress in reading. All her school reports spoke of her good behavior, noting that she was doing "good for someone at her level." "Now," Peggy asked, "what does that mean?" Peggy's requests for meetings with school personnel were ignored or subjected to lengthy delays; the few conferences that were held focused more on Peggy's "emotional needs" than on Caitlyn's academic needs. Peggy began to question herself, but as she watched her once cheerful daughter grow increasingly more withdrawn, she knew she was not imagining Caitlyn's difficulties.

The breaking point came during Caitlyn's seventh birthday party. Peggy had worked hard to make it special. All through the party Caitlyn kept asking, "When do I get to blow out my candles?" Suddenly the room was darkened, and Peggy entered with a cake that had seven candles sparkling brightly. Caitlyn ran over to the table, climbed up on a chair, and bent over the cake. She closed her eyes tightly, concentrated very hard, and then blew out all the candles. Then she ran up the stairs to her bedroom and closed the door. Peggy found Caitlyn on her bed with her favorite storybook, *Good Night Moon,* on her lap. Tears streamed down her face. "You said I would get any wish I wanted, but you were wrong. My wish didn't come true." Caitlyn still could not read any of the words on the page.

Caitlyn, of course, is dyslexic. She had difficulty pronouncing long names and trouble finding the right word to say. She had long pauses and many *um*'s when she was speaking. Her inability to identify some of the sounds of the letters of the alphabet persisted. All these symptoms were consistent with the results of a series of tests designed to determine if a young child is dyslexic. I sat down with Peggy and talked to her at length about Caitlyn and dyslexia. I knew from experience how important it was for Peggy to understand, at the most basic level possible, what a diagnosis of dyslexia meant for her daughter. I knew that once Peggy grasped that, she would become a powerful and highly effective advocate for her child.

Peggy and Caitlyn returned to California with not only a diagnosis but, most important, a plan of action, a detailed program designed to overcome Caitlyn's reading difficulty. Peggy now knew why Caitlyn could not read and knew exactly what needed to be done to fix that. Equally important, Peggy was also aware of Caitlyn's significant strengths and how these could be called into play to help her read.

Peggy followed through on our plan. She made sure that her daughter received the specific reading instruction she required. After a year, Caitlyn had made dramatic progress. No longer a little girl for whom reading was an unfathomable mystery, Caitlyn was now a self-assured young lady who understood how printed letters represent the sounds of spoken words. She could read, if not perfectly.

Caitlyn was proud of her gains. She had overcome her old nemesis— reading and pronouncing words she had never before encountered. She was able to confidently pronounce one word after another, even difficult words. "*Sk, sk-oo-oo-l, school,*" she sounded out. "Oh," she said, "I can spell it, too. Wanna see?" Then, very carefully and with great determination, she wrote *s-c-h-o-o-l* in large, bold letters. Finally, she reached into her backpack, pulled out a book, and proceeded to read with great pride and concentration:

> In the great green room
> there was a telephone
> and a red balloon
> and a picture of
> the cow jumping over the moon.

I was impressed by Caitlyn's progress, but I was also struck by the dramatic change in her mother. I strongly believe that behind the success of every disabled child is a passionately committed, intensely engaged, and totally empowered parent, usually but not always the child's mother. Peggy was a changed person. She was smiling and self-assertive. She was at ease and communicated a quiet but sizable confidence. As she told me:

> Now I am in charge of my daughter's destiny. I never again have to stand there and wait for her school principal to determine my daughter's future. Now that I know, now that I understand, I never have to be at that man's mercy again. I understand her problem, I know what she needs, and I have the power—irrespective of anyone—to act in my daughter's best interests. I feel so in control. I am a different person. To be freed of this absolute dependence on others for your child's entire future is the most exhilarating feeling imaginable. Last year I just didn't know what she needed. Now I know what to ask for her. I am no longer in the dark.

Peggy was an easygoing, soft-spoken mother of four who had become a tiger, a power to be reckoned with when it came to protecting and ensuring Caitlyn's future.

Reading is often the key to realizing a parent's dreams for her child. Early on, children are tracked, and their futures are often laid out within the school setting. In the classroom, reading is king; it is essential for academic success. Reading problems have consequences all across development, including into adult life. This is why it is so important to be able to identify dyslexia accurately and precisely early on and take the appropriate steps without delay to ensure that the child learns to read and to enjoy reading.

Most children who were not able to learn to read or to read well just a few years ago can now become competent readers. Reading may continue to be extremely difficult for a very small number of children, but even they can benefit from the application of the remarkable advances in our understanding of the reading process.

As you'll learn in Chapter 5, reading is not a natural or instinctive process. It is acquired and must be taught. How reading is taught can drastically affect the ease with which a child learns to transform what are essentially abstract squiggles on a page into meaningful letters and then sounds and then words, and then entire sentences and paragraphs. Reading represents a code; specifically, an alphabetic code. About 70 to 80 percent of children are able to break the code after a year of instruction. For the rest, reading remains beyond their reach after one, two, or even more years of schooling. Now we have the key to unlocking the reading code for these children as well.

What is so exciting about our new level of understanding dyslexia is that it explains reading and reading difficulties for all ages and at all levels of education. By identifying the primary or core cognitive weakness responsible for dyslexia, scientists now understand how children acquire the ability to read and why some do not. The model of dyslexia that has emerged can be applied to understanding and treating reading difficulties in children just entering school and in children enrolled in primary and middle grades, as well as in young adults attending high school, college, or even in graduate or professional school. The model has relevance, too, for the legions of adults who go through life without the ability to enjoy reading. These frequently neglected men and women can also benefit from our new understanding of reading. No matter who the child or adult is, what his background is, what kind of home he comes from, what his intelligence level is, or what other influences there are, a person's ability to read is routed through the same pathway deep within the brain. This pathway has been identified. In practical terms this means we know what functional system in the brain is involved. Furthermore, new discoveries now make it possible to (1) identify with a high degree of precision those children who are at the highest risk for dyslexia—even before they develop reading problems, (2) diagnose dyslexia accurately in children, young adults, and adults, and (3) manage the disorder with highly effective and proven treatment programs.

While some children who can't learn to read are identified in the first or second grade, the majority of those with dyslexia are not identified until at least third grade. In fact, it is not unusual for dyslexics to go unrecognized until adolescence or adulthood. Therefore, I will address these questions as well: How do you go about identifying a reading problem in high school or beyond, and what do you do about it? Should the student be offered special accommodations in school and for examinations, and, if so, why? What is the best school setting for a dyslexic child?

According to one father, David, this kind of information "saved" his son. He wrote:

> You saw my son Michael when he was a sophomore in high school and doing very poorly. Michael has turned around academically and emotionally. He is now a confident and secure young man. He has become his own best advocate. He knows what he needs and why. This allows him to speak up for himself and run his own interference. It is Michael who speaks to his teachers, and they respect him for it. This sense of autonomy has rescued my son.
>
> P.S. This summer we are going to visit colleges.

It is never too late. Because the new knowledge is so basic and fundamental, it is applicable to people of all ages. For example, Rachel, a highly successful self-made businesswoman and owner of a flourishing kennel and pet grooming business, was unable to read beyond a fourth grade level.

> It's so embarrassing. Salespeople come around and leave brochures for me. How can I tell them I can't read? Going into a restaurant, I can't read the menu so I'm always reduced to saying, "Hey, what's your special for the day?" During our Passover seders, I simply want to die when it's my turn to read. Now one of my sisters comes to my rescue and begins to read my passage. But in spite of her good intentions, there is always someone new and well meaning at the table who says, "Oh, didn't we just skip Rachel? Shouldn't she have a turn, too?" By now I have memorized a lot of sight words; but show me a new word, and it could just as well be Greek. Can you believe I was so desperate to read, I even ordered a reading program advertised on television? Here was a program for six- and seven-year-olds, and I bought it, but the sad part was that even this program didn't help me.
>
> Now that I'm married and looking forward to having children, I want to be a reader. I want to do the normal everyday things everyone else does: read the newspaper, read a recipe, read the instructions on a bottle of medicine.

Rachel began an intensive new program for adults. When I saw her recently, she reported:

I am going to have a baby. Each day when I get up in the morning, I open my pregnancy book and read about how my baby is growing. And when Joy is born, I am going to be able to read to her, too. It feels so good. I can read!

Caitlyn, Michael, Rachel, and their families experienced the new sense of hope that I want to share with you. I want to take you into my laboratory and show you a revolutionary new kind of science that allows us to watch the brain at work: thinking, speaking, reading, and remembering.

In the pages that follow I will examine both the scientific and the human side of dyslexia. Part I will make clear what dyslexia is and how it evolves over time. I will explain the cognitive basis for dyslexia and what the brain research teaches us about the neurobiology of dyslexia and reading. Substantial progress has been made in identifying the underlying neural mechanisms responsible for reading and for dyslexia. These studies address the most fundamental questions of all, the most abstract and yet compelling challenge facing researchers: How does the mind work and what are the relationships between brain and behavior, thinking and reading, and brain structure and function.

Parts II, III, and IV take what we have learned in the laboratory and apply it to the classroom and the home. I will discuss the impact of science on how we approach, diagnose, and treat children and adults with dyslexia. To ensure that this knowledge is used wisely, I will also discuss practical issues of special concern to many of you, including early diagnosis as well as diagnosis in older children and adults; special considerations in the diagnosis of bright young adults; the most effective treatment for children, young adults, and adults; the relation between dyslexia and standardized tests; the relation between dyslexia and attention deficit/hyperactivity disorder (ADHD); accommodations for older children; and what dyslexia does and does not mean in terms of choosing a career. We will begin by examining how the disorder was discovered more than a century ago.

2

The Historical Roots
of Dyslexia

In the late nineteenth century, physicians in rural Seaford, England, and in the heart of Scotland writing in medical journals described children in their Victorian society who were bright and motivated, came from concerned and educated families, and had interested teachers, but who, nevertheless, could not learn to read. The very innocence of the descriptions and the deep perplexity expressed by the physicians allow us to gain a unique understanding of dyslexia, one that cannot be obtained simply by reading the current literature.

On November 7, 1896, Dr. W. Pringle Morgan of Seaford wrote in the *British Medical Journal* about Percy F., fourteen years old:

> He has always been a bright and intelligent boy, quick at games, and in no way inferior to others his age.
>
> His great difficulty has been—and is now—his inability to read.
>
> He has been at school or under tutors since he was 7 years old, and the greatest efforts have been made to teach him to read, but, in spite of this laborious and persistent training, he can only with difficulty spell out words of one syllable. . . .
>
> I next tried his ability to read figures, and found he could do so easily. He read off quickly the following: 785, 852, 017, 20,

969, and worked out correctly: $(a + x)(a - x) = a^2 - x^2$. . . . He says he is fond of arithmetic, and finds no difficulty with it, but that printed or written words "have no meaning to him," and my examination of him quite convinces me that he is correct in that opinion. . . . He is what [Adolf] Kussmaul [a German neurologist] has termed "word blind." . . .

I might add that the boy is bright and of average intelligence in conversation. His eyes are normal . . . and his eyesight is good. The schoolmaster who has taught him for some years says that he would be the smartest lad in the school if the instruction were entirely oral.

Morgan captures the basic elements underlying what we refer to today as developmental dyslexia. Percy seems to have all the intellectual and sensory equipment necessary for reading, and yet he cannot. The deficit seems only to involve reading letters and words. Percy does quite well in math. As Morgan goes on to say, the numeral 7 is easily discerned and read, but not the written word *seven*.

Morgan was the first to appreciate word-blindness as a developmental disorder occurring in otherwise healthy children. However, the intriguing observation that men and women with good eyesight and strong intelligence could still lack the ability to read had been made by physicians centuries before—but always in adults who had suffered some sort of brain insult. What is perhaps the earliest recorded case of word-blindness dates back to 1676 when a German physician, Dr. Johann Schmidt, published his observations of Nicholas Cambier, a sixty-five-year-old man who lost his ability to read following a stroke. As the concept evolved, cases appearing in the medical literature described men and women like Cambier who had once read normally but then had suffered a stroke, tumor, or traumatic injury that resulted in the loss of the ability to read, a condition termed *acquired alexia*. As more cases were reported, there was an increasing interest in the nature of the reading difficulty and its associated symptoms. For example, in 1872 the distinguished British neurologist Sir William Broadbent reported a case of acquired alexia, noting that his patient also suffered from a profound difficulty in naming even the most familiar objects. When the patient was brought into a London hospital, he said, "I can see [the words], but cannot understand them."

Although Broadbent's contribution was important in providing a descriptive account of acquired reading difficulties, it was not until 1877 that Adolf Kussmaul came to the realization that "a complete text-blindness may exist, although the power of sight, the intellect and the powers of speech are intact." Kussmaul is credited with coining the term *word-blindness* (*wortblindheit*) for this perplexing condition. He narrowed the clinical entity of word-blindness to that of an isolated condition affecting the ability to recognize and read text, but with both intelligence and expressive language intact. Kussmaul then went even further in tracing the cases to lesions in the back of the brain, around the left angular gyrus.

Another German physician, Rudolf Berlin of Stuttgart, further refined our perceptions of these acquired reading problems. In his monograph *Eine besondre Art der Wortblindheit* (A Particular Kind of Word-Blindness), published in 1887, Berlin describes six cases that he personally observed over a period of twenty years. Berlin uses the term *dyslexia* to refer to what he perceives as a special form of word-blindness found in adults who lose the ability to read secondary to a specific brain lesion. If the lesion was complete, there would follow an absolute inability to read, acquired alexia. If the disruption was only partial, however, "there may be very great difficulty in interpreting written or printed symbols (dyslexia)." He conceptualizes dyslexia as a member of the larger family of language disorders called *aphasia* in which there is difficulty in either understanding or producing spoken language, or both. According to Berlin, on March 4, 1863, a Herr B. complained that he had to stop work because

> reading of printed and written characters had become so very difficult to him. . . . He had exactly the same difficulty with [Jaeger] types of all sizes [types of increasing sizes used to assess visual acuity]. . . . There was no pain or discomfort in the eyes. . . . The letters did not become dim or confused—he could simply not read further. . . . Neither the eye nor its muscular apparatus showed any abnormality on the most careful examination.

Imagine what a startling observation this was in mid-nineteenth-century Germany. The very idea that you could have perfect vision and yet could not *see* the words on the page in order to read them, that you could see and read a numeral written in a type as small as Jaeger 1 and yet still not be able to read a simple word in a type as large as Jaeger 16, must have been chilling. It is not surprising, therefore, that cases of word-blindness were often referred for consultation to specialists in the eye and vision—ophthalmologists. And it was a report of acquired alexia by an ophthalmologist at the Glasgow Eye Infirmary, Dr. James Hinshelwood, that served as the catalyst for Morgan's subsequent paper describing congenital word-blindness.

In the December 21, 1895, issue of the prestigious medical journal *The Lancet,* we can read Hinshelwood's report of the case of a highly educated fifty-eight-year-old man, a teacher of French and German, who suddenly awoke one morning to discover that:

> He could not read the French exercise which a pupil gave him to correct. On the previous day he had read and corrected the exercises as usual. Greatly puzzled . . . [and] having summoned his wife, he asked her if she could read the exercise. She read it without the slightest difficulty. He then took up a printed book to see if he could read it, and found that he could not read a single word. He remained in this condition until I saw him. On examining his visual acuity with the test types I found that he was unable to read even the largest letters of the test types. He informed me that he could see all the letters plainly and distinctly, but could not say what they were. . . . I found on examining further with figures that he did not experience the slightest difficulty in reading any number of figures quite fluently and without making any mistakes whatever. He could read figures printed on the same scale as Jaeger No. 1, the smallest of the test types, and from other tests it was evident that there was no lowering of his visual acuity. His inability to read was thus manifestly not due to any failure of visual power. . . . No other mental defect could be ascertained on the most careful examination.

It is easy to appreciate how, after reading this report, Morgan became excited when he encountered virtually the same constellation of symptoms and findings in his young patient Percy F. Although Hinshelwood's report concerns an adult who had once been a good reader, the similarities of the reading difficulties experienced by Percy F., who had never learned to read, and Hinshelwood's patient are impressive. Both had symptoms of word-blindness, and each was unable to read words, but as Morgan and Hinshelwood emphasize, each could read figures—in the smallest of types—and perform mental calculations without any hesitation. Hinshelwood's 1895 report is important for several reasons, not the least of which is the clarity of his clinical description of acquired difficulty in reading as opposed to those problems in reading that are secondary to specific ophthalmologic impairments affecting a person's sight or visual acuity. And, of course, it was Hinshelwood's paper that prompted Morgan in 1896 to submit his own report of word-blindness, but, in this instance, of congenital origin.

It is not at all surprising that, historically, cases of acquired word-blindness in adults were noted prior to cases of congenital word-blindness. Mainly, this is because in acquired cases the occurrence of word-blindness is abrupt; there is a dramatic change—a sudden loss of the ability to read. Acquired word-blindness primarily affects adults and occurs secondary to a brain insult occurring during a person's lifetime. Such insults, whether from a stroke or a tumor, typically affect the left side of the brain, where they may damage multiple brain systems. In addition to problems reading, affected patients may experience muscle weakness on the right side of the body, difficulty pronouncing words, or problems naming objects. In contrast, congenital word-blindness occurs in children and reflects an inherent dysfunction, one present since birth. Here, the clinical picture is more subtle; it evolves gradually as the child meets with continuing problems in reading as he progresses through school. And as we shall see, the reading difficulty may be overlooked for long periods of time. The congenital form is much more circumscribed, affecting primarily reading, sometimes spoken language, but never muscle strength.

From a neurological perspective, the difference in the two forms of the disorder is in the timing of the disruption to the laying down of neural systems within the brain. In the congenital form there is a glitch in the wiring when it is first laid down during embryonic development, and this miswiring is confined to a specific neural system (used for reading). In the acquired condition, a lesion blocks an already working neural system and may extend to impact other systems as well.

Morgan's sentinel report marked a watershed in our appreciation of unexpected reading difficulties in children. There soon came a flurry of reports of similar cases encountered by other physicians, almost exclusively eye surgeons, mostly from Britain but also from Europe, South America, and, eventually, the United States. But no one embraced or understood the significance of the disorder as fully as Hinshelwood did, nor was anyone as committed to bringing the disorder to the attention of as many of his colleagues.

Although Hinshelwood initially reported cases of acquired word-blindness, he soon became absorbed with the congenital form of the condition. By 1912 he had reported in a series of papers and monographs at least a dozen cases of congenital word-blindness. These reports are noteworthy for the similarities shared by the children they describe. For example, in 1900, Hinshelwood details the cases of two children who simply could not learn to read although everything about each of them suggested that they should not only be able to learn to read but should become capable readers as well.

The first case describes an eleven-year-old boy who had been at school for four years before he was dismissed because "he could not be taught to read." According to the boy's father, the child was at the school for a number of years before his problem was even noticed because

> he had such an excellent memory that he learned his lessons by heart; in fact, his first little reading-book he knew by heart, so that whenever it came to his turn he could from memory repeat his lesson, although he could not read the words. His father also informed me that in every respect, unless in his inability to learn to read, the boy seemed quite as intelligent as any of his brothers and sisters.

To demonstrate the child's sharp mind, Hinshelwood describes how he stated the address of his eye clinic and also wrote it on an envelope that the boy's father then misplaced. Fortunately, the young boy's quickness of mind allowed him and his father to keep their clinic appointment. Hinshelwood was quite impressed when the little boy was able to repeat the address after "hearing me state it once."

A second case deals with a ten-year-old boy who did well in every academic subject with the exception of reading. As Hinshelwood comments, "He was apparently a bright, and in every respect an intelligent, boy. . . . In all departments of his studies where *the instruction was oral* he made good progress." The boy's father, a physician, thought the reading problem might be due to some visual defect and thus sought a consultation with Hinshelwood. Careful examination indicated that the difficulty in learning to read was "not owing to any defect of his intelligence or to any diminution of visual acuity. His father noted that the boy never reads for amusement. As his father expresses it, 'It seems to take a great deal out of him.' "

In 1902, Hinshelwood reports two additional cases of young, intelligent children who could not read at all well. One was a ten-year-old girl who worked very hard in school and yet, "after four years of laborious effort," still reads even the most basic book "with the greatest of difficulty." He is impressed by the extraordinary effort that reading requires for this child and by the incredible patience required of someone teaching her, so much so that "on several occasions [even] her mother abandoned the task in despair." He remarks on the isolated nature of the difficulty, pointing out her general intelligence, her good vision, and her ability to do arithmetic.

In the second case, that of a seven-year-old boy, Hinshelwood notes the stress on dyslexic children of trying to read and underscores the importance of patience and support:

> He does not even know all the letters of the alphabet, but if gently told when he was wrong and if given time, as a rule he can name the letters correctly at last. He can repeat the letters of the alphabet rapidly by heart.

Consistent with previous case reports, the boy experiences no difficulties if he is taught orally; in fact, the young man was so good at learning that he, too, "for a time . . . concealed the fact of his disability." The person who perhaps knows the child best sums up his ability:

> His mother says that he is a smart, intelligent boy, even smarter and quicker in many respects than her other children, his one defect, according to her, being that he cannot be taught to read.

The Context of Congenital Word-Blindness

As clinicians, Hinshelwood and his colleagues were more than mere observers or cataloguers of their findings; they were concerned with the implications of the disorder: how long it lasts; how common it is; which groups of children are at highest risk; what treatment is best.

In addition to providing clear descriptions of his patients, Hinshelwood focuses on the central concept that underlies developmental dyslexia: an *unexpected* difficulty in learning to read. From a practical perspective this means that the weakness in reading is isolated and circumscribed, reflecting, according to Hinshelwood, a "local" rather than a generalized cerebral dysfunction. A child who is slow in all cognitive skills would not be eligible for consideration as dyslexic; a dyslexic child has to have some cognitive strengths, not only depressed reading functions.

Having examined an ever-growing number of children with congenital word-blindness, Hinshelwood was convinced that this disorder was far more common than generally appreciated:

> I had little doubt that these cases were by no means so rare as the absence of recorded cases would lead us to infer. Their rarity, I thought, was accounted for by the fact that when they did occur, they were not recognized.

Accordingly, Hinshelwood worked hard to publicize his observations through lectures and published reports. Since the clinical picture is so characteristic, he knew that once a physician was aware of the disorder, diagnosis would easily fall into place.

As I will discuss in detail later, the diagnosis of dyslexia is a clinical one based on the synthesis of information gleaned mainly from observations of the patient and from the history. Hinshelwood and other physicians of his day were able to make this diagnosis based solely on clinical presentation. Both Hinshelwood's and Morgan's reports predated the publication of the earliest version of the first standardized test, the Binet-Simon Intelligence Scale, which became available in 1905.

At about the same time, and after seeing a succession of children with congenital word-blindness, E. Treacher Collins, an eye surgeon at the Royal London Ophthalmic Hospital in Moorfields, England, concluded that the core symptoms of the disorder

> were frequently overlooked and put down to mere stupidity, or some error of refraction, very much to the disadvantage of the individual, because the individual was often blamed, bullied, laughed at, for a defect which was not his fault but his misfortune.

Physicians treating patients with congenital word-blindness were also impressed with its impact on the entire family and across generations. Many commented on the important role played by a family member, usually the wife/mother, in assisting her spouse/child.

> The father . . . who is very involved in writing and has a leading position in industry has to have all his manuscripts corrected in detail by his wife. . . . Out of 5 children, 4 require every written paper to be corrected by their mother.

Things have not changed very much for the patients I see today. For example, poor spelling is one of the telltale signs of dyslexia, and family members must offer support, sometimes in unusual ways. I once received a call from a hospital administrator who was concerned about her young son. She wanted to detect any possible reading difficulty as early as possible because her husband, an executive in a marketing firm, was dyslexic and had difficulty with spelling. To address this situation she has a separate "hot line" in her office so that he can call her to review the spelling in any letters or reports he has to complete.

Above all, Hinshelwood was a physician, a practitioner to whom patients in a state of distress came for help. Congenital word-blindness was more than a curiosity to him; he wanted to make sense of the disorder so that he could help his patients. He realized that treatment meant extending his perspective to include the educational establishment itself. In particular, he recognized the urgent need for early identification of children with congenital word-blindness:

> It is a matter of the highest importance to recognise as early as possible the true nature of this defect, when it is met with in a

child. It may prevent much waste of valuable time and may save the child from suffering and cruel treatment. When a child manifests great difficulty in learning to read and is unable to keep up in progress with its fellows, the cause is generally assigned to stupidity or laziness, and no systematised method is directed to the training of such a child. A little knowledge and careful analysis of the child's case would soon make it clear that the difficulty experienced was due to a defect in the visual memory of words and letters; the child would then be regarded in the proper light as one with a congenital defect in a particular area of the brain, a defect which, however, can often be remedied by persevering and persistent training. The sooner the true nature of the defect is recognised, the better are the chances of the child's improvement.

A model of the complete clinician, Hinshelwood was highly responsive to the needs of his patients. He urged schools to establish procedures for screening populations of children for signs of congenital word-blindness and to provide appropriate teaching to those children identified with the disorder. In 1904 he wrote:

> In these days of scholastic reform, it is evident that there should be a systematic examination of all [these] children by a medical expert who would be able to differentiate the various defects and report as to the best means of dealing with the different groups. In our educational scheme this is a subject which has met with but scant attention, and, in my opinion, special provision for dealing with the education of [these] children on a scientific basis is one of the most crying needs in our present educational methods.

Hinshelwood made specific recommendations for what amounts to special education for children with dyslexia, as in this case:

> On my advice no further attempts were made to teach him in the class, but he was advised to have special reading lessons by himself. The lessons were not to be too long, but were to be repeated frequently during the day at intervals so as to refresh and strengthen the visual impressions made in the first lesson.

This plan was adopted, and succeeded in a degree which surpassed all our expectations. . . .

And in another case,

I advised them to make no further attempt to make him read in class with other boys. His mistakes and difficulties aroused the ridicule of the others, and this excited him and made him worse. I advised frequent short lessons by himself, both at the school and on his return home.

Dr. E. Nettleship, another turn-of-the-century ophthalmologist who saw dyslexic patients, understood the challenges in serving all dyslexics equally:

The detection of congenital word-blindness is easy in the children of well-educated parents, whose children receive much individual attention. It must be much more difficult, both to recognize and deal with, in the children who crowd our Infant Elementary Schools. That the condition had been differentiated, and is receiving attention from medical men, should lead presently to its being dealt with by tutors . . . and by the teachers in all Infant Schools. The education of [these] children, by more or less special methods, is already receiving more attention than formerly. If from amongst such children, those can be sifted whose only, or principal, difficulty is real inability to learn to read, the result cannot but be useful both to the individuals and the community.

Today, as in Nettleship's time, reading difficulties are often overlooked in children from disadvantaged circumstances. It is not that children from enriched backgrounds are "over-identified" as reading disabled but, rather, that far too few poor children with the same difficulties are ever noticed, much less treated, for their reading problems.

Dyslexia was increasingly noted and reported by physicians not only in Great Britain but also in Holland (1903), Germany (1903), and France (1906). Awareness of the disorder soon traveled across the Atlantic to South America (Buenos Aires, 1903) and then to the United States. Here the first report of childhood reading difficulties came in 1905 from a Cleveland ophthalmologist, Dr. W. E. Bruner, followed within a year by a second from a Denver physician, Edward Jackson, who described two cases of "Developmental Alexia (Congenital Word Blindness)." By 1909, E. Bosworth McCready, a Pittsburgh physician interested in congenital word-blindness, was able to locate forty-one reported cases of the disorder worldwide. He noted, "While the majority of cases have been reported by ophthalmologists they have not in a single instance held the ocular conditions responsible for the word-blindness." McCready, too, takes note of the seemingly paradoxical association of dyslexia with creativity and intellectual superiority. He describes one man who "could not read but little in spite of every advantage . . . though he is now a brilliant and prominent member of a profession in which much reading is a *sine qua non*," and another dyslexic who is a judge. Still another is a "writer of verse of unusual excellence." Later, I will discuss the contemporary counterparts of these gifted dyslexics.

These cases of unexpected reading difficulties experienced by so many children and adults, and observed through the eyes of an ever-growing cadre of concerned physicians, can essentially be superimposed on one another; taken together, they create a composite image that is even stronger and sharper than the individual pictures. As such, these case reports represent a valuable legacy: They provide indisputable evidence of the unchanging and enduring nature of the characteristics of dyslexia in children.

When I first came across these reports, I was stunned by the convergence of the historical and contemporary accounts of dyslexia. The basic template provided by these early reports remains intact. In the next chapters I will tell you about extraordinary scientific advances that have added a depth and a precision to our knowledge that was unimaginable just a few years ago.

3

The Big Picture

Who Is Affected and
What Happens over Time

The year 1987 marked a watershed in our quest to understand and more effectively treat reading disability. On August 17, 1987, the Secretary of Health and Human Services, Dr. Otis R. Owen, sent to Congress the long-awaited report of the Interagency Committee on Learning Disabilities (ICLD). The ICLD, chaired by Dr. Duane Alexander and composed of representatives of the different institutes of the National Institutes of Health (NIH) and of the Department of Education, was mandated by Congress to "review and assess Federal research priorities, activities, and findings regarding learning disabilities" and to make recommendations and establish national priorities to increase the effectiveness of research on learning disabilities.

After a comprehensive investigation, the committee declared in "A Report to the U.S. Congress" that the time was right to begin an intensive, all-out drive to understand learning disabilities at a fundamental level. The report called for the establishment of NIH-supported Centers for the Study of Learning and Attention. The National Institute of Child Health and Human Development (NICHD), a branch of the NIH, issued a formal request for proposals for the establishment of such centers. Following an enthusiastic response from more than one hundred

investigators and a rigorous review process, three such centers were chosen: one at the University of Colorado, one at Johns Hopkins University,
and one at Yale University, directed by my husband, Bennett Shaywitz,
and me. Currently, there are four NIH-funded centers specifically dedicated to increasing our understanding of learning disabilities. This program of targeted research has produced unparalleled results,
particularly in our understanding of reading and reading problems.
Because I am most intimately aware of the details of the work at the Yale
Center and because our own research strategy and findings provide
valuable insights into the state of current research in the field, I will use
Yale's studies as a model for discussion.

At first we focused on the basic characteristics of the disorder,
designing a research study aimed at answering these questions: Who is
dyslexic? How many children are affected? Are boys and girls both
affected? What happens to a child with dyslexia over time, and how long
does the problem last? When does the problem go away, or is it with
someone for her entire life? Many of the answers have emerged from
the Connecticut Longitudinal Study, which has been ongoing for almost
two decades.

The Connecticut Longitudinal Study

In 1978, when I was asked to care for patients with reading difficulties, it
was unclear to me just how a physician takes care of children who are
dyslexic. There were many basic questions for which I could find no satisfactory answers; for example: Is dyslexia a common problem or a rare
one? Most of the information about dyslexia was based on studies of children who had already been identified—either by their schools or by a
clinic—as having a reading problem. I thought there might be large
numbers of children sitting at their desks in classrooms all over the country who were unable to read but never accounted for in studies of
dyslexia. To understand the full scope of the problem we needed to
count *all* children with reading problems and not only those who were
already visible and receiving help.

In order to differentiate between children who were experiencing
reading problems and those who were learning to read with ease, it was
necessary to establish exactly what rate of reading development, what
behaviors, and what characteristics are normal for children. That

required studying large numbers of children over an extended period—as it turned out, from the time they entered kindergarten and through primary school, middle school, and eventually high school and even beyond.

To begin the study we selected children who were attending kindergarten in twenty-four randomly chosen Connecticut public schools in the 1983–84 school year. Expert statisticians selected a study sample that represented the geographic and demographic diversity of Connecticut. Since we wanted to develop a more nuanced understanding of each child, we gathered information on a range of qualities that included mental ability, academic achievement, behavior at home and in the classroom, and self-perception. We obtained information from parents, teachers, and the children themselves. The criteria for those to be enrolled in the study were purposely left very broad; we did not want to influence the results by excluding any particular group of children.

We enrolled 445 children in the study. The composition of the group in terms of gender, ethnicity, and race was representative of the population of children entering public kindergarten in Connecticut that year. The participants have been regularly monitored since then. The boys and girls who began this study are now young men and women. Some are attending college, some are in the military or in civilian jobs, and some are in jail. Consistent with national trends, many have married or become parents. Although they now live in twenty-nine different states and have lived in at least seven foreign countries, the vast majority of the original participants (over 90 percent) continue to be committed to the Connecticut Longitudinal Study. Their experiences provide a panoramic view of the process of learning to read. Each of these young men and women is owed a huge debt of gratitude.

Models of Reading and Reading Disability

One of the first questions the Connecticut study addressed was the relation between good and poor readers: Do they form a continuum, or are they two distinct groups? Our educational policy for the identification of reading-disabled children for the past twenty years has been based on the belief that there exists a gap in nature that allows us to separate dyslexic readers from all other readers. "Classification is the art of carving nature at the joints; it should imply that there is indeed a joint there, that one is not sawing through bone," said Scottish psychiatrist R. E. Kendell. Results of our research suggest, however, that there is no natural joint separating dyslexic and good readers.

Evidence from the Connecticut study, as well as from Britain and New Zealand, provides a picture of an unbroken continuum of reading ability and reading disability, a conceptualization referred to as a *dimensional* model by researchers. The contrasting *categorical* model features discontinuity—a natural break in the linkage between good and poor readers. A dimensional model recognizes that there are "no natural joints in nature" to separate one group of readers from another, and that while such cutoff points may be imposed, they are arbitrary.

In truth, the need to refer to disorders, even those that occur along a continuum, by a specific diagnostic label often obscures the fact that many, if not most, disorders in nature occur in gradations and thus conform to a dimensional rather than a categorical model. Hypertension, obesity, and diabetes represent common dimensional disorders. Visual and hearing deficits also occur along a continuum. When blood pressure reaches a certain level, a patient is considered to have hypertension. But individuals just on the other side of the cutoff point, although not labeled as hypertensive, will share many traits in common with those said to have hypertension. For hypertension, as for dyslexia, there is no natural gap that separates affected people from others, and a decision is made based on an artificial cutoff point.

The demonstration that reading difficulties occur along a continuum brings with it important practical educational implications, especially since most current policies for the provision of educational services for reading disability reflect a different view of dyslexia—the categorical view, a cutoff point. As we said in the Connecticut study,

> The notion of dyslexia as a discrete entity has provided the basis for a special-education policy that provides services only to those who satisfy what are seen as specific, unvarying criteria. . . . Children who do not meet these arbitrarily imposed criteria may still require and benefit from special help.

By not recognizing shades of gray represented by struggling children who haven't yet failed enough to meet a particular criterion, schools may be underidentifying many children who will go on to experience significant reading problems. Data from the Connecticut Longitudinal Study indicate that this is more than a theoretic possibility. This is not surprising, however, given the arbitrariness of cutoff points, as *Newsweek* made clear in 1992:

> No one would accuse Kerri Schwalbe of lacking smarts or motivation. The Perrisburg, Ohio, fifth grader has an IQ of 118 and enthusiasm to spare. Unfortunately, she's never had an aptitude for linking letters to sounds. She recognizes many words by their appearance on the page, but at 11 she still can't spell or write. Common sense says she's dyslexic. But [by the standards set] in the state of Ohio . . . Kerri is not entitled to special help. "It's sad," says her mother. "She may waste her time in school until she fails badly enough to qualify as learning [reading] disabled."

Many children who do not "qualify" as dyslexic might still require and benefit from help in reading. In fact, it is often our very brightest children, children like Kerri, who would potentially benefit the most from extra help but are denied critical reading help.

The Prevalence of Dyslexia

Figures provided by schools that indicate the number of children receiving educational services for reading disability provide only a crude approximation of its prevalence. According to U.S. Department of Education statistics, 4.4 percent of children ages six to twenty-one (2.5 million out of an estimated 58 million schoolchildren) are receiving special education services in their schools. Since reading disability is estimated to comprise at least 80 percent of all learning disabilities, we can infer that about 3.5 percent of the school population, or slightly more than 2 million children, are receiving special educational services for a reading disability.

Alternatively, large-scale surveys that directly measure reading proficiency indicate that reading disabilities may be much more prevalent. For example, the National Assessment of Educational Progress (NAEP), carried out by an arm of the U.S. Department of Education, tests thousands of children annually and provides for each grade an indication of how many of these children are reading at or below a level considered standard or proficient for that grade. In a 1998 NAEP survey, 69 percent of fourth graders and 67 percent of eighth graders were reading *below* proficiency levels. Seventy-eight percent of the eighth grade students whose parents were high school graduates were reading below proficiency levels. Particularly striking was the finding that 55 percent of the children of college graduates performed below proficiency levels in reading achievement in the eighth grade. Moreover, according to the NAEP data, as many as 38 percent of fourth graders had not achieved even basic or rudimentary skills in reading. Such shocking data led the Committee on Preventing Reading Difficulties in Young Children of the National Research Council to conclude in 1998: "The educational careers of 25 to 40 percent of American children are imperiled because they don't read well enough, quickly enough, or easily enough."

The Connecticut study indicates that reading disability affects approximately one child in five. From a national perspective this means that there is not a family in America who has not been touched by a reading disability in some way.

There is an important difference in how children are identified as reading disabled by schools and by research studies. For example, in the Connecticut study each child was administered a test of intelligence and a reading test individually. Using this methodology we found that 20 percent of children were reading below their age, grade, or level of ability.

We were curious to know how many of the children identified as reading-disabled by our research study had been identified as such by their schools. Accordingly, for each child in the study we asked school personnel to tell us if that child had been identified as having a reading disability and if he had received special help for a reading problem. We found that less than one-third of the children who were reading below their age, ability, or grade level were receiving school services for their reading difficulty. This strongly suggested undiagnosed problems.

The apparent large-scale underidentification of reading-disabled children is particularly worrisome because even when school identification takes place, it occurs relatively late—often past the optimal age for intervention. Dyslexic children are generally in the third grade or above when they are first identified by their schools; reading disabilities diagnosed after third grade are much more difficult to remediate. Early identification is important because the brain is much more plastic in younger children and potentially more malleable for the rerouting of neural circuits. Moreover, once a child falls behind he must make up thousands of unread words to catch up to his peers who are continuing to move ahead. Equally important, once a pattern of reading failure sets in, many children become defeated, lose interest in reading, and develop what often evolves into a lifelong loss of their own sense of self-worth.

The high prevalence of reading difficulties in the United States is often blamed on too much television watching, lax discipline in the classroom, teaching children to read too early or too late, and too many mothers working. Most likely the problem is not a consequence of specific cultural or regional phenomena but, rather, represents the expression of a more universal vulnerability. Dyslexia occurs in some children and adults living in Europe, Australia, Israel, and North America. At one point it was thought that dyslexia affected only those who spoke alphabetic languages, such as English and German, and that those who spoke languages that are primarily logographic, such as Chinese and Japanese, were not at risk. This assumption has been proven to be false. Researchers have found comparable prevalence rates for dyslexia among American, Japanese, and Chinese children.

In 1996 my article "Dyslexia" appeared in *Scientific American*. The response was overwhelming. From all parts of the globe—Africa, Italy, Sri Lanka, Sweden, Israel, Thailand, England, Argentina—came stories of children and adults who were experiencing problems exactly like those described in the article. Diplomats, scientists, and CEOs have all told me about their difficulties with reading. Clearly, dyslexia knows no boundaries, neither geographic nor ethnic nor intellectual.

We Know Some Girls Are Dyslexic

The diagnosis of dyslexia presents a unique set of circumstances. While biologically based, dyslexia is expressed within the context of the classroom so that its identification often depends on school procedures. Since most research studies of reading-disabled children are based on children who have already been identified by their schools, we wondered if school identification processes might be biased and result in the identification of certain groups of children and the exclusion of others. For example, it had been generally assumed that reading disability was far more common in boys than in girls; studies had indicated that dyslexia affected anywhere from four to six times as many boys as girls. Could this be the result of some systematic bias in school identification procedures?

The data from the longitudinal study were ideally suited to address our question. First, the sample allowed us to examine a representative sample of children rather than only a school-identified group. Second, since every boy and girl participating in the study received individual ability and achievement tests, we were able to apply the criteria for reading disability set forth in the official school guidelines. In principle, then, our identification and the schools' identification of a reading disability were both ostensibly based on the same criteria. Theoretically, both groups were comprised of the same children. The children were in the second and third grades at the time of testing.

Figure 1 shows that according to school identification procedures, the prevalence of reading disability is three to four times more common in boys than in girls. These findings are in agreement with older reports in which the ratio of boys to girls with reading disability has varied from 2:1 to 5:1. A common thread that unites these past studies is that they were all based on samples identified through either clinic or school identification procedures. In contrast, we found no significant difference in the prevalence of reading disability in the boys and girls we identified. In general, when each child in a school or school district is individually tested, researchers report as many reading-disabled girls as boys. Similar

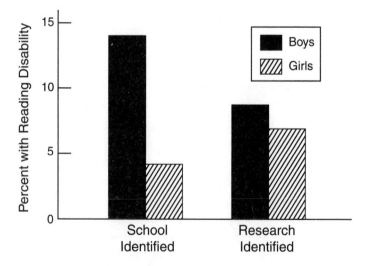

Figure 1. Prevalence of Reading Disability in Boys and Girls

Schools identify many more boys than girls; in contrast, when each child is tested (research identified) comparable numbers of boys and girls are identified as reading-disabled.

results are obtained in family studies in which, following the identification of a child as dyslexic, researchers test all other family members, both adults and children. Consistent, too, are findings from still other studies that indicate girls with reading disability are not as readily identified as boys and, in fact, are often more severely impaired in reading before they are identified for special education services.

Analysis of teacher ratings of the children's behavior revealed why girls are less readily identified than boys. There are significant differences between how teachers rate *typical* boys and girls. Teachers have incorporated a norm for classroom behavior that reflects the behavior of normal girls. As a result, boys who are a bit rambunctious—although still within the normal range for the behavior of boys—may be perceived as having a behavior problem and referred for further evaluation. Meanwhile, the well-mannered little girls who sit quietly at their seats but who, nevertheless, are failing to learn to read are often overlooked. They may be identified as reading-impaired by their school systems much later or perhaps never.

Dyslexia over Time

Dyslexia is not only common, it is persistent. For many years researchers and educators questioned whether dyslexia represented a developmental lag that children somehow outgrew or whether it represented a more persistent deficit in reading. The question is important, for if dyslexia is simply a lag in reading development—a temporary snag—then it will be outgrown, and parents and teachers need not be concerned about early reading difficulties. On the other hand, if dyslexia is not outgrown, there is real urgency in both identifying children early on and ensuring that they receive help as soon as they are identified.

Here, too, we were able to use data provided by the Connecticut Longitudinal Study. Using two complementary strategies, we determined quite decisively that dyslexia is a chronic condition and that it does not represent a temporary lag in reading development. In one approach we compared individual growth rates in reading skills across primary and middle school in two groups of readers: One was a group of boys and girls who had never experienced any reading problems, and the other was a group who met the criteria for reading disability in the early grades. To no one's surprise, we observed that both groups increased

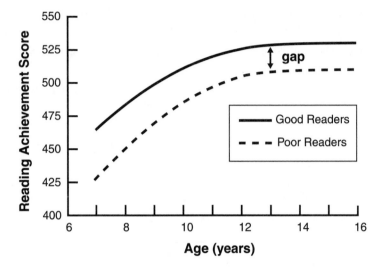

Figure 2. Dyslexia Is Persistent

Over time, reading performance improves in both good readers (upper curve) and poor readers (lower curve). However, the *gap* between the two groups remains.

their reading skills over time. However, and most important, as shown in Figure 2, the gap in reading ability between good and poor readers remains. Poor readers never catch up with their classmates who are good readers. If a child is dyslexic early on in school, that child will continue to experience reading problems unless his is provided with a scientifically based, proven intervention.

Our investigation of the so-called Matthew effect confirmed the persistent nature of reading disability. Advantage accumulates and leads to still further advantage; conversely, initial disadvantage is accentuated over time. This is referred to as the "Matthew effect" after the biblical statement: "To all those who have, more will be given, and they will have an abundance; but from those who have nothing, even what they have will be taken away." The rich get richer and the poor get poorer. Our data showed that poor readers do not become relatively poorer readers. However, the data also provided strong evidence that children who were poor readers in the early school years *remained* poor readers. After school entry, children's reading achievement changes very little relative to their peers. This only confirms that struggling children need help with their reading difficulties very early on.

One final point: About one-third of the children in the longitudinal study were receiving special help, but this help was often very erratic, occurring sporadically and consisting of what might best be described as a Band-aid approach to a gushing wound. In general we found that children received help for very limited periods of time, often from well-meaning but untrained teachers and with methods that did not reflect state-of-the-art, evidence-based instructional strategies (see Chapter 19).

Now that the pernicious nature of dyslexia has been uncovered, we must ensure that our approach to identification and intervention—in terms of age of identification, intensity and frequency of instruction, content of instruction, and skill of the teacher—is consistent with the seriousness of the disorder. In the next chapters I will discuss what we have learned about the basic nature of dyslexia. This knowledge provides the foundation for the most accurate diagnosis and the most effective interventions for reading difficulties.

4

Why Some Smart People
Can't Read

I want you to meet two of my patients, Alex and Gregory. Alex is ten
years old, and Gregory, a medical student, just celebrated his twenty-
third birthday. Their experiences are typical of children and young
adults with dyslexia. You will learn how Alex's and Gregory's seemingly
diverse symptoms—trouble reading, absolute terror of reading aloud,
problems spelling, difficulties finding the right word, mispronouncing
words, rote memory nightmares—represent the expression of a single,
isolated weakness. At the same time you will learn that other intellectual
abilities—thinking, reasoning, understanding—are untouched by dyslexia. This contrasting pattern produces the paradox of dyslexia: profound and persistent difficulties experienced by some very bright people
in learning to read. I am emphasizing the strengths of the dyslexic
because there is often a tendency to underestimate his abilities. The
reading problem is often glaringly apparent while the strengths may be
more subtle and overlooked. Later on I will discuss new insights into
dyslexia that tell us that it represents a very isolated weakness; thinking
and reasoning are intact and perhaps even enhanced.

Alex

In his first years of life, Alex was so quick to catch on to things that his parents were surprised when he struggled to learn his letters in kindergarten. When shown a letter, he would stare, frown, and then randomly guess. He couldn't seem to learn the letter names. In first grade he struggled to link letters with their sounds. By the third grade Alex continued to stammer and sputter as he tried to decipher what was on the page in front of him. Language had clearly become a struggle for Alex. He seemed to understand a great deal, yet he was not always articulate. He mispronounced many words, leaving off the beginning (*lephant* for elephant) or the ends of words, or inverting the order within a word (*emeny* for enemy). Alex had trouble finding the exact word he wanted to say even though it seemed he could tell you all about it. One evening he was trying to explain about sharks living in the ocean:

> The water, the water, lots of water, salty water with big fish, it's a lotion. No, no, that's not what I mean. Oh, you know, it's on all the maps, it's a lotion—ocean, that's what it is—a sea, no big sea, it's an ocean, an ocean!

Looking at this handsome, very serious little boy who could spend hours putting together complex puzzles and assembling intricate model airplanes, his father could not believe that Alex had a problem. Alex, however, became increasingly aware of his difficulty reading and asked more and more frequently why all his friends were in a different reading group. He practiced, he tried, but it just never seemed to come out right.

His parents brought him to the Yale Center for evaluation. We learned that Alex was extremely smart, scoring in the gifted range in abstract reasoning and in logic. His vocabulary was also highly developed. Alex could learn, he could reason, and he could understand concepts at a very high level. Despite these strengths, his performance in reading words was dismal; for example, he was able to read only ten out of twenty-four words on a third grade level. What gave Alex the most difficulty, however, was nonsense words (made-up words that can be pronounced; for example, *gern, ruck*). He struggled to decipher these words. Sometimes he used the first letter to generate a response (such as *glim* for *gern, rold* for *ruck*); at other times it seemed as if he just gave up, making seemingly random guesses. In contrast, Alex was able to read a short passage silently and answer questions about it far better than he was able to read and pronounce isolated single words. In reading a passage silently to himself, Alex made good use of clues such as pictures in the book and the surrounding words; he used them to get to the meaning of sentences and passages that contained words he could not read. "I picture what it says," he explained. However, Alex sparkled when asked to *listen* to a story and then respond to a series of questions, scoring significantly above average. Reading aloud was particularly painful for Alex. He was reluctant to read in front of the class, and it was easy to understand why. His reading was labored; words were mispronounced, substituted, or often omitted entirely. Words that he correctly read in one sentence would be misread in a subsequent sentence. He read excruciatingly slowly and haltingly. Increasingly, Alex would ask to go to the bathroom when it was nearing his turn to read. If called upon, he often acted silly, making the words into a joke or tumbling himself onto the floor and laughing so that he would be sent out of the room.

Poor spelling skills were compounded by his almost illegible handwriting. Letters were large, misshapen, and wobbly. In contrast, Alex's math skills, particularly problem solving and reasoning abilities, were in the superior range. At the close of the testing, Alex diagnosed his own reading problem: "I don't know the sounds the letters make." Furthermore, he told the evaluator that it bothered him that his friends were in a different reading group. Sometimes, he said, this made him very sad. His one wish was to be a better reader, but he didn't know exactly how that would happen.

When I met with Alex's parents, they had many questions: Does he have a problem? If so, what is the nature of the problem? What could be done to help him? Above all, they asked, "Will he be all right?" I reassured them that Alex would not only survive, he would thrive.

Gregory

In the course of my work, I have evaluated for reading disabilities not only hundreds of children but also scores of young adult men and women. Their histories provide a picture of what the future will be for a bright child like Alex who happens to be dyslexic. Gregory was a grown-up Alex. Gregory came to see me after experiencing a series of difficulties in his first-year medical courses. He was quite discouraged.

Although he had been diagnosed as dyslexic in grade school, Gregory had also been placed in a program for gifted students. His native intelligence, together with extensive support and tutoring, had enabled him to graduate from high school with honors and gain admission to an Ivy League college. In college Gregory had worked hard to compensate for his disability and eventually received offers from several top medical schools. Now, however, he was beginning to doubt his own ability. He had no trouble comprehending the intricate relationships among physiological systems or the complex mechanisms of disease; indeed, he excelled in those areas that required reasoning skills. More difficult for him was pronouncing long words or novel terms (such as labels used in anatomic descriptions); perhaps his least-well-developed skill was that of rote memorization.

Both Gregory and his professors were perplexed by the inconsistencies in his performance. How could someone who understood difficult concepts so well have trouble with the smaller and simpler details? I explained that Gregory's dyslexia (he was still a slow reader) could account for his inability to name tissue types and body parts in the face of his excellent reasoning skills. His history fit the clinical picture of dyslexia as it has been traditionally defined: an unexpected difficulty learning to read despite intelligence, motivation, and education. Furthermore, I was able to reassure him that because scientists now understand the basic nature of dyslexia, they have been able to devise highly effective strategies to help those with the disorder. I told Gregory that dyslexia reflects a problem within the language system in the brain. The understanding of the central role of language in reading and, particularly, in dyslexia is relatively recent.

Why Alex and Gregory Have Trouble Reading

Explanations of dyslexia that were put forth beginning in the 1920s and that have continued until recently held that defects in the visual system were to blame for the reversals of letters and words thought to typify dyslexia. Eye training was often prescribed to overcome these alleged visual defects. Subsequent research has shown, however, that in contrast to a popular myth, children with dyslexia are not unusually prone to *see-*

ing letters or words backward and that the deficit responsible for the disorder resides in the language system. These poor readers, like Alex, do have significant difficulty, however, in *naming* the letters, often referring to a *b* as a *d* or reading *saw* as *was*. The problem is a linguistic one, not a visual one.

As noted earlier, dyslexia represents a specific difficulty with reading, not with thinking skills. Comprehending spoken language is often at a very high level, as it was for Alex, as are other higher-level reasoning skills. Dyslexia is a localized problem.

Understanding that dyslexia reflected a language problem and not a general weakness in intelligence or a primary visual impairment represented a major step forward. Further advances have clarified the nature of the language impairment. Dyslexia does not reflect an overall defect in language but, rather, a localized weakness within a specific component of the language system: the phonologic module. The word *phonologic* is derived from the Greek word *phone,* meaning *sound* (as in *phonograph* and *telephone*). The phonologic module is the language factory, the functional part of the brain where the sounds of language are put together to form words and where words are broken down into their elemental sounds.

Over the past two decades a model of dyslexia has emerged that is based on phonological processing—processing the distinctive sounds of language. The phonologic model is consistent both with how dyslexia manifests itself and with what neuroscientists know about brain organization and function. Researchers at the Yale Center and elsewhere have had an opportunity to test and refine this model through reading and, more recently, brain imaging studies. We and other dyslexia researchers have found that the phonologic model provides a cogent explanation as to why some very smart people have trouble learning to read.

The Phonologic Model

To understand how the phonologic model works, you first have to understand how language is processed in the brain. Think of the language system as a graded series of modules or components, each devoted to a particular aspect of language. The operations within the system are rapid and automatic, and we are unaware of them. They are also mandatory. For example, if we are seated at a table in a dining room, we *must* hear what the person at the next table is saying if she is speaking loudly enough. It is nearly impossible to tune language out. That is why it is so difficult to study when others nearby are speaking.

Scientists have been able to pinpoint the precise location of the glitch within the language system (Figure 3). At the upper levels of the language hierarchy are components involved with, for example, semantics (vocabulary or word meaning), syntax (grammatical structure), and discourse (connected sentences). At the lowest level of the hierarchy is the phonologic module, which is dedicated to processing the distinctive sound elements of language. Dyslexia involves a weakness within the language system, specifically at the level of the phonologic module.

The phoneme* is the fundamental element of the language system, the essential building block of all spoken and written words. Different combinations of just forty-four phonemes produce the tens of thousands of words in the English language. The word *cat,* for example, consists of three phonemes: *k, aaaa,* and *t.* Before words can be identified, understood, stored in memory, or retrieved from it, they must first be broken

The Language System:
Reading and Speaking

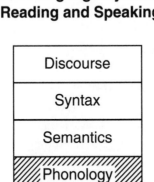

Figure 3. Pinpointing the Core Weakness in Dyslexia

Research pinpoints the weakness at the lowest level of the language system.

* The phoneme is defined as the smallest unit of speech that distinguishes one word from another.

SPEAKING

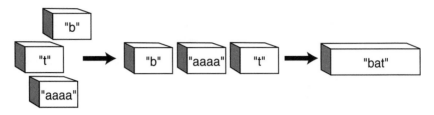

Figure 4. Speaking: Making Words

A speaker retrieves and then orders the phonemes to make a word.

down into phonemes by the neural machinery of the brain. Just as proteins must first be broken down into their underlying amino acids before they can be digested, words must first be broken down into their underlying phonemes before they can be processed by the language system. Language is a code, and the only code that can be recognized by the language system and activate its machinery is the phonologic code.

This is critical for both speaking and reading. Let's first consider speaking (Figure 4). If I want to say the word *bat,* I will go into my internal dictionary or lexicon deep within my brain and first retrieve and then serially order the appropriate phonemes—*b, aaaa,* and *t*—and then I can say the word *bat.*

In children with dyslexia, the phonemes are less well developed. Think of such a phoneme as a child's carved letter block whose face is so worn that the letter is no longer prominent. As a consequence, such children when speaking may have a hard time selecting the appropriate phoneme and may instead retrieve a phoneme that is similar in sound. Think of Alex's experience in retrieving the word *lotion* when the word he was reaching for was *ocean.* Alex knew exactly what he wanted to say but could not retrieve the exact word, so instead he picked a close but not correct phoneme. Alternatively, a dyslexic might order the phonemes incorrectly, and the result might be, as Alex said, *emeny* instead of *enemy.* Such sound-based confusions are quite common in the spoken language of dyslexics.

Not too long ago I received a note from Pam Stock, a learning disabilities teacher "deep in the trenches" in Maine. I smiled when I read what a bright six-year-old dyslexic boy said on a hot summer day. Looking over at his perspiring mother as she struggled in a traffic jam, he remarked, "You know, Mom, it's not the heat, it's the *humanity.*" (The intended word, of course, was *humidity.*) On another occasion a politician greeting his supporters said, "Welcome to this lovely *recession.*" Of course he meant to say *reception.* In each instance the confusion was a phonologic one (that is, based on the *sound* of the word) and did not reflect a lack of understanding of the meaning of the word in question. Unfortunately, such phonologic slips roll off the tongues of dyslexics fairly regularly and are often incorrectly attributed to a lack of understanding.

Reading is the converse of speaking. In reading we begin with the intact printed word on the page: The blocks representing phonemes are all lined up correctly. The reader's job is to convert the letters into their sounds and appreciate that the words are composed of smaller segments or phonemes (Figure 5). Dyslexic children and adults have difficulty developing an awareness that spoken and written words are comprised of these phonemes or building blocks. Think of the little boy who got his first pair of glasses and then said, "I never knew that building was made of red bricks. I always thought its wall was just one big smudge of red paint." Dyslexics perceive words the same way. While most of us can detect the underlying sounds or phonemes in a word—for example, *k*, *aaaa* and *t* in *cat*—children who are dyslexic perceive a word as an amor-

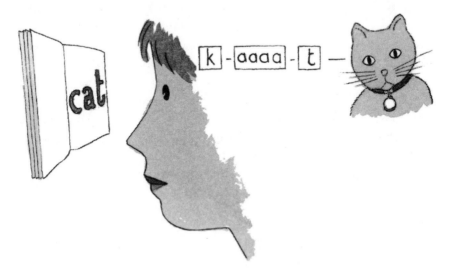

Figure 5. Reading: Turning Letters into Sounds
To read, a child converts the letters into sounds or phonemes.

phous blur, without an appreciation of its underlying segmental nature. They fail to appreciate the internal sound structure of words.

The phonologic model tells us the exact steps that must be taken if a child is to go from the puzzlement of seeing letters as abstract squiggly shapes to the satisfaction of recognizing and identifying these letter groups as words. Overall, the child must come to know that the letters he sees on the page represent, or map onto, the sounds he hears when the same word is spoken.

The process of acquiring this knowledge is orderly and follows a logical sequence. First, a child becomes aware that words he hears are not just whole envelopes of sound. Just as the little boy noted the bricks in the wall, the beginning reader starts to notice that words are made up of smaller segments, that words have parts. Next, the child becomes aware of the nature of these segments, that they represent sounds. He realizes, for example, that in the word *cat* there are three segments of sound, *k*, *aaaa*, and *t*. Then the child begins to link letters he sees on paper to what he hears in spoken language. He begins to realize that the letters are related to sounds he hears in words and that the printed word has the same number and the same sequence of phonemes (sounds) as the spoken word. Finally, he comes to understand that the printed word and the spoken word are related. He knows that the printed word has an underlying structure and that it is the same structure he hears in the spoken word. He understands that both spoken and written words can be pulled apart based on the same sounds, but in print the letters represent these sounds. Once the child has made this linkage, he has mastered what is referred to as *the alphabetic principle*. He is ready to read.

In the next chapter I will discuss the fundamental difficulty that is at the heart of dyslexia and why so many children have problems mastering the alphabetic principle. In later chapters I will focus on how to teach these children most effectively to overcome their difficulties in reading.

5

Everyone Speaks,
but Not Everyone Reads

Prospective readers must master the alphabetic principle in order to learn to read, yet one in five children is unable to do so. Why should developing an awareness that spoken words are made of smaller segments—phonemes—present such a formidable challenge? As you will learn, the answer lies with the very same mechanism that makes speaking so easy.

As linguists Noam Chomsky and Steven Pinker of the Massachusetts Institute of Technology have convincingly argued, spoken language is innate.* It is instinctive. Language does not have to be taught. All that is necessary is for humans to be exposed to their mother tongue. Through neural circuitry deep within our brains, a genetically determined phonological module *automatically* assembles the phonemes into words for the speaker and disassembles the spoken word back into its underlying phonemes for the listener. Thus spoken language, which takes place at a preconscious level, is effortless.

Some linguists like Pinker argue that language can be traced back as many as one million years. John DeFrancis, professor emeritus of Chinese at the University of Hawaii, suggests that it was some fifty thousand

---

* Virtually all humans speak except those who have rare medical conditions such as profound deafness from birth.

years ago that speech emerged as the dominant mode of communication among *Homo sapiens.* Every human society has a spoken language, and man is the only species that communicates by speaking (although there are many other species that communicate using a variety of signals— grunts, screeches, electric shock, odors, whistles, and calls). If a baby is neurologically healthy, there is almost no way she can avoid learning to speak.

Language is open-ended. It is generative. Using phonemes we can create an indefinite number of words and, with these words, an infinite number of ideas. We can tell jokes, we can muse, we can tell a story, we can imagine, we can describe. We can speak in the present, reflect wistfully about the past, or project hopefully into the future.

In contrast, animal communication systems are closed and the signals fixed. They are holistic; they do not come apart and cannot be added to or rearranged to form a new message. With animals there are a limited number of signals, and each signal is yoked to a specific meaning. There is no possibility for novelty or for indefinite variation.

The Particulate Principle

In 1989 linguist William Abler offered a brilliant insight into the language system—what he called the particulate principle of self-diversifying systems. Although this sounds like jargon, the principle itself is elegant in its simplicity. Using biological inheritance as a model, Abler suggested that chemical compounds and human language adhere to the same principles as do combinations of DNA in forming a seemingly endless number of proteins. He reasoned that these natural processes share two basic features: Each has as its core element a "particle," and each is characterized by a hierarchical structure. The particles serve as the building blocks that give rise to open-ended hierarchical systems. For chemicals it is atoms; for genetics it is the nucleotides in DNA; and for language it is the phonemes. At the next level of the hierarchy, the particles are now larger: Atoms combine to form molecules, nucleotides join to form proteins, and phonemes come together to form words.

By using a small number of phonemes, a speaker has the ability to create a seemingly infinite number of words and then sentences and paragraphs. To appreciate the vast number of combinations possible, consider that Shakespeare used 29,066 different words in his complete works (884,647 words in total).

What allows the particulate principle to operate so effectively is the special nature of the particles. Whether they are atoms of sodium, strands (nucleotides) of DNA, or phonemes, they don't change; they maintain their original identity. This means that they are able to combine with each other to form entirely new and larger units, be they compounds, proteins, or words—and yet the particles themselves are not changed in the process. (The advantage of particles over elements that do not retain their identity is shown in Figure 6. If two elements combine and blend together, the result is a mixture—somewhere in between the original two. However, when two particles combine while still maintaining their original properties, the new item formed is unique.) Forming words by combining—but not blending—phonemes brings with it the extraordinary potential to form an indefinite number of words, limited only by the number of combinations. As phonemes combine to form words, and words join together to form phrases and sentences, a larger and an entirely new structure is created at each succeeding level of the hierarchy.

A speaker can generate phonemes very quickly, with rates averaging ten to fifteen phonemes per second. In fact, the pace outstrips the

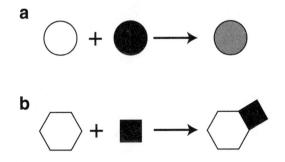

Figure 6. The Advantage of Particles Not Blending

When elements blend as they combine, as in the two circles shown, the end result is a mixture of the two, something in between. On the other hand, when two phonemes (particles) combine, as shown here with the two geometric shapes, they do not blend. Instead, they combine to form something entirely new. Endless combinations are possible, which can produce an endless number of words.

capacity of the listener's own acoustic machinery, which cannot pick up or process a series of incoming sounds that quickly. On the other hand, if the speaker uttered each phoneme very slowly, spoken language would be interminable. A further complication is that the listener has to receive the phonemes at a sufficiently fast pace so that several can be held in short-term memory at the same time and integrated to form the intended words and phrases. Phonemes can be held in the temporary memory storage bin only one or two seconds, or about five to seven unrelated words, before each, like a bubble, vanishes.

Evolution has solved this problem through coarticulation: the ability to overlap several phonemes—while maintaining the integrity of each—into one bubble of sound (Figure 7). As a result of coarticulation, bursts of sounds come at a pace compatible with the auditory system's capacity to process them, and the phonemes arrive at a rapid enough pace to meet the constraints of the short-term memory system.

Critical to the entire process is the fundamental difference between sounds—the sounds of language and the sounds of noise—and the

Figure 7. Coarticulation:
Overlapping Several Phonemes into One Burst of Sound

To say a word, a speaker first retrieves each phoneme and then coartic-
ulates or overlaps one over the other. As shown in this illustration, the three phonemes forming the word *cat* are overlapped into one packet of sound.

innate ability of the phonologic module to distinguish speech from non-speech sounds. Phonemes are presented to the sense organ, the ear and its receptors, disguised in their outer packaging as ordinary bursts of sound. For example, if I were to say the word *cat,* this would appear on an oscilloscope as one pulse of sound—and that is what it is to the listener's ear. However, camouflaged within the packet of sound are three pieces of language: the phonemes *k, aaaa,* and *t.* Once the sound is safely past the hearing machinery, the language system takes over, immediately recognizing the three phonemes as particles of language and processing them accordingly. Here, the language system is different from other systems, such as vision and hearing. The eye receives visual stimuli and the ear acoustic stimuli, but the ear is only a way station for language. Nature has provided a mechanism to allow sound, like a barge towing a valuable cargo, to guide the phonetic particles past the ear and into the safe haven of cerebral neural circuits specialized for receiving language. When the ear receives the parcel of sound, the specialized phonologic module in the brain immediately activates and recovers the phonemes contained within each pulse of sound, and automatically translates the sound into particles of language. The listener receives the exact message sent by the speaker.

What makes human speech possible as a means of communication is the coarticulation referred to earlier. In producing a word, the human speech apparatus—the larynx, palate, tongue, and lips—automatically coarticulates, that is, compresses and merges the phonemes together. As a result of coarticulation, several phonemes are folded into a single pulse or bubble of sound, without any overt clue to the underlying segmental nature of speech. Consequently, spoken language appears to be *seamless.* It is as if coarticulation has lacquered over any fissures or gaps between the individual phonemes so that what is presented to the listener is a smooth, seamless stream of speech.

Reading Is More Difficult Than Speaking

The effortless and seamless nature of spoken language has everything to do with why reading is so hard for dyslexic children. Although both speaking and reading rely on the same particle, the phoneme, there is a fundamental difference: *Speaking is natural, and reading is not.* Herein lies the difficulty. Reading is an acquired act, an invention of man that must be learned at a conscious level. And it is the very naturalness of speaking that makes reading so hard.

Just as our lungs breathe in and out for us and the chambers of our hearts contract rhythmically, highly refined neural circuitry within our brains allows us to speak and to listen without conscious thought or effort. For spoken language the phoneme comes all ready to go. This is the gift that evolution has delivered to man. Not so for reading. While reading, too, relies on the phonologic code, the key to unraveling it is not so readily apparent and can only be accessed with effort on the part of the beginning reader.

Profound differences distinguish reading from speaking. Not only are reading and writing relatively recent human accomplishments (man has had a written language for only about five thousand years), but reading is still relatively rare in the world. Reading is not built into our genes; there is no reading module wired into the human brain. In order to read, man has to take advantage of what nature has provided: a biological module for language. For the object of the reader's attention (print) to gain entry into the language module, a truly extraordinary transformation must occur. The reader must somehow convert the print on a page into a linguistic code—the phonetic code, the only code recognized and accepted by the language system. However, unlike the particles of spoken language, the letters of the alphabet have no inherent linguistic connotation. Unless the reader-to-be can convert the printed characters on the page into the phonetic code, these letters remain just a bunch of lines and circles totally devoid of linguistic meaning. This essential distinction between written and spoken language was best captured by linguist Leonard Bloomfield: "Writing is not language, but merely a way of recording language by visible marks." The written symbols have no meaning of their own but, rather, stand as surrogates for speech or, to be more exact, for the sounds of speech.

Beginning readers throughout the world must learn how to decipher print, how to convert an array of meaningless symbols on paper so that they are accepted by a powerful language machinery that recognizes only the phonologic code. I remember observing a visiting student as she tried to use her Italian lire to obtain a Coke from a vending machine at Yale. Although she literally had a pocketful of lire, her currency was essentially worthless in a machine that accepted only American coins. And so it is with reading: The most eloquent of written prose is rendered meaningless if it cannot be transformed into the phonetic code recognized by that reader's language module.

Breaking the Code

The very first discovery a child makes on his way to reading is the realization that spoken words have parts. Suddenly a child appreciates that the word he hears comes apart into smaller pieces of sound; he has developed *phonemic awareness.* ° And a remarkable discovery it is. There is little reason for a child to notice this. Since spoken language is built into our genes and takes place automatically, its segmental nature is not part of our consciousness. Furthermore, as a result of coarticulation, spoken language is seamless, further obscuring its underlying segmental nature. But once a child becomes aware of the segmental nature of spoken language, he has the basic elements—the particles of spoken language, phonemes, and their sounds—to which he can now attach the appropriate written letters. Letters linked to phonemes are no longer meaningless marks on paper but, like Cinderella, have been transformed into something truly spectacular: language. Translated into the phonetic code, printed words are now accepted by the neural circuitry already in place for processing spoken language. Decoded into phonemes, words are processed automatically by the language system. The reading code is deciphered.

Seventy to 80 percent of American children learn how to transform printed symbols into a phonetic code without much difficulty. For the remainder, however, written symbols remain a mystery. These children are dyslexic. They, like Alex, cannot readily convert the alphabetic characters into a linguistic code.

A young child *must* develop phonemic awareness if he is to become a reader. That is to say, he must understand that spoken words are made up of smaller units of speech sounds, phonemes. And, of course, it is these very same phonemes to which the letters of the alphabet must attach if the written word is to be brought into the language system. All readers—dyslexic readers included—must take the same steps. The dif-

---

° Phonemic awareness refers to the ability to notice, identify, and manipulate the individual sounds—phonemes—in spoken words.

ference is simply in the effort involved and the time it takes to master the alphabetic principle.

Of course, children vary greatly in their ease of developing phonemic awareness. For some children the process is speedy and apparently effortless; exactly how these children develop phonemic awareness is currently not known. Surely exposure to a rich language environment, one in which children are given lots of opportunity to hear and to play with spoken words—for example, to hear rhymes and to practice rhyming songs—facilitates this awareness.

In dyslexic children a glitch within the language system—at the level of the phonologic module—impairs the child's phonemic awareness

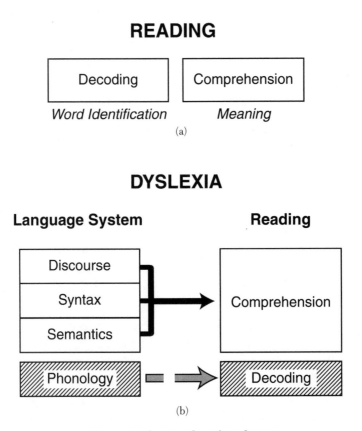

Figure 8. The Paradox of Dyslexia I

a. Two major components of reading: decoding and comprehension
b. A phonologic weakness interferes with decoding; higher abilities necessary for comprehension are intact

and, thus, his ability to segment the spoken word into its underlying sounds. The phonemes are less sharply defined. As a result of this weakness, children have difficulty breaking the reading code.

The reading process consists of two major components: decoding, which results in word identification, and comprehension, which, of course, is related to meaning (Figure 8a). When, as in Figure 8b, we consider the language module and the components of reading side by side, it becomes clear how a bright child like Alex could have trouble reading single words and yet comprehend what he is reading at a much higher level.

A phonologic weakness at the lowest level of the language system impairs decoding. At the same time, all the cognitive equipment, the higher-order intellectual abilities necessary for comprehension—vocabulary, syntax, discourse (understanding connected text), and reasoning— are intact. All the equipment that Gregory and Alex and other dyslexics require for understanding, for forming concepts, for comprehending the written text is there, unaffected by the phonologic deficit. The richness and depth of their intellectual abilities explain why identification is so often delayed in bright, dyslexic children. As one of my patient's third grade teacher remarked, "Madison is so smart, she knows the answers to the most difficult questions. She is the first one in our class to catch on to the most abstract concepts. I could never imagine that she had any problem at all." Luckily, we can now effectively treat a phonologic weakness; while, ironically, the complex reasoning and sophisticated thinking skills that dyslexic children often possess are almost impossible to teach. (My husband theorizes that since the basic circuitry for linking letters to sounds is disrupted in dyslexic readers, they develop and come to rely on other neural systems, not only for reading but for problem solving as well. Such individuals may see things in a different and perhaps more creative way and are able to think out of the box. In the Epilogue you will meet some of these people.)

We can now understand what happens to Alex and other dyslexic readers as a result of a phonologic weakness. According to the phonologic hypothesis, a circumscribed, encapsulated deficit in phonologic processing interferes with Alex's decoding, preventing word identification. This basic weakness in what is essentially a lower-level language function blocks access to higher-order language processes and to gaining meaning from text.

As shown in Figure 9, although the language processes involved in

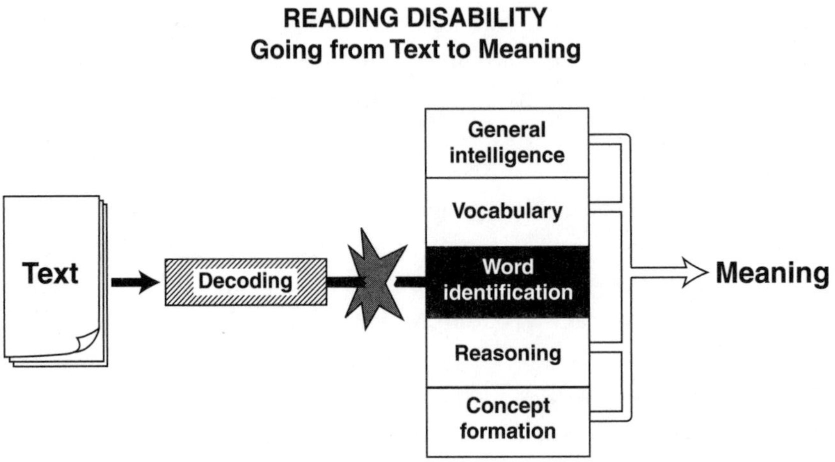

READING DISABILITY
Going from Text to Meaning

Figure 9. Going from Text to Meaning

A phonologic weakness blocks decoding, which in turn interferes with word identification. This prevents a dyslexic reader from applying his higher-level skills to get at a word's meaning. But even if he can't identify the word specifically, he can apply these higher-level skills to the context around the unknown word to guess at its meaning.

comprehension and meaning are intact in someone like Alex, they cannot be called into play because they generally can be accessed only after a word has been identified. Now we can understand why Alex, with a superior intelligence, excellent vocabulary, and boundless curiosity, cannot decipher even the simplest of words or read a passage aloud. When reading connected text silently, Alex can put his ability to think and to reason to work and use the context around the word to guess at its meaning even if he can't quite decipher a specific word. Recall that Alex did much better when asked to read a passage to himself and answer questions than when he was asked to read isolated words. And it is best for him when he can *listen* to a story because he can use all his higher-level thinking skills to follow the narrative and answer questions about it.

The impact of the phonologic weakness is most obvious in reading, but it can also affect speech in other predictable ways. Evidence began accumulating more than two decades ago that the core difficulty in dyslexia was getting to the sound structure of the spoken word. Researchers showed that between ages four and six children develop an awareness that words come apart. By age six most children (about 70 percent) can count the number of sounds (phonemes) they hear in small words. By this time many children have also had at least one full year of schooling, including instruction in reading. Reading and phonemic awareness are mutually reinforcing: Phonemic awareness is necessary for reading, and reading, in turn, improves phonemic awareness still further. The 30 percent of children who, after a year of reading instruction, still cannot separate the sounds in spoken words likely reflect the 20 to 30 percent of schoolchildren who go on to experience reading difficulties.

In the 1980s, researchers began to address that connection explicitly. British researchers Lynette Bradley and Peter Bryant found that a preschooler's phonological aptitude predicts his reading three years later. They and other investigators also found that training a young child to attend to the sounds in spoken words before he goes to school significantly improves his success in learning to read later on. In these studies one group of preschool children received specific training in attending to the sounds of words. They learned to categorize words based on their first, middle, or last sounds. For example, using pictures children were taught that words could share beginning sounds (*pig, pan*), middle sounds (*hen, pet*), and end sounds (*hen, pin*). Another group received general language training emphasizing the meaning of words. Without question the group receiving the sound-based training showed the most improvement in reading and spelling. This study was also important because it showed that the kinds of experiences a child has before he goes to school influence his ability to read years later.

In the 1990s we and other research groups demonstrated that phonologic difficulties are the most significant and consistent markers of dyslexia in childhood.

One type of test in particular seemed quite sensitive to dyslexia; this test asks a child to segment words into their phonemes and then delete specific phonemes from the words. For example, the child must say the word *stale* without the *t* sound (*sale*) or say the word *sour* without the *s* sound (*our*). A child's performance on this test was related to his ability to decode single words and was independent of his intelligence, vocabulary, and reasoning ability. When we gave this and other tests of phonemic awareness to a group of fifteen-year-olds in our Connecticut Longitudinal Study, the results were the same. Even in high school students, phonemic awareness was the best predictor of the ability to read words accurately or quickly.

If dyslexia is the result of a phonologic weakness, then other consequences of impaired phonologic functioning should also be apparent—and they are. Ten years ago the work of graduate student Robert B. Katz, for example, documented the problems that poor readers have in naming the objects shown in pictures. Katz showed that when dyslexics misname objects, the incorrect responses tend to share phonologic characteristics with the correct response; *misnaming is not a result of a lack of knowledge but of confusing the sounds of language.* For example, as in the series of drawings in Figure 10, a girl, Amy, when shown a picture of a volcano, calls it a tornado. When given the opportunity to elaborate, Amy demonstrates that she knows what the pictured object is. She can describe the attributes and activities of a volcano in great detail and point to other pictures related to volcanoes. She simply cannot summon the word *volcano.*

This finding converges with other evidence to suggest that while the phonologic component of the language system is impaired in dyslexia, the higher-level components remain intact. Phonologic abilities are not related to intelligence and, in fact, are quite independent of intelligence. Many children with superior intelligence develop dyslexia, while other children with much lower levels of intelligence catch on to reading with relative ease. People are often surprised to learn that it is phonemic

Figure 10. The Paradox of Dyslexia II

Amy has difficulty reading the word *volcano*. When shown a picture of a volcano, she retrieves *tornado,* a word that sounds similar. Once Amy hears the word *volcano,* it is clear that she knows exactly what it means.

awareness and not intelligence that best predicts ease of learning to read.

The phonologic model crystallizes exactly what we mean by dyslexia. As shown in Figure 11, a circumscribed, encapsulated weakness is often surrounded by a sea of strengths: reasoning, problem solving, comprehension, concept formation, critical thinking, general knowledge, and vocabulary. The phonologic weakness masks what are often excellent comprehension skills. Dyslexics like Gregory use the "big picture" of theories, models, and ideas as a framework to help them remember specific details. It is true that when details are not unified by associated ideas or a theoretical framework—when, for example, Gregory must commit to memory long lists of unfamiliar names—dyslexics can be at a real disadvantage. Even if Gregory succeeds in memorizing such lists, he has trouble producing the names on demand, as he often must when he is questioned on rounds by an attending physician.

Rote memorization and rapid word retrieval are particularly difficult for dyslexics. On the other hand, dyslexics appear to be disproportionately represented in the upper echelons of creativity and in the people who, whether in business, finance, medicine, writing, law, or science, have broken through a boundary and have made a real difference to society. I believe that this is because a dyslexic cannot simply memorize or do things by rote; she must get far underneath the concept and understand it at a fundamental level. This need often leads to a deeper understanding and a perspective that is different from what is achieved by some for whom things come easier because they just can memorize and repeat—without ever having to deeply and thoroughly understand.

Even when the dyslexic knows the information, the need to rapidly retrieve and orally present such information often results in the retrieval of a related phoneme, such as in substituting *humanity* for *humidity*. As a result, the dyslexic may appear much less capable than he is. On the other hand, given time and when not pressured to provide instant oral responses, the dyslexic can deliver an excellent oral presentation. Similarly, in reading, dyslexics like Gregory frequently need to resort to the context to help identify specific words. This strategy slows them down further and helps explain why the provision of extra time as an accommodation is so necessary if dyslexics are to show their knowledge.

By identifying a phonologic weakness as the heart of dyslexia, we have taken a significant step. Now, so to speak, we can see the fault in the neural system for translating print into language. In the next two chapters you will learn about the neural underpinnings of dyslexia and actually see—through brain activation patterns—what goes wrong.

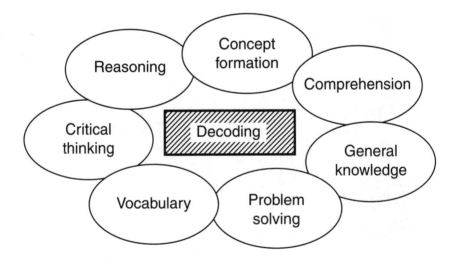

Figure 11. Sea of Strengths Model of Dyslexia

In dyslexia an encapsulated weakness in decoding is surrounded by many strengths.

6

Reading the Brain

Incredible as it may seem, today we can actually see someone's brain at work as she reads. Sophisticated imaging studies of the reading brain bring phonemes to life, allowing researchers to virtually track the printed word as it initially registers as a visual icon, is then transformed into the sounds (phonemes) of language, and simultaneously activates its meaning stored within the brain's own internal dictionary. Within milliseconds—less than the blink of an eye—assorted lines and circles in the brain's circuitry make the vast journey to meaning as a cacophony of abstract symbols is translated into a symphony of words.

And yet as recently as the beginning of the nineteenth century, scientists and philosophers weren't even sure that thinking, speaking, or reading had their roots in the brain. We've come a long way fast.

The earliest conceptions of the mind were grounded in religious and philosophical notions, and, not surprisingly, they focused on the soul. During the Age of the Pyramids (2780–2200 B.C.), the Egyptians located consciousness and intelligence in the beating heart, which was considered the hallowed center of the body. Embalming procedures to preserve the body for the hereafter provide tantalizing clues to the relative importance of each organ. The heart, considered essential for an afterlife, was quickly preserved and rapidly returned to its place within the body. Other organs—the lungs, liver, stomach, and kidney—were also replaced or were stored in special vessels arranged close to the body. In accordance with the view that the brain was a fairly useless organ, it was discarded; the priests were unable to envision a useful function for this squishy, jellylike mass.

The Egyptians were not the only civilization to trivialize the brain. Ancient Chinese medicine developed a system, Zang Fu, for assigning functions and different levels of importance to the various organs of the body. Based on the belief that the human soul resided within the heart, Zang Fu considered the heart the most important organ. The brain was considered peripheral, irrelevant to thinking or feeling. Mental functions and spirituality were thought to reside in the heart.

On reflection, the relative value ascribed to the heart and brain is understandable in the context of the times. The ancients could only deduce an organ's function from what they could observe through their senses. They noted that the heart beat, contained bright red blood, and when it stopped, so did life. The brain, on the other hand, seemed pale, lifeless, and uninteresting. It should not be surprising, therefore, that even Aristotle, the preeminent anatomist and student of animal behavior in ancient Greece, attributed the control of sensation and motion to the heart and not to the brain. The brain was viewed as a "cold" organ, a refrigeration device of sorts whose usefulness was its ability to cool off the heat generated by the "warm" heart. Aristotle believed that man's larger-size brain accounted for his supreme intelligence over animals, but not for reasons we might imagine.

> The heart is hottest and richest and must be counterbalanced, for man's superior intelligence depends on the fact that his larger brain is capable of keeping the heart cool enough for optimal mental activity.

Cooling off the hot heart meant that man could maintain mental superiority over all other creatures.

By the second century animal experiments were beginning to provide clues to the central importance of the brain. Most influential were the experiments of Galen which demonstrated that the brain was critical for movement, for sensation, and for thinking. This brilliant physician-scientist associated all varieties of higher cognitive activities—memory, imagination, and intelligence—with the brain, and he also related brain injury to disruptions of these processes. Galen made no attempt to further localize specific functions to discrete brain regions.

The view of the brain as a holistic and undifferentiated organ reigned virtually unchallenged for hundreds of years. When attempts at brain localization first emerged, they did not focus on the actual substance of the brain. Here the overriding influence of religious beliefs on science is evident. It was unthinkable to the church leaders of the fourth and fifth century that the essentially holy spirit of man should be contaminated by association with the lowly and impure flesh that made up the substance of the brain. Accordingly, the ethereal spirits were placed not in the brain matter but in the ventricles, the system of spaces within the brain that contain the cerebrospinal fluid (see Figure 12). In accordance with ecclesiastic teaching, man's spirit and ideas could literally flow through the cavities. A Byzantine church leader, Nemesius, the bishop of Emesa, even developed a system that organized brain functions and related each to one of the four ventricles in the brain. According to Nemesius, perception was found in the two side or lateral ventricles, thinking in the middle (third) ventricle, and memory in the back (fourth) ventricle. Although ultimately wrong, this view paved the way for the concept that specific cognitive functions were localized in different areas of the brain.

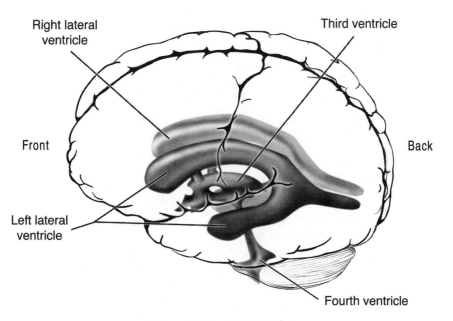

Figure 12. Brain Ventricles

Shown here are the brain ventricles, the connecting spaces within the brain that contain the cerebrospinal fluid.

The belief that thinking originated in the ventricles prevailed in Europe and the Middle East for centuries. Even Leonardo da Vinci, who could produce the most exact and precise drawings of the ventricles, placed the qualities of imagination, cognition, and memory in these cavernous spaces. Finally, in the latter half of the sixteenth century, Volcher Coiter, a German physician and surgeon and also an inspired experimentalist, cut into the ventricles of a living creature and observed no harmful results and no effects on behavior. With this experiment the ventricular theory of the mind was no longer tenable. Beginning in the seventeenth century, astute clinicians (Thomas Willis, Emanuel Swedenborg, and Joseph Baader) began publishing reports in which they related their patients' symptoms to general areas of brain damage. As crude as these descriptions were, at least higher cognitive functions (thought, imagination, and memory) had finally made their way to the brain itself.

Localizing Brain Functions

By the late eighteenth century, physicians had taken a great interest in the origins of human personality traits as well as mental illness and were eager for a conceptual framework that would allow them to organize these behaviors with regard to the brain. The doctrine that came to be known as *phrenology* was ideally suited for this purpose. Phrenology preached that a range of human behaviors and cognitive abilities originated within the brain and that each individual trait was housed within a particular region or self-contained *organ* of the brain. The larger the organ (brain area) responsible for a personality characteristic, the stronger that attribute in the person. According to the phrenologists, as a brain organ grew in size, it necessarily stimulated the overlying cranium to grow, producing protuberances on the surface of the skull. Performing cranioscopy—palpating the skull—according to a phrenologic map would determine the size of the various organs and therefore indicate how much of a trait was present (Figure 13). To many, the idea that psychological attributes could be deduced from external inspection of the skull, face, or body was somehow reassuring and gave a sense of order to an array of often puzzling, if not frightening, symptoms.

The first phrenologist was the highly controversial Austrian-born physician and anatomist Franz Joseph Gall, the man responsible for

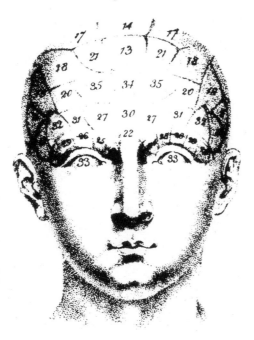

Figure 13. Phrenologic Map of the Brain

The phrenologic system relating specific psychologic traits to associated protuberances on the skull is shown in this drawing by Johann Spurzheim.

modern concepts of brain localization of cognitive functions. Gall advanced the idea that specific brain functions originate in separate and discrete areas of the brain. He based his theory on a personal observation made when he was nine years old. He loved to relate the story of his classmate who was exceptionally good at memorizing words. Gall thought his classmate's unusual facial appearance—protuberant eyes—might be related to his keen memory. Gall reasoned that his classmate must have had an overly developed frontal brain region that was responsible for his excellent memory; in turn, the excessive development of this brain area literally pushed the child's eye sockets forward, causing the bulging eyes. And so the doctrine of phrenology was born. This nine-year-old's fantasy captured the mind of an entire generation.

Eventually, Gall localized twenty-seven different psychological traits to their associated brain organs. His reasoning left something to be desired. He localized "carnivorous instinct, tendency to murder" to "organ 5," the area just above the helix of the ear, because this region was accentuated in an executioner he observed and was also pronounced in a child who liked to torture animals.

Together with his disciple Johann Caspar Spurzheim, Gall lectured to enthralled audiences all over Europe, spreading the belief that qualities such as courage, love of offspring, the tendency to steal, vanity, wisdom, and even poetic talent could be assessed according to the size of a specific associated bump or depression on the head.

While scientists dismissed the premise by about 1840, the more fundamental notion that cognitive functions could be localized within specific brain regions took hold and continues to influence neuroscientists to this day. Scientists and physicians began trying to localize those functions in the only way they could at the time: by studying the brains of individuals who had suffered an accident of nature such as a stroke or a traumatic injury to the brain. After a patient died, examination of the brain revealed the area of injury caused by the stroke or trauma, and it was, in turn, related to the patient's symptoms. It was just such a circumstance that allowed the first cognitive process (expressive language) to be localized in the brain.

In 1861 a fifty-one-year-old Frenchman, Leborgne, was transferred to the clinical service of Paul Broca, a highly respected French physician. The long-suffering Leborgne had been hospitalized for at least two decades with a range of neurological ills that included epilepsy, loss of speech, and paralysis of his right side. Leborgne had been nicknamed Tan by the other patients because that was the only word he could say, and he repeated it over and over. His ability to understand spoken language, however, was relatively unaffected. Leborgne was a patient of Broca's for less than a week when he passed away. Examining Leborgne's brain afterward, Broca was at once struck by a rather large irregular lesion on the surface of the left frontal region (the inferior frontal gyrus, to be precise; see Figure 14). Located just behind the left temple, this portion of the brain is now commonly referred to as Broca's area. Today, neurologists classify a loss of language as an aphasia, and the specific kind of language difficulty observed in Leborgne—a loss of fluent speech while retaining the ability to understand language—is known as Broca's aphasia.

Broca's observation ushered in a new era of brain exploration of cognitive functions. There were to be no more quarrels over the brain's role in cognition; loss of a highly specific cognitive function—not just any speech problem but the loss of the ability to articulate words—was

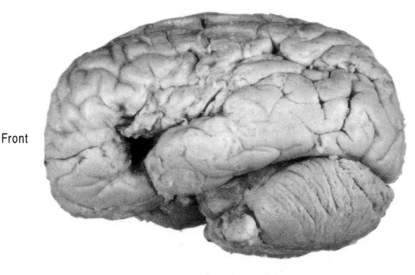

Front   Back

Figure 14. Tan's Brain Showing Defect in Broca's Area

A view of the left side of Tan's brain indicates a large, irregular defect in the inferior frontal gyrus, a region now referred to as Broca's area.

linked to the destruction of a particular brain region. Broca went on to define different types of speech difficulties. For example, he noted that the expressive aphasia he had initially described could be accompanied by retention of the ability to swear. In describing the case of a beleaguered parish priest decades earlier (1843), another physician, Jacques Lordat, had unknowingly provided one of the most striking cases of this dissociation. Following a stroke, the priest could say very few words, but he was able to utter "the most forceful oath of the tongue, which begins with an 'f' and which our Dictionaries have never dared to print."

Broca also clearly established that the roots of reading—language and speech—originate in the cerebral cortex.* As self-evident as this may seem today, the logical source of our ability to speak was long thought to be the tongue. In ancient Rome, for example, the treatment for the inability to speak was to tone and massage the tongue—like any weak or lazy muscle—and to gargle vigorously. Although perceptive physicians seemed to disentangle *loss of speech* (aphasia) from *loss of*

---

* Cortex refers to the *gray matter,* that is, the nerve cells close to the surface of the brain; *white matter* refers to the long tails or axons of the nerve cells that carry the message from the nerve cells to other neurons in the brain or spinal cord.

movement (paralysis) of the tongue, the view that the tongue was the primary organ for speech was firmly entrenched and lingered through at least the seventeenth century. When William Harvey, who had electrified the scientific world with his discovery of the circulation of blood, suffered a stroke in 1651 and was unable to speak, his apothecary provided this renowned physician-scientist with what he considered the very best aphasia treatment available: He crisply clipped Harvey's frenulum, the thin sliver of tissue tying the tongue to the base of the mouth. The hope was that if his tongue was freed, Harvey's aphasia would improve. Although we can surmise that Harvey's tongue was now looser, we can also conclude with great assurance that his aphasia was not improved.

The precocious German neurologist Carl Wernicke, who by the age of twenty-six had completed the three-volume *Der aphasische Symptomenkomplex* (The Aphasic Symptom Complex), used a combination of astute clinical observation and deductive reasoning to suggest that damage to an area along the upper part of the temporal lobe (the brain region behind the helix of the ear; see Figure 15) would produce still another type of aphasia. This speech disturbance, now referred to as

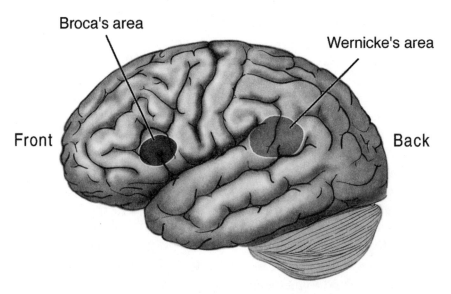

Figure 15. Brain Localization of Expressive and Receptive Language
The left side of the brain, with the two major areas associated with language highlighted: expressive language (Broca's area) and receptive language (Wernicke's area).

Wernicke's aphasia, was almost the inverse of the expressive aphasia localized by Broca. In contrast to Broca's aphasia, in which the patient cannot get the words out but usually fully understands language, in Wernicke's aphasia the patient speaks with ease but does not understand language and utters gibberish.

How the Brain Reads

Broca's discovery opened the door to learning how the brain reads. Remember, in order to read we must enter the language system; at a neural level this means that reading relies on the brain circuits already in place for language. Although not appreciated at the time, the identification of Broca's area as a site critical for language marked the first step in the quest to map the neural circuitry for reading.

The strategy used by Broca and legions of neurologists since is straightforward. In a patient who has passed away, areas of damaged tissue are identified, localized according to anatomic landmarks, and correlated with the patient's symptoms. It is important to appreciate what this type of evidence can tell us as well as its limitations. To pinpoint a site that disrupts the circuitry for spoken language is not quite the same as mapping out the neural machinery responsible for language. Broca's contemporary, British neurologist John Hughlings Jackson, appreciated this distinction when he said, "To locate the damage which destroys speech and to locate speech are two different things." Let's say a patient, almost always an adult, suddenly loses his ability to read. This condition, acquired alexia, typically follows a stroke in an individual who had been a good reader. Here, destruction of brain tissue produces a break in the circuitry and, one could say, causes a power outage that interrupts the pathway for reading. The wiring had originally been laid down correctly, but it is now disrupted. Locating the area of disruption tells us that this area is necessary for reading, but it doesn't identify the complete neural circuitry responsible for reading.

In the condition of developmental dyslexia, where reading fails to develop normally, something has gone awry right from the beginning. Consequently, we would *not* necessarily expect to find a distinct lesion, a cut in the wiring; instead, the wiring may not have been laid down correctly in the first place, a glitch having taken place during fetal life, when the brain is hard-wired for language. As a result, the tens of thousands of neurons carrying the phonologic messages necessary for language do not appropriately connect to form the resonating networks that make skilled reading possible.

The enormous complexity of the brain in its initial development presents a myriad of opportunities for a misconnection or a false connection. Within this context we can begin to consider the genesis of the difficulties in dyslexia. Most likely as a result of a genetically programmed error, the neural system necessary for phonologic analysis is somehow miswired, and a child is left with a phonologic impairment that interferes with spoken and written language. Depending on the nature or severity of this fault in the wiring, we would expect to observe variations and varying degrees of reading difficulty.

But there are many possible scenarios for developmental dyslexia. What is really needed to understand dyslexia is the ability to map the full neural circuitry for reading. That was not achieved, however, until the 1980s.

In the interim, physicians tried to make sense of dyslexia in the best way they could. In the late 1970s the neurologist Drake Duane, who had a longstanding interest in dyslexia, organized and coordinated a brain bank that would make available to scientists the brains of dyslexics who had passed away. One such individual had already been examined and the results reported in the *Annals of Neurology*. Spearheaded by Duane and sponsored by the Orton Dyslexia Society, the dyslexia brain bank provided the brains of four additional individuals with histories of reading problems as children. Examination showed a number of differences between these brains and the brains of people who did not have dyslexia, primarily differences in the structures associated with language on the left side of the brain. These abnormalities coincided with hypotheses offered by the neurologist Norman Geschwind twenty years earlier that dyslexia results from damage or improper development of language regions in fetal life. These findings played an important role in focusing attention on the neurobiological substrate of dyslexia.

A Revolution: Reading the Mind

In 1973, using computed tomography (CT, which is a computerized series of X rays that build a three-dimensional image of the brain), scientists were able to *see* the brain for the first time. For this groundbreaking discovery Godfrey N. Hounsfield and Allan M. Cormack were awarded the Nobel Prize for Physiology or Medicine in 1979.

Using CT and, later, magnetic resonance imaging (MRI), which is discussed below, neuroscientists could see the finest details of brain anatomy. But these pictures provide information about structure and not about function, so it wasn't until functional brain imaging became possible in the early 1980s that scientists were able to see the brain at work in a healthy person. Brain *function* could be observed as a person read, spoke, thought, or imagined.

Positron emission tomography (PET) was the first technology developed to study the brain at work; it involves measuring blood flow to brain regions through the use of a radioactive compound injected into the bloodstream. Though much has been and continues to be learned about brain function from this technology, it is hampered by its invasive nature and the elaborate equipment required to make up the radioactive materials. For the most part, PET has been supplanted by a newer technology, functional magnetic resonance imaging (fMRI), which allows neuroscientists to visualize the inner workings of the human brain in a completely noninvasive way; there is no radiation or injections. Currently, fMRI is the most widely used method to study the brain at work.

In a seminal paper, "On the Regulation of the Blood-Supply of the Brain," published in 1890 in the *Journal of Physiology,* British scientists C. S. Roy and C. S. Sherrington argue for the principle of *autoregulation of cerebral blood flow.* Basically, they provide evidence that, within the brain, local blood supply varies in response to functional activity in that region. In their own words:

> These facts seem to indicate to us the existence of an automatic mechanism by which the blood-supply of any part of the cerebral tissue is varied in accordance with the activity of the chemical changes which underlie the functional activity of that part.

Much more recently, in 1981, Louis Sokoloff, a scientist at the National Institutes of Health, showed that it is the changes in energy metabolism that directly influence alterations in blood flow:

> It is, therefore, clear . . . that energy metabolism and functional activity are closely coupled in the nervous system and that local

blood flow is distributed and adjusted in the cerebral tissues to local metabolic demand and thereby to local functional activity.

This makes it possible to envision the sequence of events at the associated brain region as a person reads: increase in functional activity of local neurons $\longrightarrow$ increase in local metabolism $\longrightarrow$ increase in local blood flow.

This concatenation of brain events makes sense. Performing a cognitive task like reading is work and consumes energy. Suppose a child is asked to determine if two words rhyme. As he attempts to rhyme these words, a chain of events is set in motion: The neural systems necessary for carrying out this task are activated and consume energy; to meet the increased energy requirement, more blood flow is needed to bring additional fuel (oxygen) and nutrients to that location. This concept, the autoregulation of cerebral blood flow, is the underlying principle of functional brain imaging. This principle, together with the fact that increased blood flow produces alterations in the magnetic properties of blood, is what allows fMRI to work.

Functional MRI is based on the magnetic properties of a basic component of blood: oxygenated hemoglobin. In red blood cells oxygen is bound to hemoglobin and transported through the body for delivery to working cells. The magnetic properties of the hemoglobin molecule change depending on the amount of oxygen bound to it: Blood with high oxygen concentrations produces a stronger magnetic signal than blood with less oxygen. Thus, as a person carries out a specific cognitive task, responsible neurons in sites distributed throughout the brain become activated, blood flow to these brain regions increases—bringing with it rich, highly oxygenated blood—and the fMRI apparatus picks up its stronger magnetic signal.

In the next chapter you will learn how fMRI experiments are carried out and what fMRI is teaching us about how the brain reads.

7

The Working Brain Reads

Functional MRI is remarkably patient-friendly and easily accomplished for both adults and children. In our research we have imaged hundreds of people of all ages with uniformly positive feedback.* Virtually the same scanner used for MRIs to evaluate headaches and torn knee ligaments is also used in functional imaging. For those readers who have not had an MRI, I will explain briefly what it's like by telling you about the experience of Kacie, age eight.

When Kacie and her mother first arrived at the MRI center, Jennifer, a research coordinator, greeted them, introduced them to the center, and helped Kacie feel at home. Jennifer then reviewed with Kacie the tasks she would be asked to perform as she was being imaged. Kacie quickly caught on and was soon ready for the imaging. In the scanning room she lay down on a sliding table that had a large open tube at one end. At the start of the imaging, the table moves so that Kacie's head lies comfortably within the open tube (Figure 16).† While lying in the scanner Kacie responded to each stimulus by pressing a *yes* or a *no* button on a device she was holding in her hands. The device measured how accurately and how rapidly she responded.

---

* For this discussion I have chosen to focus primarily on our own imaging program at Yale, the studies I know best.

† The tube contains the electromagnet that produces the images.

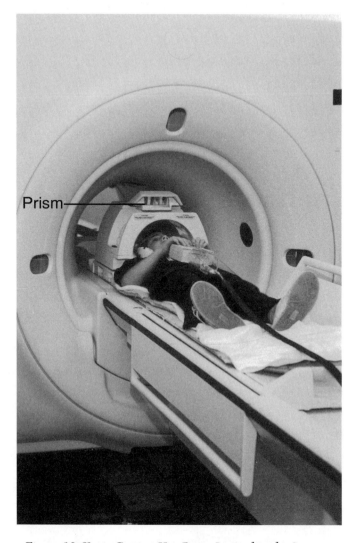

Figure 16. Kacie Getting Her Brain Imaged in the Scanner

Kacie is holding the response box and looking through the prism just above her head.

Once Kacie glided into the scanner, she looked up through a prism (periscope) just above her head to see stimuli, pairs of words, as they were rapidly projected one after another on a screen. Nonsensical but pronounceable words such as *LETE* and *JEAT* were used as stimuli, and Kacie was asked whether each pair rhymed. As shown in Figure 17, if the words rhymed, she pressed the YES button. Since these words are made up and Kacie had never seen them before, they could not have been memorized and had to be sounded out, ensuring that the neural pathways for phonologic analysis would be activated. As each pair of words flashed on the screen and Kacie sounded out the words to herself, the MRI scanner recorded her thinking process. If the process activated neurons in Broca's area, fresh oxygenated blood would flow into this area and into each region connected to the neural network responsible for phonologic analysis. Within this circuit of actively firing neurons, newly

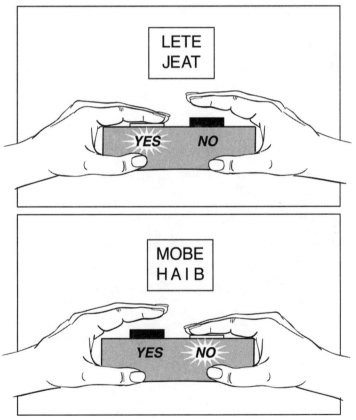

Figure 17. Reading and Responding While in the Scanner

Kacie reads the words and presses the YES button if the words rhyme and the NO button if they do not.

arriving oxygenated blood was replacing oxygen-poor blood, and the scanner was recording it all. After the imaging was completed, Kacie was none the worse for wear (see Figure 18).

Immediately after imaging, we give each participant a copy of her *structural* brain MRI—essentially a photograph of her brain anatomy, which is invariably normal in people who are dyslexic.* While my colleagues and I anticipated that dyslexics would be reassured when shown

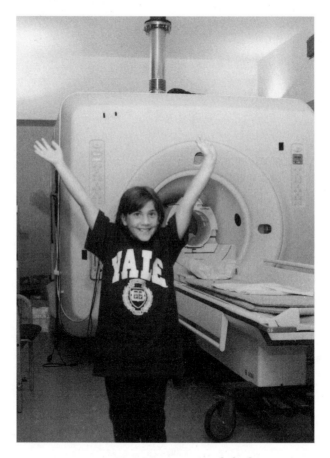

Figure 18. Mission Accomplished.
Kacie after her imaging was completed.

* It takes more time to complete the processing necessary for the functional MRI. Remember that for dyslexics the problem is in the brain wiring—a disruption exposed by a functional MRI. The basic anatomic structures are intact.

their brain images, we didn't realize how meaningful and moving an experience it would be. Children and adults alike have embraced their brain images as if they were being reunited with a long lost and deeply mourned relative. When I point out the various normal anatomic structures, the subject, no matter how old, invariably lights up with wide-eyed amazement. An adult will invariably remark, "You may not believe this, but I always thought I was retarded and that my brain would look abnormal, with some parts missing or holes or something not right. I can't believe I have a normal brain. What a relief."

Basic Landmarks of the Brain

The brain is an extraordinary organ, and for all its complexity in functioning, its organizing structure is relatively straightforward. I am going to digress here to point out some of the basic landmarks that I will refer to as we move forward.

The brain is made up of two mirror-image sides or hemispheres: right and left. As shown in Figure 19, the front of the brain, near the forehead, is referred to as *anterior,* and the back of the brain, behind the ears and farther back, is called *posterior.* Each hemisphere of the brain is divided into four lobes or sections: *frontal, parietal, temporal,* and *occipital.* The frontal lobes are anterior, the occipital lobes posterior, and the parietal and temporal lobes somewhere in between. The parietal lobe sits above the temporal lobe. There are mirror-image lobes on each side of the brain. Classically, the left side of the brain has been associated with language.

Connecting the left and right hemispheres is a broad band of tissue made up of the tails or axons of nerve cells that busily carry messages from one hemisphere to the other; this band of connecting insulated fibers is called the *corpus callosum* and appears as a white band. In contrast, the brain cells that are the command center and originate the message are not insulated and appear as gray matter. If the right and left lobes are viewed as the vertical poles of the letter *H,* the corpus callosum is the horizontal band that connects the two sides. Finally, tucked beneath the occipital lobes is the *cerebellum,* the part of the brain that controls movement and coordination.

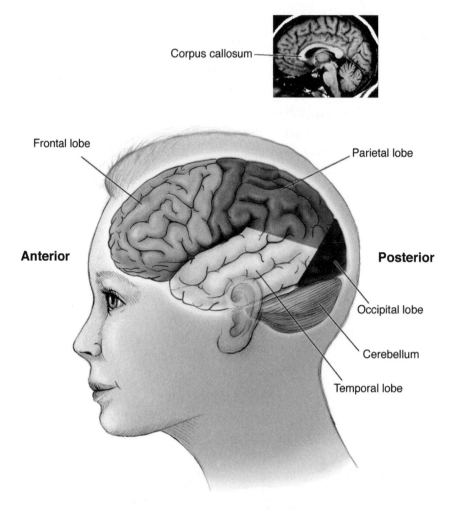

Figure 19. Brain Landmarks

The left side of the brain is shown. The inset is an MRI image of the structures in the center of the brain; note the corpus callosum.

Watching the Brain Read

Our functional imaging studies are focused on mapping the neural circuitry for reading. In planning our research, our first goal was to identify the neural pathways for breaking words into their underlying sounds.

To begin we recruited subjects, nineteen men and nineteen women, all of whom were good readers. To activate the circuitry for phonologic analysis, we asked our subjects to judge whether two nonsense words rhymed. After all the participants had been imaged, we examined the data and saw a surprising difference between the brain activation patterns in men and women (see Figure 20). As shown in the brain images, men activated the left inferior frontal gyrus, while women activated the right as well as the left. While all nineteen men activated only the left side of the brain, most but not all women—eleven out of nineteen—showed activation on both sides (eight women activated only the left side). This represented the first demonstration of a visible sex difference in brain organization for language. (By the way, women performed the task as accurately and as quickly as men.)

We were excited by our discovery of sex differences in brain organization, but what most excited us was the identification of specific neural sites for sounding out words. The very same brain region that demonstrated sex differences, the inferior frontal gyrus, was also involved in reading. Having established to our satisfaction the feasibility of using

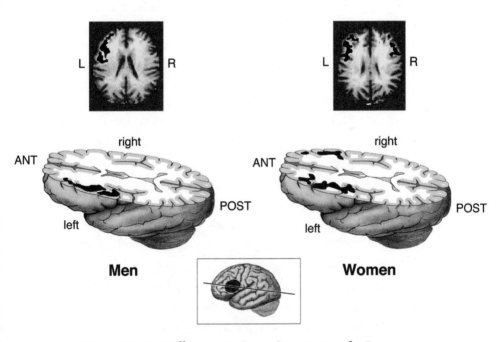

Figure 20. Sex Differences in Brain Organization for Language

The black areas indicate sites of activation in men and women as they rhymed nonsense words and show that men activate the left side of the brain and women activate both the left and right sides of the brain. The insets are the fMRI images showing the brain activations.

fMRI to study reading, we felt comfortable proceeding to the next step: a series of studies that would begin to teach us—at the level of brain organization and function—why some very smart people have trouble reading.

These studies began less than a decade ago, and the progress has been breathtaking. First, the neural systems for reading in children and adults are rapidly being mapped out. Imaging studies have identified at least two neural pathways for reading; one for beginning reading, for slowly sounding out words, and another that is a speedier pathway for skilled reading. Next, careful examination of brain activation patterns has revealed a glitch in this circuitry in dyslexic readers. Studies from around the world leave no doubt that dyslexic readers use different brain pathways than do good readers.

As they read, good readers activate highly interconnected neural systems that encompass regions in the back and front of the left side of the brain (see Figure 21). Not surprisingly, the reading circuitry includes brain regions dedicated to processing the visual features, that is, the lines and curves that make up letters, and to transforming the letters into the sounds of language and to getting to the meaning of words.

Most of the reading part of the brain is in the back. Called the posterior reading system, as noted above, it is made up of two different pathways for reading words, one sitting somewhat higher in the brain than the other. The upper pathway is located primarily in the middle of the brain (technically, the parieto-temporal region), just above and slightly

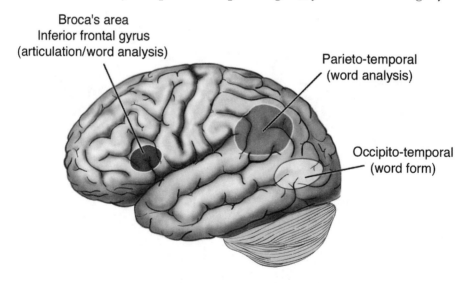

Figure 21. Brain Systems for Reading

behind the ear. The lower path runs closer to the bottom of the brain; it is the site where two lobes of the brain—the occipital and the temporal—converge (referred to as the occipito-temporal area). This hectic region serves as a hub where incoming information from different sensory systems comes together and where, for example, all the relevant information about a word—how it looks, how it sounds, and what it means—is tightly bound together and stored. The lower circuit is behind the ear, near the area where children often get swollen glands associated with scalp or ear infections.

Scientists have long focused on these areas as important in reading. As early as 1891 the great French neurologist Jules Dejerine suggested that the parieto-temporal region was critical for reading, and just one year later he was also the first to link the occipito-temporal area to reading.* These two subsystems have different roles in reading, and their functions make sense in light of the changing needs of the reader: Beginning readers must first analyze a word; skilled readers identify a word instantaneously. The parieto-temporal system works for the novice reader. Slow and analytic, its function seems to be in the early stages of learning to read, that is, in initially analyzing a word, pulling it apart, and linking its letters to their sounds. In contrast to the step-by-step parieto-temporal system, the occipito-temporal region is the express pathway to reading and is the one used by skilled readers. The more skilled the reader, the more she activates this region (see Figure 22). It responds very rapidly—in less than 150 *milliseconds* (less than a heartbeat)—to seeing a word; instead of analyzing a word, the occipito-temporal area reacts almost instantly to the whole word as a pattern. One brief glance and the word is automatically identified on sight. Not surprisingly, the occipito-temporal region is referred to as the *word form* area or system.

Here's how we think the word form system works: After a child has analyzed and *correctly* read a word several times, he forms an exact neural model of that specific word; the model (word form), reflecting the word's spelling, its pronunciation, and its meaning, is now permanently stored in the occipito-temporal system. Subsequently, just seeing the word in print immediately activates the word form and all the relevant information about that word. It all happens automatically, without conscious thought or effort (see Figure 23). As skilled readers speed through the text, the word form area is in full gear, instantly recognizing

---

* Based on postmortem studies of adults with acquired reading difficulties.

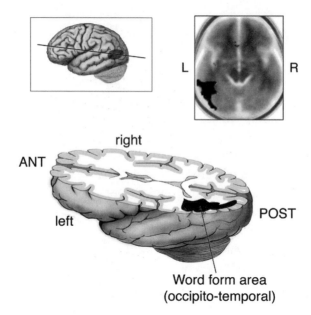

Figure 22. An Area for Skilled Reading: The Word Form Area

This is a correlation map. In the area shown in black there is a strong correlation between children's reading scores and activation in the word form area in the left side of the brain; the higher the score, the more activation is observed. The inset shows the correlation in an MRI image of the brain.

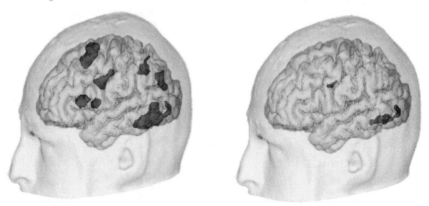

Visible words　　　　　　　　**Masked words**

Figure 23. Brain Activation Responses to Visible and Masked (Subliminal) Words

fMRI brain activation responses to visible words are shown on the left; multiple regions including the word form area are activated. In contrast, when words are presented for very brief periods of time (subliminally) and not consciously perceived, the word form area continues to be activated, indicating that this brain region responds automatically to words.

one word after another. Not surprisingly, the best readers, those with the highest scores on tests of reading, are the ones who show the most activation of the word form region during imaging. Thus, there is a strong link between reading skill and reliance on the word form area. A third reading pathway, this one in Broca's area in the front of the brain, also helps in slowly analyzing a word. There are therefore three neural pathways for reading: two slower, analytic ones, the parieto-temporal and frontal, that are used mainly by beginning readers, and an express route, the occipito-temporal, relied on by experienced, skilled readers.

Fortunately, mapping the neural pathways in good readers opened the door to understanding the nature of the difficulty in dyslexic readers. As mentioned earlier, imaging studies revealed markedly different brain activation patterns in dyslexic readers compared to those in good readers. As they read, good readers activate the back of the brain and also, to some extent, the front of the brain. In contrast, dyslexic readers show a fault in the system: underactivation of neural pathways in the back of the brain. Consequently, they have initial trouble analyzing words and transforming letters into sounds, and even as they mature, they remain slow and not fluent readers. (Fluency in reading is discussed in Chapter 17.)

At all ages good readers show a consistent pattern: strong activation in the back of the brain with lesser activation in the front. In contrast, brain activations in dyslexic children appear to change with age. Imaging studies reveal that older dyslexic children show increased activation in frontal regions so that by adolescence they are demonstrating a pattern of *overactivation* in Broca's region—that is, they are increasingly using these frontal regions for reading (see Figure 24). It is as if these struggling readers are using the systems in front of the brain to try to compensate for the disruption in the back of the brain. This coincides with what is known about the reading style of many dyslexics. One means of compensating for a reading difficulty, for example, is to subvocalize (say the words under your breath) as you read, a process that utilizes a region in the front of the brain (Broca's area) responsible for articulating spoken words. Under the guidance of this frontal system, a dyslexic reader can develop an awareness of the sound structure of a word by physically forming the word with his lips, tongue, and vocal cords. This process of subvocalization allows him to read, albeit more slowly than if the left posterior systems were working.

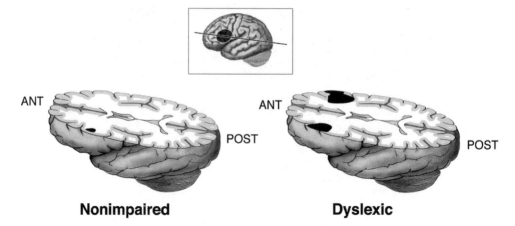

Figure 24. Changes in Brain Activation Patterns With Age:
Older Dyslexic Children Use Frontal Brain Regions

These are correlation maps. Areas that are black have a high correlation with age. As children get older, these areas become more activated. In the image on the left, nonimpaired readers show little change in brain activation with age, hence, there is very little black. In contrast, on the right, dyslexic children show increasing activation in frontal brain regions as they get older, as indicated by prominent black areas.

This pattern of underactivation in the back of the brain provides a neural signature for the phonologic difficulties characterizing dyslexia (see Figure 25). This signature seems to be universal; it is true of dyslexics in all languages and of all ages. Even high-achieving university students with childhood histories of dyslexia, who are accurate but slow readers, continue to show this pattern (see Figure 26).

These findings are helping us understand the roots of dyslexia. For example, we observed the disruption in young children that indicated that the wiring glitch is present from the start of reading and does not represent the end result of years of poor reading. The identical posterior disruption is observed in children and in adults—neurobiologic proof that reading problems don't go away. They are persistent, and now we know why.

We have also learned that dyslexic children and adults turn to alternate compensatory reading systems. Brain images recorded as dyslexic readers try to sound out words show the posterior system on the left side of the brain is not working; instead, these slow but accurate readers are relying on alternate secondary pathways, not a repair but a different

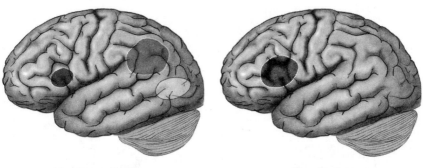

Nonimpaired   **Dyslexic**

Figure 25. A Neural Signature for Dyslexia:
Underactivation of Neural Systems in the Back of the Brain

At left, nonimpaired readers activate neural systems that are mostly in
the back of the left side of the brain (shaded areas); at right, dyslexic
readers underactivate these reading systems in the back of the brain
and tend to overactivate frontal areas.

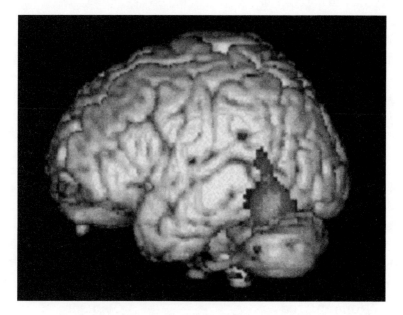

Figure 26. Universal Disruption in College Students
with Childhood Histories of Dyslexia

fMRI brain activations (shaded area) show left posterior brain regions
activated by French-, English-, and Italian-speaking university students who are good readers, but not by those with childhood histories
of dyslexia and who are now accurate, but slow, readers.

83

route to reading. In addition to their greater reliance on Broca's area, which was mentioned earlier, dyslexics are also using other auxiliary systems for reading, ones located on the right side as well as in the front of the brain—a functioning system but, alas, not an automatic one (see Figure 27). These findings explain the previously puzzling picture of bright adult dyslexic readers who improve in reading words accurately but for whom reading remains slow and draining. The disruption in left posterior systems prevents rapid, automatic word recognition; the development of ancillary right side (and frontal) systems allows for accurate, albeit very slow, reading. These dyslexic readers have to rely on a "manual" rather than on an automatic system for reading.

Having identified the neural components of skilled reading, scientists are now wondering about how these systems talk to one another. Without going into too much detail, it is thought that sophisticated behaviors such as reading originate within widely distributed neural systems, and not at individual local anatomic sites, by a symphony of neurons rather than by a single section of the orchestra.

The brain's reliance on patterns of connectivity may have particular relevance to the teaching of reading since within these systems patterns of neural connections are continually reinforced and strengthened as a result of repeated practice and experiences. We can then imagine that

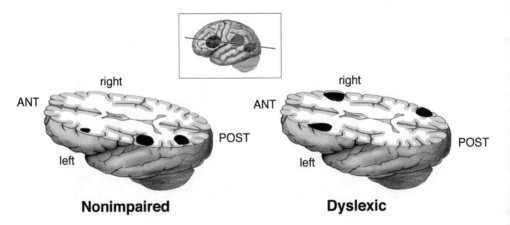

Nonimpaired　　　　　**Dyslexic**

Figure 27. Dyslexic Readers Use Compensatory Systems to Read

The nonimpaired reader, on the left, activates neural systems that are mostly in the back of the left side of the brain; the dyslexic reader, on the right, activates systems on the right side and in the front of the brain on the left.

each time a six-year-old is able to associate a particular sound with a letter, the neural pathways responsible for making this linkage are further reinforced and even more deeply imprinted within her brain.

The latest imaging studies continue to probe deep into the brain to better understand reading difficulties. Tantalizing new data suggest that we are on the verge of being able to tease apart different groups of poor readers. For example, imaging studies of our longitudinal sample are providing clues that there may be two major groups of poor readers. One, the classic dyslexic, is born with a glitch in his posterior reading systems. This group has higher verbal abilities and is able to compensate somewhat—improving in accuracy but remaining slow readers. The second group seems to have developed into poor readers mainly, we speculate, as a result of experience. It may be the result of a combination of poor reading instruction in school and a disadvantaged language environment at home. In this group the wiring for the posterior reading system may have been laid down early on but never activated appropriately; the system is there, but it is not functioning properly. Without effective intervention (discussed in Chapter 19), individuals in this group remain poor readers, reading both inaccurately and slowly.

One of the most exciting applications of brain imaging is just coming into use: directly evaluating the effects of specific reading interventions on the neural systems for reading. In later chapters you will learn about interventions that work, programs that help disabled readers learn to read. A key question relates to whether such effective reading programs are band-aids that cover up a reading problem and perhaps encourage the development of secondary manual pathways, or whether they can actually rewire or "normalize" the brain.

Can dyslexic readers develop the fast-paced word form reading system? We asked this question in a recent study. We used fMRI to study boys and girls who were struggling to learn to read and who then received a yearlong experimental reading program. The progression of changes we observed was remarkable.

Images obtained immediately after the intervention showed the tentative emergence of primary left-side systems used by good readers as well as the development of right-side secondary pathways for reading. The final set of images obtained one year after the intervention had ended was startling. Not only were the right-side auxiliary pathways much less prominent but, more important, there was further development of the primary neural systems on the left side of the brain. As shown in Figure 28, these activation patterns were comparable to those obtained from children who had always been good readers. We had observed brain repair. And the children improved their reading. This may explain why children who receive effective interventions early on develop into both accurate *and* fluent readers. As previously mentioned, while right-side systems can support accurate (but slow) reading, left-side posterior circuits are essential for rapid, automatic reading. These findings provide powerful evidence that early intervention with an effective reading program (like those described in Chapter 19) leads to the development of primary, automatic reading systems and allows a child to catch up to his classmates. This is consistent with accumulating evidence that experience (such as exposure to effective reading instruction in school) drives the development of the fast-paced word form system. After more than a century of frustration, it has now been shown that the brain can be rewired and that struggling children can become skilled readers.

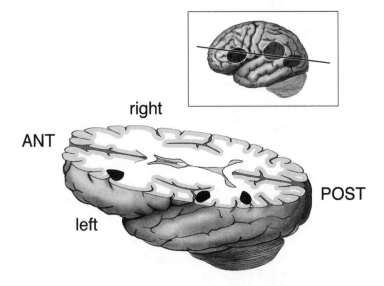

Figure 28. Effective Reading Interventions Result in Brain Repair

One year following an effective reading intervention, dyslexic children have developed left-side reading systems (shown in black) in both the front and back of the brain.

Putting It All Together

Because so much ground has been covered in this chapter, let me summarize what we've learned so far.

Reading is a code, and no matter who we are, each of us must somehow represent print as a neural code that the brain can decipher. Functional imaging makes this process transparent, allowing scientists to watch (and record) the neural systems at work as they attempt to transcribe letters into sounds. For most people this process is incredibly quick, smooth, and effortless. For others it's an entirely different story. Imaging provides the neurobiological—the physical—evidence of the difficulties that dyslexic readers have in transforming this written code into the linguistic code that is the key to reading.

Seeing these images leaves no doubt that the core problem in dyslexia is phonologic: turning print into sound. Only when dyslexic readers are asked to map letters into sounds do we see evidence of a fault in the circuitry. Neuroscientists now have the holy grail that we have been searching for since Morgan first introduced us to Percy F.—a neural explanation for dyslexia.

Now that we have the ability to pinpoint the specific neural networks serving reading, our quest to understand, treat, and perhaps even prevent dyslexia has taken a quantum leap forward. There is now a neural target for reading interventions: the word form area. Having identified the neural networks engaged by reading and the anatomic location of the disruption in dyslexia, we are now probing deeper into these systems. In this exciting new frontier we are examining the basic chemistry of the neural cells in the disrupted brain regions. The technology of magnetic resonance spectroscopy may help us identify potential metabolic mayhem within the nerve cell itself. Such studies are now under way in our laboratory.

As mentioned earlier, dyslexia is a hidden disability, and because there was no physical proof of it, like a broken bone visible on X-ray, skeptics tried to explain it away. At long last, thanks to functional imaging, dyslexic readers have the proof they have been seeking. These remarkable images provide concrete evidence of the physical reality of their reading difficulty. They also explain how adolescent and young adult dyslexic readers can read accurately but slowly. In the future, functional imaging may allow early detection (and possibly prevention) of dyslexia—even before children learn to read—and its detection in bright adults. The application of functional imaging may also guide us in the development of more effective, more precisely targeted, treatments. Meanwhile, it is possible to use what we have learned about the basic phonologic weakness and the substantial strengths of the dyslexic reader to provide better solutions for struggling readers at all levels.

Making Scientific Discoveries Work for You

The new science of reading has direct application to identifying and treating reading difficulties. It allows us to spot early-warning signs of a reading problem; to know what specific clues to look for at any age; and to understand which are the most scientifically sound approaches to teaching reading. The science happily dovetails with practical everyday needs; this knowledge can be used to answer all the common questions concerning dyslexia. The possibilities for someone with dyslexia are just about limitless; the potential for success and for a happy, fulfilling life is greater than ever before. Applying all that we know allows virtually every dyslexic child to dare to dream.

This information should bring welcome relief to parents like Joyce Bulifant, an actress and comedian who is dyslexic and whose only child is dyslexic. She sums up what all parents who are dyslexic must feel: "Once you have struggled with your own dyslexia, it's bad enough, but to watch a child go through it is unbearably painful."

Even people with dyslexia who are successful by most standards still want to know more about their problem. Paul Grossman, a brilliant lawyer living in San Francisco, refers to his own sense of frustration: "No one seemed to know what the problem was. They couldn't figure it out—I was so smart in so many things and yet I couldn't read. It was hard when no one could tell you what the problem was—much less what to do about it."

The serious concerns of men and women like Joyce and Paul about their or their child's reading problems have not, for the most part, been adequately addressed. But it is important for you to know—indeed, it is the central premise of this book—that it does not have to be this way. It is possible to diagnose dyslexia early and accurately, to provide effective interventions, and for children who are dyslexic to reach adulthood feeling confident and able to achieve their potential. It is also possible to diagnose, to remediate, and to alleviate many of the problems of dyslexic adults. The greatest stumbling block preventing a dyslexic child from realizing his potential and following his dreams is the widespread ignorance about the true nature of dyslexia. The remainder of this book is devoted to eradicating this ignorance by applying scientific knowledge to the identification and management of dyslexia.

Part II

Diagnosing Dyslexia

8

Early Clues to Dyslexia

The most helpful guide to accurate identification and effective treatment of dyslexia comes from our "sea of strengths" model: an isolated weakness in getting to the sounds of words surrounded by an array of strengths in thinking and reasoning. Using this simple model, many parents and teachers have become experts at recognizing the signs of dyslexia, and you can, too. In the next sections I will describe exactly how a phonologic weakness impacts spoken language and then written language.

Applying our model, the essential ingredients of a successful program for the dyslexic child are *identifying*

- a weakness in getting to the sounds of words
- the strengths in thinking and reasoning

and then *providing*

- early help for the weakness
- accommodations to help access the strengths

I cannot emphasize enough the importance of focusing on the strengths as well as the weaknesses. The goal is to make sure that the strengths and not the weaknesses define the child's life.

We will now turn our attention to how the sea of strengths model helps us recognize the signs of dyslexia in our children.

The Earliest Clues to Dyslexia

You will discover the earliest and perhaps the most important clues to a potential reading problem by *listening* to your child speak. Listening for subtle signs that your child's phonologic skills are not developing as they should is a lot easier than it sounds. That is because fuzzy phonemes leave their distinct mark on everyday language in highly predictable ways, influencing how well your child is able to pronounce certain words, sing nursery rhymes, and, eventually, learn the names and sounds of the letters of the alphabet.

The first clue to dyslexia may be *a delay in speaking.* As a general rule, children say their first words at about one year and phrases by eighteen months to two years. Children vulnerable to dyslexia may not begin saying their first words until fifteen months or so and may not speak in phrases until after their second birthday. The delay is a modest one, and parents often ascribe it to a family history of late talking. My patient Sam's grandmother shrugged off his late speech when he was two, saying that his father, too, was a late talker. Interestingly, in the course of our evaluation of Sam, we discovered that his father was a compensated dyslexic who had gone undiagnosed. While a delay in speaking may be familial, so is dyslexia. A seemingly innocent speech delay may be an early warning signal of a future reading problem—especially in a family that has a history of dyslexia. Then again, some dyslexic children may not demonstrate a speech delay or it may be subtle and go unnoticed.

Once a child begins to speak, *difficulties in pronunciation*—sometimes referred to as "baby talk"—that continue past the usual time may be another early warning. By five or six years of age, a child should have little problem saying most words correctly. Attempts to pronounce a new word for the first time or to say a long or complicated word can reveal problems with articulation. It is as if there is a jam in the articulatory machinery that churns out spoken language, and the phonemes are tripping over one another as they come out of the child's mouth. Typical mispronunciations involve either leaving off beginning sounds (such as *pisgetti* for spaghetti or *lephant* for elephant) or inverting the sounds within a word (*aminal* for animal). As part of one of our research studies, a group of six-year-olds with early signs of language difficulties were asked to repeat a series of words. Looking at the words and their pronunciations, you could just feel the phonologic mayhem that was occurring as each child tried to gather the appropriate phonemes and spew them out in some perceived order:

physicist ———> *sysitist*

pistachio ———> *stipachio, sputachio*

specific ———> *pacific, spestickit, pacissic, spastific*

statistics ———> *satislicks*

Even older children and adults are not immune to tripping over phonologic debris, as Gregory the medical student came to know when he tried to pronounce the long (anatomical) names of body parts, or other dyslexics soon discover when they attempt to say unfamiliar or complicated words.

Most preschoolers love to play games with sounds and with rhyming words, and, indeed, much of the humor in books geared to this age level exploits the young child's fascination with rhyme. Three- and four-year-olds derive great glee out of hearing and repeating sounds, such as *Peter, Peter, pumpkin eater* and *Hickory, dickory dock, the mouse ran up the clock.* Dyslexic children, on the other hand, have trouble penetrating the sound structure of words and as a result are less sensitive to rhyme. Sensitivity to rhyme implies an awareness that words can be broken down into smaller segments of sound and that different words may share a sound in common; it is a very early indicator of getting ready to read. Children's familiarity with nursery rhymes turns out to be a strong predictor of their later success in reading. In England, researchers asked three- and four-year-olds, "Can you say [for example] 'Humpty Dumpty' for me?" Regardless of intelligence or family circumstances, the children who were the most familiar with nursery rhymes were also the top readers three years later. Conversely, children who demonstrate reading difficulties may show early signs of *insensitivity to rhyme.* Parents may notice that at age four their son is still not able to recite popular nursery rhymes and he may confuse words that sound alike. By the beginning of kindergarten, when most boys and girls are able to judge if two words rhyme, dyslexic children may still not be able to demonstrate that they *hear* rhyme. For example, when asked, "Do *food* and *foam* rhyme?" or "What about *talk* and *walk*?" dyslexic children are often unable to tell which word pair rhymes. They are unable to focus on just one part of a word—in this example, *alk*—to determine that *talk* and *walk* rhyme.

The British researchers also compared a group of children with reading difficulties to a group of younger children who read well. Each child was asked to listen to a list of words such as *fun, pin, bun,* and *gun* and then select the word that did not belong. The reading-disabled child's troubles with rhyme became apparent. Although several years older, the poor readers experienced much more trouble choosing the correct word. It is not a matter of intelligence, just an insensitivity to the sound structure of language.

Not infrequently, an incorrect phoneme is accessed. As mentioned earlier, a child may look at a picture of a volcano that she has seen many times, and the word she pulls up is *tornado*—close in sound but not in meaning. Because of difficulties in accessing the intended phonemes, a child may *talk around a word,* as Alex did when he could not retrieve the word *ocean,* or he may begin to say a word and end up with a series of um's or "um, um, um . . . I forgot." Such children often point instead of speaking or become tearful or angry as they become increasingly frustrated at being unable to utter the word they have in mind.

As a child gets older, she may resort to using words that lack precision or specificity to cover up her retrieval difficulties, such as using vague words like *stuff* or *things* instead of the actual name of the object. Sometimes it is hard to follow the conversation of a dyslexic because the sentences are filled with pronouns or words lacking in specificity: "You know, I went and picked up the stuff and took it there. The things were all mixed up, but I got the stuff anyway." It is important to remember that the problem is with expressive language and not with thinking. She knows exactly what she wants to say; the difficulty is with pulling out the right word. These expressive language difficulties continue as the child matures. She may be quiet, appear inarticulate, or in general experience difficulties expressing herself. This is a frequent pattern, but it is not invariable; some dyslexic children may be quite articulate when they speak.

As with Alex and Gregory, the ideas are often advanced; it is the need to produce a word on command that is problematic for the dyslexic child. Parents and teachers may become irritated with a child because he seems so bright, and they cannot understand why he spits out the wrong word. However, the frustration of the adults is nothing compared to the frustration and shame experienced by the child as he says the wrong word. Demand for instant responses, to hurry up with an answer—as when Gregory was questioned by his attending physician on rounds—only serve to increase anxiety, which further interferes with rapid and smooth word retrieval. As a dyslexic child matures into adulthood, his speech continues to show evidence of the difficulties he has getting to the sound structure of words. His speech is littered with hesitations; sometimes there are many long pauses, or he may talk around a word, using many indirect words in place of the single word he can't seem to come up with (technically referred to as circumlocution). He is neither glib nor fluent in his spoken language.

Given a choice, the dyslexic can almost always *recognize* the correct word. For example, if asked whether a sudden ghostly appearance is an *apparition* or a *partition,* a dyslexic will invariably choose the correct response, *apparition.* However, when confronted and put on the spot to recall or to come up with the word for a sudden ghostly appearance, the dyslexic may reach into his lexicon and pull out a word that sounds similar to the word he intended—in this instance, *partition* instead of *apparition.* For those who do not understand the phonologic basis of this confusion, it may appear that the child guessed or is totally confused. Parents must always keep in mind (and remind their child's teacher) that these are phonologic slips and that the child most likely knows the meaning of the word but just can't get it out. The child or adult may say, "It was just on the tip of my tongue," or "I just can't get the word out. It's stuck."

Finally, and perhaps most critically, fuzzy phonemes interfere with the beginning reader's ability to learn the names and the sounds of the letters of the alphabet. This series of accomplishments—learning the alphabet, learning the names of individual letters, and then learning the sounds that the letters make—marks an important transition for the would-be reader. For the first time the child is expected to link the abstract squiggles that we call letters with their names and with their sounds. This *is* the beginning of reading. It is a necessary if not entirely sufficient accomplishment that must be in place in order to read. Conversely, difficulty in acquiring these skills is an early warning signal that the child may have a reading problem.

As children mature, they develop a sensitivity to the parts of language. Initially, spoken language is like a strip of movie film—it appears continuous and without any breaks. With time, children begin to appreciate the segmental nature of language: Just as strips of film on closer examination are composed of individual frames, ribbons of speech can be broken down into separate words; words, in turn, can be pulled apart into syllables, and syllables into particles—phonemes.

Children's increasing sensitivity to the sounds of language and to the segmental nature of language can be observed in the preschool child. Beginning at close to three years of age, preschoolers love to learn and to sing their ABCs. At this stage the alphabet is really an undifferentiated string going from A to Z; children generally are not aware of the individual letters. If you stop a three-year-old child in the middle of singing the ABC song and ask what letter comes next, she most likely will have to start to sing the song all over again. This is perfectly normal; the ABC song helps a child become familiar with the names of the letters, and it is not expected that she will be able to differentiate individual letters until she is a little older. A year or so later, by about age four, a child begins to recognize and to name individual letters; she is typically most interested in learning the letters of her own first name. By the time she is ready to enter kindergarten, she will know the names of most, if not all, of the upper- and lower-case letters. Of course, the accomplishment of this critical milestone may vary reflecting differing preschool and home experiences. Certainly, by the time a child has had a full year of instruction in kindergarten, she should be able to recognize and to name all of the letters of the alphabet, both uppercase and lowercase. Learning letter sounds, which is critical for reading, is intimately linked to learning the names of letters. Mastering letter-sound relationships is the focus of intense activity during kindergarten, and children generally leave kindergarten knowing the sounds of most of the letters of the alphabet. Gradually and sequentially, from the time they are toddlers through their first year of formal education, children are busily acquiring the raw materials for becoming a reader: knowledge of the alphabet, recognition of individual letters, and the ability to associate sounds with letters. Failure or delay in acquiring these skills is an early clue to a potential reading problem.

Digging into Your Genetic Roots for Clues

In addition to early clues provided by difficulties with spoken language, your own family history can often provide helpful clues regarding a vulnerability to a reading problem. Dyslexia runs in families; having a parent or a sibling who is dyslexic increases the probability that you are, too.

Between one-quarter and one-half of the children born to a dyslexic parent will also be dyslexic. If one child in a family is dyslexic, almost half of his sisters and brothers are also likely to be dyslexic. Not surprisingly, in cases where a child is identified as dyslexic and his parents are then evaluated, in one-third to one-half of the cases a parent turns out to be dyslexic, too. The writer John Irving and the financier Charles Schwab both discovered they were dyslexic following the diagnosis in a child.

A child who has a dyslexic sibling or parent should be monitored extremely closely for early indications of oral language difficulties. This is one of those instances in which parents must really be tuned in to their child's spoken language. And knowing that a child has a family history of reading problems clearly provides an unusual opportunity for early identification of affected siblings. As I will discuss later, it is now possible to test young children (optimally, at around four or five years of age) for early indicators of dyslexia. Children with family histories of reading disability should be standing right in the front of the line for such testing.

Recent studies have shown that not only does dyslexia run in families but it is carried as a genetic trait. A characteristic that is familial may not necessarily be passed down to succeeding generations through genetic mechanisms. Traits may also go from one generation to the next as a result of environmental exposure to certain behaviors or habits. Even if a child does carry a gene or a set of genes that predispose him to dyslexia, it just means he is at higher risk for it. If dyslexia was entirely genetic, then both members of a set of identical twins (sharing the exact genes) would have reading problems. In reality, in only 65 to 70 percent of the cases are both twins dyslexic; in 30 to 35 percent one identical twin is dyslexic and the other is not. And so the ultimate expression of dyslexia depends on an interaction between a child's genetic endowment and his environment. In addition to his innate predisposition, being read to at home, playing rhyming games, and, particularly, the effectiveness of his reading instruction at school will all play a role in determining what kind of a reader he becomes.

As if to emphasize this point, I am often asked if anything can be done to help when dyslexia is inherited. Of course there is. Many disorders with a strong genetic predisposition respond well to treatment (such as Type 2 diabetes mellitus). Knowing a child has a reading problem that may be inherited does mean, however, that it has to be taken very seriously and may require a very strong effort to build up his skills.

In Chapter 19 I will discuss such reading programs and how they meet with significant success, particularly if the problem is identified early.

Is there a dyslexia gene? The complexity of the reading process suggests that no single dominant gene gives rise to dyslexia; there are several genes involved. At this time there is promising research regarding a number of them. Some of these genes may enhance reading ability, while others depress it. The genetics of dyslexia is an area of very active research, and scientists are finding that the search for the genes responsible is more complicated than they originally anticipated.

Myths and Misunderstandings About Dyslexia

In being alert to clues to dyslexia, it is also important to be aware of some of the popular misconceptions and myths surrounding the disorder. Sometimes a child's diagnosis is wrong or delayed because she fails to demonstrate one or more of the presumed "symptoms."

One of the most enduring misconceptions is that dyslexic children *see* letters and words backward and that reversals (writing letters and words backward) are an invariable sign. While it is true that dyslexic children have difficulties attaching the appropriate labels or names to letters and words, there is no evidence that they actually *see* letters and words backward. In one study, primary school children who had reading problems and also a tendency to make reversals were asked to copy a series of letters and words. They had no difficulty doing so. What they did find troublesome was having to *name* the words accurately. For example, the children were able to copy the word *was* and to say the individual letters making up the word in the appropriate order. They typically then would name the word as *saw*. This study confirmed that dyslexic children have problems in naming but not in copying letters. A related misconception is that mirror writing invariably accompanies dyslexia. In fact, backward writing and reversal of letters and words are common in the early stages of writing development among dyslexic and nondyslexic children.

Because these beliefs about dyslexia are so prevalent, many dyslexic children who do not make reversals are often undiagnosed. One frustrated father who was trying to obtain help for his daughter commented, "They say she doesn't have a problem, she just has to work harder and that she can't have dyslexia because she doesn't transpose letters or write backward."

On the other hand, some parents and teachers worry unnecessarily when a young child shows reversals. It seems that A.J., six years old and starting first grade, was beginning to read, making the kinds of phonological errors discussed earlier, such as reading *hop* as *hob.* Unaware that A.J.'s beginning attempt to code sounds to letters was a very positive indication of his progress in learning to read and appropriate for his age and grade, his grandmother was concerned that he was "mixing up his p's and b's." I reassured her that this was not a sign of dyslexia. Reversals are irrelevant to the diagnosis of dyslexia.

Left-handedness, difficulties with spatial (including right-left) orientation, trouble tying shoelaces, and clumsiness are also said to be associated with dyslexia. These are certainly not core findings that we would expect in most people with dyslexia, but of course there are clusters of people within the larger population of individuals with dyslexia who are also left-handed or who have spatial difficulties. Whatever subgroups of children with dyslexia may exist, it is clear that the vast majority of the dyslexic population share a common phonologic weakness (about 88 percent, our research team determined).

We will now move beyond the earliest clues to dyslexia and focus on the later clues which can alert you that your child is not progressing along the path to becoming a skilled reader and may need extra help.

9

Later Clues to Dyslexia

Breaking the reading code allows a child to cross the threshold into the world of reading. But learning to read marks only the beginning of a continuing process. Just as we now understand how a child first learns to read, a clear picture has emerged of how a child becomes a skilled reader. Surprisingly, it involves an increasing focus on the details—the letters making up a word.

When a child first begins to read, the *logographic stage,* he does not use knowledge of letter names or letter sounds to "read" a word. We are all familiar with four- and five-year-olds "reading" familiar signs such as Stop or McDonald's or words on boxes of breakfast cereal. These very young children are relying on visual cues of various sorts, such as the shape of the red Stop sign or the famous golden arch. In one study, researchers pasted a *Coca-Cola* logo over a Rice Krispies box, and the majority of preschoolers continued to "read" it as Rice Krispies. This level of reader will recognize only a few words, invariably associated with a highly distinctive visual cue. These young children are not paying attention to the word itself but are memorizing some associated visual cue and relying on that to memorize and later recognize the word. Using such arbitrary cues is obviously of limited value. Children can memorize hundreds of words, but by the time they reach fifth grade, they will come across as many as ten thousand new words during the school year. Relying on memorization simply won't do. To make progress in reading, they must learn how the alphabetic code works. Linking letters to sounds and then sounding out words is the only guarantee of being able to decode the thousands of new words. This is exactly what primary school children do.

Generally during kindergarten, or as early as nursery school, as children learn letter names, a type of early or primitive reading becomes evident. If a child knows the letter names *j* and *l*, for example, she can *read* the word *jail* by just saying the first letter name (*jay*) and the last (*ell*). This type of reading is considered primitive because the reader is not paying attention to the full complement of letters in the word; she is relying on letter names and not letter sounds. To read effectively a child needs to pay attention to all the letters in a written word so that she can link them to the sounds she hears in the spoken word and then decode the word. Otherwise she will confuse words that have the same initial and final consonants but differ in their interior vowels (such as *book* and *beak*). As children progress in learning to read, they rely more and more on trying to relate letters and groups of letters to the sounds they hear in spoken language.

One group of researchers discovered how important it is for early readers to try to match letters to sounds even if the children don't always succeed. They found that the kinds of errors children make while reading in the first grade offer important clues to their ability to use the phonologic code and, ultimately, to become proficient readers. Children whose reading errors reflected an attempt to match letters to sounds (for example, reading *big* for *beg*) tended to be good readers at the end of the school year. Conversely, children whose errors indicated a lack of awareness of the relation of letters to sounds typically ended the year as poor readers. (Such children might read *like* for *milk,* words that have some letters in common but do not sound the same.) These children were not flexing their phonologic reading muscles. Parents should be concerned when their children act in a similar way. Above all else, the transition to being a skilled reader requires a child to focus her attention on the *internal* details of the word, on the specific letters that make up the word and the sounds they represent. There is no other way.

But reading is more than associating letters with sounds. The aspiring reader must build his reading vocabulary so that eventually he can read complex, long, or unfamiliar words. Since he has stored each letter that has been transformed into a sound, he has accumulated within his brain an entire storehouse of letter representations. If our young reader were to stop here, his reading would be very slow and laborious since he would have to read letter by letter. But as a child reads, he builds up his vocabulary and with it his storehouse of saved words, and now things really begin to accelerate. The child goes from storing images of individual letters associated with specific sounds to storing larger and larger chunks of printed material—common letters that frequently go together (*-at, -gh, -th*), larger groups of letters that recur (*-ight, -eight, -ought*), and, finally, after the child has read many books and successfully decoded thousands of words again and again, he has accumulated a storehouse of entire words. All the child needs to do now is look at the printed word on the page and a match is made with a word that is stored within his brain. As noted earlier, as a person becomes proficient in reading, the different kinds of relevant information—the word's spelling, its pronunciation, and its meaning—are more tightly linked together as part of the same resonating neural circuit in the occipito-temporal (word form) area. Once the person plugs into the word, the whole circuit lights up, and the word is immediately recognized and understood.

A skilled reader has a huge internal dictionary of stored words. The aspiring reader must use the phonetic code to create her own individual storehouse of words and then continue to rely on the phonetic code throughout life, even as a literate adult. Recent scientific evidence indicates that advanced readers, too, demonstrate some degree of reliance on phonology to activate the stored word.

The beauty of this process is that it allows the reader to decipher and read a word that she has never before encountered. She sees a word and scans all the letters. Do any of the letters fall into a familiar pattern? Do they resemble letter groups—parts of words—that she has stored? If so, she is able to take these letter patterns and connect them to a known pronunciation. For example, if she sees the unfamiliar printed word *architect,* she may know that the letters *t-e-c-t* go together and how they are pronounced. She may also know from experience that the letters *a-r-c-h* are often grouped together and that *arch* sounds either like the arch of your foot or like Noah's ark. She tries to pronounce the unknown word both ways, *arch-itect* or *ar-ki-tect,* and uses the surrounding text to judge which pronunciation fits. From the context she realizes that the word is *architect,* meaning a designer of buildings, and is pronounced like ark (ar-ki-tekt). Once she has successfully decoded this word, it joins the other words stored in her lexicon. Each time she reads the word again, the connection from the printed word to its stored model becomes stronger. After reading it correctly several times, she will activate its stored model—including its spelling, pronunciation, and meaning—instantly, thus adding it to her growing list.

Fluency—reading a word accurately, quickly, smoothly, and with good expression—is acquired by practice, by reading a word over and over again. This is consistent with what we know about neural circuits that are reinforced and strengthened by repetition. A reader must have four or more successful encounters with a new word to be able to read it fluently. (As will be discussed later, I use the word *fluent* to describe how a skilled reader reads; I reserve the term *automatic* for describing the neural processes that underlie fluent reading.) And once a word can be read fluently, the reader no longer has any need to rely on context. Fluency does not describe a stage in which a reader is able to decode *all* words instantly; rather, we become fluent word by word. Studies in which the eye movements of readers are tracked have shown that a skilled reader pauses at between 50 and 80 percent of the words in a text. He needs to fixate on the words, essentially to scan them in, but does so very, very quickly because the words—their spelling patterns and pronunciations—are well known to him. If you meet someone on the street you don't know well, you may continue to stare at him until some shred of recognition appears; however, if you know someone well, a glance is enough.

Initially, small common words are read instantly; as the reader progresses, larger and more complicated words, including words that appear infrequently, join the storehouse of words read at a glance. Although children's books may contain thousands of words, only a relative few make up most of the text. In the primary grades, for example, 50 percent of the entire text is comprised of about one hundred words; 75 percent of the text, one thousand words; and about 90 percent of the text, five thousand words. The remaining 10 percent are words that occur infrequently. Since as few as one hundred words make up half of those in a typical book for schoolchildren, you can understand how boys and girls who are good readers can become fluent quite quickly and are soon reading with relative ease.

In addition to reading words accurately and quickly, a skilled reader understands what he reads. Reading comprehension develops gradually so that, over time, the balance tips from learning mostly from listening to learning through reading. Thus, the beginning reader learns much more from what he hears than from what he reads in print. This gap narrows in the primary grades as the child becomes a better reader. By seventh grade the balance begins to favor reading; at this point the reader is said to have *mature* reading comprehension. Gradually, the student gains more and more from reading so that by the time he is in college most of his knowledge and vocabulary is acquired through book learning.

A large vocabulary is a key element in facilitating reading comprehension; in turn, reading itself is a powerful influence in developing a child's vocabulary. Indeed, it is difficult to overestimate the importance of reading to a child's intellectual growth. Reading researcher Keith Stanovich has emphasized how dependent a child's vocabulary is on reading. A child learns about seven new words a day, which amounts to a staggering three thousand words a year. To acquire a new word for his vocabulary, a child must scrutinize the inner details of the word and not gloss over it. For the most part, analyzing each letter and letter group in a word is the only way an accurate stored representation is formed and the most effective means of having a new written word become a part of the child's working vocabulary.

Books offer almost three times as many interesting or complicated words—words outside the general vocabulary of a sixth grader—compared to even the most educated speakers. Books for adult readers have about fifty rare words for every one thousand words; the spoken language of a college graduate has only about seventeen rare words per one thousand spoken words. Children's books, too, "have 50 percent more rare words in them than does the conversation of college graduates." And so simply relying on even the most sophisticated conversations to increase vocabulary falls short of what can be gained through reading.

The powerful influence of early reading on later reading and vocabulary growth was demonstrated when researchers had children keep diaries of how they spent their time when they were not in school. As shown in Figure 29, the very best readers, those who scored better than 90 percent of their peers on reading tests, read for more than twenty minutes a day (about 1.8 million words a year), while those at the fiftieth percentile read only 4.6 minutes a day (282,000 words yearly). The poorest readers, those children reading below the tenth percentile, read less than one minute each day (a meager 8,000 words a year), and would require one year to read what the best readers read in two days. Given such worrisome consequences of poor reading, it is desirable to identify, early on, a child who is not on track to becoming a skilled reader.

Fortunately, the process of becoming a skilled reader is well mapped

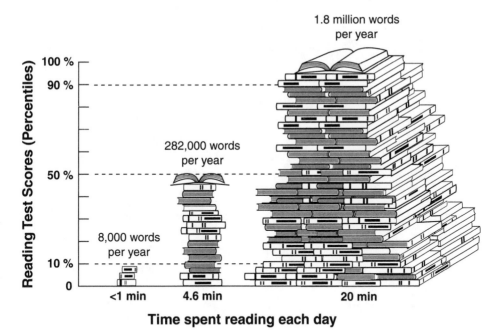

Figure 29. Good Readers Read Many Words Per Year;
Poor Readers Read Very Few

Good readers spend more time reading each day so that they read many more words in a year compared to poor readers.

out. It consists of a series of discrete and discernible accomplishments, ones you can look for and monitor to determine if your child is on track. To help you do this, I've included a guide for the expected developmental sequence and timing of specific reading-related skills or benchmarks. Keep in mind, though, that these are general guidelines for the typical child, and they are certainly not written in stone. Each of these expected steps represents a single point. What we are looking for is a series of points that together, over time, can help affirm that a child is on course or alert you early on that there might be a problem. Because teaching or learning experiences influence phonologic skills, the child's level of schooling, rather than age, may at times be the more appropriate guide to expectations.

A Guide to the Development of Reading-Related Skills

Early Preschool Accomplishments (age 3–4)

- Begins to develop awareness that, like a roll of perforated postage stamps, sentences and then words come apart
- Shows an interest in the sounds of language: repeats and plays with sounds, especially rhymes; recites nursery rhymes ("Humpty Dumpty," "Jack and Jill")
- Identifies ten alphabet letters, most likely from his or her own name

Late Preschool Accomplishments (age 4–5)

- Breaks spoken words into syllables (such as today ⟶ *to-day*) (50 percent of children can count the number of syllables in a spoken word)
- Begins to break words into phonemes (20 percent of children can count the number of phonemes in a spoken word)
- Recognizes and names a growing number of letters

Beginning Kindergarten Accomplishments (age 5–5½)

- Compares whether two spoken words rhyme: Do *cat* and *mat* rhyme? Do *hop* and *mat* rhyme?
- Names a word that rhymes with a simple word like *cat* or *make*
- Recognizes and names just about all upper- and lowercase letters

End of Kindergarten Accomplishments (age 5½–6)

Spoken language:

- Continues to progress in breaking spoken words into syllables (90 percent of children can count the number of syllables in a word)
- Identifies which of three spoken words or pictures begins with the same sound as a given word (when instructed: Tell me which word begins with the same first sound as *car: mat, can,* or *dog*—he answers *can*) or with a different sound than the other two (when asked which word begins with a different sound—*man, dog,* or *mud*—he answers *dog*)
- Pronounces the beginning sound in a word (when asked to say the first sound of the word *mat,* he answers "*mmmm*")
- Counts the number of phonemes in a small word (when asked to

count the sounds he hears in *me,* he finds two; accomplished by 70–80 percent of children)

- Blends (pushes together) phonemes into a complete word (when asked what word the sounds "*zzzz,*" "*oo*" make, he answers *zoo*)

Print:

- Names all the letters of the alphabet
- Knows the sounds of almost all the letters of the alphabet
- Masters the alphabetic principle; understands that the sequence of letters within a written word represents the number and sequence of sounds heard in the spoken word
- Begins to decode simple words
- Recognizes a growing number of common words by sight (*you, my, are, is, the*)
- Uses *invented spelling,* such as writing *krr* for *car*
- Writes many uppercase and lowercase letters
- Writes his or her own name (first and last) and names of family members or pets

First Grade Accomplishments (age 6–7)

Spoken language:

- Counts the sounds in longer (three-phoneme) words (when asked, Can you count the sounds you hear in *same?*, he answers *three*)
- Says what word remains if a given sound is taken away from the beginning or end of a three-phoneme word (when instructed, Say *bat* without saying the "*b,*" he says *at*)
- Blends the sounds in three-phoneme words (when asked, What word do the sounds, "*m,*" "*aaaa,*" "*n*" form?, he answers *man*)

Print:

- Reads aloud with accuracy and comprehension any text that is meant for first grade
- Links letters to sounds to decode unknown words
- Accurately decodes one-syllable words (real words like *sit* and *bath,* and nonsense words like *zot* and *shan*)
- Knows sounds of common letter groups or word families such as *-ite* and *-ate*
- Recognizes by sight common irregularly spelled words (which do not follow the pattern of a word family), such as *have, said, where, two*

- Has reading vocabulary of three hundred to five hundred words, including sight words and words that are easy to sound out
- Monitors his or her own reading
- Self-corrects if an incorrectly identified word does not fit with cues provided by the letters in the word or with cues provided by the context surrounding the word
- Reads simple instructions such as "Open your book"
- Begins to spell accurately short, easy words

Second Grade Accomplishments (age 7–8)

Print:

- Routinely links letters to sounds to decode unknown words
- Begins to learn strategies for breaking multisyllabic words into syllables
- Accurately reads some multisyllable real and nonsense words, such as *Kalamazoo*
- Begins to read with fluency—reads accurately, smoothly, rapidly, and with inflection
- Reads and comprehends fiction and nonfiction meant for second grade
- Represents the complete sound of a word when spelling
- Reads on his own voluntarily

Third Grade Accomplishments (age 8–9)

Print:

- Reads aloud with fluency and comprehension any text meant for third grade
- Uses knowledge of prefixes, suffixes, and roots to infer meanings of words
- Reads longer fiction selections and chapter books
- Summarizes the main points from readings
- Correctly spells previously studied words
- Uses a dictionary to learn the meaning of unknown words

Fourth Grade and Above Accomplishments (age 9 and over)

- Reads to learn
- Reads for pleasure and for information

Slow Readers

For dyslexic readers the process of learning to read and of becoming a skilled reader is torturously slow. Benchmarks are significantly delayed. At the beginning, difficulties linking letters to sounds interfere with learning to read. Over time, as the dyslexic learns to read, he, too, begins to build up his own storehouse of letter and word representations. Unfortunately, the dyslexic reader may match only a few of the letters in a word to their sounds. As a result, the stored model of that word is a bit off and incomplete. Later on, when the dyslexic reader comes across that word again, he may find it hard to locate an exact stored match or to recognize the printed word at all.

As mentioned previously, part of the process of becoming a skilled reader is forming successively more detailed and complete representations of familiar words. Generally, dyslexic readers require many more exposures to a printed word over a much longer period of time before the stored representations are clear and true to the printed word. In some instances, stored representations continue to be imperfect, impeding the ready retrieval of words. As a result, even when dyslexic readers are able to decode words accurately, they are still not quick in their reading of these words. The phonologic weakness clearly affects not only learning to read but also the ability of dyslexic readers to become skilled readers.

As a further consequence of their imperfectly stored word models, dyslexic readers are forced to continue to rely on context to get to a word's meaning; consequently, the benefit is limited to that particular situation. Because a dyslexic reader often gets to the meaning without having first fully decoded the word, there is no true stored representation added to his memory bank. The next time he comes across that word it is as if he has never seen it before, and he will have to go through the same exercise of using context to get to the word's meaning.

Context also explains a common puzzling symptom of dyslexia. Many dyslexic readers complain of difficulties in reading the little words, such as *in, on, the, that,* and *an.* The parents of a nine-year-old dyslexic boy, Noah, described his peculiar difficulty with reading small words while at the same time

reading without apparent hesitation longer, more difficult words, such as *museum* and *Metropolitan Opera,* and shorter words representing *things* such as *tree, bat,* etc. Our son, a baseball fan, when in third grade could read *Metropolitan Stadium,* but the word *on* gave him real difficulties.

Since dyslexic readers rely so much on context, it is often difficult to figure out a small, so-called *function* word whose meaning cannot be gleaned from the context. For example, a ball could be *on, over,* or *under* the table, which makes it difficult to decide which of these choices is the one the author intended. For the same reason a dyslexic might be able to read words such as *tree* and *bat* because they represent concrete objects that can be predicted from the text as well as visualized. The small function words are so neutral that it is difficult for the dyslexic child to find something in the text to help him anchor and remember the word.

Finally, the ability of a child—an avid baseball fan—to read the name of a local baseball stadium and not other, seemingly simpler words presents an example of the importance of reading material that is relevant and meaningful to the reader. Rather than having to be pushed, he finds the content itself so interesting that he is pulled into the reading material. Whether it's science or baseball, even those with severe dyslexia can learn to read, not only decoding isolated words, but comprehending the materials—for, after all, that is the pull.

Judging Your Child's Progress

In the first part of this chapter I focused on how skilled reading develops and when to expect the successive milestones characteristic of skilled reading. This knowledge demystifies reading; it allows you to observe your child's reading in a new, *informed* way. You know when to expect your child to walk and to talk, and now you will be able to know what to anticipate in your child's reading development and when to expect it.

You will also learn how to recognize the danger signs, the specific clues that alert you that your child's reading is not progressing smoothly. *Just as a parent would not think of ignoring her child's scheduled physical with his pediatrician, every parent should regularly observe her child reading. Given the high prevalence of reading difficulties, it is much more likely for your child to have a reading problem than almost any other physical problem for which he is being checked.*

I recommend reading with your child as often as possible, at least several evenings a week. Part of that time should be devoted to hearing your child read to you. Listening to your child read prevents a problem from developing without your knowledge; moreover, it's fun. I have wonderful memories of reading with my children, and although they are now adults, they often surprise me with details of stories we read together years ago.

Listen carefully as your child begins to read. For a first grader, is there evidence that he is trying, although imperfectly, to link letters with sounds? Has he taken that important first step of matching the initial letter of a word with its sound? As the year progresses, you should notice that he is matching sounds to letters in each position in a small word (beginning, end, and middle). He should also be recognizing common letter groups (such as *-ate, -at, -ite*) and associating them with their sounds. He should leave first grade reading.

By second grade his basic tools for reading should be in place. In particular, second grade should see the emergence of a child's ability to read easy multisyllabic words (such as *rabbit, butter* and *sleepy*). This important step involves paying attention to the individual parts *within* the word. He is matching not only the first and last parts of the word but the inner details of longer words as well. Follow along as he reads aloud and listen carefully. You should be concerned if your second grader is not yet sounding out words, is taking wild stabs at words, is not able to read new or unfamiliar grade-level words, has not yet penetrated the inside of a word when he is reading, cannot decode most single or some easy multisyllabic words, is not building a vocabulary of words that he can read fluently, or doesn't seem to enjoy reading.

While most children with reading problems are not identified until third grade, the ideal time to identify and help a child is during the very first few years of school, which is why I have concentrated on clues that are easy to observe during kindergarten and grades one and two. Good help can be given later, but it is much more difficult.

As your child progresses through third and higher grades, your focus shifts from wondering if she is learning to read to wanting to know if she is learning to read a critical core of words fluently. Reading is changing in character now. Words are more complicated, and there are many more of them. In class the emphasis is less on teaching reading than on using reading to gain information. It is therefore easy to understand why reading problems are so often diagnosed for the first time in third grade. Since dyslexic readers often do not use a decoding strategy to identify a word and instead rely heavily on the surrounding context to figure out its meaning, you should notice if your daughter uses word substitutions; these replacement words make sense in the context of the passage but do not resemble the pronunciation of the original word. For example, a child might read *car* for *automobile.* Making repeated substitutions is a sure sign that the reader is using context to guess at the meaning of words she has been unable to decode. Because these substitutions often make literal sense, you may find it helpful to obtain a second copy of the books your child is reading so that you can actually look at each word as she reads it. Otherwise, you may not always notice that she is substituting one word for another.

Pay attention to the overall rhythm of her reading. Is it smooth or hesitant? She should be reading most of the words on the page fluently. Does she instead tend to trip over the words? Slow or choppy oral reading with words omitted, substituted, or misspoken are important clues that a third grader is not on track for becoming a skilled reader. Such children are in terror of being called on to read aloud and often go to great lengths to avoid such embarrassment; they often stay home, ask to leave the room, or act out and have to be sent out of the room.

In addition to problems with reading, poor spelling is often a sign of dyslexia. Spelling and reading are intimately linked; to spell correctly a child relies on his stored representations of a word, and these are imperfect in dyslexia. Spelling difficulties may be an indication that the child is not paying attention to all the letters in a word and not storing that word correctly. As a child who is dyslexic goes on in school, difficulties with spelling persist. In fact, spelling errors may remain long after a dyslexic child or adult has learned to decode most words accurately. Analysis of spelling errors often reveals omissions of entire blocks of sounds or confusion of the order of sounds. These comments from Daniel, a thirty-something computer programmer, reflect the experience of many dyslexics:

> My spelling is atrocious. . . . So often I compensate by using a smaller word or words (often a poor compromise). Spell checkers are a great help but not always. Often the spelling is mangled so much that the spell checker can't find a match.

I have found handwriting to be an important clue to dyslexia. Children who are dyslexic frequently have abominable handwriting—a problem that continues into adulthood. I believe this difficulty reflects the dyslexic child's problem of appreciating the sounds that make up a word. While speaking, the lips and mouth form phonemes in articulating words. In writing, the fingers express phonemic awareness (they form the fine motor correlates of the phonemes). Not hearing the phoneme distinctly results in an inability to write it clearly. This is my own theory, and I am unaware of any evidence to confirm or refute it. Oddly, the same fingers of a dyslexic reader that clutch pencils awkwardly and form letters hesitantly gracefully whiz across the keyboard as they type. Word processing is often an incredible relief to dyslexic children and adults alike (perhaps it is the freedom of not having to form the letters that is so liberating). Matt Fisher, who is dyslexic and head of his own architectural firm, describes his experiences with the keyboard:

> None of my friends type as fast as I do. I think it's because I memorize the words, not the parts. So I'm just reproducing words. . . . I guess I'm really just memorizing all the words and using them as tokens both for input and output.

I think Matt is absolutely right. He is not interacting with the word, nor is he sounding it out; he is acting as a pass-through—just lifting the word as a whole and placing it on the page via the keyboard.

The inability to read fluently leaves its mark on young adults who are dyslexic. By adolescence, good readers have built huge storehouses of word representations and are reading thousands of words instantly. Decoding is not a problem for them, so their energies can be devoted to thinking about what they read. Bright dyslexic adolescents love to think, but for them it's hard to take in the raw material—the printed words— that serve as the source of inspiration for new ideas. They must devote their full concentration to decoding words instead of attending to issues of comprehension. Reflecting the lack of fluency, they read slowly—a hallmark of dyslexia. The lack of fluency causes significant problems for dyslexic adolescents as they try to cope with large volumes of written work. For example, homework assignments are often incomplete or take a great deal of time to complete. Fluency is what binds a reader to the text. If a child cannot effortlessly decode a critical mass of words on the page, he cannot engage the text. He'll be at odds with it. I frequently hear people say, "My son is not paying attention to his homework." If you cannot penetrate and decode enough words on a page, reading is like gliding over ice: You never get into the words and, of course, their meanings. Why would someone continue to pay attention to words that have no meaning for him? Would you continue to read what is in essence a foreign text that you cannot decipher? After a while you would lose attention, start daydreaming, stare out the window, and then give up.

Furthermore, the necessity of devoting all his attention to decoding the words on the page makes a dyslexic reader extremely vulnerable to any noises or movements. Reading for him is fragile, and the process can be disrupted at any moment. Any little sound that draws his attention away from the page is a threat to his ability to maintain his reading. He needs all his attention to try to decipher the printed words. In contrast, a fluent reader has attention to spare, so room noises are not likely to interfere with his reading. The practical consequences of this fragility are that dyslexic readers often require an extremely quiet room in which to do their reading or to take tests.

The difficulties that a dyslexic reader has in gaining command of the phonology of his primary language are exacerbated when he tries to learn a new language. Persistent difficulties in learning a foreign language provide an important clue that a student may be dyslexic.

As was said earlier, a person who has not mastered the phonetic code and developed into a skilled reader must often rely on brute memorization, as does this fifty-two-year-old man with particularly severe dyslexia. (I have left the text as he wrote it.)

> I have had to memorize every word that I use in speaking or in writing. If I have not memorized that word, I can't pronounce it either. I leave off parts of words when I write and I leave of parts of woulds when I pronounce them. I also leave of words in a sentence if I am writing something. If I have memorized a word now [and I] see that word highfinated in a song book, I do not recognize that word. I have to take that word and squash highfins and get that word back to how it looks when I memorized it before I can recongize it again.

There is one final clue to dyslexia in children and adults alike: the fact that they say they are in pain. Dyslexia inflicts pain. It represents a major assault on self-esteem. In grade school children, this may be expressed as a reluctance to attend school or moodiness or spoken expressions such as "I'm dumb" or "I get teased a lot." Adolescents may develop feelings of shame and work hard to hide their reading problem by avoiding school, pretending to have forgotten assignments, and doing anything not to read aloud in class. Adults invariably harbor deep pain and sadness reflecting years of assaults to their sense of self-worth. A highly successful student summed it up for most bright young dyslexics:

> My experiences resulting from my dyslexia have had a serious impact on me. . . . I have particularly low self-esteem when it comes to my schoolwork, and I rely very heavily on encouragement from my teachers. Positive reinforcement has been the driving force behind most of my academic success.

At the same time I want to make clear to the dyslexic reader that in spite of these difficulties, he shouldn't be discouraged. The work of one reading researcher, in fact, offers great encouragement. Rosalie Fink has studied a very intriguing and accomplished group of dyslexic men and women, highly intelligent individuals who exemplify the paradox of dyslexia. Possessing at the same time a persisting phonologic deficit and extraordinary intellectual accomplishments, the group includes such distinguished scientists as Baruj Benacerraf, chair of comparative pathology at the Harvard Medical School; Ronald Davis, professor of biochemistry at Stanford University Medical School; Florence Haseltine, director of the Center for Population Research at the National Institute for Child Health and Human Development; and Robert Knapp, emeritus director of gynecology and gynecologic oncology at the Brigham and Women's Hospital and the Dana Farber Cancer Institute at the Harvard Medical School. Some of these scientists are authors of highly acclaimed textbooks and scholarly articles, and their honors include a Nobel Prize and election to the National Academy of Sciences and the Institute of Medicine. These individuals provide a wonderful example of how dyslexic readers, under the right circumstances, can become skilled readers.

What seems to distinguish this group is the development of an unusually strong interest in a very narrow area of study, often while still children or adolescents. As Fink describes it,

By focusing on a single domain of knowledge, many of the individuals with dyslexia became virtual "little experts" about their favorite topic, sometimes beginning at an early age. For some, early reading interests later developed into high-powered careers; for others, early reading interests developed into life-long hobbies.

Their passionate interest in a subject drove them to read everything they could about it. This allowed them to concentrate on a restricted range of words—the relatively small group of words that makes up the repeating vocabulary of any discipline. By reading material on the same topic over and over again, these dyslexic readers were able to become fluent. Their intense interest in what they were reading spurred them on to not gloss over words but to try to pronounce each word and then use the surrounding context to make sure that the word fit in the passage. In this way they behaved like nonimpaired readers, constantly trying to refine the spellings and pronunciations so that what they read made sense. This small group of words was eventually added to their memory bank, allowing otherwise dyslexic readers to become fluent for these words.

Many of these people are still struggling with getting to the sounds of words and continue to rely on context to get to meaning. Baruj Benacerraf, a 1980 Nobel Laureate in Medicine or Physiology, said, "Even today, when I can't figure out a word, I guess from the context. Yes, I guess what makes sense." Moreover, seeing "the big picture" allows dyslexic readers to master what might seem to be overwhelming amounts of reading material. For example, Sylvia Law, professor of law, medicine, and psychiatry at New York University School of Law, does it this way:

> When you're immersed in a field, you kind of know what the forest looks like, and you're looking to see if there's a particular tree in here. So it's easy to just skim and zero in on the important stuff in the law, you know, the most important sentence in a 100-page document, where it says, "The court says. . . ." There are a lot of techniques and filtering devices that I use to get through lengthy legal documents.

Clearly, dyslexic men and women are able to make significant, even profound, contributions. Their stories prove that dyslexics can gain competence in the most complex areas of knowledge and explain why dyslexics often find high levels of success in careers in which they can become superspecialists.

The key to success and to avoiding much of this frustration is to recognize dyslexia as early as possible, even before a child is expected to begin to read. It is now possible to diagnose dyslexia reliably in children at the cusp of school entry; in school-age children; in young adults attending college, graduate, or professional school; and in parents and other adults who harbor a desire "to finally find out what is wrong with me." Because dyslexia springs from a common phonologic weakness, there is a great similarity and consistency to the difficulties most dyslexics experience. The clues you have just read about can alert you to the possibility that a person you know is dyslexic. The presence of several of these clues is a sign that you need to take the next step: consider a more systematic and formal evaluation for dyslexia. In the following chapter I will focus on who should seek an evaluation.

10

Should My Child
Be Evaluated for Dyslexia?

Having described how spoken language and skilled reading develop, and how a phonologic weakness might impact each, I now want to gather together all the clues that combined will serve as an early-warning system for recognizing dyslexia. The clues will help you answer the question: Should my son or daughter (or I) be evaluated for dyslexia?

No one wants to be an "alarmist" and put her child through an evaluation for trivial or transient bumps along the road to reading. Evaluations can take time, and those carried out privately can be expensive. But I think we have to remind ourselves that our children are precious, one-of-a-kind individuals and have only one life to live. If we elect not to evaluate a child and that child later proves to have dyslexia, we cannot give those lost years back to him. The human brain is resilient, but there is no question that early intervention and treatment bring about more positive change at a faster pace than an intervention provided to an older child. And then there is the erosion of self-esteem that accrues over the years as a child struggles to read.

Childhood is a time for learning. A child who delays breaking the phonetic code will miss much of the reading practice that is essential to building fluency and vocabulary; as a consequence, he will fall further and further behind in acquiring comprehension skills and knowledge of the world around him. To see this happen to a child is sad, all the more because it is preventable.

Joseph Torgesen, a reading researcher at Florida State University who has carried out many of the critical studies on intervention, has this to say about the need to identify children early on and the cost of waiting:

> To the extent that we allow children to fall seriously behind at any point during early elementary school, we are moving to a "remedial" rather than a "preventive" model of intervention. Once children fall behind in the growth of critical word reading skills, it may require very intensive interventions to bring them back up to adequate levels of reading accuracy, and reading fluency may be even more difficult to restore because of the large amount of reading practice that is lost by children each month and year that they remain poor readers.

Most parents and teachers delay evaluating a child with reading difficulties because they believe the problems are just temporary, that they will be outgrown. This is simply not true. Reading problems are not outgrown, they are persistent. As the participants in the Connecticut Longitudinal Study have demonstrated, at least three out of four children who read poorly in third grade continue to have reading problems in high school and beyond. What may seem to be tolerable and overlooked in a third grader certainly won't be in a high schooler or young adult. Without identification and proven interventions, virtually all children who have reading difficulties early on will still struggle with reading when they are adults.

Luckily, parents can play an active role in the early identification of a reading problem. All that is required is an observant parent who knows what she is looking for and who is willing to spend time with her child listening to him speak and read.

The specific signs of dyslexia, both weaknesses and strengths, in any one individual will vary according to the age and educational level of that person. The five-year-old who can't quite learn his letters becomes the six-year-old who can't match sounds to letters and the fourteen-year-old who dreads reading out loud and the twenty-four-year-old who reads excruciatingly slowly. The threads persist throughout a person's life. The key is knowing how to recognize them at different periods during development. Therefore, I have gathered the clues together to provide three distinct portraits of dyslexia: first, in early childhood from preschool through first grade; next, in school-age children from second grade on; and, last, in young adults and adults.

Clues to Dyslexia in Early Childhood

The earliest clues involve mostly spoken language. The very first clue to a language (and reading) problem may be delayed language. Once the child begins to speak, look for the following problems:

The Preschool Years

- Trouble learning common nursery rhymes such as "Jack and Jill" and "Humpty Dumpty"
- A lack of appreciation of rhymes
- Mispronounced words; persistent baby talk
- Difficulty in learning (and remembering) names of letters
- Failure to know the letters in his own name

Kindergarten and First Grade

- Failure to understand that words come apart; for example, that *batboy* can be pulled apart into *bat* and *boy,* and, later on, that the word *bat* can be broken down still further and sounded out as: "*b*" "*aaaa*" "*t*"
- Inability to learn to associate letters with sounds, such as being unable to connect the letter *b* with the "*b*" sound
- Reading errors that show no connection to the sounds of the letters; for example, the word *big* is read as *goat*
- The inability to read common one-syllable words or to sound out even the simplest of words, such as *mat, cat, hop, nap*
- Complaints about how hard reading is, or running and hiding when it is time to read
- A history of reading problems in parents or siblings

In addition to the problems of speaking and reading, you should be looking for these indications of strengths in higher-level thinking processes:

- Curiosity
- A great imagination
- The ability to figure things out
- Eager embrace of new ideas
- Getting the gist of things
- A good understanding of new concepts
- Surprising maturity
- A large vocabulary for the age group
- Enjoyment in solving puzzles
- Talent at building models
- Excellent comprehension of stories read or told to him

Clues to Dyslexia From Second Grade On

Problems in Speaking

- Mispronunciation of long, unfamiliar, or complicated words; the *fracturing* of words—leaving out parts of words or confusing the order of the parts of words; for example, *aluminum* becomes *amulium*
- Speech that is not fluent—pausing or hesitating often when speaking, lots of *um*'s during speech, no glibness
- The use of imprecise language, such as vague references to *stuff* or *things* instead of the proper name of an object
- Not being able to find the exact word, such as confusing words that sound alike: saying *tornado* instead of *volcano*, substituting *lotion* for *ocean*, or *humanity* for *humidity*
- The need for time to summon an oral response or the inability to come up with a verbal response quickly when questioned
- Difficulty in remembering isolated pieces of verbal information (rote memory)—trouble remembering dates, names, telephone numbers, random lists

Problems in Reading

- Very slow progress in acquiring reading skills
- The lack of a strategy to read new words
- Trouble reading *unknown* (new, unfamiliar) words that must be sounded out; making wild stabs or guesses at reading a word; failure to systematically sound out words
- The inability to read small "function" words such as *that, an, in*

- Stumbling on reading multisyllable words, or the failure to come close to sounding out the full word
- Omitting parts of words when reading; the failure to decode parts within a word, as if someone had chewed a hole in the middle of the word, such as *conible* for *convertible*
- A terrific fear of reading out loud; the avoidance of oral reading
- Oral reading filled with substitutions, omissions, and mispronunciations
- Oral reading that is choppy and labored, not smooth or fluent
- Oral reading that lacks inflection and sounds like the reading of a foreign language
- A reliance on context to discern the meaning of what is read
- A better ability to understand words *in context* than to read *isolated* single words
- Disproportionately poor performance on multiple choice tests
- The inability to finish tests on time
- The substitution of words with the same meaning for words in the text he can't pronounce, such as *car* for *automobile*
- Disastrous spelling, with words not resembling true spelling; some spellings may be missed by spell check
- Trouble reading mathematics word problems
- Reading that is very slow and tiring
- Homework that never seems to end, or with parents often recruited as readers
- Messy handwriting despite what may be an excellent facility at word processing—nimble fingers
- Extreme difficulty learning a foreign language
- A lack of enjoyment in reading, and the avoidance of reading books or even a sentence
- The avoidance of reading for pleasure, which seems too exhausting
- Reading whose accuracy improves over time, though it continues to lack fluency and is laborious
- Lowered self-esteem, with pain that is not always visible to others
- A history of reading, spelling, and foreign language problems in family members

In addition to signs of a phonologic weakness, there are signs of strengths in higher-level thinking processes:

- Excellent thinking skills: conceptualization, reasoning, imagination, abstraction
- Learning that is accomplished best through meaning rather than rote memorization
- Ability to get the "big picture"
- A high level of understanding of what is read *to* him
- The ability to read and to understand at a high level overlearned (that is, highly practiced) words in a special area of interest; for example, if his hobby is restoring cars, he may be able to read auto mechanics magazines
- Improvement as an area of interest becomes more specialized and focused, when he develops a miniature vocabulary that he can read
- A surprisingly sophisticated listening vocabulary
- Excellence in areas not dependent on reading, such as math, computers, and visual arts, or excellence in more conceptual (versus factoid-driven) subjects such as philosophy, biology, social studies, neuroscience, and creative writing

Clues to Dyslexia in Young Adults and Adults

Problems in Speaking

- Persistence of earlier oral language difficulties
- The mispronunciation of the names of people and places, and tripping over parts of words
- Difficulty remembering names of people and places and the confusion of names that sound alike
- A struggle to retrieve words: "It was on the tip of my tongue"
- Lack of glibness, especially if put on the spot
- Spoken vocabulary that is smaller than listening vocabulary, and hesitation to say aloud words that might be mispronounced

Problems in Reading

- A childhood history of reading and spelling difficulties
- Word reading becomes more accurate over time but continues to require great effort
- Lack of fluency

- Embarrassment caused by oral reading: the avoidance of Bible study groups, reading at Passover seders, or delivering a written speech
- Trouble reading and pronouncing uncommon, strange, or unique words such as people's names, street or location names, food dishes on a menu (often resorting to asking the waiter about the special of the day or resorting to saying, "I'll have what he's having," to avoid the embarrassment of not being able to read the menu)
- Persistent reading problems
- The substitution of made-up words during reading for words that cannot be pronounced—for example, *metropolitan* becomes *mitan*—and a failure to recognize the word *metropolitan* when it is seen again or heard in a lecture the next day
- Extreme fatigue from reading
- Slow reading of most materials: books, manuals, subtitles in foreign films
- Penalized by multiple-choice tests
- Unusually long hours spent reading school or work-related materials
- Frequent sacrifice of social life for studying
- A preference for books with figures, charts, or graphics
- A preference for books with fewer words per page or with lots of white showing on a page
- Disinclination to read for pleasure
- Spelling that remains disastrous and a preference for less complicated words in writing that are easier to spell
- Particularly poor performance on rote clerical tasks

Signs of Strengths in Higher-Level Thinking Processes

- The maintenance of strengths noted in the school-age period
- A high learning capability
- A noticeable improvement when given additional time on multiple-choice examinations
- Noticeable excellence when focused on a highly specialized area such as medicine, law, public policy, finance, architecture, or basic science
- Excellence in writing if content and not spelling is important
- A noticeable articulateness in the expression of ideas and feelings

- Exceptional empathy and warmth, and feeling for others
- Success in areas not dependent on rote memory
- A talent for high-level conceptualization and the ability to come up with original insights
  - Big-picture thinking
  - Inclination to think out of the box
  - A noticeable resilience and ability to adapt

These clues across the life span offer a portrait of dyslexia. Examine them carefully, think about them, and determine if any of these clues fit your child, you, or someone else you are close to. Look for clues in the weaknesses *and* strengths. Identifying the weaknesses makes it possible to spot dyslexia in children before they are expected to read and in adults after they have developed some degree of reading accuracy but are continuing to show the remnants of earlier problems, reading slowly and with great effort.

If you think you or your child has some of these problems, it is important to note how frequent they are and how many there are. You don't need to worry about isolated clues or ones that appear very rarely. For you to be concerned, the symptoms must be persistent; anyone can mispronounce a word now and then, or confuse similar-sounding words occasionally. What you are looking for is a persistent pattern—the occurrence of a number of these symptoms over a prolonged period of time. That represents a likelihood of dyslexia.

Getting Help

Identification of a problem is, of course, the key to getting help. The sooner a diagnosis is made, the quicker your child can get help, and the more likely you are to prevent secondary blows to her self-esteem. If your preschool child struggles with language, particularly with rhymes and pronouncing words, and especially if there is a family history of reading problems, you should not keep your worries to yourself. You need to seek help. Children with a history of dyslexia within their immediate family have a substantial risk of being dyslexic. The combination of a family history of dyslexia and symptoms of difficulties in spoken language can help identify a vulnerable child even before she begins formal schooling.

A preschooler can be seen by her pediatrician, who can then make a referral for further evaluation if appropriate. Since the focus of the evaluation of such a young child is on her spoken (rather than her written) language, I often turn to a speech and language pathologist to carry out this type of assessment. These specialists are quite knowledgeable about early language development and are often extremely helpful in assessing phonologic skills in young children. Parents can call the American Speech-Language-Hearing Association (301-897-5700) for the names of certified speech and language pathologists in your area or go to its Web site (www.asha.org/proserv).

Parents and teachers must closely monitor a child's progress in learning to read, beginning no later than kindergarten. Kindergarten is in many ways a watershed in identifying children who are vulnerable to dyslexia. For the first time a child is in a public environment where he is exposed to a formal curriculum geared to teaching those skills necessary for reading, and he is surrounded by his peers who are exposed to the same teaching. The child is now a student, and there are expectations for what must be learned. Even acknowledging that children come from different backgrounds and that children may intrinsically differ in their pace of learning, the clues I have listed are such important signals that reading is not progressing that they should not be ignored. The cost to your child and to you is too great. I have yet to meet a family that feels they acted too soon.

If you observe these signs, I urge you to speak to your child's teacher. Before doing so, it often helps to list your observations and your concerns. Parents are often so nervous when speaking to their child's teacher that they forget why they were worried. The teacher will appreciate having such a list as well. Ask her to categorize your child's progress. Ask her to be quite specific. Ask what the expectations are for a child at that particular time and where he is in relation to these expectations and to the progress of his classmates. Ask how much he has progressed since the beginning of the school year. What does the teacher predict for his progress by the close of the school year? What specifically is being done to ensure that your child increases his reading progress? This is a vitally important question. Remember, scientific data show that reading problems are persistent; they do not represent a temporary lag in development. It is wishful thinking to believe there will be a sudden magical improvement. Schools often have a tendency to want to wait; sometimes parents have this same tendency. (Why don't we see how things go until after Thanksgiving? We can't spoil his Christmas. Let's wait until after his birthday.) You don't want to be like the mother of one of my patients who was surprised to be told by her son's teacher on the very last day of school, "I really hope he has a better year next year."

Many of my patients have found this brief checklist helpful in setting up a meeting with their child's teacher:

- Make a written list of your concerns
- Set up a specific time to speak to your child's teacher; don't catch her on the run
- Find out how your child is progressing in reading; you want specifics, not generalities or euphemisms (you can check these against the benchmarks listed in Chapter 9)
- Pin down exactly how her reading progress is being measured
- Ask what reading group she is in and what level reader that group represents
- Ask how she compares to others in her class and in her grade
- Ask what the expectations are for her by year's end
- In very specific terms, ask what help she is receiving (the type of reading program, size of group, and minutes per day)
- If you can, visit the class and observe your child along with her classmates during a reading lesson

You are now an informed parent who is an effective advocate for your child. Your child is depending on you. It is a good feeling to be in control and to know what is and what is not acceptable. As a knowledgeable parent you will not accept allusions to a temporary or developmental lag or that "some children are just slow readers" or that girls are not dyslexic. Nor will you accept that there is "no such thing as dyslexia." Anyone who says this needs to be educated. If you are unhappy after your discussion with the teacher, seek a second opinion. Speak to the school psychologist, to the principal, or to the reading specialist (if there is one in your school). Be persistent. Parents are often fearful of antagonizing school personnel, and justifiably so; however, the alternative, waiting, can be even more harmful to your child. Your daughter's classroom teacher may have been worrying, too, and your interest may be just enough to jump-start the process of treatment. The worst thing you can do if you suspect a reading problem is to do nothing.

Under no circumstances should you allow yourself to be talked into waiting. This is not an option. Within schools, time just seems to ooze away. Set a deadline for a response. And do not depend solely on your school for an evaluation. Your pediatrician can refer you for testing as well. If you need help, contact the International Dyslexia Association (www.interdys.org), the International Learning Disabilities Association (www.ldanatl.org), the National Center for Learning Disabilities (www. ld.org), or Schwab Learning, a program of the Charles and Helen Schwab Foundation for Learning (www.schwablearning.org). Don't be intimidated. Act quickly. Trust your instincts. Remember, you know your child best.

Even if school personnel are not aware that your child is having difficulties reading, your child may know. A six- or seven-year-old is capable of recognizing that his reading is not going well. Attorney Paul Grossman describes his experience in first grade:

> I knew as soon as they started teaching reading. I remember in first grade we were reading Dick and Jane, and when it would come my turn, I didn't know where we were in the reader. It wasn't that I couldn't read at all, but I couldn't read well enough to keep up with where the kids before me had read. I knew I had a problem.

Evaluations are not only for children. An evaluation can sometimes turn an adult's entire life around and point him in a new and better direction. If you recognize your own problems (or those of your spouse or an adult child) in the clues given in the previous pages, I encourage you to get help. Start by getting an evaluation. You may find the answer to a puzzling array of observations you have made that includes signs of high intelligence seemingly contradicted by persistent difficulties with reading (or pronouncing) the simplest of words or by problems with rote memory or spelling. If you often wonder how you can seem so smart and yet be backward in reading at the same time, seek an evaluation. Don't hesitate or be frightened. One forty-two-year-old engineer confided to me, "I'm afraid that you'll find out that I am really dumb." But in fact we find that such people are much smarter than they ever expected; they just have a problem that needs attention. Worry never solves anything, nor does fear. It is never too late to get help, either in the form of remediation or, often, in the form of accommodations that may allow you to access your strengths for the first time.

Now that you are aware of the warning signals, I will tell you about the evaluation itself—how we go about making a diagnosis of dyslexia.

11

Diagnosing Dyslexia
in the School-Age Child

As common as reading problems are, and as much as we have learned about them, dyslexia is often missed. Take the experience of one of my colleagues. Here is the e-mail she sent me about her granddaughter Ashley:

> In order for Ashley to keep up [in third grade], my daughter spends up to four hours a night working with her on homework. She has to read *everything* to Ashley. Even then it is clear that she is not progressing at the same rate as her peers. You can't imagine what an effect reading is having on Ashley and on all of our lives. Her father, too, has a reading problem, and watching Ashley struggle brings back terrible memories.

I spoke with Ashley's mother, and she was indeed overcome with worry.

> Everyone seems to be saying there is no problem, and yet that doesn't mesh with what we are seeing day in and day out. Is it all our imagination? I don't think so. Deep down I know there has to be some sort of problem. Despite all of Ashley's hard work and her good attitude, despite all the kind support she receives from her school and from us, she isn't learning to read.

Ashley's story is not unusual. Tens of thousands of children who are struggling to read are going undiagnosed. Ashley has one of the most important predictive factors—a family history of a reading problem—and was having reading problems, yet no one made a diagnosis. You listen to her conversation and you hear *you know* and *stuff* and lots of *um's*. The clues were there, but no one asked the right questions.

There were enough clues in her spoken language, in her school history, and in her family history to tell us that Ashley warranted a full evaluation for dyslexia. Today's evaluation for dyslexia puts into practice all that we have learned about reading and reading problems. It is focused, it follows a structure, and it reflects a scientific rationale. The evaluation follows the rules set in place by the definition of dyslexia: a reading difficulty in a child or adult who otherwise has good intelligence, strong motivation, and adequate schooling.*

Rather than pulling away from the reality of the daily experience of dyslexia, today's scientifically based evaluation is genuine—you might say it is *organic*. It reflects the very real experiences that dyslexic children and their families have endured.

The diagnosis of dyslexia reflects a reading difficulty that is unexpected for a person's age, intelligence, level of education, or profession. It is a clinical diagnosis based on a thoughtful synthesis of information—from the child (or adult's) personal and family history; from observations of her speaking and reading; and from tests of reading and language. As in other conditions in medicine, the history is the most critical component and is afforded the most respect. Wise clinicians appreciate that tests are only approximations of the reality that is the individual's real life experience. And, in fact, the tests that are ultimately selected must be chosen with great care.

Obviously, an evaluation must be tailored to the individual so that it

---

* Under the leadership of G. Reid Lyon, a working group of the International Dyslexia Association meeting in Washington, D.C., in August 2002 developed the following, more detailed definition: "Dyslexia is a specific learning disability that is neurobiological in origin. It is characterized by difficulties with accurate and/or fluent word recognition and by poor spelling and decoding abilities. These difficulties typically result from a deficit in the phonological component of language that is often unexpected in relation to other cognitive abilities and the provision of effective classroom instruction. Secondary consequences may include problems in reading comprehension and reduced reading experience that can impede growth of vocabulary and background knowledge."

reflects the expression of problems appropriate to that person's age and education.* The three steps of the evaluation process are

1. Establish a reading problem according to age and education.
2. Gather evidence supporting its "unexpectedness"; high learning capability may be determined solely on the basis of an educational or professional level of attainment.
3. Demonstrate evidence of an isolated phonologic weakness, with other higher-level language functions relatively unaffected.

Step one is the most critical. Reading tests are easy to understand once you recall that there are two major components of reading: *decoding* (identifying words) and *comprehension* (understanding what is read). Accordingly, the assessment focuses on how well the child reads words and on how well she understands what she has read. While accuracy is critical early on, the ability to read fluently gains in importance as the child matures. *A child who reads accurately but not fluently is dyslexic.* In a young school-age child like Ashley, the reading evaluation first determines how accurately she can decode words, that is, read single words in isolation. Ashley, for example, was asked to read increasingly difficult words, going from *go, the,* and *me* to words like *pioneer, inquire,* and *wealth,* and finally to the most complex: *epigraphist, facetious,* and *shillelagh.*

Even more central to the diagnosis of dyslexia is how Ashley reads so-called nonsense or made-up words; she would never have seen these words before and could not have memorized them. We might begin with *ree, ip,* and *din.* The words increase in difficulty to *rejune, depine,* and *viv,* and then to the most challenging of all: *pnir, ceisminadolt,* and *byr-cal.* The point of these strange but pronounceable words is that they test a child's ability to "sound out words," that is, to map letters to sounds. Each word can be sounded out if you have acquired what is referred to as "phonologic decoding" ability.

The ability to read nonsense words is the best measure of phonologic decoding skill in children. Reading tests often refer to this skill as "word attack." The reader literally has to penetrate the sound structure of the

---

* A simple test of reading a word list that is useful for Ashley, a third grader, might be misleading for a twenty-two-year-old college student who now reads words accurately but who continues to read very slowly and laboriously.

word and sound it out, phoneme by phoneme; there is no other way. Most children generally reach their full capacity to sound out nonsense words by adolescence.

Tests of reading comprehension are generally read silently. Accordingly, someone's score on such a test depends less on the accurate pronunciation of each word than on her being able to infer the meaning of the passage in order to answer questions based on it. That is, the test taker can use the context to guess at the meaning of some words and still answer the comprehension questions correctly. For example, if Ashley cannot read the word *giraffe* or pronounce it, she can still guess at its meaning by reading the words preceding it: "A tall animal with a very long neck is called a *giraffe.*" As a result, dyslexic readers often do better on tests of reading comprehension than on measures that ask them to decode isolated single words. The Woodcock-Johnson III and the Woodcock Reading Mastery Test, Revised/Normative Update include tests of reading real and nonsense words, and of reading comprehension. Both tests provide state-of-the-art measures for assessing reading in school-age children; the Woodcock Reading Mastery Test has more test items and may provide a more in-depth assessment of reading skills.

Tests of oral reading—reading passages aloud—are often particularly helpful in identifying any uncertainties a child may have in decoding a word. By its very nature, oral reading forces the reader to pronounce each word. Listening to a dyslexic reader as she painfully tries to decode one word after another leaves no doubt about her reading ability. We can observe how much effort it requires for her to pronounce each syllable of each word; we can hear words that are mangled or newly made up. We can note that some words that should be there are not. We can note the lack of cadence or inflection in her reading. We can thus identify a struggling reader who still has not fully mastered the connection between letters and sounds. And as you know by now, such labored oral reading can be a sign of dyslexia in an otherwise extremely gifted and accomplished person.

Currently, the Gray Oral Reading Tests are the only ones that measure accuracy, rate, and comprehension as someone reads passages aloud. This provides a valuable index of fluency. The Test of Word Reading Efficiency assesses how accurately and how quickly someone reads single words and pseudowords; this is helpful, but it does not measure true fluency, which is based on reading connected text aloud. Still another test, Test 2 Reading Fluency of the Woodcock-Johnson III, asks a student to read a series of sentences silently as fast as she can and answer a question about each sentence as she goes along; she is stopped after three minutes. It is assumed that more fluent readers will read the sentences faster and more accurately, and answer more questions correctly; the number of correct answers is the child's fluency score.

Children who have difficulties reading typically struggle with spelling where they have to encode the words, that is, convert the sounds into letters. Helpful spelling tests include the Test of Written Spelling-4 and the Wide Range Achievement Test, Revised, and Wechsler Individual Achievement Test-II, as well as the Woodcock-Johnson III which measures spelling as one of the skills on its written language subtest.

After a child is evaluated, we know exactly what pattern to look for in the test results to diagnose dyslexia:

- Difficulty reading single words
- Particular difficulty decoding nonsense or unfamiliar words
- Reading comprehension often superior to decoding individual words
- Inaccurate and labored oral reading of passages
- Trouble reading small "function" words—*that, is, an, for*
- Slow reading
- Poor spelling

Ashley, of course, fell within this pattern. Once her reading difficulty was established, we focused on Step Two of the evaluation; we wanted to gain a sense of her learning capability. There is no single way to do that, so common sense comes in handy here. Depending on a person's age and education, the assessment of her learning capability can be accomplished by taking a history and listening for indicators of her strengths as well as the problems she has experienced; by interviewing and observing her; by tests of cognitive ability in a school-age child; and by knowledge of educational or vocational attainment in young adults or adults.

For students attending competitive colleges, graduate degree programs, or professional schools, the texture of their lives and their accomplishments tell us more than tests of cognitive ability. (Over time, dyslexia limits reading, which may artificially depress IQ scores.) If a student is thriving at a highly competitive college, am I to believe that an IQ test is a better measure of his potential for learning than his documented performance in the classroom? As Richard Pryor said, "Who are you going to believe, me or your lying eyes?"

The discovery of the phonologic model has drastically diminished the role of tests of intelligence in the diagnosis of dyslexia. Traditionally, the concept of dyslexia as an "unexpected" difficulty in reading was interpreted as underachievement in reading relative to ability (or learning potential). This was based on the belief that in the average person, ability (as measured by IQ) and reading achievement are very closely correlated. In other words, simply knowing a person's IQ should have predicted his level of reading achievement. For example, a person with an IQ of 115 was predicted to have a reading achievement score of approximately 115; if he scored 90 instead of 115 on a reading test, this discrepancy of twenty-five points meant that he had a reading disability.* Eligibility for special education programs in public schools has traditionally been based on the demonstration of such a discrepancy. That should no longer be the case.

These procedures were established before we understood the phonologic basis of reading and dyslexia. Fortunately, science and our understanding of reading have progressed dramatically, and it is essential that the approach to the diagnosis of dyslexia be consistent with and reflect this new knowledge. Here is why.

Ashley scored in the high average range on an IQ test; her verbal reasoning ability was in the very superior range. It was clear by reviewing her prior evaluations that she had shown evidence of a reading disability from her first test. But the size of the discrepancy between her IQ and reading scores was not large enough to meet her school's criteria for a reading disability. Now, having failed reading for three successive years and with her reading achievement scores spiraling downward, Ashley was showing an ever-widening discrepancy between her ability and her reading achievement. Overlooked in her initial evaluation by her school two years earlier were the hallmarks of dyslexia that Ashley was already demonstrating: a family history of reading difficulties (her father), prominent oral language problems involving the sounds of language, and an inability to master the reading code despite every indication of high intelligence and strong motivation. As her mother said, Ashley just did not "get it." The whole idea of linking letters to sounds was foreign to her. Her critical first years in school were pretty much wasted. When her

---

* Discrepancies of twenty-two points or more were considered meaningful.

teachers and testers heard her read aloud, why didn't they suspect dyslexia?

There is an emerging consensus among researchers and clinicians that the dependence on a discrepancy between IQ and reading achievement for a diagnosis of dyslexia has outlived its usefulness except in very limited circumstances. Now that the central role of a phonologic deficit has been proven, the diagnosis of dyslexia can be far more specific. Indicators of phonologic difficulties can be detected by a child's history, by observation, and/or by specific tests. As with Ashley, rather than noting a child's struggles as she tries to read and to speak, the discrepancy approach mandates that to be eligible for help a child must fall far enough behind in reading to develop a discrepancy sufficiently large to satisfy administrative concerns. To do so is to ignore modern science.

For Step Three we want to know if there is a phonologic weakness and if it is part of a more generalized language problem affecting all components of the language system. Fortunately, there have been important advances in our ability to assess phonologic skills in school-age children. In a struggling reader, the presence of a phonologic deficit in the context of relatively intact overall language abilities is the *sine qua non* of dyslexia. As mentioned earlier, a phonologic weakness and strengths in thinking and reasoning can be recognized. For example, parents can often observe problems with rhyming or with pronouncing words or, as with Ashley, difficulty in retrieving words, having words on the tip of the tongue and not being able to pull them out.

Phonologic skills can be directly and reliably measured in a school-age child. The Comprehensive Test of Phonological Processing assesses a particularly broad array. One specific kind of phonologic test that is quite sensitive to dyslexia in children asks a child to pull apart a word and then delete a specific phoneme. Not surprisingly, this is called a phoneme deletion (or elision) test. The examiner asks the child: "Can you say *sold* without the *sss*?" (old). "Can you say *crane* without the *r*?" (cane). The old-fashioned game of pig latin also makes an effective test of phonemic awareness. Here, too, children are asked to separate the phonemes in a word and move them around. For example, the examiner might ask, "What would *photo* be if you took the first sound off, moved it to the end of the word, and added *ay*?" (otophay). Children who cannot break apart spoken words into phonemes will not be able to link letters to sounds. Tests of phonemic awareness are related to reading abilities in both primary school and high school.

A child's vocabulary—her familiarity with the meanings of a range of common and uncommon words—provides a good index of her general language skills. In the most commonly used test (Peabody Picture Vocabulary Test), she is asked to point to which one of four pictures shows, for example, a *giant,* a *canoe,* a *mammoth,* or an *equestrian.* This contrasts with the Boston Naming Test, which asks children to name a series of pictured objects, a process much more difficult for dyslexic readers who have difficulty retrieving words. In this test a child's score may better reflect her ability to retrieve the sounds making up a word than her knowledge of the word's meaning.

Once Ashley had completed her evaluation, we examined all the information: what her parents (and teachers) had told us about her development and school history; what we observed during our interactions with her; and what her pattern of performance on tests of reading, language, and intelligence told us about her style of learning. In each of these elements we looked for evidence of a reading problem, of intact higher-level thinking and language skills, and of a phonologic difficulty. Ashley struggled to read words. She experienced the most problems when trying to sound out nonsense words. She was able to pronounce only the first few words, performing at the level of a first grader. In addition to her difficulties deciphering isolated words, Ashley labored over reading passages out loud. She read the stories very slowly and haltingly as she tried to decode the words. Sometimes she would skip two lines and not seem to notice. In oral reading, Ashley scored dismally. Clearly, Ashley was not a fluent reader. In contrast, she scored much higher on a test of reading comprehension based on silent reading.

Ashley's high learning capability was evident. Her parents (and grandmother) told us about her development. They described a bright, highly inquisitive, and creative child who constantly wanted to know *why,* who put together two-hundred-piece puzzles herself, who spent hours looking at the globe of the world and finding different countries by their shapes, and who especially loved to be read to. She could listen to stories from Greek mythology over and over again. Ashley's teachers corroborated these accounts by relating their own observations of her performance in class when, for example, she listened to stories and absorbed even the most abstract and subtle points. Ashley's ability to understand what she heard and her ability to read were, according to her teacher, "like day and night." Although not a good reader, Ashley was apparently an excellent thinker.

Her performance on tests of phonemic awareness demonstrated just how difficult it was for her to get to the sounds of words. On the phoneme deletion test Ashley just could not seem to pull apart the sticky phonemes in the test words. To her a word was a solid impenetrable whole. There was no question that Ashley had a phonologic weakness.

On the Peabody Picture Vocabulary Test, where she could point to pictures of words, Ashley performed in the superior range. (Dyslexics often have large vocabularies.) She was able to demonstrate her strong vocabulary, and since she did not have to summon up the word itself and say it, she was not penalized by her phonologic difficulty in retrieving words. In contrast, on the Boston Naming Test, which required her to actually *name* a pictured object such as *wreath, escalator,* and *abacus,* Ashley did much worse. (This is typical of dyslexics.) She called an *escalator* a *calculator,* and an *abacus* a *tobaccus.* In each instance, when asked to describe the object in her own words, it was clear that she was confusing the sounds of the words and not their meanings. She knew the meaning of *escalator* ("it's like moving stairs for people to go on") and of *abacus* ("something the Chinese count with"), but she could not easily retrieve and say the exact word.

Tests of reading (accuracy, fluency, and comprehension), spelling, and language represent a core battery for the diagnosis of dyslexia in children. In young children, tests of cognitive abilities may be helpful in pointing to strengths that might otherwise be obscured by their reading disability. For this reason I have included IQ tests as one of several indices of cognitive ability, and not as a gatekeeper. (The achievements and professional attainments of adolescents and adults provide evidence of their cognitive capability.) Of course, additional tests of academic achievement (in arithmetic, for example), language, writing, or memory may be administered as part of a more comprehensive evaluation. For example, if a child performs much better on a test of math concepts compared to reading, that adds to the impression of an isolated reading deficit in the context of other well-developed academic abilities. (Keep in mind that at times dyslexic children experience difficulty with remembering the names of numbers, in memorizing multiplication tables, or, sometimes, in reading word problems.) But there is no single test score that ensures a diagnosis of dyslexia. It is the overall picture that matters. Thus, an extremely bright child who has a reading score in the average range but who struggles and cannot learn to read fluently, and who has all the signs just described for dyslexia, has dyslexia. This pattern is so consistent and so replicable among dyslexic readers that use of the three-step approach I have just described should ensure that each struggling reader is identified *before* she endures years of frustration and failure.

There are other disorders that may impact reading. Dyslexia is distinguished from these problems by the unique, encapsulated nature of the phonologic weakness, one not intruding into other language or thinking domains. For ease of comparison I will briefly summarize the characteristics of developmental dyslexia so that it may be compared with, and not confused with, the other disorders that feature reading difficulties.

In *developmental dyslexia* the phonologic weakness is primary, other components of the language system are intact, and the reading impairment is at the level of decoding the single word, initially accurately and later fluently. Intelligence is not affected and may be in the superior or gifted range. The disorder is present from birth and not acquired.

In *language-learning disability* the primary deficit involves all aspects of language, including both the sounds and the meanings of words. The reading difficulty is at the level of both decoding and comprehension, and language difficulties of all sorts are prominent. Measures of verbal intelligence are significantly affected by language deficits, and intelligence may be in the subaverage range. People are born with the disorder.

In *acquired alexia* there is a loss or a diminution of reading ability resulting from brain trauma, a tumor, or a stroke affecting the brain systems necessary for reading. There may be other accompanying symptoms, such as loss of speech or weakness of the right side of the body, depending on the exact region affected by the injury to the brain. In contrast to developmental dyslexia, this disorder is acquired and is most often observed in middle-aged or elderly men and women.

Hyperlexia is a relatively rare disorder whose cause is unknown. In many ways it is the mirror-image of dyslexia. Children who are born hyperlexic learn to decode words very early, sometimes even as toddlers or preschoolers. They show an early and intense interest in words and letters, and their exceptional word recognition ability is often apparent by the age of five. But they have extremely poor reading comprehension.

In addition, there are deficits in reasoning and abstract problem solving. Not infrequently, affected children have difficulties forming relationships with other children as well as adults.

It is also important in diagnosing dyslexia to eliminate other potential contributing factors in school-age children who struggle to read. For example, children should be evaluated for hearing or vision problems. At one time it was thought that subtle hearing problems resulting from chronic ear infections might interfere with the acquisition of language and, later, with reading, but the most recent evidence indicates that ear infections typically do not interfere with language development and reading. The same is true of problems relating to the ability of eye muscles to converge, which have often been blamed for reading difficulty; there is a scarcity of hard evidence to support such a relationship. I also want to mention some tests I am often asked about that are unnecessary in the evaluation of dyslexia. For example, laboratory measures such as imaging studies (MRIs, CT scans, X-rays), electroencephalograms (EEGs), and genetic studies are not indicated in the general evaluation for dyslexia and should be taken only if there are specific clinical indications.

Many people confuse attention deficit/hyperactivity disorder (ADHD) and dyslexia. Some even use the two terms interchangeably. But ADHD and dyslexia are two entirely different disorders. Dyslexia is a language-based disorder affecting reading; ADHD is a problem reflecting difficulties allocating, focusing, and sustaining attention. Between 12 percent and 24 percent of those with dyslexia also have ADHD.

Reading failure is one of a small group of public health problems that we have the ability to detect reliably early on, treat effectively, and even perhaps prevent. We must ensure that each child who is not learning to read in the first year or so of school is identified and treated. It is now possible to protect children against reading failure, but in order to do so, such children must first be identified. The earlier the diagnosis is made, the better the results. This is why I now want to turn our attention to the question of evaluating younger children for the first signs of a reading problem.

12

Identifying the At-Risk Child

Ashley was diagnosed as dyslexic in third grade, at the age of nine, after she had suffered three years of frustration and had fallen further and further behind her peers. In this chapter you will learn just how unnecessary this destructive holding pattern—failing in reading but also failing to have it recognized—is for children with dyslexia. Today it is possible to reliably identify boys and girls at high risk for dyslexia *before* they fall behind.

Earlier I discussed the general clues to a reading disability. Here I want to zero in on the specific assessment approaches that help identify potential reading problems in a young child.

Two different types of assessment are used for identifying young children at risk for reading problems; the basic difference is between the requirements for screening a population (large numbers) of children and for carrying out an in-depth evaluation of an individual child because of specific concerns.

Kindergarten screening is meant to be used by school systems with their kindergarten populations to determine which children seem prepared for reading and which children may be at risk for reading problems. These screenings, often administered by classroom teachers, are very brief.

Kindergarten screening has become a routine part of getting ready for school. Until very recently screening programs were terribly unfocused and represented a nonscientific hodgepodge of so-called early childhood measures that related very little to predicting future reading achievement. Now reliable tests are available that have a high—but not absolute—degree of accuracy. By design they overidentify many children who then receive further, more detailed testing. The rationale is that it is better to overidentify than it is to overlook a child who is at risk and would benefit from early intervention programs.

Children come to school with a wide range of experiences. Some come from homes where letters are noticed and made a part of their everyday life with ABC books, letter games, and magnetized plastic letters on the refrigerator. Others may not have had even the most minimal exposure to letters or to books in the preschool period. Consequently, many experts recommend that large-scale screening for phonologic difficulties be carried out during the second semester of kindergarten, when the child is about five and a half or even six years old. At this point all the children have been exposed to at least one semester of formal schooling and should have developed some degree of phonologic ability. (Specific kindergarten screening approaches are discussed in Chapter 15.)

The assessment approach I will focus on here is an in-depth evaluation of the skills (especially phonologic) known to be related to reading success. This evaluation is appropriate for preschool and kindergarten children who show signs of a potential reading problem, and it is administered on an individual basis by a professional who is knowledgeable about reading and dyslexia: a speech and language pathologist, a learning disabilities specialist, or an experienced psychologist. The results of this comprehensive evaluation establish a child's readiness for reading and pinpoint specific areas of strengths and weaknesses.

Children's phonologic abilities follow a natural progression and are relatively straightforward to assess across development, beginning at about age four. Phonologic sensitivity refers to the ability to focus on the sounds rather than on the meaning of spoken words. The child can tell you what word rhymes with *cat* rather than simply if a cat is a kind of animal. As I mentioned earlier, phonologic skills develop gradually over time and in a predictable, logical sequence. Awareness of this sequence and its timing makes it possible to recognize when a child is veering off course. And the great news, of course, is that you can identify that child and help him get back on track before any serious damage is done. We know that, in general, as a child develops phonologic skills, he gains the ability to focus on smaller and smaller parts of the word rather than on the word as a whole, indivisible unit. At the same time he works his way from attending to the outside or ends of words into the inside or middle parts of words. At first children are able to separate out only the beginning sounds of words, then the end sounds, and finally the inside sounds. Penetrating the inside of a word is much more difficult than noticing either end, and it is the ability to notice and code each of the parts within a word that marks the maturing reader.

In describing a child's phonologic skills, two terms are often used: *phonologic* awareness and *phonemic* awareness. Phonologic awareness is a more general and more inclusive term; it includes all levels of awareness of the sound structure of words. It is also used to refer to the earliest stages of developing an awareness of the parts of words, such as sensitivity to rhyme or noticing larger parts of words such as syllables. Phonemic awareness is a much more specific term. As noted earlier, it refers to the more advanced ability to notice, identify, and manipulate the smallest particles that make up a word: phonemes. Phonemic awareness has the strongest relationship to later reading, and most tests focus on this level of awareness. The most helpful tests include three kinds of measures: sound comparison, segmentation, and blending.

For sound comparison we would ask a child to tell which word begins with the same first sound as *rat: man, sat,* or *run.* For segmentation we might ask a child to count or pronounce the individual parts of a word, for example, "Can you count the sounds you hear in *man?*" (three). Alternatively, we could ask him to blend together the parts of a word that has already been pulled apart: "What word do the sounds 's' 'aaaa' 't' form?" (*sat*). In addition, as he develops increasing phonemic awareness, we can have him add, move around, or delete a part of a word by asking, for example, "What word remains when you take the 'r' sound away from *frog?*" (*fog*).

Research has opened our eyes to how important it is to have phonologic skills in place during the first years of school. By the end of first grade, most children have just about mastered their basic phonologic skills. From second grade on, a child's development of these competencies is more a matter of refining and gaining efficiency or automaticity in the phonologic skills previously acquired. And, as was said previously, these phonologic skills influence reading from the start. In fact, a group of Florida researchers demonstrated the profound impact that these skills have on a child's later reading. As the accompanying graph demonstrates (Figure 30), children who began first grade with poor phonologic

144

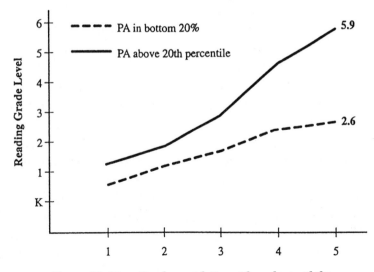

*Figure 30. First Graders with Poor Phonologic Ability
Are Poor Readers in Fifth Grade*

Children scoring in the lowest 20 percent on a test of phonology in first grade (dashed line) were reading at a low level (2.6) when they were in fifth grade. In contrast, children who scored higher on phonology in first grade (solid line) were reading at a 5.9 grade level in fifth grade.

skills (in the lowest 20 percent of their class) were two grade levels below their classmates in a test of word reading in fifth grade.

In addition to tests of phonemic awareness, there are two other tests that add valuable information about a young child's readiness for reading. The first, which measures *phonologic memory,* evaluates a child's ability to temporarily store bits of verbal information. We see how well he can remember a series of numbers or words that were just presented to him orally. (Both spoken numbers and words are stored as phonemes.) In this type of test a child may be asked to repeat the numbers given, such as *five seven three one six.* This type of memory plays an important role in reading at every level, even for a first grader who is trying to sound out a word. As a child reads a sentence, he has to hold several bits of information in mind in order to put it all together and make sense of what he has just read. Think of the process: He first decodes the letters into sounds, then holds these sounds in his memory as he tries to decode the remaining letters in the word, and then he takes these stored sounds, blends them together, and forms the word. Words are stored primarily on the basis of their sounds, so the ability to hold words temporarily is really a kind of phonologic skill. And the clearer the phonemes, the more efficiently words can be retrieved.

A second kind of test, the *rapid automatic naming test,* or RAN, examines still another aspect of phonologic processing, what is technically referred to as *phonologic access.* The RAN tries to determine how easily and rapidly a child can retrieve verbal (phonetic) information held in long-term storage. The child is typically shown a card with several rows of pictures of familiar objects and asked to name them one after another as quickly as he can. Highly familiar stimuli are used so that this does not turn into a test of the child's vocabulary. Both accuracy and speed are measured. The child's facility in rapid naming is related to just the sorts of processes he must perform as he reads, when he must be able to go into his long-term memory and rapidly retrieve the stored phonemes. A number of studies have shown that the faster a child is able to name (especially series of letters or numbers), the better a reader she is likely to become later on. First-rate tests of the full range of phonologic skills are now available.

Tests to Evaluate Phonologic Skills and Reading Readiness (with Applicable Ages/Grades)

Comprehensive Test of Phonological Processing in Reading (CTOPP) (PRO-ED, Inc.), age five through adult*

Lindamood Auditory Conceptualization Test (LAC) (PRO-ED, Inc.), kindergarten through sixth grade

Rosner Test of Auditory Analysis (Walker & Company), kindergarten through sixth grade

Test of Phonological Awareness (TOPA) (PRO-ED, Inc.), kindergarten through second grade*

The Phonological Awareness Test (PAT) (LinguiSystems), age five through seven*

Yopp-Singer Test of Phoneme Segmentation (available from "A test for assessing phonemic awareness in young children", by H. K. Yopp, in *The Reading Teacher* 49 [1995]: 20–29), kindergarten through first grade

*Indicates tests that are standardized.

In addition to phonology, a child's knowledge of letter names and sounds serves as a helpful guide to how ready he is to read. Testing letter knowledge is straightforward; it can be assessed informally by asking the child to name letters presented one at a time on a card. Similarly, knowledge of letters and sounds is tested by also asking the child, "Can you tell me a sound this letter makes?" More formal testing can be obtained by using a reading test that contains a letter identification section, such as American Guidance Service's Woodcock Reading Mastery Test, Revised/Normative Update.

Emerging data suggest that these tests are quite effective, although not perfect. Researchers still must tinker to get a firmer handle on just which combination of tests is the best. Right now I would say that the two most valuable tests for predicting reading—in addition to the factors I've identified—are knowledge of letter names and of letter sounds, and phonemic awareness. In kindergarten the child's ability to name the letters of the alphabet is the better predictor of future reading abilities; in first grade it is the child's knowledge of letter sounds.

Teachers are also critical when it comes to identifying who is at risk. Too often, however, their unique insights and depth of experience are underutilized. A kindergarten or first grade teacher's impressions of a student's skills noted on a brief questionnaire, the Multigrade Inventory for Teachers (MIT), add significantly to predicting who will experience reading problems.* In addition, it is often helpful to assess a child's familiarity with the conventions of print—for example, that there are spaces between words and that books are read from top to bottom and from left to right—to ensure that a young child is aware of what books are and how they work.

Interestingly, IQ tests given to young children are comparatively not good predictors of later reading difficulties. Furthermore, IQ is not a strong indicator of how well a young child will respond to intervention programs for reading. Therefore, I do not recommend IQ tests as essential for the earliest identification of boys and girls at risk for reading difficulties.

---

* The MIT, developed for use in the Connecticut Longitudinal Study, enables teachers to rate students on a range of behaviors and academic skills.

What a Parent Can Do

Here is what I believe is the most scientifically sound and sensible approach to identifying young at-risk children before they experience reading failure:

• Observe your child's language development. Be on the alert for problems in rhyming, pronunciation, and word finding.

• Observe your child's ability to connect print to language. Notice if he is beginning to name individual letters.

• Know your family history. Be alert to problems in speaking, reading, writing, spelling, or learning a foreign language. Some families with more than the average complement of dyslexics seem to have an abundance of photographers, artists, engineers, architects, scientists, and radiologists. Somewhat less frequent, but still impressive, are the large number of families sprinkled with great writers, entrepreneurs, and jurists who are dyslexic.

• If there are clues to problems with spoken language, learning letter names, and especially if there is a family history, have your child tested.

In this regard, here is my recommendation for a sensible and effective battery of tests for the early recognition of reading problems. The battery includes tests of

phonology (awareness, memory, and access)

letters (names and sounds)

vocabulary (receptive and expressive)

print conventions

listening comprehension

reading (real words, nonsense words, and comprehension)

Tests of receptive vocabulary (in which a child points to the picture that illustrates a spoken word) and listening comprehension (a child answers questions after listening to a story) are important. Rather than probes for weaknesses, they are measures of strengths in the dyslexic child and serve as useful reminders of a child's thinking potential when she is not limited by her difficulties in phonology and reading. As opposed to the difficulties dyslexic children encounter in gaining information from print, they score well on these tests. I have included tests of reading for children in the first and second grades because they provide an indication of a child's reading skills compared to his peers at a time when he should be reading.

All the steps I have recommended here can help you judge if your child is ready to read or if he requires special attention or education to help him begin to read. If his testing indicates that he is not quite ready to read, you have the choice of delaying kindergarten or allowing him to enter kindergarten *and* receive the kinds of intensive, evidence-based prevention programs that are discussed in Chapter 19.

I strongly recommend not delaying kindergarten entry; this will only delay needed help.

While many parents believe that a child will respond better to the demands of kindergarten if he is a year older than his classmates, the evidence says otherwise. A group of researchers took advantage of what was in essence a natural experiment to test whether it was biological maturity or exposure to reading instruction that most influenced early reading. The researchers compared two groups of young children who were hovering on either side of the cutoff date for kindergarten entry. One group had birth dates that allowed them to begin kindergarten. A second group was similar in every way except they just missed the cutoff for kindergarten entry. They were a month younger and had to wait a year before starting. When tested later, those in the group that entered kindergarten were reading better than the delayed entry group. Rather than age or maturity, it is reading instruction that leads to better reading. The evidence seems clear: Delaying a child's entry to school does not help him become a better reader.

On the other hand, early identification, when linked to effective programs of intervention, can make a difference. Such intervention can ensure that the vast majority of today's children will never have to experience reading failure. Good help is available to them now as never before.

13

Diagnosing
Bright Young Adults

Almost two decades ago I received a call from the dean of undergraduate studies at an Ivy League university. That call introduced me to the world of bright young adults with reading difficulties. The dean wondered if I could help him with an unusual request from Briana, an undergraduate about to enter her senior year, who wanted to spend an extra semester at the school. She said she was dyslexic and required the extra semester. The dean was astonished. "I've reviewed her records, and she is absolutely brilliant!" Having had little experience with dyslexic young adults, I, too, was puzzled. So I started where every diagnostic journey must begin: with the history.

Briana came from a family brimming with dyslexics, including her two sisters and a brother. She had struggled early on and since age eight had attended specialized schools where she was able to receive close attention and specific help for her reading disability. An evaluation in third grade seemed to reflect the comments of many of her teachers.

Her oral reading is characterized by frequent pauses and repetitions. Although she is working diligently to master reading subskills, she is not yet successful in using them to figure out new words. Comprehension, however, is quite good.

The indicators—her family history of dyslexia; her early and continuing difficulties with the mechanics of reading, despite good comprehension; her slowness in reading—were clear. I knew Briana was dyslexic. I was impressed that a dyslexic could be successful in a school where there was such a heavy demand for reading, and I wondered how many students like Briana attended topflight colleges. Although Briana's standardized test scores were not stratospheric, her qualities as "a creative thinker, an inquisitive scholar, and an independent leader"—as described by one of her high school teachers—must have caught the eye of an admissions staffer.

Briana explained that she had completed her first three years "at a great cost." Reading very slowly and with great effort, she had devoted all her time and energy to just keeping up. Now that she was approaching her senior year, she did not want to see the quality of her education diminished because of lack of time:

> Though my grades in [my] courses are not bad, I feel that to the degree to which grades can reflect any truth at all, they reflect a level of mediocrity inappropriate to my intellectual aptitude, earnest scholarship and industriousness. . . . I am requesting an additional term of study in which to complete these courses in a manner befitting my intellectual aptitude and earnest studentship. . . .
>
> The point is not that I am almost inarticulate, nor that I can barely struggle through a page of text. . . . I want the stuff of a liberal education, for whatever it's worth, to carry with me in my life. I want to possess, to understand, to challenge and to recreate the ideas, knowledge and visions of the liberal tradition.

Briana was given permission to extend her studies for one semester and graduated the following year. She is now an accomplished writer.

Although no one is ever cured of dyslexia, highly intelligent, exceptionally hardworking, and strongly motivated young men and women with dyslexia can attend and successfully complete their education, as hundreds have, at Yale, Brown, Harvard, Stanford, and other excellent colleges and professional schools. I know that at Yale our dyslexic students have performed well, reflecting the full range of abilities and personalities of all our students. Admissions officers are clearly attuned to the competencies of these students; they appreciate that the qualities they are looking for go far beyond what test scores have to say about a person.

From my twenty years of working directly with dyslexic students at Yale and other universities, and from my research and that of others, the "sea of brilliance interspersed with isolated islands of weakness" model has held up. In particular, the students at Yale have shown me what it means to be bright and dyslexic. I consult about issues relating to dyslexia in students and faculty at Yale and, in the process, read through their records—essentially minibiographies. As I peruse these documents, I read of little boys and girls who struggled to read or couldn't quite form their letters or print their names neatly, who could not spell, who stuttered and stammered as they mispronounced words, who puzzled their teachers and parents, and who were poked and prodded to try to understand why. I think of their mothers and all that they and their children endured. I cannot help but think of the worries each mother must have had: What will ever become of my child? Reading one report after another, I imagine how much parents (and children, too) must have worried and how gratifying it must be to see their dyslexic child now as a successful student at such a high level.

I have come to know dozens of brilliant, extraordinary students and faculty at all levels; I have met with them, talked with them, problem-solved with them, and reviewed their testing records in great detail. I have learned, as I said earlier, that at the level of college and beyond, IQ and other tests tell us very little of a dyslexic individual's potential for academic success and for future contributions to society. Some of the most outstanding and successful students and faculty—by any measure—score only average on tests of intelligence. Obviously these tests are not tapping into and measuring some of the essential qualities that converge to bring about brilliance, creativity, or perseverance.

At the same time so-called average scores on reading tests for a dyslexic student cannot measure the extraordinary effort that went into reading each word, to laboriously pronouncing it bit by bit, to rereading it over and over again until it began to sound right and make sense. What a juxtaposition: the tremendous cognitive strengths and conceptual ability of the bright dyslexic adult on one level and, on another, his ongoing struggle, at the most basic level of language, to try to decode and to identify the printed word. He is all geared up—his powerful intellectual equipment is waiting to be fed its nourishment of words so that he can assimilate and feast on the ideas and the thoughts they contain—but to get to the basic substrate, the printed word, he must first decode and identify that word. What frustration. What perseverance.

Diagnosis

In 1996, in celebration of the hundredth anniversary of the first description of developmental dyslexia, I wrote an article for *Scientific American,* "Dyslexia," in which I discuss Gregory, the medical student whom we met earlier, who typifies many bright young adults with dyslexia. He was extremely bright, understood the most difficult concepts, and yet had trouble pronouncing anatomic names and memorizing isolated facts. Following the publication of that article, I received many letters and e-mails from students and parents of students. Some of the students had already been diagnosed as dyslexic, while a substantial minority had never been evaluated for dyslexia. For example, Brandon Rogers, a philosophy major in a liberal arts college in the Midwest, wrote:

> I have always done well in school. . . . If I didn't get something, I would study it and study it until I did. If it meant staying up much (or even most) of the night, I would put in whatever work was necessary to do well. Until recently, I never thought anything of this. I figured that the problems that made me have to put in so much overtime were the same problems everyone had. No one ever thought I might have dyslexia. I always did well in school. I was the smart one. I got A's. . . .
>
> When I first heard about dyslexia, it was one of those meaningless terms thrown around, and seen as an excuse for people who don't like to work hard. But the more I have learned about it, the more I feel it might be affecting me. The pronunciation problems I have, the absurd spelling errors, the abysmally slow pace of my reading, the needing to read things over and over again, the problems getting down what the professor says, I

thought that maybe I had figured out what has been causing some of the issues I've always had. I just want to know for sure. I have never been tested for anything before, but, as I said, I just want to know.

Brandon's questions echo those I hear from many college students and other young adults concerned about their reading. Yes, it is both possible and, I think, worthwhile to obtain a specific diagnosis of your learning difficulties. No, Brandon's constellation of problems is not normal, but it is exactly what we would expect to see in a bright young man or woman who is dyslexic. Following scores of dyslexic children as they matured into young adults has given us a picture of the evolution of dyslexia over time. This clinical information is now enhanced by research studies of reading in adults (both dyslexic and nonimpaired) and by studies of brain function during reading. These research findings have important implications for the diagnosis of dyslexia in young adults.

As children mature, bones elongate, muscles strengthen, voices deepen, fingers grow steadier, strides lengthen, knowledge accumulates, and skills sharpen. Yet the core phonologic deficit in dyslexia remains, even in the brightest and hardest-working children. Numerous studies conducted on college students and other adults document the persistence of the phonologic deficit.

The implication of all this for the diagnosis of dyslexia in adults is that, as Johns Hopkins researcher Maggie Bruck noted, phonologic deficits are constant throughout the lives of men and women who are dyslexic. This means that data gathered from a dyslexic as a child won't change as the person gets older; phonologic deficits persist in virtually all those diagnosed as dyslexic in childhood. Of course, dyslexic readers can learn to read more words accurately and can learn to read with good comprehension, but the persistent phonologic deficit prevents fluency. The difficulties during childhood evolve into slow, labored reading in adulthood. Thankfully, it is our cognitive capability and not our phonology that allows us as humans to reason, to analyze, and to solve problems at the very highest levels—and to be capable of great accomplishment.

Researchers discovered that dyslexic college students take a very long time to identify words, even words they can eventually identify correctly. If dyslexic readers attempt to (or are made to) read too quickly, they simply will not be able to identify words. This may be misinterpreted as a lack of understanding. Just how important the issue of speed is for dyslexic adults was demonstrated in what is referred to by researchers as a reading match study. College students with histories of dyslexia were compared to sixth grade children reading at the same level of accuracy. The dyslexic college students were the slower readers.

In order to understand how college-age dyslexics read, we must separate the number of words a person can read from the manner in which he goes about reading those words. Two college students, one dyslexic and the other a nonimpaired reader, may read the same word accurately, but via two entirely different neural routes.

Earlier I talked about evidence from brain research that offers tantalizing clues to how dyslexic and nonimpaired adults diverge in their reading pathways. Recall that in skilled readers the fast-paced word form system automatically recognizes a word; the word is read rapidly and effortlessly. In a dyslexic reader a disrupted word form system prevents automatic reading. Instead, he is dependent on secondary reading pathways, those in the front and right side of the brain. Dependence on these secondary routes to reading has important implications for how he reads. First, they allow him to read a large number of words, albeit very slowly. Second, rather than the sound-based route to reading, the dyslexic reader relies on higher cognitive abilities to infer the meaning of the unknown word from the surrounding context. And this is why the bright dyslexic reader does so much better in reading words in context compared to words in isolation or with scanty contexts.

Slow reading is the price the dyslexic pays for this more indirect route to getting to the meaning of an unknown word. At the same time, dyslexic young adults—with much perseverance and sufficient time— are able to comprehend college-level materials. Studies have confirmed the universal nature of this faulty wiring; dyslexic students worldwide, speaking different languages, share a disruption of the primary neural systems for reading (see Chapter 7, Figure 26).

Understanding that the dyslexic reader relies on neural systems that permit accurate but not fluent reading helps explain why the kinds of tests and approaches used for diagnosing dyslexia in children are not suitable for older individuals. For the most part, these rely on measures of reading accuracy and not fluency. It also explains why scores on traditional tests of word recognition may not differentiate accomplished adults with dyslexia from adults who are good readers and why timed tests of reading are more valid measures of dyslexia in these adults. In the next section I will apply this knowledge to the diagnosis of dyslexia in bright young adults. My goal is to translate scientific data into everyday clinical practice so that decisions made about dyslexic young men and women are based on science and not on misconceptions or outmoded views.

For the most part, the heart of a diagnosis of dyslexia in a bright young adult lies in her history. At this stage of life, dyslexic readers have accumulated enough life experiences to document a trail of phonologic and reading difficulties. For some, like Briana, it is a history of reading difficulties leading to evaluation, tutoring, or special schooling; for others, like Brandon, often because they are so bright, the diagnosis of dyslexia is delayed, the symptoms brushed aside with the explanation "Oh, but he's too smart. Let's wait." This is the kind of child who falls between the cracks and escapes diagnosis until he is an adult.

In making a diagnosis, a person's history is critical. We look for a pattern of findings pointing to a phonologic deficit that permeates almost every aspect of his life. Each case will differ as to the specific ingredients of that pattern; there is no single event, symptom, or test score that in itself allows a diagnosis. The phonologic weakness is always present, but we must know how to recognize it in different settings and during different life stages. A developmental history of difficulties with language, particularly phonologically based components of language, often provides the clearest and most reliable indication of a reading disorder. Slow reading is the primary symptom of dyslexia in an accomplished young adult. And as was just explained, in these bright individuals, standard assessment procedures used with children are inadequate and often misleading. For now, therefore, the history—of laborious reading and writing, of poor spelling, of requiring additional time in reading and in taking tests—represents the most sensitive and accurate indicator of a reading disability in young adults.

The diagnosis of dyslexia at any age is not about formulas or magical cutoff scores; it is about understanding how a phonologic deficit impacts people's lives. Theory provides the template, but true understanding comes from developing an intimate sense of the disorder as it is expressed day in and day out over a span of time. There is simply no substitute for personal knowledge of real people who are dyslexic. Though by now you are thoroughly versed in the component parts of dyslexia, I want to take you through an in-depth history of one of my patients to show you how all the pieces come together and how a diagnosis is made.

Nikki

Nicholas (Nikki) Romerio, now age twenty-two and with a history of dyslexia in his mother and grandmother, showed a delay in his language early on; by nursery school his parents were already worrying about it, especially his production of sounds. At the same time, Nikki's mother felt his comprehension of language was excellent and that he understood "everything." A speech and language evaluation concluded that Nikki had a problem forming the sounds of words.

Once in school, Nikki could not seem to get started in reading. He would hide under the table so he wouldn't be asked to name the letters of the alphabet when it was his turn. He was diagnosed as dyslexic in first grade, after the other children had already nicknamed him "Nikki Know Nothing."

Although not wealthy and, in principle, committed to public education, Nikki's parents made the difficult decision to educate him in private schools. They worried that he would be "eaten up" in public schools where "Nikki Know Nothing" might evolve into the truth. Nikki benefited from small classes and extensive tutoring and, especially, his own perseverance.

Nikki's history and prior evaluations clearly pointed to a phonologic deficit that had robbed him of his ability to read fluently. In particular, observations in early evaluations were especially helpful, because they tended to address the key question in the diagnosis of dyslexia: Is there evidence of a phonologic deficit affecting reading? To answer this central question we need to know how a young man like Nikki goes about the task of reading. The specific tests used and the scores obtained are often far less important than the description of what the examiner observed as the child read or tried to read.

Nikki's earliest evaluation, now almost two decades old, does not use the term *phonology.* Yet when reading the evaluator's comments, we know at once that Nikki had experienced phonologic difficulties: "Nikki has difficulty in recognizing consonant and vowel sounds and synthesizing these into words."

As early as first grade, Nikki was already feeling the burden of a phonologic deficit. According to his teacher, "His serious approach and his ability to focus on the reading task aid him positively; but he is very much aware of the difficulty reading presents for him, and at times appears terribly anxious and frustrated."

In second grade science, his report card notes that Nikki "needs to work on his word attack skills and to increase his reading fluency. He is a slow, methodical reader and demonstrates good reading comprehension when given enough time."

Grade three assessment continues the pattern, noting that "he has no developmental delay with the exception of speech and language." In reading a list of words, "Nikki worked slowly and made many errors such as *flit* for *felt* and *impolite* for *imply,* but with time he was able to decode words on a third grade level. However, when time was limited, his immediate sight vocabulary was at a second grade level."

Nikki's score on an oral reading test that measured speed and accuracy was also at a second grade level. He tried to read quickly but made many errors, even on the easiest, pre-primer passages. He used a finger to help hold his place but still frequently omitted words or made errors such as reading *bark* for *break.* His comprehension of the third grade passage was good as long as he had enough time. Nikki's performance was summed up in this way:

> Nikki is a highly motivated nine-year-old who has not been able to achieve up to his intellectual potential. . . . He does not remember letter sounds, and blending sounds into meaningful words has been very difficult for him. Nikki also has trouble remembering the names of places and may confuse some sound-similar words such as *nuisance* and *nonsense.* He does not perceive the details in words correctly, thus he easily confuses words such as *bowl* and *blow.* Nikki still does not hold his pencil in a mature fashion; he does not seem to oppose his thumb and forefinger in holding the pencil, much like a younger child. He is inconsistent in sizing his letters, writes slowly and still seems to need to attend to the mechanics of forming his letters.

Nikki's ninth grade evaluation, more than seven years ago, is extremely useful in understanding him today. Describing his perform-mance on a word discrimination task, the examiner indicates that Nikki "made only two errors and one self-correction, but worked slowly and was unable to complete more than ¾ of the items on a timed subtest. His score, at an early fifth grade level, indicates how much time and effort Nicholas must use to read the volume of material required at the high school level."

Nikki's scores, like all dyslexics, are highly dependent on how and on what he is tested. The large disparity in Nikki's skills emerged when he was questioned about a passage he read. He excelled at grasping the ideas expressed in the passage (he scored more than 90 percent); on the other hand, retrieving rote facts mentioned in the same reading was much more difficult. Such isolated bits and pieces, stored in their pho-netic form (as fuzzy phonemes), are, as we know, often difficult for a dyslexic to retrieve on demand.

Repeat assessment in Nikki's senior year of high school continued this same pattern: inefficient word identification skills, trouble with non-sense words, difficulty reading aloud, a very low reading rate (18th per-centile), and "abysmal" spelling (8th percentile).

And what about today? An evaluation of Nikki as a medical school student:

Observation:	Strong motivation; serious work ethic, very hardworking; cooperative; not good at small talk; yet talks inces-santly—exhibiting need to verbalize and work through problems; checks and rechecks his work; repeats ques-tions to himself; subvocalizes during reading; reads and rereads materials; examiner tired from watching him.
Coping Strategies:	Uses laptop computer for word pro-cessing; follows text with a ruler; underlines specific words or phrases; writes down notes on everything he reads, then recopies the notes over and over until he has learned them; must have quiet when studying and when

	taking tests; requires full concentration to read.
Silent reading rate:	5th percentile
Oral reading rate:	8th percentile
Phonologic awareness:	Not proficient
Pencil grip:	Awkward
Handwriting:	Slow, illegible
Spelling:	Relies on spell checker
Reading words:	
Word attack	45th percentile
Word identification	53rd percentile
Oral reading	
comprehension:	99th percentile
Math concepts:	99th percentile
Visual-spatial skills:	Excellent, "tops in anatomy"

Some corporate leaders are described as "24/7 guys." Well, dyslexic readers are 24/7 people, too. Nikki was obviously working very hard, trying to manage his studies and carry out all the necessary reading. When asked about the possibility of tutors, he replied, "No time for tutors." For him, reading for pleasure is a fantasy. Indeed, one gets the sense that the word "fun" is not part of his lexicon; since he has never experienced life any other way, he accepts it. A painful aspect of dyslexia for Nikki is the constant assault on his self-esteem. When he tells you, "I can't think of anything I'm good at," he is sincere. Asked about reading aloud, he replies, sounding very much like the first grader hiding under his seat, "I can't do it. I get very nervous if called on to read." Reflecting his repeated difficulties with tests, he has developed test anxiety. "After taking so many hits on tests, I kind of feel shell-shocked. Just going into that room brings back so many bad memories. I have to work really hard not to think of that and instead to focus on the questions. It's never easy. But you have to understand, I'm not one to give up."

What can we learn from Nikki about the diagnosis of dyslexia in bright young adults? The Nikki who was first assessed in grade school is still the same Nikki who is now a medical student. Then and now he exhibits just about every indicator of a phonologic weakness surrounded by a sea of strengths:

- A strong family history of dyslexia
- Early language problems in articulation but not in comprehension
- Trouble learning the alphabet
- Problems associating letters and sounds
- Trouble sounding out words
- Confusion of words that sound alike
- Difficulty perceiving the details in words
- Absolute terror of reading aloud
- Slow reading
- Disastrous spelling
- Immature pencil grip
- Poor handwriting
- Diminished self-esteem
- Strong secondary test anxiety
- Time as a critical factor in his performance
- Extremely variable performance depending on format of test
- Results of multiple choice tests underestimate his knowledge
- Superior learning capability along with deficient reading skills
- Comprehension superior to rote memory
- Grasps the main idea much better than details

As predicted, the tests that are most likely to reveal Nikki's persistent phonologic deficit are tests of reading speed. They are the most sensitive measures we have to assay the impact of a phonologic deficit in a bright young adult. In the not too distant future we may be able to image the brain of someone like Nikki and determine that his reading is not on track, that he has not switched to the automatic reading system.* Until that day comes, timed reading tests offer a window on whether someone is or is not a fluent reader. And here they tell us without a doubt that Nikki, as brilliant as he is, remains on the laborious slow track for reading.

The approach to the diagnosis in young adults comes naturally from all that we have learned about reading and the brain. Above all it calls upon clinical judgment. It is a thinking man's or woman's approach and is not based on unproven formulas or arbitrary decisions; rather, cutting-edge science and good old-fashioned common sense drive the process. If

---

* Currently, fMRI is used solely as a research tool.

one understands the basic nature of dyslexia, the diagnosis unfolds easily and naturally.

Young men and women who are dyslexic may manifest what seems to be a confusing array of contradictory findings: honors and failures; commendations and warnings; the 99th percentile in some areas and the 9th percentile in others; brilliant thinker and hopelessly slow reader—all in the same person. Dyslexic readers experience awesome highs and devastating lows. One day they are praised for incisive thinking so that they feel they must be very smart, and the next day a disappointing performance on a multiple-choice test makes them feel, as Nikki told me, "really dumb. I can't understand how I could have fooled so many people for so long."

Understanding the phonologic model allows you to sort through this seeming mess and to make sense of it all. Although there is now a mountain of evidence about the evolution of reading and phonology, I have found that the relevant information can be summarized in a relatively simple and straightforward way. Here are the essential facts about dyslexia in an adult:

- The phonologic weakness persists; it never goes away.
- In children the phonologic weakness primarily affects reading accuracy; over time, accomplished dyslexic adults learn to read a core of words accurately.
- In bright young adults the phonologic weakness affects the speed of reading.
- Skilled adult readers read accurately and rapidly; while adult dyslexics read slowly and laboriously—they are not fluent.
- Brain imaging studies indicate adult dyslexics never switch over to the automatic reading circuit necessary for fluent reading.
- Reliance on secondary reading pathways results in accurate but slow reading.

Science and common sense say that if a person reads extremely slowly and yet is able to comprehend materials at a college level or beyond, he has a phonologic deficit as well as significant strengths. He is dyslexic. In my experience the diagnosis becomes straightforward once the diagnostician understands the basic nature of dyslexia.

This knowledge can now be applied to the three-step process we established earlier for the diagnosis of dyslexia.

Step 1. Establish a reading problem according to age and education.

A reading problem in an accomplished adult is established by a careful history, as I have described above. The most consistent and telling sign is slow and laborious reading and writing. The failure to recognize or to measure the lack of fluency in reading is probably the most common error in the diagnosis of dyslexia in bright young adults. Keep in mind that a simple word identification task is not sensitive enough to identify dyslexia in someone accomplished enough to graduate from college and attend law, medical, or any other advanced degree school. Accordingly, tests relying on the accuracy of word identification are inappropriate for diagnosing dyslexia in these individuals. Observing a person read aloud and administering timed tests such as the Nelson-Denny Reading Test and tests of oral reading of connected text such as the GORT-4 can establish the lack of fluency in accomplished adults.

Step 2. Gather evidence supporting dyslexia's "unexpectedness." High learning capability may be determined solely on the basis of an educational or professional level of attainment.

An accomplished adult's level of education or professional status pro-vides the best indication of learning capability. Graduation from a good college or status as a graduate, medical, or law student indicates high capability. A lack of fluency (slow reading) in such an adult signifies an unexpected reading problem or dyslexia. Furthermore, any scores obtained on testing must be considered relative to peers with the same degree of education or professional training.

Step 3. Demonstrate evidence of an isolated phonologic weakness with other higher-level language functions relatively unaffected.

Slow reading in the face of high levels of educational or professional achievement is evidence of an encapsulated phonologic weakness. In particular, strong conceptual and verbal reasoning abilities or strengths in vocabulary and reading comprehension indicate strengths in non-phonologic language domains.

Following these three basic steps and applying research-based knowledge of the developmental pattern of reading and dyslexia results in a precise and scientifically valid diagnosis of dyslexia in an accomplished young adult or adult.

There are a few additional points to be made about the evaluation of young adults. First, a body of science tells us that the phonologic weakness is persistent and that the clearest evidence documenting such a weakness will come from a person's life history. Once a person is dyslexic, he is dyslexic for life. Accordingly, there is no reason for college students to be retested once they have been diagnosed in childhood—unless there has been an extraordinary change in their symptoms or life circumstances. Not only is retesting not helpful but it may be harmful, placing unnecessary psychological and financial burdens on an already overwhelmed dyslexic student.

In a legal case brought by students with learning disabilities at Boston University, Judge Patti Saris ruled that there was no basis for requiring retesting of college students every three years, noting that "defendants have produced no peer-reviewed literature or scientific testimony that provides evidence for the idea that a person's learning disability will show any change after adulthood, or that a student's test scores will show substantial change during [his or her] college career." Thus legal opinion joins with scientific fact to rule against such a misguided policy.

Second, I am puzzled by the often-repeated notion that some students *pretend* to be dyslexic. When asked about this, I always respond by asking in turn, "Do you know this for a fact? Are you personally aware of such a case?" Invariably the person shakes her head and replies, "Oh, no, it's just something I've heard." Such notions are nonsense. In all my experience with scores and scores of students, I have yet to encounter a young man or woman who falsely claims to be dyslexic. For those who understand dyslexia and its tremendous costs to the individual, the very idea that someone would willingly seek such a diagnosis is absurd. Sally Esposito, who was coordinator of disability services at Yale, explained:

> The students just don't want to identify themselves. They don't want to be labeled. I guess they simply don't want to be viewed as different or disabled. They are so embarrassed by the stigma. They panic when they think their professors or classmates will find out. One of my biggest problems is getting students to iden-

tify themselves and come to the office for the services that they are entitled to. Often, they just won't do it. They say the cost is just too high.

Lastly, I often hear that the diagnosis of dyslexia is somehow vague or lacking precision. As a physician I am always amused by these comments. The diagnosis of dyslexia is as precise and scientifically informed as almost any diagnosis in medicine. Each time I take my turn as attending physician on our acute inpatient pediatric wards, I am humbled by the lack of precision—even in this day of molecular medicine—in making even the seemingly most simple and most common diagnoses. So often we simply don't know and have to use our best judgment. In the case of dyslexia, our knowledge of the phonologic weakness and its impact across the life span now allows us to make a remarkably informed clinical judgment with a high degree of confidence. In fact, there are times when I wish other diagnoses in medicine could be made with the same degree of precision.

Now I want to turn to the highly effective steps we can take to teach reading: first to the typical reader, and then to the dyslexic reader, young or old.

Part III

Helping Your Child
Become a Reader

14

All Children
Can Be Taught to Read

One of the most rewarding experiences I can imagine is seeing a child who once was sad and defeated transformed into one who glows with an eagerness to learn. The new scientific breakthroughs in the teaching of reading are responsible for exactly that. Talia Matthews is one of these happy children.

Talia is a bright, bubbly, red-haired nine-year-old who radiates self-confidence. According to her mother, Talia was not always this way. She was identified as dyslexic in third grade as part of a joint research project by Yale University School of Medicine and Syracuse University. This is what her mother told me:

> Before, no one had said anything—not one word to even suggest that Talia had a reading problem. But the other children knew. They called her a loser. They'd say, "Loser. You can't read."
>
> I thought that she was very lazy, that she was just being obstinate because she seemed so smart in other ways. She knew stuff. I remember saying, "What's the Queen of England's last name?" And Talia just looked over and said, "Windsor. You know, Windsor Castle." And she just gave this whole spiel on something that had been read to her.

I asked how old Talia was when she said that.

> Seven. And yet she couldn't read any books. And she would get so mad because her little brother would sit there, and he would shout it out. We'd all feel bad. And she'd run to her room. That was really awful.
>
> She would fake being sick. She didn't want to go to school. She would want to come home. The nurse would call me and say she's throwing up. She'd make herself physically sick so she could come home from school, so she wouldn't have to have reading time.

I asked Ms. Matthews if she had spoken to the teachers or if a teacher had spoken to her.

> Oh, yes. They told me, "We think it would be good if she buckled down and tried harder. . . . Maybe she just isn't as smart as you think she is." I can still hear them say, "Parents tend to think all kids are geniuses—when they are not."
>
> And then the folks at Syracuse . . . told me, "Your daughter is extremely smart. Her IQ is very high. Talia has a reading problem." When I heard that, I cried. I said, "Oh, my God." And they said they had a possible way they could work with her and teach her.

Talia was identified as dyslexic and placed in a reading program for one hour a day, four days a week, for a year.

> I noticed a real change in Talia. I saw her being interested in coming home and wanting to do her homework. It just clicked. They taught her a new way.
>
> She did exactly what they were showing her. It was completely different from what they were teaching her in school. And if she didn't know a word, she didn't want any help from anyone. And that was a big difference. Before, she would beg someone else, "Please just do it for me."
>
> She is like night and day. She doesn't have bellyaches. I think she missed one day of school this year; the year before, thirty. And when she has to read out loud in class, she can't wait.

It's unbelievable how this has affected our family. Before, we felt so much guilt for how we had been treating her. I would say, "What's wrong with you? Your brother has his homework done. And we can't even get you to do two answers." We were grilling her, you know, like in her face. So my husband and I had a lot of guilt about how we were treating her until she was diagnosed with dyslexia and went into the reading program.

Life is better in our family; it's normal. And she has friends, and she feels better about herself. She has girls call her, and she says, "Mom, they think I'm really cool."

She tells everyone, "I couldn't read. And I was tested. And there was actually a problem with me, and they taught me how to fix it."

She's getting A's and B's. It clicked. She even likes to read for pleasure.

I asked Ms. Matthews what she would want to tell other parents whose children might have a reading problem.

There is a way to teach your child. You just have to find the right method. Reading can be the most important thing in the world because it affects everything—everything.

I would say don't give up. Try to find someone who can evaluate your child and see what way she needs to be taught.

Now Talia can do anything. She already has a vision of what she wants to do with her life. She wants to be a veterinarian.

Your dyslexic child can become a reader just like Talia did. Rather than a magic wand, such a transformation requires two essential ingredients: early diagnosis *and* effective treatment. In previous chapters you learned how to identify a reading problem early; in the following chapters you will learn what to do once a child is identified. I will provide you with the basic principles to guide you and allow you to determine what is best for your child. They are the same ones that were helpful in identifying a reading problem; now you can apply them to obtain the most effective treatment.

Principles to Guide You

Principle One.

Develop a life span perspective. An effective program is tailored to a child's or adult's specific developmental needs. What works best for a six-year-old is not going to be the most helpful approach for a sixteen-year-old. Accordingly, the first step in designing an effective reading program is to determine where your child is on the developmental continuum. Within such a framework, the focus early on is on remediation and, if possible, identifying a child at risk and preventing reading difficulties. As the child progresses in school and reaches middle school and then high school—particularly those who have the potential to participate in demanding academic programs—the emphasis shifts from providing remediation to providing accommodation.

Principle Two.

Remediate the phonologic weakness and access the higher-level think-ing and reasoning strengths (through accommodations). This is important because it places emphasis not only on the child's reading difficulty but on his strengths. It reminds everyone that the isolated phonologic weakness is only one small part of a much larger picture. Far too often the focus is only on the weakness, and the child's strong capabilities (and potential) are overlooked. Whatever those strengths are—the ability to reason, to analyze, to conceptualize, to be creative, to have empathy, to visualize, to imagine, or to think in novel ways—it is imperative that these strengths be identified, nurtured, and allowed to define that child. For many children, accommodations represent the difference between academic success and failure, between a growing sense of self-confidence and an enduring sense of defeat.

Before discussing specific approaches to teaching reading, I want to discuss other important factors that can significantly influence your child's eventual success in reading and in life. These include, in addition to the nature of the reading program, the intrinsic qualities of the child and the significant adults who interact with him.

Considering solely the child's characteristics, his long-term outlook will reflect the severity of his phonologic weakness and the degree of his cognitive strengths. Not surprisingly, children with milder phonologic difficulties and higher intellectual capabilities tend to do better. There is now evidence, however, that children all along the spectrum can benefit from research-based reading programs. Upon discovering your child's dyslexia, her unique blend of strengths and weaknesses reflects her past: the genes she inherited and her experiences growing up. But you can brighten her future by maximizing the two factors over which you have some control: the reading program your child receives, which will be addressed in the following chapters, and how she is treated by the adults around her.

The significant adults in a dyslexic child's life—typically her parents and her teachers—play an enormous role in determining her future outlook. While this would seem to be self-evident, I have witnessed far too many instances where the most loving and well-intentioned parents or teachers have taken an uncharacteristically passive stance and assumed that somehow "things will work out." It is not easy to be the parent of a vulnerable child, particularly a child with a hidden disability that can escape diagnosis, as Talia's mother so poignantly demonstrated. But the reality is that in the overwhelming number of cases, the only way things will improve is if a knowledgeable and caring adult takes the lead and actively creates change. Most of the time it is a patient, persevering, and positive "activist" parent.

A child with dyslexia is in need of a champion, someone who will be his support and his unflinching advocate; his cheerleader when things are not going well; his friend and confidant when others tease and shame him; his advocate who by actions and comments will express optimism for his future. Perhaps most important, the struggling reader needs someone who will not only believe in him but will translate that belief into positive action by understanding the nature of his reading problem and then actively and relentlessly working to ensure that he receives the reading help and other support he needs. Experience has shown me that if a child receives such help, he will succeed. I can point to a couple of parents as models: Ken Kilroy, of Los Angeles, who with unfailing grace and persistence has championed his child's learning needs and also worked hard to ensure that his son's strengths in math and science are not overlooked, and Norma Garza, a businesswoman and civic leader who continually strives to understand her son's academic needs and wages a tireless campaign to bring the newest research knowledge about dyslexia to his small school in Brownsville, Texas. A child who has such a champion will not only succeed academically but will maintain his sense of self and the possibilities for a happy future. One of my purposes in writing this book is to give parents who want to be champions for their children the know-how that will allow them to make a real difference in their child's life.

Our knowledge of what works in teaching reading has come to us through science. This new information can be put to use to provide a sensible and successful approach to teaching children to read—children without any reading difficulties, children who are at risk for reading problems, and children who are already known to be dyslexic. Constantly bombarded by information about different approaches to teaching reading and about new "miracle" treatments for reading disability, parents (and often teachers, too) are confused about reading instruction. As a parent, how do you know where to begin or how to determine what is the best reading program for your son or daughter? The good news is that data coming in from laboratories all over the world are providing a clear picture of the process of learning to read. Finally, a growing number of scientists, clinicians, and educators agree about what every child needs to know to become a good reader.

For the first time ever there is an "evidence-based" guide to what works in teaching children to read. It is an outgrowth of a grassroots concern that while a substantial number of children were failing to learn to read, little was available to help parents and teachers make important choices among different approaches to reading instruction. And so in 1997, Congress directed the creation of a National Reading Panel of experts to come together to objectively and comprehensively review the existing research relating to the teaching of reading. As a member of the panel, I can attest to how seriously the group took its mission, traveling to all parts of the country to listen to parents, teachers, and others; developing rigorous criteria to review the existing research; initially identifying more than six thousand studies and then subjecting those that met criteria to careful analysis. On April 13, 2000, after more than two years of effort, the panel released its findings in the "Report of the National Reading Panel, Teaching Children to Read: An Evidence-Based Assessment of the Scientific Research Literature on Reading and Its Implications for Reading Instruction." It was with great pride that I, along with the panel chair, Dr. Donald Langenberg, and the director of the National Institute of Child Health and Human Development (NICHD) Dr. Duane Alexander, presented the report to Congress. The most thorough report ever to be undertaken in American education, it provides a road map to guide parents and teachers to the most effective, scientifically proven methods for teaching reading. Now in education, as in medicine, we can look to the scientific evidence as the basis for choosing a treatment. Before selecting a reading program, parents and teachers can and must ask, "What is the evidence of its efficacy?" I will discuss the findings of the National Reading Panel throughout the remainder of this book.

The findings of the panel are now part of the groundbreaking No Child Left Behind Act, which was passed by Congress overwhelmingly and signed into law by President George W. Bush on January 8, 2002. The Reading First program, a component of this legislation, makes substantial financial awards available to states that demonstrate through a rigorous review process that the funds will be used to support scientifically based reading programs for children and scientifically informed professional development programs for teachers. As a reviewer for the Reading First grants, I can attest to the extremely high criteria that must be met by a state in order to receive an award. This landmark legislation signals the beginning of a revolution in how children are taught to read, ensuring that every child will be provided with a reading program that works.

In the following chapters I will discuss in detail what approaches to the teaching of reading are most effective (evidence-based) at different points along the reading continuum. I will devote an entire chapter to "breaking the reading code," because that is the most critical and for many children the most difficult step. Then, in subsequent chapters, I will focus on how to ensure that a child becomes a skilled reader, that is, a reader who reads accurately and rapidly, and understands what he reads. I will discuss what to do for the child who continues to experience difficulties and answer some of the most pressing questions that have come from parents. I will conclude this section with a discussion of the important role of specific accommodations in helping a dyslexic student access his strengths.

15

Helping Your Child
Break the Reading Code

One of the most exciting things to happen to your child between the time he enters kindergarten and the time he leaves the next spring is that he breaks the reading code. To do so he must solve the two parts of the reading puzzle: one involving spoken language, and the other involving written language. For the past five thousand or so years since man has been reading, each potential reader has faced the same challenge.

To solve the first part of the puzzle, each would-be reader must begin to understand that spoken words come apart and that they are made up of very small bits of language. As you read earlier, these tiny particles of language are called phonemes, and the development of this insight about words is called phonemic awareness. Once a child appreciates that spoken words can be pulled apart into distinct sounds, he is well on his way to solving the spoken language part of the reading code. Then he is ready to take the next big step: figuring out how printed letters link to these sounds—for example, knowing that the first sound of the spoken word *sat,* "ssss," is represented by the letter *s,* and the final sound, "*t*" by the letter *t*. And then one day he solves the puzzle: He makes the critical insight that the written word *sat* has the same number and sequence of sounds, "ssss," "aaaa," "t," as the spoken word *sat* and that the letters represent these sounds. He has broken the reading code! The child has mastered the alphabetic principle. He is ready to read.

This step is extremely important because once a child knows the code, printed words are no longer a mystery. He has a *strategy;* he knows how to link the letters to the sounds they represent and then to blend the sounds together to read the word. He applies his knowledge of how letters relate to sounds to analyze and to read more and more unfamiliar words. This is referred to as *decoding.* The better a child gets at decoding words, the more accurate his reading. A child who knows how to sound out printed words is freed from having to memorize every word he wants to be able to read. Sounding out words allows him to unlock the mystery of reading and to read words he has never seen before.

Recent brain research allows us to link our understanding of the sequence of steps a child goes through in learning to read to the work that must go on within the brain to solve the reading code as well as to the teaching of reading. Within his brain, the child is literally building the neural circuitry that links the *sounds* of spoken words, the phonemes, to the print code, the *letters* that represent these sounds. A major role of kindergarten is to provide a child with the kinds of experiences that allow him to build those brain connections as accurately, as strongly, and as quickly as possible.

Part One of the Code: Sound Advice

At the very beginning stage of reading, the initial goal is to draw the child's attention to the *sounds* of language. It is important to keep in mind that children will vary in their progress along this road. Some will need to go through each step slowly, while others will progress more rapidly, not requiring instruction for every step of the process. The end point is for a child to develop phonemic awareness, the most important and sometimes most difficult task in learning to read and the foundation of all subsequent reading and spelling instruction. Teaching it requires only about fifteen minutes a day during the course of a school year, and children benefit from this instruction as early as preschool and kindergarten. Progressively, a child's attention is drawn to the sounds in words, first through noticing rhymes, then by comparing sounds in different words, and finally by learning how to "work on words," pulling them apart, pushing them together, and moving the parts around within the word. While phonemic awareness refers to the sounds of spoken words, it often helps to use letters to emphasize the different sounds and to facilitate transferring this skill to reading. Always keep in mind that we are teaching phonemic awareness not as an end in itself, but because of its central importance in helping a child understand the relation of letters to sounds and, ultimately, to become a reader.

Step One: Developing an Awareness of Rhyme

The very first step for a child is to develop a growing awareness that words can rhyme. Tuning into rhymes sensitizes very young children to the fact that words come apart. For example, to know that the words *fig* and *jig* rhyme, a child must attend to just a part of each word—the ending, *ig*. The child begins to appreciate that words have parts. His natural joy in playing with rhymes (words ending with the same sound) and alliteration (a series of two or more words beginning with the same initial sound, such as *click, clack, clock*) helps lay the groundwork for teaching phonemic awareness.

You can help sensitize a child to rhyme by reading stories and poems to him aloud. One richly illustrated rhyming book that he will enjoy is *Chugga-Chugga Choo-Choo* by Kevin Lewis and Daniel Kirk. Listen:

> Chugga-chugga
> choo-choo,
> whistle blowing,
> whoooooooo! whoooooooo!

And

> Into tunnels, underground.
> See the darkness. Hear the sound.
> Chugga-chugga choo-choo, echo calling,
> whoooooooo! whoooooooo!
> whoooooooo! whoooooooo!

Children often love to pump their fist up and down as they make the sounds of the train whistle.

There are many books that you can read with your child to help prepare him for reading. Knowing you are building a foundation for reading provides added incentive for making reading aloud a routine part of your special time together. Here is a list of children's books that joyfully play with the sounds of language.

Bemelmans, Ludwig, *Madeline* (New York: Penguin Putnam, 2000).

Brown, Margaret Wise, *Four Fur Feet* (New York: Hyperion, 1996).

Bunting, Eve, *The Pumpkin Fair* (New York: Houghton Mifflin, 2001).

de Paola, Tomie, *Hey Diddle Diddle and Other Mother Goose Rhymes* (New York: Putnam, 1998).

Fleming, Denise, *In the Tall, Tall Grass* (New York: Henry Holt, 1995).

Fox, Dan, and P. Fox (eds.), *Go In and Out the Window: An Illustrated Songbook for Young People* (New York: Henry Holt, 1987).

Galdone, P., *Henny Penny* (New York: Houghton Mifflin, 1984).

Hawkins, C., and J. Hawkins, *Tog the Dog* (New York: Penguin Putnam, 1991).

Heidbreder, Robert, *I Wished for a Unicorn* (Toronto, Canada: Kids Can Press, 2001).

Ho, Minfong, *Hush! A Thai Lullaby* (New York: Orchard Books, 1996).

Karlin, Nurit, *The Fat Cat Sat on the Mat* (New York: Harper-Collins, 1998).

Kellogg, Stephen, *Aster Aardvark's Alphabet Adventures* (New York: Morrow, 1992).

Krauss, Ruth, *Bears* (New York: Scholastic, 1993).

―――. *I Can Fly* (New York: Golden Books, 1999).

Larrick, Nancy (ed.), *Songs from Mother Goose* (New York: HarperCollins, 1989).

―――. *When the Dark Comes Dancing: A Bedtime Poetry Book* (New York: Putnam, 1982).

LeSieg, Theo, *Please Try to Remember the First of Octember!* (New York: Random House, 1988).

―――. *The Eye Book* (New York: Random House, 1999).

LeTord, B., *An Alphabet of Sounds: Arf Boo Click* (New York: MacMillan, 1981).

Lewis, K., and D. Kirk, *Chugga-Chugga Choo-Choo* (New York: Hyperion, 1999).

Lewison, W., *Buzz, Said the Bee* (New York: Scholastic, 1992).

Lobel, Arnold, *Whiskers and Rhymes* (New York: Morrow, 1988).

Martin, B., J. Archambault, and L. Ehler, *Chicka Chicka Boom Boom* (New York: Simon and Schuster, 1991).

Ochs, C. P., *Moose on the Loose* (Minneapolis: Carolroda Books, 1991).

Pretlusky, Jack, editor, *Read-Aloud Rhymes for the Very Young* (New York: Alfred A. Knopf, 1986).

———. *The Frog Wore Red Suspenders* (New York: Greenwillow Books, 2002).

Seuss, Dr., *There's A Wocket in My Pocket* (New York: Random House, 1996).

———. *Hop on Pop* (New York: Random House, 1976).

———. *One Fish, Two Fish, Red Fish, Blue Fish* (New York: Random House, 1988).

———. *Green Eggs and Ham* (New York: Random House, 1976).

Silverstein, Shel, *A Giraffe and a Half* (New York: HarperCollins, 1975).

Van Allsburg, C., *The Z was Zapped* (Boston: Houghton Mifflin, 1987).

Yee, Josie, *Classic Sing-Along Rhymes* (New York: Scholastic, 2002).

Zeifert, Harriet, *I Swapped My Dog* (Boston: Houghton Mifflin, 1998).

It is great fun to read these books aloud with your child; they are full of rhymes and alliterations. As he listens to them or even joins in singing the little ditties, he is taking a step toward becoming a reader. Hallie Kay Yopp, who teaches reading courses at California State University and recommended many of the books on the list, suggests some activities that children can enjoy as they listen to the stories. First, she says, "Read the story aloud several times simply for the pure joy of reading and sharing." Then draw the child's attention to the sounds. (I can hear the children giggle as they listen to C. P. Ochs's *Moose on the Loose* about the zookeeper who runs through the town of Zown asking everyone if they've seen a "moose on the loose in a chartreuse caboose.") As you read these stories, simple comments such as "Isn't it funny that so many of the words rhyme?" help stimulate rhyme awareness. You can also ask your child to predict the next word in a rhyming story or ask if she notices that all the words in a sentence begin with the same sound: "Listen to the beginning sounds in these words: *Pink pigs picked pretty petals.* What sound do you hear? Yes, the *'p'* sound. What are some other words that begin with that sound?"

Here are some more selections you can practice reading to your child. I've chosen one of my children's favorites, *One Fish Two Fish Red Fish Blue Fish* by Dr. Seuss:

> Bump!
> Bump!
> Bump!
> Did you ever ride a Wump?
> We have a Wump
> with just one hump.
> But
> we know a man
> called Mr. Gump.
> Mr. Gump has a seven hump Wump.
> So . . .
> if you like to go Bump! Bump!
> just jump on the hump of the Wump
> of Gump.

Or some children may prefer *Madeline* by Ludwig Bemelmans, also written in rhyme. Here he describes little Madeline:

> She was not afraid of mice—
> she loved winter, snow, and ice.
> To the tiger in the zoo
> Madeline just said, "Pooh-pooh,"

and nobody knew so well
how to frighten Miss Clavel.

As you read these rhyming stories aloud, it is helpful if you exaggerate
the sound of the rhyming words.

In addition, you can invite your child to join in reciting poems and
jingles. These activities are easily fitted into a child's daily schedule; for
example, you can do something as simple as having your child sing along
with you as he prepares for bed:

Twinkle, twinkle little star,
how I wonder what you are.
Up above the world so high,
like a diamond in the sky.
Twinkle, twinkle little star,
how I wonder what you are.

Step Two: Working on Words

After getting to know rhymes and developing the sense that words have
parts, children are ready for the next big step on the road to reading: taking words apart and putting them back together. Pulling apart a word
into its sounds is often referred to as *segmenting;* pushing sounds
together to form a word is called *blending.* These are the two key
processes involved in learning to spell and to read. In spelling, for example, a child *segments* the spoken word into its sounds and transforms
each sound into a letter. In reading the letters are converted into sounds,
which are then *blended* together to form the word. Working on words is
the initial work of reading and forms the central focus of reading programs for young children. Just as a surgeon must learn the smallest
details of human anatomy, budding readers must develop a keen awareness of the internal anatomy of spoken and printed words.

In practice, children are introduced to the sounds of language gradually. Most reading programs begin by showing the child how to dissect
words into their biggest chunks of sounds, syllables, and then introduce
the smaller pieces, phonemes.

Separating Words into Syllables. There are good reasons to begin
with syllables. They are the largest units of sound that make up a word,

and they are relatively easy for children to identify and manipulate within words. One activity that helps a child pull apart the sounds in a word is to count (actually clap) the number of syllables in his own name: *Jay . . . son.* (Clap, clap). *Jon . . . a . . . than.* (Clap, clap, clap). Alternatively, children can take turns clapping out the syllables for each day of the week (*Tues . . . day*); each month of the year (*Sep . . . tem . . . ber*); recognizable objects (*cow . . . boy, scare . . . crow*); fun words such as cucumber (*cu . . . cum . . . ber*), or Cinderella (*Cin . . . der . . . el . . . la*).

Children can also practice pushing syllables together to form words: "Can you tell me what word *rain . . . bow* makes?" (*rainbow*). "And now *a . . . corn*" (*acorn*).

Or a child may be asked to blend the sounds of his own name: "Tell me the word that *Jay . . . son* makes" (*Jason*).

If you have any questions about the number of syllables in a word, you can consult the dictionary.

Separating Syllables into Phonemes. Separating words into syllables is relatively easy; the words are already perforated and readily come apart. In contrast, the next major step, appreciating that spoken words can be pulled apart into even finer divisions—phonemes—is difficult for most beginning readers, and particularly so for dyslexic children. As you have read, the ability to focus on these smallest units of sound is one of the best predictors of a child's later reading ability.

In the most effective programs, children first practice comparing or matching sounds in different words. The aim is to start a child thinking about how the sounds in these words compare to one another. Always begin by asking him to match the very first sounds in words and then the final sounds. It is often helpful to have a set of cards with pictures of everyday objects (such as a man, map, door, cat, dog, mom, mitt, can, cup, tag, top). You can cut the pictures out of a magazine and paste each one on a card, or you can use those from children's board games.

You can begin by asking your child to identify the first sound in a word such as *map*. Show him a picture of a map, clearly saying, "This is a *mmmap*." Ask him to name the picture. Next say, "The first sound in *mmmap* is '*mmmm*.' Can you say the first sound?" Then lay out four or five picture cards, some beginning with the "*mmmm*" sound. Ask him to say the names of each of the pictures and then to group together all the objects beginning with the "*mmmm*" sound.

You may also show him three picture cards with, for example, a fan, a dog, and a cake, and ask him to name each picture. Then ask, "Can you show me which one of these pictures begins with the '*d*' sound?" You can point to one of the pictures (dog), name it, and then ask, "Can you find something else in the room that also begins with the same '*d*' sound?" Or you can simply ask him to produce a word that begins with the same sound as a target word: "Can you tell me a word that begins with the same sound as *ssssnake*?" (*sit, soup,* and *smile*).

Sound-matching games are relatively easy because they do not require the child to manipulate phonemes and are ideal for the budding reader in kindergarten.

Once a child is successful at matching sounds, he is ready for the more difficult task of pulling apart words: first the beginnings, then the endings, and then the middle sounds. Children carry out these kinds of activities with spoken words first, and then they progress to games involving the letters and sounds that make up written words.

There are all sorts of ways you can pull words apart. You can ask your child to clap for the number of sounds he hears in a word. For example, you can say, "*ssss . . . ee, see.* Clap for the number of sounds you hear, *ssss . . . ee, see.*" She should clap twice for the two sounds, "*ssss*" and "*ee.*" Interestingly, most kindergartners seem to be successful in separating the sounds in two-phoneme words such as *eat, it, say,* and *zoo,* but they are stymied when asked to pull apart even relatively simple three-phoneme words such as *fan* and *mop.* So go slowly. Start with the most basic two-phoneme words and then work your way up to three or more sounds.

You could also add a sound and ask: What word do you get if you add the sound "*t*" to the word *see*? (*seat*).

You could take away a sound, first a beginning sound, and ask: What word do you get if you take the "*ssss*" sound from the word *seat*? (*eat*). Then take away an ending sound: Can you say *seat* without the "*t*" sound? (*see*).

The above tasks require segmentation. The converse, phoneme blending, is one of the most important and, surprisingly, difficult jobs for the beginning reader to master. (Recall that in reading a child must transform the letters to sounds and then blend the sounds together to form the word.) You may want to practice blending activities at home with your child. One method is to line up three pictures, such as a man, a map, and a fan. Choose a word represented by one of the pictures, for example, *man,* and slowly pronounce each of its sounds:

"*mmmm*" . . . "*aaaa*" . . . "*nnn.*" Ask your child to point to the picture that shows the word made by pushing these sounds together.

For a slightly more difficult variant, rather than asking your child to point, you can ask him to tell you the word made by pushing these sounds together.

For both segmenting and blending activities, you can use the following two- and three-phoneme words. Notice that the number of letters and the number of sounds in a word are not always equal. *Zoo* has three letters and only two sounds.

Two-phoneme words:

is	tie	zoo	shy
to	see	chew	knee
do	toe	row	my
sew	be	mow	it
shoe	hay	key	day

Three-phoneme words:

cat	bat	cab
sheep	pan	map
can	jeep	cub
mice	fish	book
feet	man	dog
nap	jet	tag
zap	nip	top
sun	net	mom
cup	bag	tap
bed	bug	top

Hints for Building Success

The goal of these activities is to draw your child's attention to the smallest parts of words. Here are some of the things you might want to keep in mind as you do so:

• You want your child's active involvement. When you have it, he is paying attention, and learning is going on. The activities should be short and enjoyable. If he is not interested, let it go. Little is accomplished if he sits there passively with you talking at him. Try to do these activities when both you and he are alert and in a good mood.

- You want him to notice each word or word part you say, so speak slowly and clearly and pronounce each sound very carefully.
- Exaggerate sounds—for example, *mmmman*—and have him do the same when he repeats it back to you.
- Make up your own jingles, rhymes, or silly stories to highlight a particular sound, or even sing a song together. Funny and visually absurd rhymes and alliterations often work best in making a sound more salient to the child. To highlight the "*ssss*" sound, for example, sing with him "*Silly Sammy seal slept soundly in the silent silver sea.*"
- Use concrete objects (blocks or coins) to represent the sounds in words. Your child should indicate how many sounds he hears in a word by the number of coins (or blocks) he places on the table. For example, for the two-phoneme word *zoo*, he would say each sound ("*zzzz*" "*oo*") as he lays out one and then a second coin (see Figure 31).

Figure 31. Helping Your Child Count Phonemes in Words

As your child pronounces each sound in a word, such as *zoo*, he puts a coin in the center of the table.

Overall it helps to keep in mind that there is a logic to these activities. They should reinforce what is happening in your child's classroom. Always check with his teacher to ensure that you, she, and your child are working in synchrony. Ask her about what specific activities he is doing in class and how you can help at home to further his reading skills.

Teachers and parents who prefer a ready-made program for teaching phonemic awareness can purchase one of several excellent commercial products. Geared to children in preschool or kindergarten, they are especially helpful for children at risk for reading difficulties: "Phonemic Awareness in Young Children: A Classroom Curriculum," "Ladders to Literacy," and "The Sounds Abound Program: Teaching Phonological Awareness in the Classroom" are meant for instructing entire preschool or kindergarten classes; in contrast, "Phonological Awareness Training for Reading" and "Road to the Code: A Phonological Awareness Program for Young Children" work best with small groups or on a one-to-one basis. Good computer programs to stimulate phonological awareness include DaisyQuest and Daisy's Castle, and Earobics. All should be used as an addition to a classroom program.

These programs are listed below with their contact information and targeted grade.

DaisyQuest and Daisy's Castle (Adventure Learning Software), kindergarten and first grade

Earobics (Cognitive Concepts), preschool through elementary school

Ladders to Literacy (Paul Brookes), kindergarten

Phonemic Awareness in Young Children: A Classroom Curriculum (Paul Brookes), kindergarten, weaker first grade, and special education students

Phonological Awareness Training for Reading (PRO-ED), kindergarten through second grade

Road to the Code (Paul Brookes), kindergarten and first grade

The Sounds Abound Program: Teaching Phonological Awareness in the Classroom (LinguiSystems), preschool through first grade

Part Two of the Code: Put It in Writing

Once a child has learned about the segmental nature of spoken words and is becoming familiar with individual sounds, she is ready for letters. Most children have already learned to sing the ABC song as preschoolers and enter kindergarten knowing the names of most of the letters. In kindergarten, knowledge of the letters is reinforced—not only their shapes and names but their sounds. By the second half of the year most children can identify and print each of the letters. Now they can begin to use them for the purpose of reading.

Learning about and using different sound and letter combinations to decode words is called *phonics.* In English there are more sounds than letters—about forty-four phonemes and just twenty-six letters. These forty-four sounds provide the means by which the developing reader can attach letters and create print, or "visible speech."

Linking letters and letter groups to sounds has traditionally been taught in the first grade, though children may be ready for phonics long before their teachers believe they are. Depending on the child's own readiness, this instruction can start as early as kindergarten with excellent results. As mentioned earlier, knowing how letters represent sounds helps children pay better attention to the individual sounds when they occur in a spoken word.

The A to Z of Teaching Beginning Reading

Although awareness of sounds and letters is necessary for learning to read, children need practice in reading stories. They need to apply their newly acquired skills to sounding out and decoding familiar and less familiar words, to reading words in sentences and in books, and to understanding the meaning of the word and the sentence. Let's consider each of these activities in turn, beginning with practice.

Practice. New brain imaging technology shows the powerful positive effect of practice in creating neural circuits related to the development of what scientists call expertise or skill. Basically, the brain learns by practice. The old dictum repeated by mothers and teachers about the importance of practice, practice, and more practice turns out to be right. Whether it is for learning how to pitch a baseball, to play a musical instrument, or to read, nothing is more important for the formation and reinforcement of neural systems. That is what leads to perfection and expertise. The 2002 Olympic bronze medal winner in men's figure skating, Timothy Goebel, who electrified the Salt Lake City judges with his quadruple jumps, said, "I just practice a lot. I'm always practicing. So I don't have to think about it anymore." It is the same with reading: Once a child gains an awareness of how letters relate to sounds, he benefits greatly from opportunities to put into practice what he has just learned.

After an introduction to the specific letter-sound relationships, the next critical step is for a child to practice the words, both in isolation and then in reading simple sentences and books. To improve his accuracy a child needs to practice reading, both silently and, especially, out loud to others. Each time he stumbles on a specific word and, with his teacher's or parent's guidance, makes corrections and refinements, he is establishing increasingly more accurate word representations within his brain. Eventually he builds an exact neural replica of the word. His internal representation of the word reflects its precise spelling, pronunciation, and meaning. Writing the word and learning to spell it also contribute to establishing accurate representations of that word in his neural circuitry.

Learning spelling-sound patterns, practicing them in different words and in reading books, learning how to form letters and to spell the words—all contribute to forging and then reinforcing the connections that will eventually form the neural code for that word. Think of beginning reading as solving a mystery—the mystery of the unknown word. The more clues, the greater the chance of solving the mystery. The more detailed and accurate the replica of the word built into the child's neural circuitry, the more likely he is to recognize the word when he comes across it again.

Even kindergartners, at the cusp of literacy, can practice their new skills. Children love to read even when they know only a few letter-sound linkages. Simple booklets, about twelve to twenty-four pages—so-called decodable texts (containing the words with letter-sound patterns that a child has already been taught)—can help him apply his newfound skills by actually reading words in a book. The "Bob Books" series (see Chapter 16) is a good example. Alternatively, parents and children can have fun creating their own personal minibooks. It takes little more than keeping a list of the words your son has learned and combining them into simple sentences: "Pat the cat. The hat is on the cat." As he learns new words, you can keep adding to the series, thereby showing your child how much he has learned. Then he has his very own library to call on when he wants to "read" a book. Generally, these little books are most helpful in kindergarten and early first grade.

Sight words. Once a child learns about letter-sound relationships in specific words, he eventually generalizes and uses these principles to read other, new words that have the same letter pattern and are pronounced the same way. If a child can read *cat* and is able to divide it into *c-at,* he will also be able to decode other words in the same *at* family: *mat, sat, bat.* With time he will go on to acquire knowledge of more and more complex word families.

Sometimes, however, difficulty arises where you might least expect it. I am thinking of words such as *a, is, are, one, two, said, again, been, could, the,* and *once,* which pop up frequently in books for young children but don't seem to follow the rules. These words do not follow a pattern and cannot be sounded out. Consequently, they must be committed to memory and recognized on sight; not surprisingly, they are often referred to as *sight words.** (Because of the inconsistencies in their letter-sound linkages, they are also sometimes called "irregular" words.) Since sight words are sure to be found in children's books, it is important that they become part of a child's reading vocabulary at a very early stage. Making flash cards and reviewing them regularly helps a child learn these common words. Having him print his own card and say the word as he writes it often helps reinforce its pronunciation. (See Chapter 16 for a list of the most common sight words.)

Writing. Recognizing and writing letters represents a major milestone in learning to read. More emphasis is directed toward writing lowercase letters because they are more common. Once children can write letters, no matter how poorly, they can engage in a variety of writing exercises that further encourage awareness of the sounds that make up words and of how letters represent these sounds. Writing out his own name and then other common words such as *cat, mom,* and *dad* reinforces that awareness. Early on in kindergarten, children can use alphabet blocks or letter cards to "write" the words. By the time the children are ready to

---

* *Sight word* can have two meanings: one as I have described, referring to words that don't follow rules for pronunciation, and the other meaning words that can be read "on sight," that is, automatically and without having to go through a decoding process. Here I am employing the first usage.

leave kindergarten, they are using letters to spell words phonetically, although not necessarily correctly. These earliest attempts at such spellings are referred to as "invented" or temporary spelling.

Spelling. Spelling is intimately linked to reading not only because sounds are being linked to letters but because words are being encoded—literally put into a code instead of merely being deciphered or decoded. As I mentioned earlier, in spelling, the spoken word is being pulled apart into its sounds and then each sound is encoded or transformed into the letters representing that sound. Invented spelling functions as a transitional step as kindergartners try their hand at matching letters to sounds. When children try to form print words based on the sounds they hear in spoken words, it is a good indication that they are on the road to reading. This is why children in kindergarten and in the beginning of first grade are encouraged to practice "invented spelling" and to write a word as they think it sounds, such as *knd* for *candy, hrs* for *horse,* or *kt* for *cat.* As you can see by these examples, beginning readers commonly omit vowel sounds, so a child's invented spelling for the word *house* might well progress from *hs* to *hws* to *house.* Notice that the pronunciation of the invented spelling is very close to that of the intended word. A child may have the sounds down, but he may not have quite mastered the link between sound and letters. In kindergarten that's okay.

Listening, playing, and imagining. A kindergarten child's reading program is rounded out by a range of activities that enhance her language skills and her enjoyment of literature. Whether at school or at home, being surrounded by books, listening to stories read aloud, talking about the characters and events in the story, and playing with blocks or puppets all help a child develop her thinking skills and her imagination, build her vocabulary, and become aware of the world around her.

Reading and word knowledge are mutually reinforcing. Reading builds a child's vocabulary, and knowledge of word meanings helps in decoding words and improves reading comprehension. A primary goal of reading is to get to the printed word's meaning; to do so requires that a child first decipher the word and then have the word in his vocabulary. Initially, the words a child learns to read are quite simple and invariably in his oral vocabulary, but before long the words get more complicated and unfamiliar. At this stage, knowing the meaning of a word helps facilitate its decoding. As a child encounters an unfamiliar printed word, he tries out different pronunciations: Is the *i* in *ink* pronounced like the *i* in *ice* or like the *i* in *it?* If he knows the meaning of the word *ink,* he is far more likely to pronounce it correctly. The larger a child's vocabulary, the more words—and the more difficult and complex words—he is going to be able to decipher and to read. Consequently, it is never too early to introduce a child to new words and their meanings, which strengthens his neural model for each of the new words he encounters. Parents can help by making it a point to talk about each new word (or concept) you come across in a story, to define it in simple words, and then to have your child use the word in a sentence. Learning about the meanings of new words reinforces a child's worldly as well as his word knowledge, both key ingredients for strengthening a child's reading comprehension, which is the goal of reading.

In addition to improving a child's vocabulary, listening to stories has many other positive benefits for reading. At home you can enhance these positive effects by having your daughter sit next to you as you read, watching as you point to each word as you pronounce it. She will soon notice that words that take longer to say look longer on the page. *Caterpillar* sounds longer than *cat* and looks longer when you see the word printed on a page. Such observations help the child learn that the spoken word and the printed word are related. At a later stage she will begin to associate the printed word with the sound and meaning of the spoken word. Eventually she will learn to use her finger to point to each of the words as you read them, and then she will want to read and point out the words herself. To get started, I suggest reading aloud the books listed below. They are just right for a child on the cusp of reading.

Cohen, Caron Lee, *How Many Fish?* (New York: Harper-Collins, 1998).

Davis, Katie, *Who Hops?* (New York: Harcourt Brace & Company, 1998).

Eastman, P. D., *Go Dog Go!* (New York: Beginner Books, 1961).

Emberley, Ed, *Drummer Hoff* (Englewood Cliffs, N.J.: Prentice-Hall, 1967).

Hutchins, Pat, *Rosie's Walk* (New York: Macmillan, 1968).

Kraus, Robert, *Whose Mouse Are You?* (New York: Macmillan, 1970).

Martin, Bill, Jr., *Brown Bear, Brown Bear What Do You See?* (New York: Henry Holt, 1992).

Martin, David, *Monkey Trouble* (Cambridge, Mass.: Candlewick Press, 2000).

Neitzel, Shirley, *The Jacket I Wear in the Snow* (New York: Greenwillow Books, 1989).

Seuss, Dr., *The Foot Book* (New York: Random House, 1968).

Tafuri, Nancy, *The Ball Bounced* (New York: Greenwillow Books, 1989).

Kindergarten children also love to make up stories and to dictate them to their teacher or to their parent, who magically transcribes each word onto paper. As a child dictates his little story and then watches as you point to and read each word back to him, he is learning to associate sound, letters, and meaning. He is building the integrated neural circuits necessary for reading. He is also building his imagination.

Self-confidence. This is probably the most important ingredient in ensuring that a child is ready to read and is setting out on a good path. After all is said and done, the most significant development for your child as he leaves kindergarten is how he feels about himself. A critical role of the kindergarten experience is to ensure that every child achieves some degree of success in what he does, that he receives positive comments from his teacher, and that he is encouraged. That will keep him motivated to read. Without motivation and the sense that he can succeed, a child will have little reason to struggle as he tries to pull apart words that seem to be inseparable.

The Importance of the Right Fit in Kindergarten

Each child is different, and it is important to pinpoint where your child is along the reading pathway. Rather than a student trying to keep up with (or slow down to) a pace that is uncomfortable for him, instruction must be fitted to the child.

Once instruction begins, there are inevitable questions: Is this approach working? Is my child making progress and catching up, or is he falling behind? If he continues at this pace, what does this mean for his future as a reader? The only way to answer these questions reliably is by assessing the kinds of skills discussed here—rhyming, phonemic awareness, knowledge of letter names and sounds—and the child's ability to apply these skills to reading.

In kindergarten it is best to administer an initial screening, followed by ongoing monitoring of a child's progress and then an end-of-the-year evaluation of his reading skills to determine the child's actual progress and exactly which skills he has acquired and how well he has mastered them. As noted in Chapter 12, because children enter kindergarten with a wide range of language-related experiences—some barely able to recognize letters and others already reading—we wait one semester before the initial screening to ensure that all children have had access to the same instruction. The initial screening assessment is key because it pinpoints the state of the child's prereading skills, confirms he is on track, identifies any precursors of reading difficulties, and may indicate the need for further evaluation. This assessment and a fuller testing of the child, if necessary, help ensure that his first formal reading instruction will be appropriate, neither too easy and repetitive nor too difficult and frustrating.

Such assessments need not be elaborate or time-consuming. The Texas Education Agency has developed the Texas Primary Reading Inventory (TPRI, which can be found at www.tpri.org), a sensible approach to teaching beginning reading in which instruction is tied to ongoing assessment of the child. In January or February each kindergartner receives an initial screening that is short and to the point—under ten minutes. If a child needs further assessment, a follow-up, more detailed reading inventory takes only twenty-five to thirty minutes. What I like about the Texas model is that instruction can be linked to the results of the testing. If a child is found to be weak in a particular area, such as knowledge of how letters map onto sounds, suggested activities are provided to teach that specific skill.

The University of Virginia's Curry School of Education, in conjunction with the Virginia Department of Education, has developed a screening assessment called the Phonological Awareness Literacy Screening (PALS) that through its Web site (http://curry.edschool. virginia.edu/go/pals/) provides activities to foster early reading, if any shortcomings are detected.

A relatively new approach, DIBELS (Dynamic Indicators of Basic Early Literacy Skills), was developed to identify children who are at risk for reading difficulties. I recommend it highly. DIBELS provides a set of brief (one-minute-long) individually administered tests of pre- and early-reading skills that are given three times during the school year. If a child performs well, three assessments are adequate. If not, the DIBELS can be administered more frequently, even on a weekly basis, to monitor progress and to make any necessary instructional refinements. DIBELS' Web site can be accessed at http://dibels.uoregon.edu. In addition, a number of excellent assessments (mainly phonologic skills) for beginning reading appear in Chapter 12.

The Reading First program also provides funding incentives for schools to carry out research-supported screening programs and assessments. As a consequence, more and more educational publishers are now incorporating such assessments into their beginning reading programs.

Of course, good teachers monitor each child's progress throughout the school year, generally through observations in the classroom. These observations are helpful, but by themselves they cannot pinpoint exactly where a child is on the reading continuum. On the other hand, taken together, the results of the testing, the teacher's classroom observations, and samples of a child's work provide a powerful up-to-the-minute assessment of his progress and his needs.

Every child deserves to get off to a running start in reading, so it is critical that the reading skills of every kindergarten child be formally— that is, systematically—reassessed before the close of the school year. This removes any guesswork as to the precise level of his reading performance. It also provides data with which to plan for the coming year—to determine, for example, whether a child needs to be in an accelerated program or a more intensive reading program, or if he can continue at his current pace. If he is not making progress, plans can also be made for summer programs or individual tutorial help.

Above all, do not keep the child back a year in school. Research indicates that retention is not effective. These data come from studies that compared two groups of children for whom the only difference was that one was retained and the other went on to the next grade. Students who were not retained were better off academically and emotionally. Staying back did not help the children in their learning and seemed to carry an additional negative psychological burden. This should come as no surprise. Earlier I discussed data which indicated that there is no such thing as a developmental lag. If a child is experiencing a problem in learning, it is not going to get better by allowing more time to pass before he receives the appropriate help. He needs a proven intervention, which I will talk about in Chapter 19. Here I want to emphasize that *instruction that fails a child once is not going to help him the second time around.* I recommend against retention. Keep in mind that if a reading problem is caught early and the child receives effective intervention, he can catch up; in contrast, a child who is delayed in receiving such instruction has great difficulty in closing the gap.

It is critical to identify a child's reading problem before he fails. Even some children whom one might assume do not need early assessment and monitoring should have it just the same. Some especially bright children, for example, may learn to read early and seem to leapfrog over learning phonologic skills. These children memorize lots of words with seeming ease and quickly build a large reading vocabulary. They simply memorize words without learning how to analyze them and pull them apart, let alone figure out how to pronounce a new or unfamiliar word. Invariably there comes a time when such children cannot decipher the insides of these new, relatively long words—especially technical names, as in the sciences (*bicarbonate, polynomial, stegosaurus*), or names of people or places in history or around the world (*Picasso, Lafayette; Laramie, Timbuktu, Kathmandu*). They have no strategy to deal with them. It is therefore best to ensure that all children's basic phonologic skills are assessed right from the start and that they receive early and intensive instruction if necessary.

Is Your Child on the Right Road to Reading?

Here is a checklist to help you determine where your child is on the road to reading by the end of kindergarten. You should ask yourself or your child's kindergarten teacher, based on her own observations and your child's performance on more formal assessments, if your child has reached these milestones:

- Knows that spoken words come apart and that letters represent these sounds
- Easily names the letters of the alphabet, both uppercase and lowercase
- Writes the letters of the alphabet

- Is beginning to learn about letter-sound matches
- Is beginning to decode simple words
- Is beginning to recognize some common sight words
- Uses invented spellings
- Knows about print conventions—reading from left to right, from the top of the page to the bottom
- Has a growing vocabulary
- Looks forward to reading

If your child has these skills, she's off to a running start in reading.

16

Helping Your Child
Become a Reader

First grade is one of the most important for a child on the road to reading. He has taken the first and most profound step on the pathway to reading: He has broken the reading code. Now he must take the next step by learning the mechanics of reading, focusing on identifying the words on a page and understanding what those words mean.

Most children enter first grade *ready to read;* they should leave as "real readers," with a reading vocabulary of about four hundred words. They should be able to read easy books and even simple directions, spell many short words accurately, and self-correct their reading errors when the identified word doesn't fit with cues provided by the letters in the word or with the surrounding context. These major accomplishments don't occur by chance; they are made possible by well-structured and systematic activities that draw the child ever closer to understanding how words work. First grade builds on the foundation provided in kindergarten. The most successful reading programs follow the model discussed for teaching children how to break the reading code, and they include the following activities:

- Learning to read words by:
  sounding out small simple words (first grade)
  taking apart bigger words (second grade and later)
- Learning to spell words

- Memorizing sight words
- Practicing oral and silent reading
- Practicing fluency
- Writing, including letters and stories
- Building word and worldly knowledge
- Learning comprehension strategies

Continuing efforts to create a sense of self-esteem strengthen the program and hold the ultimate key to its success.

In this chapter I will focus on the basic skills necessary for reading regular words (both big and small), on memorizing sight words, and on practicing reading. Building on these accomplishments, in the next chapter I will emphasize the approaches necessary for becoming a skilled reader: developing fluency, building word and worldly knowledge, and learning comprehension strategies. Later on (Chapters 18 and 19), I will focus on the child who is struggling and fails to respond to good instruction.

Sounding Out Small Words

An early step in becoming an accurate reader is learning to sound out words, beginning with simple two- and three-phoneme words like *zoo* and *pan* and going on to longer clusters of letters and sounds that make up more complicated words such as *play, chick,* and *mask.* Children in first grade more rigorously begin to pull apart words and learn how to analyze and decode progressively more challenging ones. They accomplish this by learning more about the relation of letters to sounds and by learning how to apply this knowledge to reading. As mentioned in the last chapter, this kind of knowledge is technically referred to as *phonics.*

Because in the past phonics has been associated with a particularly boring and repetitive approach to teaching reading, some have questioned its value as part of a reading curriculum. But the criticism of phonics was never a reflection of a lack of effectiveness in helping a child learn to read; rather, phonics was reviled because of the way it was taught. Phonics has now had a makeover, retaining its core educational value but redesigned to draw children into the reading process. This is good news since phonics provides the foundation for all subsequent reading. Phonics helps build the exact neural replica of a word, combining the way the word sounds with its spelling. For your child to obtain maximum benefit from phonics, it is important that you be aware of some of the less visible and often overlooked aspects of its instruction.

The Essentials of Phonics

There are many phonics programs, of varying degrees of effectiveness. The National Reading Panel found that programs that teach phonics *systematically* and *explicitly* (I will discuss this shortly) are the most effective. Systematic phonics is an organized method of teaching children about how letters relate to sounds. Children learn how to convert letters to specific sounds and then how to blend the sounds together to read a word. They learn how different patterns of letters represent different sounds. They learn rules, and then they learn exceptions to these rules. After a while a child has the knowledge required to analyze and identify just about any word he encounters. This is the goal of systematic phonics instruction. What is so critical and so unique about learning phonics in this way is that it allows the reader to apply his accumulating knowledge to deciphering and reading words he has never seen before. No other method of teaching reading can make this claim.

In general, systematic phonics programs progressively introduce the child to different letter-sound pairings, beginning with the simplest, most consistent, and most frequent combinations and then gradually expanding to cover more complex and unusual ones. A typical program might begin by teaching:

Simple one-to-one, letter-sound relationships. The focus here is on those consonants that occur frequently, tend not to look or sound like one another, and have a predictable one-to-one relationship between their letter and their sound. One suggested sequence for introducing consonants is *m, t, s, f, d, r, g, l, h, c, b, n, k, v, w, j, p, y.* Children can make many words from just the first few consonants and vowels (see below).

Vowel sounds. In order to read words, children need to learn about vowel sounds, too. Vowels tend to be more difficult to pronounce than consonants. They can be *long* or *short*. Children are taught that long vowels "say their names" (the "*a*" sound in *cake,* the "*e*" sound in *key,* and the "*i*" sound in *time*). Short vowels do not—for example, *cap, help,* and *tip.*

In systematic programs, specific sets of letters, generally six to eight consonants and two vowels, are taught as a unit. Once they are mastered, children go on to another set. Initial groupings typically contain several of the consonants noted above plus the vowels *a* and *i* because the sounds of these two vowels are the easiest to distinguish from one another. Once a child knows the sounds of her first group of consonants and vowels, she is excited because she can now begin to link these letters to their sounds and then to blend these sounds together and read the word on the page. These simple consonant and vowel combinations are used to make the words in a child's first books and are the focus of reading instruction in first grade. By the middle of first grade, a child should be able to sound out a growing number of these words.

Complex letter-sound patterns.   Having mastered one sound–one letter linkages, the child is ready for links where letters and sounds do not invariably have a one-to-one relationship. The focus is on patterns where, for example, two letters may represent one speech sound; these combinations are referred to as *digraphs.* Although they sound quite technical, digraphs are very common—*sh-* as in *ship, ch-* as in *chip, -ng* as in *sing, th-* as in *thing, wh-* as in *when.* These and other, more complicated letter-sound relationships are generally taught during first grade and continue into second. As children progress they are surprised to learn that not only are there digraphs but there are also *trigraphs* (*-dge* as in *wedge, -tch* as in *itch*) or even *quadrigraphs* (*-eigh* as in *weigh, -ough* as in *tough*). To give you a sense of how helpful it is to learn these patterns, imagine trying to pronounce the letters *-dge* (*ledge*) or *-eigh* (*sleigh*) if you haven't been taught that they group together to make one pronounceable sound.

Rules.   Children are taught useful rules that help them figure out the correct pronunciation of different letter patterns. A child learns that the pronunciation of a letter sometimes depends on what letters come after it. In first grade children are taught the *silent e rule:* a vowel followed by a consonant and then an *e,* such as in *take, dime,* or *home,* is typically pronounced as a long vowel. They also learn that the letter *c* may be pronounced as "*k*" when it is followed by *a, o,* or *u* (such as in *cake, come,* and *cup*) or followed by any consonant (*clap* and *crack*), or as "*ssss*" if followed by *e, i,* or *y* (*cent, cinema,* and *cyclone*). Such rules help encourage the rising reader to look at all the letters in a word.

Spelling. Although technically not part of phonics instruction, I have included spelling here because it is intimately related to reading and to the relation of letters to sounds. As children learn to read words, they also begin to learn how to spell these words. In general, a child should not be asked to spell a word she can't read. Serious spelling instruction begins in mid–first grade, although children are typically not held to accurate spelling until second grade. Effective spelling instruction is more than rote memorization of word lists. Spelling (going from sound to letter) strongly reinforces reading (going from letter to sound), and its instruction should be linked to a child's reading lesson. Like reading, spelling instruction follows a logical sequence that begins with phonemic awareness and then learning which letters represent which specific sounds. As a child reads more and learns more words, he begins to appreciate that the same sound can have different spellings; for example, he learns that the "*a*" sound can be spelled *mate, weight,* and *straight.* Through spelling lessons as well as his own reading, a child learns the most frequent letter patterns for different sounds. (A word of caution: Initially it is best to stress the most frequent spellings and not try to overwhelm a child with every possible spelling of a sound. In this case, *mate* would be the most common spelling for the "*a*" sound.)

As children progress they are introduced to spelling strategies they can apply to help spell new words. They also learn about so-called irregular (sight) words whose sounds and spellings don't match the rules they have been taught (such as *should* and *colonel*); the spelling of these words must be memorized. Children vary widely in their spelling abilities, although children who are dyslexic experience by far the most severe and longest-lasting difficulties in producing accurate spellings.

Two Approaches to Identifying Words

In teaching reading, not only is what is taught important but *how* it is taught. As I mentioned, effective reading programs teach children about phonics not only systematically but *explicitly* as well. There is no subtle or subliminal teaching here; children are not left to their own devices. In general, systematic phonics programs also directly teach letter-sound relationships. "Synthetic phonics" is a prime example of one such program type. Children are taught to transform letters into sounds and then blend (synthesize) the sounds together to form a pronounceable word. This is in contrast to "whole language" reading programs that teach phonics without having children work on words; words are not systematically analyzed or pulled apart. The focus is not on the sounds of language but on meaning. Early on, children are given books to read or to have read to them. It is assumed that reading is acquired naturally, just as speech is (which is, as we know, an incorrect assumption). In this view, letter-sound relationships will be learned naturally, seemingly by osmosis, as children are surrounded by literature and exposed to printed materials. According to this view, there is no reason to teach phonics systematically or explicitly; children will figure it out on their own.

The two approaches differ markedly in how children are instructed to approach unfamiliar printed words. Phonics instructs a child to try to analyze the word and to sound it out, while whole language emphasizes guessing the word from the context of the story or from pictures accompanying the story. In phonics the clues to identifying the word lie *within* the word itself, and children are encouraged to attend to the finer points of the word's structure. In whole language the clues are *external* to the word and are to be derived from the meaning of the story. The National Reading Panel found that children who are taught phonics systematically and explicitly make greater progress in reading than those taught with any other type of instruction.

The panel found that beginning the teaching of phonics in kindergarten or first grade produces the best results. Once a child demonstrates that she has some understanding of how spoken language works, it is time to learn how letters link to these sounds. In general, phonics instruction extends over two school years. All children benefit from it.

First grade instruction in phonics not only helps children learn how to sound out and pronounce words, improving reading accuracy, it also helps reading comprehension. As children reach higher grades, reading more complicated texts, phonics tends to influence reading comprehension far less. This is reasonable since reading comprehension in lower grades involves reading very simple words that are usually quite familiar to a child. If he can decode the word, he generally knows what it means. At higher grades, reading involves more complicated and unfamiliar words. To comprehend what he is reading, the reader must not only be able to pronounce the word, but he must also know what the word means—and this is not taught as part of phonics instruction.

Phonics also helps spelling, and the earlier it is taught, the more effective it is. This is not surprising since phonics concentrates on how letters represent sounds in words, which, after all, is what spelling is about. As a child progresses in school, he learns new words that are more likely to contain irregular spellings; that is, their spelling is not fully predictable by phonics rules. And so with time phonics has less of an effect on a child's spelling.

The quality and quantity of materials available to teach phonics are better than ever. The report of the National Reading Panel and the Reading First legislation's stress on using effective reading programs have provided a strong stimulus to produce top-quality phonics programs. Before I discuss good reading programs that include systematic phonics instruction, I want to mention two more focused, ready-made beginning phonics programs from England that incorporate all the effective components.

According to the National Reading Panel, Jolly Phonics (which you can find at www.jollylearning.co.uk) seems to have gotten it right. It is a highly effective program that, according to children, is also fun. The program is intended for the youngest beginning readers in school; this means four- and five-year-olds in England and five- and six-year-olds in the United States. It includes teaching letter shapes and sounds, how to blend sounds to form words, how to identify sounds in written words, and sight words. Helpful hints that enable children "to develop their understanding and their confidence" are provided, such as the one stating that when two vowels are together, the first vowel provides the long vowel sound and the second vowel is silent. This hint is rendered as "When two vowels go walking, the *first* does the talking." This is amusing to a child while helping him work out words such as *team, mail,* and *boat.* Children are taught clever mnemonics and hand movements to help associate the letters with their sounds. As an example, the letter *a* is taught by association with the word *ant* as children run their fingers up their arm while singing *a, a, a, a, a, ants.* To teach the letter *m* and its sound, *"mmmm,"* children are asked to describe their favorite meal and then rub their tummies as they say *m, m, m, m, m, meal.* According to the panel's review, when groups of children using Jolly Phonics or a whole-language approach were compared after one year of instruction, the children in the phonics programs were reading and writing significantly more words. A year after the instruction had ended, the Jolly Phonics group continued to outperform the other group. Another engaging and helpful phonics program, also from the United Kingdom, is Letterland (found at www.letterland.com), in which animate characters take on the names and shapes of the letters they represent, as in Fireman Fred and Sammy Snake.

As noted earlier, a typical course for phonics instruction is in full gear in first grade and continues through second grade. Once a child is able to read most one-syllable words comfortably, the emphasis switches from phonics to learning strategies for figuring out increasingly longer and more complex words. Children will vary in their progress, however; some may experience difficulty and need phonics instruction to continue into later grades. The classroom time devoted to the instruction of phonics per se need not be long, perhaps fifteen to twenty minutes a day. This is reinforced many times a day via all the other activities in a child's reading program and by encouraging the child to read and write independently.

After first grade, reading instruction systematically moves along. Instruction in the second and third grades reinforces the basic principles of teaching reading with the goal of encouraging the child to read more and to read increasingly more complex books independently. By the end of second grade a child should be selecting, reading, and enjoying chapter books as well as spelling words correctly and writing his own little stories.

Taking Apart Bigger Words

In third grade and especially fourth grade and higher, reading instruction adds a new dimension by focusing on big words. In the same way that a beginning reader learns how to pull apart simple words, a maturing reader requires a strategy to analyze the longer and more complicated words he encounters. A child *learns to read* in grades one through three but *reads to learn* (acquire new information) in grades four through eight. Certainly by fourth grade a child begins to study specific subject areas and to do so in increasing depth, bringing about a sharp increase in the number and complexity of printed words he will confront in his daily schoolwork. He is now expected to read multisyllabic words, and the strategies he adopts to tackle them are straightforward and revolve around the basic idea of systematically breaking a multisyllabic word into smaller chunks. The goal is to teach a child how to figure out where there are natural breaks in a word. Once the printed word is pulled apart, the child uses his knowledge of letter-sound relationships to further analyze each smaller part.

Children progressively learn how to tackle these longer words over time. This instruction often begins during first grade when a child is introduced to compound words such as *inside* and *goldfish,* and taught that they can be separated into two parts (*in* and *side, gold* and *fish*). During second grade, children are taught explicit strategies for figuring out how to analyze longer and more complicated written words, and this is emphasized even more in third grade. The most useful approach is, first, to divide a word according to where its syllables naturally break. Syllables contain one vowel *sound* (although they may have more than one vowel letter, such as in *toe* and *bait*). Vowel sounds are made by opening the mouth. (Because of this anatomical relationship, you can often tell the number of syllables by counting the number of times your jaw moves as you say a word. You can also put your fingers on your jaw and feel its movement as you articulate different words. Say the word *jaw,* and you'll note one movement; say the word *scarecrow,* and you'll sense two.)

Using these strategies a child can break apart a surprising number of words. And once a student is able to pull apart a word into its syllables, he can then analyze each syllable into its phonemes, blend the sounds together, and pronounce the word. And as I said earlier, practice is critical. Children do best when they feel confident enough to take a stab at pronouncing these strange words and are able to laugh at their own errors, and at the same time work to self-correct their mistakes. There is no substitute for practice, guidance, and feedback; and practice, self-correction, and more practice.

There are several helpful strategies to use with children who are learning to divide multisyllabic words. Here are the most useful.

Dividing a long word between the two consonants

A word like kitten becomes *kit-ten.* The child sounds out each syllable, *kit* ⟶ "k" . . . "i" . . . "t," and *ten* ⟶ "t" . . . "e" . . . "n," then blends the sounds together, and the word *kitten* is pronounced perfectly.

Knowing word derivations

If a child knows how words are built, how they are put together, he will also know how to take them apart. Children progressively learn about prefixes, suffixes, and word origins—first Anglo-Saxon and then Latin roots, and later Greek origins of English words. These forms are referred to as *morphemes,* the smallest parts of words that convey meaning. The prefix begins a word (*im-* means not; *im*pure means *not* pure). The suffix ends it (*-er* means one who does; a photograph*er* is one who photographs). If your child recognizes a prefix or a suffix, and in some cases both, he is better prepared to unhitch the parts of a potentially unwieldy word. For example, the word *unsinkable* has two common affixes:* the prefix *un,* meaning not, and the suffix *-able,* meaning having the ability to. Once your child knows frequently used affixes such as *un-* and *-able,* he can pull apart a long word such as *unsinkable* (*un-sink-able*), pronounce it correctly, and know that it refers to something that cannot be sunk.

Knowing the etymology or the roots of a word is a very powerful aid to reading, shedding light on a word's pronunciation, its spelling, and its meaning. For example, knowing the Latin root *script,* meaning to write, can be helpful in subdividing such words as *manuscript* and *transcript,* and in knowing that each has to do with writing. In the same way, a knowledge of Greek roots is indispensable to those interested in science or technology. It is very useful for a student to know *ology* (*ol-ogy*), which means the study of; he can then decipher and know the meaning of a whole range of potentially difficult and academically important words, including *zoology* (the study of animals), *biology* (the study of living organisms and life processes), and *meteorology* (the study of the atmosphere, especially the weather). Even the most obscure and complicated-appearing words can be broken down into more manageable units and deciphered if the reader is aware of their derivation or roots. Without this knowledge it is difficult for students to read any but the simplest of texts. Children who are not able to unhitch long words are forced to skip over these words or give them made-up names, such as *asty* or *Amy* for *astronomy.* Doing so allows the child to read through the text, but since the child guesses a different word each time he encounters the word *astronomy,* he does not form a permanent neural model of it. As a result, he will not recognize the word when his teacher talks about astronomy the next day in class or when he comes across the word *astronomy* again in a book.

* An affix is a letter or a group of letters attached to the beginning or ending of a word or word root that changes its meaning. Prefixes and suffixes are affixes.

Children learn how to read words in a systematic, logical progression. Children who can read most small words easily and have a strategy for approaching longer, more complex ones are mature readers. They are ready to apply their skills to technical or specialized words in textbooks and to uncommon words in literature. They are also adept at using the dictionary to confirm spellings or to look up exact meanings.

What You Can Do to Help Your Child

I have gathered together the most important information you will need to help your child become a reader. I've divided the information into two sections. The first focuses on school and includes the questions to ask about your child's reading program. The second directs its attention to the home and the kinds of activities you, as a parent, can do with your child to encourage his development as a reader.

At School

One of the questions I am asked frequently concerns how to choose a reading program that works. Since the publication of the findings of the National Reading Panel in 2000, publishers have worked very hard to update their reading materials to incorporate the most effective, scientifically based teaching methods. Nowhere has the impact of the panel's report been felt more strongly than in California, where due to the efforts of one grandmother, Marion Joseph, who was concerned that her grandson was not learning to read, there has been a revolution in the teaching of reading. California has set the highest standards nationally for the preparation of reading materials. They are published in the *Reading/Language Arts Framework for California Public Schools, Kindergarten Through Grade Twelve*. This publication states what must be included in a comprehensive reading program for each grade. It includes each of the elements that the National Reading Panel found to be effective, gives the amount of time needed to teach reading and language arts (as much as 150 minutes a day in grades one and two), and stipulates that extra time (thirty to forty-five minutes a day) should be built in to permit practice and reinforcement for those children who need extra help or enrichment for those who are ahead of the curve.

Every child should have the benefit of such excellent reading instruction. Accordingly, educators and parents in other states should demand that their state adopt comparable standards. For this reason I recommend the two reading programs that have been adopted by California: *Open Court Reading,* California 2002 edition (Columbus, Ohio: SRA/McGraw-Hill; sra-4kids.com) and *A Research-Based Framework for Houghton Mifflin Reading: A Legacy of Literacy,* California 2003 edition. (Boston: Houghton Mifflin; hmco.com)* These programs are complete and incorporate each of the elements of an effective reading program, including phonemic awareness, phonics taught systemically and explicitly, spelling, sight words, stories to read aloud and silently, fluency practice, writing, and strategies for building vocabulary and developing comprehension. If your school is using a program that has been adopted by the State of California, you are in good hands. Your child will learn to read. There are other programs, of course, that can effectively teach your child to read. As I have been emphasizing, reading programs are being updated and improved constantly, and it is therefore important to ask the right questions about your child's reading program if it is not one I have mentioned. These are the questions to ask and the things to investigate to determine if your child's reading program works.

A Brief Checklist Concerning
Your Child's Beginning Reading Program

What method is used to teach reading?

The key questions to ask are these:

- Is there scientific evidence that the program is effective? You may want to ask for specific evidence, such as an article on the efficacy of the program or method in a peer-reviewed scientific journal.[†] (Keep in mind that testimonials, no matter how moving, are not scientific evidence, nor are articles in newsletters and magazines or mentions in the media or online.)
- Was the program or its methods reviewed by the National Read-

---

* These versions were tailor-made to meet California's high standards.

[†] Peer review is the gold standard for scientific review; it means that independent scientists carefully reviewed the evidence and found it worthy of publication.

ing Panel? If not, how does this program compare to those found effective? You want specifics.

- In teaching beginning reading, are phonemic awareness and phonics taught systematically and explicitly?
- How are children taught to approach an unfamiliar word? They should feel empowered to try to analyze and sound out an unknown word first rather than guess from the pictures or context. Illustrations and context can be used as a second step to verify if the pronunciation seems to make sense.
- Does the program also include many opportunities to practice reading, to develop fluency, to build vocabulary, to develop reading comprehension strategies, to write, and to listen to and talk about stories?

How is instruction matched to a child's individual needs?

The critical elements to look for are these:

- *Individualization:* The size and flexibility of instructional groups are important. Some components of reading such as vocabulary may be taught as a class activity. However, given the variability in reading skills within a class, other components such as basic phonologic skills and oral reading are best addressed in smaller groups. A portion of each day's reading instruction, therefore, should be carried out in small groups. A class of twenty is divided into three groups of six to seven students so that each child receives individualized attention at least once a week as he tries to sound out words or read aloud. This grouping should be flexible for each component of reading, so that a child can move in and out of a group depending on his progress and level of skill in that particular area. Children who are progressing more slowly will benefit from smaller groups and more intensive attention to that skill.
- *Feedback and guidance:* Learning should be *active,* with many teacher-child interactions. Ideally, the teacher models reading for the child and then provides feedback and guidance as the student rereads the selection aloud. This is best determined by direct observation while visiting your child's classroom.
- *Ongoing assessment:* The child's reading skills should be assessed

both by informal teacher observation and by more formal measures. As I will discuss in Chapter 19, measuring your child's progress in reading needs to be an ongoing process in order to reflect his changing needs. In the primary grades (one to three) his reading should be assessed at least three times during the school year to monitor growth, and more often if there are indications of failure to make progress.

At Home

While a parent should not become her child's primary teacher, she can become her child's biggest helper. With a light hand, good humor, and the suggestions found here, you can help accelerate your child's progress. In most instances I strongly caution parents against setting out to teach their child all of the phonics rules or a complete reading curriculum. Teaching reading is a complex task and one that should be left to a professional. Keep in mind that your child is in class for perhaps six hours a day. You will see him after school when he is tired and less receptive to learning and when you, too, are not at your most energetic or patient. I recommend that you work with your child fifteen or twenty minutes a few evenings a week; it should remain fun and not a chore for either of you. For the most part, weekends should be left for enjoyment and not to play catch-up.

Focus on reinforcement. School is where *new* learning should take place; home is ideal for *practice* and *reinforcement*. School helps him build the necessary neural models for reading; home practice strengthens and solidifies the model. Try to coordinate any home reading activity with what your child is learning in school. The goal is to reinforce and strengthen what he is learning. Children do best when they can focus on one procedure or approach at a time. Work in harmony with your child's teacher.

I encourage you to reinforce selected basic skills that will make reading more understandable and ultimately more enjoyable for your child. I will give you a list of children's books that are right for him, books that he will be able to read, that he will enjoy reading, and that will stimulate him to read more. The activities are easy to do and require little more than a stack of index cards, magnetic letters, a felt marking pen, and a highlighter pen. For some of the activities I recommend colored as well as white index cards.

Sounding out smaller words.   Like most other behaviors, how we read reflects the habits we develop through instruction and practice. You can play an important role in ensuring that your child develops good reading habits by encouraging certain behaviors. One of the most important is to learn to sound out words and to do so early. Whenever your child comes across a word he is unsure of, encourage him to try to sound it out. You can begin by asking him about the first sound. For example, if the word is *mat,* you can say with some exaggeration, "The first letter is *mmm.* What is the sound of *mmm?*" Repeat the process with the last sound, "*t,*" and then the middle sound, "*aaaa.*" Once he is able to articulate "*mmmm,*" "*aaaa,*" "*t,*" ask him to blend the sounds together rapidly and say *mat.* Ask him if this sounds right to him. Does it make sense in the story? Here he is practicing good reading habits by, first, decoding an unknown word, and then verifying that his pronunciation is accurate. By teaching him to ask himself these questions automatically, you are also fostering his independence as a reader and building his confidence.

Speak to your child's teacher and ask what sounds and strategies your child is working on and what you can do to help him practice. If she isn't able to provide any suggestions, you can ask her about some of the activities listed below. These simple and useful strategies are relatively easy for you to practice with him and will help him pull apart literally hundreds of words that he might otherwise give up on. They are also helpful when you are reading with your child. If he stumbles on a word that is dependent on one of these strategies for its pronunciation, after you finish a page or story you can use the troublesome word as an opportunity to review the rule. These strategies will allow your child to pronounce the following correctly:

- Words following the *silent e rule* so that he knows the difference between words like *mate* and *mat*
- Words containing the letter *c* and to determine when a *c* is said softly, as in *cereal* and *cinder,* or makes a hard sound, as in *camel* and *clock;* I refer to this as the *saying c's rule*.

Taking Apart Bigger Words.   Once your child is comfortably reading easy one-syllable words, you can help him develop strategies for longer, more complex words. You can help him read

- compound words such as *newspaper* and *backpack* which are composed of two smaller real words

- other longer words by learning how to divide those with specific letter patterns—those having two consonants surrounded by two vowels such as *goblet* and *mitten.*
- the beginning, middle, and end of words by calling on prefixes, suffixes, and word roots.

Below are specific details about each of the activities described above. Begin with the ones focused on short words and then, after checking with your child's teacher, introduce him to the other strategies meant for older children with stronger reading skills. The most useful rule and the one taught earliest is

The secret of the silent e rule.   Focus on and reinforce the *silent e rule* more than the others. Since it affects many words, it is extremely useful to a novice reader. It is also simple to teach: (1) tell your child the rule, (2) show him several examples, and (3) practice applying the rule to different words. You will need a stack of index cards with pairs of words printed on them, words with and without the *silent e* at the end. A list of such pairs of words appears on page 214. For step one, tell your child:

> Some words have a secret code that tells you how to say them. The *silent e* code helps you read many, many words. Here is the code: Look for a word where there is a vowel followed by a consonant and then a final *e,* which makes the vowel say its own name (vowel, consonant, *silent e*).

Next, give him the examples (write each one down):

> Here are some examples: *rate, fine, same.*

Sequentially, point to the vowel, the consonant, and the *silent e* at the end and then say each word.

For step three, play a game in which one form of a word is magically transformed into another. You will need the index cards with the pairs of words (such as *pan/pane*) printed on them. Practice reading one form of the word and then the other. For example, first read the word *hid,* then point to its cousin with the *silent e* at the end, *hide,* and read it, *hide.* Repeat this for each of the words, and then ask your child to do the same. Once he seems to have grasped the idea, alternate, sometimes beginning with the word with the *silent e* and then reading the other word (*rate*, then *rat*). At other times start with the short form (*rat*) followed by the word with the *silent e* at the end (*rate*).

You can then apply the rule to real-life reading. Ask your child to get a book that he is familiar with and enjoys. With you by his side, have him take a highlighter and mark and read each word following the *silent e* code. Your child will master the exercise and enjoy his ability to read the many words he can now decipher with his secret code.

Here are forty word pairs to begin with. Copy each pair onto an index card.

bit, bite	cub, cube	cut, cute
can, cane	cap, cape	cod, code
con, cone	Dan, Dane	dim, dime
fad, fade	fat, fate	fin, fine
fir, fire	hat, hate	hid, hide
hop, hope	kit, kite	Jan, Jane
man, mane	mad, made	mat, mate
not, note	pal, pale	pan, pane
pin, pine	rat, rate	rid, ride
rip, ripe	rob, robe	rod, rode
Sam, same	Sid, side	sit, site
tam, tame	tap, tape	Tim, time
Tom, tome	tub, tube	van, vane
win, wine		

You can also use magnetic letters to make word pairs with and without the *silent e*. Spell out *pal*, for example, and ask your child to spell out *pale*. Conversely, begin with *pale*, ask him to pronounce the word, and then ask if he can transform *pale* into *pal* by removing the magnetic *e*.

Saying c's. You can help your child understand why the *c* in *cent* is pronounced one way and the *c* in *can* another. Share the rule with him, give him some examples, and then practice applying the rules governing how to say the letter *c* whenever it is encountered in words. The rule is: When the letter *c* is followed by the letters *e, i,* or *y,* it is pronounced softly like an *ssss*, as in *cent* and *cinnamon*. When the letter *c* is followed by a consonant or the vowels *a, o,* or *u,* it makes a hard *c* or *k* sound, as in *car* and *cup.*

You can help your child practice the different sounds by writing different *c* words on your index cards, some followed by the letters *e, i,* or *y* that produce the soft *c,* and others followed by either a consonant or the vowels *a, o,* or *u* that make the *k* sound. Here are some words to help you get started:

Soft *c*'s: *cent, center, cell, cellar, cinder, Cinderella, cite, city, cycle*

Hard *c*'s: *cab, cake, call, can, cap, car, cat, clam, clap, Coke, cop, cup*

Once you have made up about five or six cards in each of the two pronunciation groups, ask him to group the words pronounced like *cent* in one pile and the ones pronounced like *cat* in another. Next, have him read aloud the words in each group. If he misses a word, put that card back into its original pile so he will have another chance to read it correctly.

Compound words.   Compound words serve as a wonderful introduction to longer words. Because they are made up of two real words, it is easy for children to see how the compound word can be divided into smaller pieces. One fun activity that helps your child become aware of compound words is to go through your house or the pictures in a book or magazine, pointing to and saying the name of common household objects such as *toothpaste, toothbrush, hairbrush, washcloth, highchair, dishwasher, staircase, doorway, doorknob, lightbulb, bedroom, baseball,* and *driveway.* In each case indicate how the spoken word can come apart, such as saying, "*Toothpaste* is really made up of two words, *tooth* and *paste.*" Then say and write each half of the word on a separate index card and show him how they come together to form the word and how they can also be pulled apart. This will help make your child aware that longer words are made of parts that can be pulled apart and pushed back together again.

Two consonants surrounded by two vowels.   This strategy is also relatively easy to master and can make a big difference in the progress your child makes as he comes to slightly longer words. This tool tells a child that in words where there is a vowel that is followed by two consonants

Figure 32. Pulling Apart Longer Words

Above (depicts strategy): When there are two consonants surrounded by a vowel on either side, imagine the vowels pulling the consonants apart. Below: This strategy applied to the word *magnet*.

and then followed by another vowel, you can divide the two consonants down the middle. Although this rule is a mouthful, don't let it put you off. It's really not hard for children to learn. Sometimes I find it helps to refer to this sequence as two consonants surrounded by a vowel on either side (*v, c, c, v*). As shown in Figure 32, you can tell your child to picture the vowels trying to pull the consonants apart. Examples always help, such as *attic* (*at-tic*) and *magnet* (*mag-net*).

After telling your child the rule, use a few of the words below as examples, showing her how to divide the words. Give her an opportunity to practice. Write each of these words on a separate index card and ask her to show exactly where she would separate the word. (The first several should show the division; ask your child to split the remainder.) If she hesitates, repeat the strategy and point to the middle consonants as you pronounce each part of the word, such as *pic-nic*.

ab-sent	com-mon	hap-pen	pen-cil	suc-cess
attic	cotton	helmet	picnic	sudden
basket	custom	hidden	plastic	tablet
blanket	dentist	himself	possum	tennis
blossom	fallen	insect	problem	traffic

216

bottom	funnel	kidnap	public	triplet
button	gallop	kitten	puppet	trumpet
cactus	goblet	lesson	rabbit	tunnel
cannot	gossip	magnet	ribbon	upset
cobweb	gotten	mitten	signal	velvet
		napkin		

Prefixes, suffixes, and word roots. As mentioned earlier, teaching these meaningful parts of words is a favorite strategy for breaking up multisyllabic words. Learning these small but meaningful bits of language often captures even the most blasé child's interest. He will look at words in an altogether new way and be delighted that he can literally deconstruct a word and know its pronunciation and its meaning. Introduce your child to a prefix (or suffix), explain its meaning, and then show her the examples below. The prefixes below account for almost two-thirds of all prefixed words. (For more on prefixes see Chapter 17.)

For each of the words listed, have her practice as described below for the word *imperfect.*

For the prefix *im,* you can first write, pronounce, and define it: "*Im* means *not.*" Then ask your child to pronounce it. Next select a word with the prefix and write the word, underlining the prefix (*im*perfect). Ask her to pronounce the underlined prefix (*im*) and then read aloud the entire word (*im*perfect). Once she has correctly pronounced the word, you can talk about its meaning: how the addition of the *im* prefix turns *perfect* into *not perfect.* Lastly, use the word in a sentence to ensure that your child has a true sense of the meaning of that word. Many of these words are most appropriate for late third graders or fourth graders. Keep in mind that it is not until fourth grade that students are expected to read multisyllabic words easily.

Prefixes

dis-	*im-* or *in-*	*mis-*	*pre-*	*re-*	*un-*
(not)	(not)	(bad)	(before)	(again)	(not)
disagree	impatient	misbehave	prearrange	reappear	unable
disappear	imperfect	mislay	precook	rearm	unbend
disarm	impolite	mislead	prepaid	rearrange	uncover
disconnect	impossible	misplace	preschool	recount	undo
dishonest	impure	mispronounce	pretest	redo	unequal

dislike	inactive	misread	preview	reenter	unfair
disloyal	incomplete	misspell		refill	unhappy
dismount	independent	mistreat		refresh	unkind
disobey	invisible	misuse		reheat	unlock
disorder				renumber	unwrap
disown				replay	
distrust				retell	

Suffixes

-able (is, can be)	-ful (full of)	-less (without)	-ly (resembling)	-ment (action/ process)	-ness (state/ quality of)
admirable	careful	ageless	bravely	agreement	cleverness
agreeable	cheerful	beardless	brotherly	amazement	darkness
breakable	colorful	bottomless	cleverly	arrangement	fairness
curable	delightful	careless	fatherly	development	fullness
desirable	fearful	fearless	foolishly	entertainment	goodness
enjoyable	forgetful	jobless	freely	experiment	happiness
excitable	helpful	painless	honestly	government	kindness
laughable	joyful	sleepless	loudly	payment	loudness
moveable	painful	worthless	neatly	punishment	sadness

Learning to sound out smaller words and to unhitch longer ones are only part of a total reading program. Children must also be taught how to read words that don't follow the rules and to apply this knowledge to reading and writing.

Memorizing Sight Words. Introduce your child to the most common sight words found in books and have her commit them to memory. Having a core of words that she can read makes it so much easier when a child first attempts to read books on her own. As said earlier, there is no way to learn sight words other than by rote memory. The process is simple: Introduce the word, use it in a sentence, write it on a card, and ask your child to say it. Then have her write the word on a card as well. The act of writing a word as she says it aloud helps reinforce its pronunciation in her memory. Write the word in a sentence, too, since it is important to practice reading words in a sentence as well as when they are alone. Printing each word on a colored index card of its own also helps your child remember a word; linking a bright color with a particular word helps to establish memory links for these mystery words. Once you have made the mystery word cards, take a large shoe box, decorate it together with your daughter, label it "Word Bank," and keep the growing number of sight words in it. Each week you can reach into the bank, take two or three cards initially—and, later on, four or more—and review the words on the cards for a few minutes throughout the week. Resist the temptation to take too many words at once. It is much more effective to focus on fewer words and do so intensively. Let your child's progress guide you. If your child seems to have trouble with a word, add it to the next week's words as well. Try to point out and highlight the week's special words whenever you come across them in books, magazines, or newspapers.

Since sight words are so common and so well represented among the most frequently used words in print, the best long-term approach to mastering them is to help your child gradually memorize these words, a few at a time. Here is a list of the 150 most common words found in printed English according to the *Word Frequency Book*. The words are listed in order of their frequency. As you skim them, you will notice immediately that the vast majority are sight words.

Most Common Words

the	not	into	water	think
of	but	has	long	also
and	what	more	little	around
a	all	her	very	another
to	were	two	after	came
in	when	like	words	come
is	we	him	called	work
you	there	see	just	three
that	can	time	where	word
it	an	could	most	must
he	your	no	know	because
for	which	make	get	does
was	their	than	through	part
on	said	first	back	even
are	if	been	much	place
as	do	its	before	well

219

with	will	who	go	such
his	each	now	good	here
they	about	people	new	take
at	how	my	write	why
be	up	made	our	things
this	out	over	used	help
from	them	did	me	put
I	then	down	man	years
have	she	only	too	different
or	many	way	any	away
by	some	find	day	again
one	so	use	same	off
had	these	may	right	went
	would	other	look	old
				number

Because these words are so common, it is necessary for a would-be reader to be able to decipher these little words "on sight." Reviewing a few each week should give your child a head start in reading most beginning books. Begin with the first ten or so words; they make up a staggering 25 percent of all words appearing in print.

Practicing Reading. Practice is the key to becoming a skilled reader. Without it a child may see a word and then have it float out of his mind forever. With it he strengthens the neural connections for the word so that it is in ready reserve until it is needed again.

Very simple principles guide the choice of reading materials your child should practice with. Children need to be exposed to books that are easy and fun to read. With these books the child is in familiar territory since most of the words they contain are already registered in the reading circuits of his brain. These books help consolidate reading skills already learned; repeated practice with them is the key to reinforcing and strengthening the neural wiring for specific words and word families. Children also benefit from reading somewhat more difficult books as well. With a teacher or parent available to provide guidance and to answer questions, reading such books allows the child to expand his knowledge of letter-sound linkages and of exceptions to the rules, and to learn new vocabulary words and concepts.

In practice, a child starts with the simplest books, and as he learns more letters and sounds and more sight words, he gradually works his way up to longer and more interesting books. But at the very beginning, for the sheer pleasure of being able to read on his own—and for the confidence it builds—nothing works as well as the small decodable booklets discussed in the previous chapter.

Once you read one to your child, chances are that she will want to reread it on her own over and over again. Children like to read these simple books because they *can*. A good series to start with is "Bob Books" by Bobby Lynn Maslen. There are three sets of these little books that are just right. I recommend the first set, Reading Level A, for kindergartners who are just breaking the code. Reading Level B and Reading Level C are appropriate for a first grader. The books systematically present newly learned letter-sound combinations in words. Level C features compound words and long vowels, including the *silent e rule:* "Jane likes to play baseball." "Jane made it to the base. Jane was safe on first base." Bob Books are published by Scholastic Inc. (www.bob-books.com). Another excellent decodable booklet series, the "Books to Remember" collection, is published by Flyleaf Publishing (www.flyleaf-publishing.com).

At the beginning I would make it a habit to read a book to your child first and then sit with her as she reads it back to you. This ensures that

Figure 33. Reading with Your Child

she can read the book and that you will be there to offer assistance if she comes across an unexpectedly difficult word. When you read with her, you can support her by

• reminding her that part of the fun of reading is figuring out the word and that it often takes more than one try.

• encouraging her to first sound out the word and listen to how the word sounds and ask herself: Does it sound right? Does it fit in?

• encouraging her to trust her instincts, and if a word doesn't seem right, to apply the strategies she knows and to check her word bank to see if it is a tricky word that must be memorized. If so, she can check its pronunciation with you.

• sharing with her your own missteps in reading.

To read a book with ease, a child should be able to read about nineteen out of twenty words on a page correctly. If not, the book is probably too difficult for her to read alone. There are aids to help you gauge accurately a book's level of difficulty. One, the Degrees of Reading Power (DRP) system, lists children's books according to their reading level. The information is available in the form of Readability Reports in two broad categories: "Readability of Literature and Popular Titles" and "Readability of Textbooks." The listing for literature and popular books is available on a CD-ROM, DRP-Booklink, that can be purchased (www.tasaliteracy.com); the textbook information is available online at their Web site. Book difficulty is ranked from zero to 100 units. Most books range from an easy reader level of 30 units to much more difficult books around 85 units. Using this system I learned the relative difficulty of some very popular children's books:

Book	Units	Readability
Are You My Mother? by P. D. Eastman	34	*Easiest*
Cat in the Hat by Dr. Seuss	35	
Clifford the Big Red Dog by Norman Bridwell	37	
Nate the Great by Marjorie Sharmat	38	
Frog and Toad Are Friends by Arnold Lobel	41	
Amelia Bedelia by Peggy Parish	43	
The Boxcar Children		
by Gertrude Chandler Warner	44	
Superfudge by Judy Blume	45	
Freckle Juice by Judy Blume	45	

Charlotte's Web by E. B. White	50	
Harry Potter and the Sorcerer's Stone by J. K. Rowling	54	*Difficult*
Baseball's Greatest Games by Dan Gutman	56	
Ethan Frome by Edith Wharton	59	
The Red Badge of Courage by Stephen Crane	60	
Great Expectations by Charles Dickens	60	
Roots by Alex Haley	62	
The Works of Edgar Allan Poe edited by Gary Richard Thompson	64	
Silent Spring by Rachel Carson	68	
Profiles in Courage by John F. Kennedy	69	*More Difficult*

In general, the very beginning primary textbooks average 40 units, later elementary textbooks 50 units, middle school textbooks 56 units, and high school textbooks 62 units. Children's magazines tend to range between 48 and 57 units, comparable to *Charlotte's Web.* Teen magazines are somewhat more difficult, falling into a range of 58 to 64 units, about the same as *Roots* and *The Works of Edgar Allan Poe.* Popular magazines for adults typically range from *People,* with a difficulty level of about 62, to national and business magazines that are somewhat more challenging at levels of 69 to 71. The front pages of newspapers average 69 units. State driver's license manuals average anywhere from a low of 55 units in Missouri and 58 units in California to a grueling high of 70 units in Alabama and Ohio. School systems can participate in the DRP program, which provides tests of reading comprehension and reports scores in DRP units. The child's DRP score can then be directly matched to reading materials at that same level of difficulty.

Another program called the Lexile Framework also matches students to books through tests with a common measure, the Lexile unit. The company that distributes the Lexile system provides collections of books for different groups of readers. Lexile levels extend from zero to about 1700. In this system *The Cat in the Hat* is scored at 150 Lexile units, *Charlotte's Web* at 680, *Ethan Frome* at 1160, and *Silent Spring* at 1340. Parents and others can access the Lexile Framework at www.lexile.com.

For discovering a book's level of difficulty when you are at a bookstore or a library, use *Children's Books in Print,* which has volumes sorted by title, author, or subject matter; all versions indicate the recommended grade level for each book listed (available as a book or online at www.booksinprint.com).

Here is a list of picture books you can read to a young child.

Allard, Harry, *Miss Nelson Is Missing* (Boston: Houghton Mifflin, 1977).

Bridwell, Norman, *Clifford the Big Red Dog* (New York: Scholastic, 1985).

Brown, Margaret Wise, *Good Night Moon* (New York: Harper & Row, 1975).

Christelow, Eileen, *Henry and the Red Stripes* (New York: Clarion Books, 1982).

Cronin, Doreen, *Click, Clack, Moo: Cows That Type* (New York: Simon & Schuster, 2000).

Denenberg, Julie, *First Day Jitters* (Watertown, Mass.: Whispering Coyote, 2000).

Depaola, Tomie, *Strega Nona: An Old Tale* (Englewood Cliffs, N.J.: Prentice-Hall, 1975).

Henkes, Kevin, *Chrysanthemum* (New York: Greenwillow Books, 1991).

Hoffman, Mary, *Amazing Grace* (New York: Dial Press, 1991).

Howe, James, *Horace and Morris but Mostly Dolores* (New York: Atheneum, 1999).

Kellogg, Steven, *The Mysterious Tadpole* (New York: Dial Press, 1977).

Lester, Helen, *Hooway for Wodney Wat* (Boston: Houghton Mifflin, 1999).

Modarresi, Mitra, *Yard Sale!* (New York: DK Publishers, 2000).

Polacco, Patricia, *Thunder Cake* (New York: Philomel Books, 1990).

Seuss, Dr., *The Cat in the Hat* (New York: Random House, 1957).

Small, David, *Fenwick's Suit* (New York: Farrar, Straus and Giroux, 1996).

Viorst, Judith, *Alexander and the Terrible, Horrible, No Good, Very Bad Day* (New York: Atheneum, 1972).

Waber, Bernard, *Ira Sleeps Over* (Boston: Houghton Mifflin, 1972).

Williams, Linda, *The Little Old Lady Who Was Not Afraid of Anything* (New York: Crowell, 1986).

Williams, Vera B., *A Chair for My Mother* (New York: Greenwillow Books, 1982).

Yaccarino, Dan, *Deep in the Jungle* (New York: Atheneum, 2000).

Poetry

Florian, Douglas, *Mammalabilia* (San Diego: Harcourt Brace, 2000).

Pretlusky, Jack, *A Pizza the Size of the Sun: Poems* (New York: Greenwillow Books, 1996).

Zahares, Wade, *Big, Bad, and a Little Bit Scary: Poems That Bite Back!* (New York: Viking, 2001).

Easy Readers

Lobel, Arnold, *Frog and Toad Are Friends* (New York: Harper & Row, 1970).

Mills, Claudia, *Gus and Grandpa Ride the Train* (New York: Farrar, Straus and Giroux, 1998).

Parish, Peggy, *Thank You, Amelia Bedelia* (New York: Harper & Row, 1964).

Rylant, Cynthia, *Mr. Putter and Tabby Toot the Horn* (San Diego: Harcourt Brace, 1998).

——— *Henry and Mudge in the Family Trees* (New York: Simon & Schuster, 1997).

——— *Poppleton Has Fun* (New York: Blue Sky Press, 2000).

Seuss, Dr., *Mr. Brown Can Moo! Can You?* (New York: Random House, 1970).

——— *One Fish Two Fish Red Fish Blue Fish* (New York: Random House, 2001).

Sharmat, Marjorie Weinman, *Nate the Great, San Francisco Detective* (New York: Delacorte Press, 2000).

Wiseman, B., *Morris and Boris at the Circus* (New York: Harper & Row, 1988).

Yolen, Jane, *Commander Toad and the Space Pirates* (New York: Coward-McCann, 1987).

Ziefert, Harriet, *The Little Red Hen* (New York: Viking, 1995).

——— *The Three Little Pigs* (New York: Viking, 1995).

Poetry

Kuskin, Karla, *Soap Soup and Other Verses* (New York: Harper-Collins, 1992).

Lobel, Arnold, *Book of Pigericks* (New York: Harper & Row, 1983).

Maestro, Marco and Giulio, *Geese Find the Missing Piece: School Time Riddle Rhymes* (New York: HarperCollins, 1999).

Pretlusky, Jack, *Awful Ogre's Awful Day* (New York: Greenwillow Books, 2001).

Prelutsky, Jack and Arnold Lobel, *Random House Book of Poetry for Children,* (New York: Random House, 1983).

Silverstein, Shel, *Where the Sidewalk Ends* (New York: Harper & Row, 1974).

Stevenson, James, *Sweet Corn* (New York: Greenwillow Books, 1995).

Viorst, Judith, *If I Were in Charge of the World and Other Worries: Poems for Children and Their Parents* (New York: Atheneum, 1981).

Picture Books with Rhymes/Pattern/Repetition

Adlerman, Daniel, *Africa Calling: Nighttime Falling* (Boston: Whispering Coyote Press, 1996).

Alarcon, Karen Beaumont, *Louella Mae, She's Run Away!* (New York: Holt, 1997).

Aylesworth, Jim, *The Gingerbread Man* (New York: Scholastic Press, 1998).

——— *Old Black Fly* (New York: Holt, 1992).

Buehner, Mark and Carolyn, *Fanny's Dream* (New York: Dial Press, 1995).

Cooney, Barbara, *Miss Rumphius* (New York: Viking, 1982).

Hennessy, B. G., *Jake Baked the Cake* (New York: Viking Penguin, 1990).

Hutchins, Pat, *Don't Forget the Bacon!* (New York: Greenwillow Books, 1976).

Lobel, Arnold, *The Rose in My Garden* (New York: Greenwillow Books, 1984).

London, Jonathan, *Froggy Gets Dressed* (New York: Viking, 1992).

Macauley, David, *Black and White* (Boston: Houghton Mifflin, 1990).

Meddaugh, Susan, *Martha Blah Blah* (Boston: Houghton Mifflin, 1996).

Raffi, *Down by the Bay* (New York: Crown, 1987).

Shannon, David, *Bad Case of Stripes* (New York: Blue Sky Press, 1998).

Silverstein, Shel, *A Giraffe and a Half* (New York: Harper and Row, 1964).

Taback, Simms, *Joseph Had a Little Overcoat* (New York: Viking, 1999).

Wing, Natasha, *Jalapeño Bagels* (New York: Atheneum, 1996).

Winter, Jeanette, *The House That Jack Built* (New York: Dial Press, 2000).

Transitional Chapter Books

Adler, David, *Young Cam Jansen and the Library Mystery* (New York: Viking, 2001).

——— *Cam Jansen and the Catnapping Mystery* (New York: Viking, 1998).

Cameron, Ann, *Stories Julian Tells* (New York: Pantheon, 1981).

Cleary, Beverly, *Ramona's World* (New York: Morrow, 1999).

Duffey, Betsy, *How to Be Cool in the Third Grade* (New York: Viking, 1993).

Hesse, Karen, *Sable* (New York: Holt, 1994).

Hinton, S. E., *The Puppy Sister* (New York: Delacorte Press, 1995).

King-Smith, Dick, *Jenius: The Amazing Guinea Pig* (New York: Hyperion, 1996).

Kline, Suzy, and Frank Remkiewicz, *Horrible Harry in Room 2B.* (New York: Viking Kestrel, 1988).

LeGuin, Ursula, *Catwings* (New York: Orchard Books, 1988).

Sachar, Louis, *Marvin Redpost* (New York: Random House, 2000).

Spinelli, Jerry, *Tooter Pepperday* (New York: Random House, 1995).

Consider this selection a starting point for further exploration. Your local library has a treasury of good books, and you might also want to consult the lists of recommended works in such guides as these:

Books That Build Character by William Kilpatrick et al. (New York: Simon and Schuster/Touchstone, 1994).

Books to Build On: A Grade-by-Grade Resource Guide for Parents and Teachers edited by John Holdren and E. D. Hirsch, Jr. (New York: Dell, 1996).

The New Read-Aloud Handbook by Jim Trelease (New York: Penguin, 1995).

The New York Times Parent's Guide to the Best Books for Children by Eden Ross Lipson (New York: Three Rivers Press, 2000).

Beginning readers eagerly anticipate the latest arrival of their very own magazine full of simple stories that they can read as well as other fun activities and puzzles. For children ages two to six, *Ladybug* magazine introduces poems, rhymes, and songs. *Spider* is geared for children age six to nine who are independent readers. *Cricket's* audience is maturing nine-to-fourteen-year-olds; it has wonderful stories, puzzles, and contests that are appealing to children who are now reading to learn and to enjoy themselves. You can subscribe to *Ladybug, Spider,* and *Cricket* by contacting Cricket Magazine Group, 315 Fifth Street, Peru, Illinois 61354, or online at www.cricketmagazine.com. *Ranger Rick,* devoted to nature, science, and the outdoors, is filled with beautiful photographs and ideal for curious children age seven to twelve. Subscriptions to *Ranger Rick* are available from the National Wildlife Federation, P. O. Box 2038, Harlan, Iowa 51593, or online at www.nwf.org. Children in grades four through nine will enjoy *Calliope,* an unusual children's magazine that explores history and builds word and worldly knowledge in a highly entertaining format. *Calliope* can be ordered from Cobblestone Publishing, 30 Grove Street, Peterborough, New Hampshire 03458-1454 (www.cobblestonepub.com).

To introduce children to current events, I suggest *Time For Kids,* which has three junior versions (*Big Picture* is just right for kindergarten and first grade, *New Scoop* is geared to grades two and three, and *World Reports* is aimed at children in grades four through six). They feature news stories, many contributed by children. Suggested activities and subscriber information for *Time for Kids* are available at www.time-forkids.com. For older children (age eight through fifteen) craving sports-related stories, *Sports Illustrated for Kids* (www.SIKIDS.com) covers all major organized sports teams (NBA, NFL, NHL, and MLB) as well as extreme sports.

Magazines provide inviting bite-sized reading materials for every age and every interest. Providing materials of genuine interest helps make reading a habit, encouraging the practice that builds automatic reading systems.

Even if you choose a book or magazine that turns out to be too difficult for your child, you can always do shared reading in which you read most of the book but pause when you come to a word your child can read or sound out successfully.

Once your child learns to read words accurately, she is ready for the next step in which she will not only read words correctly but will read them smoothly and rapidly—without giving it a second thought. How she becomes that fluent reader and what you can do to help her achieve that is the subject of the next chapter.

17

Helping Your Child
Become a Skilled Reader

Fluency, the ability to read a text quickly, accurately, and with good understanding, is the hallmark of a skilled reader. Children who are fluent readers love to read. Since it requires little energy, reading is relaxing. It is easy for fluent readers to get lost in a book. They are the ones who come to the dinner table with book in hand or who want to keep their bedroom light on at night to finish "just one more chapter." For a nonfluent reader, opening a book is hardly a welcome event.

To appreciate fluency let me introduce you to a pair of young readers, Megan and Christy, who are classmates in the fourth grade. Both girls are extremely bright and attend their school's TAG (Talented and Gifted) program.

Recently, Christy developed headaches that often keep her at home. She was never considered a problem reader, although her reading skills seemed to lag behind her capacity to understand stories that were read to her. Christy will do anything to avoid reading. When she does read, she must devote all her attention to deciphering the words—often making several attempts before correctly reading a word aloud—and therefore has little energy left to consider the meaning of the passage she is reading. She reads in an expressionless monotone that is difficult to follow. Megan, on the other hand, glides across the lines of text, adjusting her tempo or modulating her voice to reflect their meaning. Megan is fluent, Christy is not.

If parents and teachers understood the essential role of fluency in skilled reading, and how easily and effectively it can be taught, fluency would no longer be the most neglected reading skill. The National Assessment of Educational Progress reported that 44 percent of fourth grade boys and girls were not yet fluent readers. These are shocking data given the fact that children are expected to develop into fluent readers by the end of second grade. Perhaps this is because many educators believe that once a child can read words accurately, the work of becoming a reader—and of teaching reading—is complete. Reading words accurately brings a child only to the cusp of skilled reading. And this is where a parent and teacher can play a significant role in helping to transform a beginning reader into a skilled reader.

Children learn to read a word accurately and then, after much practice, fluently. It can be taught. Fluency describes how a skilled reader reads aloud. As I noted earlier, I reserve the term *automatic* for the brain processes that make fluent reading possible. Remember, we believe that the neural circuitry within the brain has integrated all the features of a word so that a mere glance at that word instantly activates its stored model in the word form area located in the back of the left side of the brain. That is why we believe fluent readers are able to read rapidly and with good pronunciation and understanding. Fluent readers no longer have to sound out words part by part.

Fluency forms the bridge between decoding and comprehension, and children acquire fluency word by word, by repeated exposures to a word—*if* they begin pronouncing the word correctly. I want to emphasize that fluency is not a stage where suddenly a child reads all words fluently. Fluency is acquired word by word, reflecting the words a child has read and fully mastered. At least four correct readings are necessary for automatic recognition of a word. And while accuracy is a necessary precursor to fluency, accuracy does not necessarily evolve into fluency. This is especially true of a dyslexic child who is not able to call upon the specialized word form area and must instead rely on slower, ancillary neural pathways for reading. These pathways are okay for accurate reading but not for fluency.

Teaching Fluency: What Works Best

When the National Reading Panel analyzed almost a hundred research articles on teaching fluency, they made an important discovery: The programs that work most effectively and produce the largest gains share three key features: (1) a focus on a child's oral reading, (2) opportunities for practice, allowing a child to read and to reread words aloud in connected text, and (3) ongoing feedback as a child reads. Reading aloud makes feedback possible. Silent reading does not. The feedback component is essential because it allows a child to modify his pronunciation of a specific word and simultaneously correct the stored neural model of that word so that it increasingly reflects the exact pronunciation and spelling of the word. Needless to say, the feedback must be carried out in a constructive and positive manner. You must not risk a child's losing self-confidence or developing a fear of reading in front of others.

You may hear this overall technique referred to as *guided repeated oral reading*. Such guidance can come from a teacher, a tutor, or a parent. Once a child has received feedback from an adult and is fairly fluent, he can practice with a peer or even by listening to what he has read into a tape recorder. Approaches using this method are also referred to as repeated reading, paired reading, shared reading, assisted reading, and echo reading. In echo reading, for example, the child's teacher first models by reading a paragraph aloud, and then the student reads the same paragraph aloud under the teacher's guidance. The child reads the same selection at home that evening, and a parent listens and gently provides corrective feedback. Students then pair up in class the next day and take turns reading each page (or paragraph) to one another. Within this method a single teacher can keep track of and monitor a large number of children as they read in pairs. Children also read silently on their own for twenty or thirty minutes each day. This approach works well for primary school children, whether accomplished readers or not.

Interestingly, guided repeated oral reading may help poor and good readers in different ways. For someone struggling, reading a passage over and over while receiving feedback is a means of obtaining input to master a specific word. It helps the student build a more accurate neural representation of that word within her brain and pronounce the word correctly. In contrast, rereading a passage out loud helps a good reader integrate the word's meaning with the surrounding text, allowing him to get a better sense of the prosody or the rhythm of the passage.

From its extensive review, the NRP concluded that guided repeated oral reading programs "help improve children's reading ability, at least through grade 5, and they help improve the reading of students with learning problems much later than this." Still, the proven effectiveness of guided repeated oral reading to increase fluency is too often ignored. That is unacceptable. In fact, the evidence is so strong that I urge the adoption of these reading programs as an integral part of every school reading curriculum throughout primary school. Guided repeated oral reading may even be helpful to some students in middle or high school. It may well be that this approach will help readers master the special language peculiar to different academic disciplines, for example, biology or history. Remember, if a child has trouble pronouncing a word, he is unlikely to have an accurate representation of that word in his brain, and it will be difficult for him to store or to retrieve any information associated with that word. If troublesome words are pre-identified and practiced aloud with guidance, the child will more easily build the neural model for that word and connect relevant information to it.

Fluency training, one component of a comprehensive reading lesson, takes perhaps fifteen minutes or less per lesson. Keep in mind that a child must first read a word accurately before she can read it fluently. And so in carrying out guided repeated oral reading with a child, it is important that she practice reading passages at her own comfort level. As mentioned earlier, children are comfortable with a book's text when they can read about nineteen out of twenty words correctly; such a book is at the child's *independent reading level.* You can ask her teacher to recommend books that she feels are appropriate. If your school participates in either the DRP or the Lexile reading programs, her teacher will be able to give you a list of books matched to your child's reading level and interest.

Parents Can Help Build Fluency

As an informed parent you can play a strong and active role in helping your child become a fluent reader. He should begin to read fluently by the middle of second grade. You can gauge his fluency by listening to how smoothly he reads at his own level and how well he is able to read with expression.

Listening to him read aloud often is the single most meaningful activity you can do in this process. Put aside time for it each evening or at least three or four times a week. I want to stress that consistency is far more important than the amount of time devoted to each practice session. In these sessions you can have him read to you, or you both can take turns reading aloud to each other—a paragraph, a page, or a short chapter at a time. For a child who is struggling, it is often useful for you to read a little and then have him reread aloud the same material that you have just modeled reading for him. If you can, get a duplicate set of books so that each of you can follow along as the other reads. It is helpful to give him a ruler or other level marker to place under each line as he reads or follows along so he keeps his place.

Evenings spent reading together build a lifelong pattern of enjoyment. I believe that the pleasures associated with this experience become built into the reading networks within a child's brain. Thus, as a child matures into a teenager and then a young adult and no longer reads aloud with his parent, each time he picks up a book and begins to read, he resurrects this happy memory of days gone by when he snuggled next to his mother or father and learned about the *The Cat in the Hat, Good Night Moon, Danny and the Dinosaur,* and, later on, *The Pumpkin Smasher* and *The Westing Game.*

If your child hates to read and doesn't read very well, reading aloud regularly with him will quickly alert you to a problem if one exists. A child who avoids reading is among those most in need of practice and guidance, and is especially helped by your reading aloud with him. That will avoid a common downward spiral often observed in struggling readers: Such children avoid reading and as a result never receive practice in reading or the helpful feedback and correction that would improve their reading. These children become less and less involved with reading and fall further and further behind their classmates. They never build the fast-paced neural circuits necessary for rapid and automatic word recognition. It is possible even with the most reluctant reader to find books that are comfortable and interesting for him to read aloud with you. The goal is to practice reading the printed word aloud and not teach literature.

Reading should always be encouraged for pleasure and for knowledge; however, *if a child is a halting or tenuous reader, simply encourag-*

ing him to read silently to himself will not make him a better reader. He may simply be repeating errors—or daydreaming. It is only by reading and rereading aloud, with feedback and correction, that real gains in reading are noted. I am pleased that the Reading First program that I referred to earlier stipulates that schools requesting funds must include scientifically based fluency instruction in their reading curriculum.

The methods described here are meant for the typical reader; a dyslexic reader may require more. In Chapter 19 I have provided a full range of effective fluency programs for these struggling readers.

Once a child begins to read more and more words accurately and rapidly, he can turn his attention to more complex texts. At this stage his higher thinking and reasoning skills come into play and, together with his vocabulary and his knowledge of the world around him, help him derive meaning from his reading.

A mature reader must have the vocabulary and the background knowledge to understand and place in context what he has just read. If he comes across the words *Eiffel Tower,* for example, he needs to know how to pronounce each word. But to give the words meaning he also needs to know what the Eiffel Tower is—a huge tower in France. This calls on his word knowledge, his vocabulary. It is even better when he can place the word more fully in context, that he knows the Eiffel Tower is located on the Champs de Mars in Paris, that it was designed by Alexandre Gustave Eiffel for the exposition of 1889, and that it is a major tourist attraction. This sort of information is the reader's worldly knowledge that helps him gain meaning from what he is reading. Word knowledge is found in the dictionary, worldly knowledge more likely in an encyclopedia.

And so a child does not simply open a book, decode the words, and magically understand the content. The extent and depth of his vocabulary and background knowledge will determine how well equipped he is to gain meaning from the text. Important, too, are the active thinking processes that the reader uses to integrate his existing knowledge with the new information he encounters. In a general sense these thinking processes can be thought of as reasoning. Based on this model, approaches to teaching comprehension focus on strengthening and extending the child's word and worldly knowledge and providing him with a series of strategies to organize and direct his thinking as he reads.

The Meaning of Words

The size of a child's vocabulary is one of the best predictors of his reading comprehension; children with the biggest vocabularies tend to be the strongest readers. This becomes increasingly true as a child gets older. And so we turn our attention now to building a child's vocabulary.

At the beginning, most of the words a child encounters in print will be in his spoken vocabulary. Then sometime around third grade the words he comes across in print are less likely to be familiar to him. This marks a pivotal point in the child's growth as a skilled reader. He must build up his spoken vocabulary so he can recognize these less familiar words when he reads them.

First, in teaching vocabulary the intent is for the child to regard any new word as more than just a label but as a fully formed idea. Rather than rotely reciting a word's definition or rattling off a synonym, the goal is for the child to make that word an active part of his thinking process. A word is most likely to spring to life if a child can integrate it with familiar ideas or with his own past experiences. For example, if the new word is *transmission* and the student is familiar with cars and how they work, he will quickly integrate *transmission* into his knowledge base and use the word as part of his active vocabulary. It is important to keep in mind that it is the ideas that take precedence and that the lion's share of the time spent teaching should be devoted to discussions of the ideas represented by specific words. In fact, it is often better to discuss the word's meaning and relevance before naming it. In effect, this creates a cradle within which to catch and hold the word once it is mentioned.

Vocabulary instruction that works best actively involves the child in getting to the word from every possible perspective. The more connections he can make between the new word and the words and world he knows, the more salient the word is, the more likely he is to make it a part of his usable vocabulary. Once a new word is introduced, an essential part of the learning process is to encourage the child to use the word as much as possible—initially just to make sentences with it and then to incorporate it in his everyday life. Having repeated encounters with the same word also helps ensure that its meaning is tightly woven into the automatic reading circuits within the child's brain and that subsequently it can be retrieved quickly.

A child's vocabulary grows by about three thousand new words a year. These words can be directly and explicitly taught as part of a vocabulary program, or the words can be acquired implicitly, as most of them are, through everyday life experiences—hearing his parents' conversations and those of his peers and teachers, via television and the movies, on trips to the museum and the supermarket—or through reading. (In the case of a dyslexic child, words can be acquired from listening to stories read to him or from hearing books on tape.) Only a small proportion of a child's vocabulary comes from direct instruction. This has a number of implications.

Both teachers and parents need to be selective about the words that a child is expected to learn. The prime criteria for selection are those words that are most likely to stretch the child's mind, those that are conceptually difficult (but not beyond his grasp)—that is, words he would not likely get on his own. It is not a contest to cover the most words superficially or to select the most unusual words but for the child to integrate and use words he might encounter and ordinarily not have learned on his own. Above all, a word should be relevant and useful; for example, you can preread an assigned book and select specific words for intensive vocabulary instruction. A child can also suggest words that give him a hard time. A word chosen for vocabulary instruction should tie into a central concept of a story or theme he is learning. It often works best to focus on a group of words unified by a common theme or topic so that learning each individual word reinforces learning the other words in the group as well. Words that relate to that common theme but have opposite meanings also work well.

In one approach the theme was "fear." The teacher and her students both contributed to generating a word list based on "fear," writing each of the words on the board. When a large number of words accumulated, the words were subdivided into categories. Students were also encouraged to think of words that conveyed not being fearful—words such as *intrepid, heroic,* and *brave.* In this so-called brainstorming method, several other categories were developed as well:

Emotions/reactions: terror, horror, fainting, quaking

People/creatures: monster, ghost, bogeyman, alien, humanoid, poltergeist, Dracula

Places: cemetery, graveyard, haunted house, funeral parlor, unlit street, dark alley

In the process of generating all these words, children engage in far-ranging discussions of their own experiences relating to fear, activating their own background knowledge and relating it to the current book that the class is reading. An important by-product of this activity is that the children enrich and extend their understanding of fear. They now possess a new arsenal of words. The very act of forming categories for these words gives structure and direction to the children in how to think about words and their potential meanings.

The Parents' Role

A parent can easily follow the teacher's lead. As your child delves into a book, for example, you can ask her to pick out one or two new words in each chapter for later study and discussion. She can highlight the words, place a Post-it on the page, or jot the word down. Later the two of you can look at how the word was used in the text and talk about what it might mean. Look for clues in the surrounding words. Does it elicit any images or connections to your child's life experiences? Does she know any similar words? Talk about what the words have in common, how they differ. What other words can you both think of that bring to mind the same idea or concept? Write the words down. Take a pad and pencil and see how many words the two of you can generate as part of your personal brainstorming. Categorize the words together. Have your daughter use each word in a sentence. Have her play word detective and see how many times she sees or hears the word in the next twenty-four hours, and then revisit the word and continue your discussion. Creative teachers and parents have developed other useful aids for vocabulary instruction that go beyond books and beyond the classroom. In one highly successful program, children competed to become a "Word Wizard," receiving points for bringing to class a newly learned vocabulary word they had used, seen, or heard in a different context outside of school.

Dictionaries are useful as a starting point but often provide sparse definitions of words. All children in third grade and above benefit from knowing how to look up words in a dictionary, but learning about words should not be limited to this one source. Dictionary.com is a helpful online resource for looking up word definitions, synonyms, and antonyms, with an additional "word of the day" feature that produces a constant stream of new words. This site also features "Dr. Dictionary," to whom you can e-mail your questions about words and word usage.

The nature of instruction should be *flexible* and depend on the word itself. Some words, such as *democracy*, require a full discussion along with examples; other words, such as *the double helix*, are best learned through images as well as explanations. Everything is fair game—even using English muffins or a Tennyson poem, "Flower in the Crannied Wall," to learn about "nooks and crannies." Learning new words also benefits from *repetition* and *reinforcement.* Conceptually challenging words need to be introduced and discussed over and over again; a child does not assimilate and use a word after meeting it once, twice, or even three times. It takes many repetitions.

Children can be encouraged to use their knowledge of word parts, specifically prefixes, suffixes, and Latin and Greek roots to pull an unknown word apart and determine its meaning. And just as you don't try to teach your child every unfamiliar word in a story, it is helpful to focus on learning only the most important of the hundreds of affixes and roots. If your child comes to know these really well, he will be able to add substantially to his reading vocabulary. Fortunately, only a relative few of these word parts occur with any real frequency: Just twenty prefixes account for 97 percent of all words with prefixes found in English schoolbooks, and nine of these prefixes account for 75 percent of all pre-fixed words. Here are the most common ones:

Rank	Prefix	Percentage of All Prefixed Words
1	Un- (*not*)	26
2	Re- (*again*)	14
3	In-, im-, il-, ir- (*not*)	11
4	Dis- (*not*)	7
5	En-, em- (*put into*)	4
6	Non- (*not*)	4
7	In, im- (*in*)	3
8	Over- (*excessive*)	3
9	Mis- (*bad*)	3
10	Sub- (*below*)	3
11	Pre- (*before*)	3
12	Inter- (*between*)	3
13	Fore- (*earlier*)	3
14	De- (*reverse*)	2
15	Trans- (*across*)	2

Rank	Prefix	Percentage of All Prefixed Words
16	Super- (*above*)	1
17	Semi- (*half*)	1
18	Anti- (*opposite*)	1
19	Mid- (*middle*)	1
20	Under- (*too little*)	1
All others		4

Since a child gains much of her vocabulary incidentally, it is important to maximize her ability to learn new words as a result of her everyday experiences. The guiding principle here is that the richer and denser her network of worldly knowledge, the greater the possibility that a new word will find a relevant "hook" to latch on to, activate her existing knowledge, and be integrated within this network. Similarly, the larger a child's vocabulary, the more likely she is to understand and relate to a new idea or bit of information. The more she is exposed to a range of meaningful experiences and the more she reads, the greater her vocabulary and knowledge network.

Parents and teachers can encourage children to pay attention to and learn new words. One father I know, Hayden, used his hobby of keeping an aquarium as a learning experience for his son, Jeremy. Jeremy accompanies his father to the pet store to buy supplies and select new fish. Before setting out, father and son look through their many books on fish, read about the different types of fish and their care, select the ones they are most interested in, and write the names down. At first Hayden did all the reading, with Jeremy looking at the pictures and following along. Soon Jeremy was able to recognize the words in print and pointed to the words *zebra fish, shark, angelfish, parrot fish,* or *clownfish* whenever that name appeared. After a while father and son began to read together aloud. And now Jeremy, a fourth grader, reads more and more of the selections to his father. Discussions between father and son have centered not only on fish but on algae, coral, anemone, chlorophyll, predators, infections that fish are prone to, evolution, and ecology. What began as an interest in aquarium fish expanded into a much broader interest in the sea and creatures of the sea. Other parents have used a child's interest in sports, dogs, cars, skateboarding, dollhouses, politics, space, or horses as the impetus for the development of a larger vocabulary and a broader, enriched view of the world.

There is no one formula for teaching a child new words. Rather, it is important to keep in mind that each and every experience is an opportunity for learning—going fishing, visiting Grandma, playing baseball, putting groceries away after shopping, taking a walk in the woods, hearing news on television, and reading (books, magazines, newspapers, and even labels and signs). The key is to expose a child to many different kinds of experiences, to talk with him about these experiences and the words they generate in an open-ended way so that there are no wrong answers, and then to encourage him to use the new words as often as possible.

How Parents Can Nurture Reading Comprehension

Just as parents can have a positive effect on fluency and vocabulary, they can have a similar effect on reading comprehension. A recent study carried out with seven- and eight-year-olds determined that home reading habits were strong predictors of a child's later performance in reading. Skilled readers were read to more often by their parents and were more likely to read with their parents and talk about books and stories with them.

The basic idea is to encourage your child to be an active listener, the forerunner of an active reader. All the steps you take to accomplish this are directed toward capturing his attention and pulling him into the reading. The goal is for the words and the ideas they represent to take on meaning. And so you are continually looking for ways to connect what is happening in the pages of the book to what is familiar or meaningful to your child.

I like to divide reading comprehension activities into three parts: those you can do before opening the book, those that are most helpful as the child reads, and those that help him organize his thoughts and sum up the events of the story after he finishes reading. These activities are fun but intensive. By no means should you feel obligated to go through each one of these for each book you and your child read together. I am offering a range of possibilities. You must decide which of these best suit you and your child. There is no one right way or one set formula to teach comprehension skills to your child. The idea is to transfer a way of thinking about reading to your child. Once he has assimilated this way of actively thinking about reading, he is an independent reader.

Before the Book Is Opened

Right from the start it is important to establish a purpose for reading—for example, to find out what is going to happen to the main character or how the mystery will be solved. There are a number of ways you can start a child thinking about purpose. Point out the book's title and author. If there is an illustration on the cover, you might talk about what it says about the book and its purpose. Scanning through a book prior to reading helps familiarize the reader with its content and give him a sense of where the book or chapter is going. Consider *The Story About Ping* by Marjorie Flack and Kurt Wiese. The cover drawing is of a scampering duck against a background of Chinese junk boats, resting in a river as the sun is going down. If you turn the pages, you will find images of Ping, the scampering duck, as well as other ducks, boats, water, a little boy holding Ping, and Ping surrounded by a host of ducks amidst lots of hay at the book's end. You can ask your child what he thinks this book seems to be about and what he anticipates will happen in the story.

The cover picture of Ping can spawn a discussion of ducks, visits to a farm, or what you know about ducks. Do ducks like water? Do they swim? What do you think Ping is doing in the water? What about the boat? Looking at the cover, you can see a setting sun visible in the distance. Ask your child what time of day he thinks the cover portrays and why. Ask him if he thinks this is going to be a happy or sad story and why. You are modeling for your child how a good reader proceeds. A skilled reader is an active reader, not someone adrift; he reads purposefully, makes predictions, and wants to know if his predictions are validated or if he needs to alter them. Making predictions draws a child into the story and makes him eager to go on.

It is always a good idea to anticipate any potentially difficult or unfamiliar words or concepts. If you have the time, you should preread or scan through the chapter or book to identify the worrisome words. In this story the word *Yangtze* is likely to be a new one for your child. You could show him on a globe where the Yangtze River is located, or you could talk about rivers, including any that are in your local area or that you have visited. In this way you help activate your child's background knowledge by relating this story to things that he already knows about or that are meaningful to him. Finally, you might try to relate it to other stories, such as those about ducks. These strategies are quite flexible. You can apply them while you read to your child or later on as he reads to you.

During Reading

Start out by commenting on the first few sentences or first paragraphs of the story. This ensures that your child is actively involved from the very beginning. Opening sentences are critical because they often set the stage for the entire story and introduce you to the place and characters. In *The Story About Ping* we immediately meet Ping and his "mother and father and two sisters and three brothers and eleven aunts and uncles and forty-two cousins." We find out that "their home was a boat with two wise eyes on the Yangtze River." And just a few short paragraphs later we learn that "Ping was always careful, very careful not to be last, because the last duck to cross over the bridge always got a spank on the back." At this point you can pause to reflect on what has been learned so far and what the author might be preparing the reader for. You can ask, "Do you think there's a chance that Ping might be last on the boat when we turn the page? Why? And if he is, what do you think he might do? What would you do?" By talking about the story and how your child relates to it, you are drawing him into the narrative and raising his interest level. This is important to do right at the start because once a child loses interest, it is hard to bring him back into the flow of the story. On the other hand, once he is part of the unfolding events, he is hooked and will want to know what happens next.

It is also important to establish the *who, what, where, when* and *why* right from the beginning. This information represents the structure of the story; it provides reference points for discussion and anchors the narrative. Knowing these story facts can also help your child visualize what is happening and encourage him to bring up images that he associates with the place or people. Holding such an image in mind is one more connection to the action in the book and to better comprehension. And just as you did earlier, you can identify and talk to him about difficult words or concepts; in *Ping* these could be *wise, scurrying, running away,* or *reunion.* Ask your child to point out what he sees as the difficulties that are affecting the characters in the story and then suggest some possible solutions. You can talk about the ramifications of each. As you read on, ask him if his predictions need to be changed or modified, and ask him to explain his thinking.

From time to time you can ask your child to summarize the plot, to recount the sequence of events that has occurred, or to tell you the main idea in a paragraph you have just read. The last of these helps your child differentiate important from trivial or redundant information, a key factor in getting the gist of a story. To help enrich the story and bring your child closer to it, ask him more about the characters; you can talk about Ping or the Master of the Boat who calls out, "La-la-la-la-lei!" each evening, or even the little boy who plucks Ping from the water. Does he like each of them? Why? Do they remind him of anyone he knows or someone he has read about before? How does the story make him feel— happy, sad, lucky, frightened, eager, or excited? Why? Follow the same pattern as you read other stories, always integrating your child and his experiences into the fabric of the story.

After Finishing the Book

Ask your child to summarize the book's plot, to tell you what happened and his feelings about it. See if he can retell the events in order. If not, this is the time to use paper and pencil to chart the aspects of the story visually, such as cause and effect or a particular sequence of events. Ask your child if he wants to read the story again. Ask if he wants to read more stories about the same topics; in this case, ducks, boats, rivers, or China.

Because these activities involve basic reasoning skills, you can introduce them to your child even before he learns to read, and certainly before decoding instruction begins. Reading aloud to your child is an excellent way to get him started, and one of the first things to teach your child is that the purpose of reading is to gain meaning from the printed word. You can show him what to look for and listen for in a story (discussed below). You and your child can even act out characters. These kinds of activities bring the child into the story, encourage him to be an active listener, and help him acquire the kinds of skills that build meaning. They help develop his oral language skills, his vocabulary, his background knowledge, and his understanding of how books work.

Books are the center of a child's reading development, and there are many wonderful children's books available for every age, interest, and reading level (see Chapter 16). Introduce your child to books and reading very early. Read to him as he gets older. Make sure that he reads books (at his reading level) aloud to you and that he reads books to himself as well. Initially he should be reading at least twenty minutes daily, and later, thirty minutes or more. Reading *consistently*—at least four or five days a week even if for short periods of time—is more important than the length of time spent reading each day. Reading more frequently, especially aloud, will improve his reading skills, and that, more than anything else, will encourage him to want to read for longer periods of time.

The basic skills required in order to comprehend and the strategies he will need to call on remain relatively stable over time. Once he begins reading instruction, vocabulary and comprehension skills should be taught alongside those focused on decoding.

Activities to Guide You

Here is a summary of the activities that have been discussed. Focus on a few of them each time you read together.

- Establish a purpose for reading
- Identify the title and author
- Comment on the cover illustration
- Scan through the pages
- Establish the W's: who, what, where, when, why
- Relate the story and events to your child's existing knowledge and interests
- Predict future events (read a passage, pause, comment, and ask your child to predict what will happen next)
- Summarize the main ideas
- Generate questions as you read
- Make inferences
- Clarify difficult words or confusing concepts
- Use imagery or visualization
- Organize ideas, perhaps graphically on paper
- Retell the sequence of events
- Enjoy the story

In addition, take your child to the library early, even before she is a reader. As soon as she is eligible, get your child her own library card. Going to the library frequently, attending story hour, getting to know the children's librarian at the neighborhood public library (and later on at school, too) is a smart thing to do for your child. The children's librarian is an expert in children's books and can be a wonderful resource for you and your child. As she gets to know your child and develops a sense of her interests, of her favorite books and authors, and of the kind of child she is, the librarian can alert her to books of interest, to upcoming events, and to newly arrived additions.

Comprehension: The Trouble Signs

One of the added benefits of sitting alongside your child and reading with him is that it gives you insight into his ability to comprehend what he is reading. Below are some of the signs of a child who is having trouble comprehending what he is reading:

- He doesn't seem to get much from his reading.
- He has trouble answering the question "What was the book about?"
- He doesn't enjoy reading.
- He spends the same amount of time on easy passages as he does on difficult ones.
- He doesn't finish what he begins to read.
- He doesn't seem to be able to relate his reading to things he knows.
- He has trouble drawing inferences from his reading; his interpretations are always extremely literal.
- He can't quite come up with main ideas or summarize what he has read.
- He can't distinguish important ideas from lesser ones in the text.
- He has trouble making predictions.
- He rarely looks back at earlier pages to check his reading.
- He says reading is boring or tiring.
- He avoids reading.

If this seems to describe your child, you need to confirm your impressions. Speak to his teacher and perhaps have him tested at school. It is important to determine not only if he has a problem reading but the nature of the problem. Most often when a child is experiencing reading problems, it is a reflection of difficulty in decoding words accurately and fluently. He may be struggling with trying to get to the word itself. Comprehension skills generally mature when a child has all the prerequisite skills in place: decoding accuracy, fluency, vocabulary, background knowledge, and strategies. A weakness in any of them will affect comprehension.

This discussion has been directed to you as I would direct it to a parent in my practice. Knowledge is empowering, and when you understand reading, you should have the confidence to help your child. Don't worry about each and every detail. Once you understand the logic, you will know what to do and act accordingly.

Part IV

Overcoming Dyslexia: Turning Struggling Readers into Proficient Readers

---

18

Sam's Program

A Model That Works

Sam has not had an easy time at school. The son of a professional writer and his wife, an architect, Sam was identified as having a speech problem before entering kindergarten and placed in a program to encourage articulation development. After six months his speech was considered to have improved sufficiently, and he was dismissed from the program. When he struggled to read in first grade, his mother was told to "give him time."

When Sam reached third grade, his parents were very concerned. He never picked up a book on his own. When his mother tried to read with him, Sam found every excuse to avoid it. She felt Sam should be tested, but his teacher said it wasn't necessary; after informal testing, his teacher had concluded that Sam did not have a reading problem. Sam's parents were fearful of antagonizing his teacher and school officials. The situation deteriorated. At home Sam sulked and was starting to avoid schoolwork of any kind. At school he was given extra time on the computer. Nothing seemed to make a difference. Desperate, the family went to the Yale Center; Sam was tested and found to have a significant reading disability. With that evaluation in hand, Sam's parents returned to their school where a Pupil Placement Team (PPT) meeting was held, and Sam was identified as a special needs child with a reading disability. It was now February. He started on a reading program quite popular with teachers in the New England area. By June there was little progress. One moment he was a self-assured, graceful shortstop; the next, an insecure stumbling reader soon to enter fourth grade. Then I met with all parties concerned.

The school personnel were genuinely interested and caring, but the reading program was misguided. It included a hodgepodge of phonics activities that were not taught systematically or explicitly. As far as I could ascertain, there was no scientific evidence to support the general effectiveness of the reading instruction being employed. Moreover, this nine-year-old was being taught with two different reading programs (one with his special education teacher and one in his regular classroom), reflecting two very different reading strategies. Vocabulary growth and reading comprehension were virtually being ignored.

I was especially concerned because, as you now know, in fourth grade the emphasis is no longer on learning to read but on reading to learn. Sam continued to have difficulty with isolated words and struggled to read the required textbook for social studies. Sam was sure to fail subjects he had the intellect and motivation to master. That to me was—and is—unacceptable, because effective reading programs for dyslexic children exist. Even a program as lacking as Sam's can be transformed into an effective one. It happened for Sam, and it can happen for almost any child.

The program we designed for Sam focused on three major goals:

1. to provide a proven type of reading intervention delivered with sufficient intensity by a knowledgeable teacher
2. to integrate Sam's special reading program with the rest of his regular classroom work
3. to ensure that his reading status is steadily monitored

From the beginning it was critical that a responsible, knowledgeable educator take charge of Sam's educational plan. This role seemed natural for the school's new reading specialist, whom I will call Ms. Griffin. She and I reviewed a list of evidence-based interventions and chose *Language! A Literacy Intervention Curriculum.* We were impressed by the program's success with children in the upper elementary and middle school grades and its comprehensive nature. Reading is taught as part of an enriched total language experience that integrates reading, writing, spelling, grammar, language use, and vocabulary, and devotes substantial time to reading aloud as well as to reading independently. Since Sam had much catching up to do, we wanted to ensure that the intervention was delivered with sufficient punch. He needed to receive instruction for a large block of time and in a small group, with maximal student-teacher interaction. We were also pleased that *Language!* offered an intensive professional development program for teachers, helping ensure that the program would be taught effectively.

Here is what Sam has been doing. In place of his regular classroom instruction, Sam receives ninety minutes (two school periods) of *combined* reading and language arts daily in a small group of three students. Fluency practice—with single words, phrases, and connected text—is provided daily. The competitive part of Sam particularly enjoys the regular graphing of his fluency rates when he can actually see the steady increase in the number of words he can read correctly per minute. (See Chapter 19 for more on fluency.)

Sam receives another forty-five minutes of resource room instruction four days a week. The resource room functions as a bridge both to his regular classroom and to his home. Much of this time is devoted to integrating Sam's reading needs with his instruction in other subject areas; the focus is on *prereading* and *rereading.* Working alongside his teacher, Sam is able to preread his reading assignments (for social studies and science) before he tackles them alone. At this time he practices pronouncing difficult words by copying each word onto an index card (and, time permitting, looking up its meaning, using it in a sentence, and drawing a relevant cartoon to remind himself of the meaning). He reads it aloud as quickly as he can several times. All classroom handouts are also reviewed. Sam takes his written tests here, and his teacher helps him read the questions. He receives additional time on his class tests as well as on the statewide proficiency tests.

Rigorous efforts are under way to help Sam in his regular class. As I've said, of all in-class activities, reading aloud in front of classmates is the one feared most by students with reading difficulties. In Sam's case, when he is to read aloud in class, he is told the day before and practices the assigned passage with his resource room teacher and/or with a parent at home. (A child often feels more confident when he has recorded himself reading the passage aloud several times and is able to listen to how he sounds.) If he feels ready to read aloud in class, he simply raises his hand.

Spelling and writing activities are integrated across regular and special classrooms. Sam is expected to spell accurately the words he has learned as part of his reading program. Since spelling is more difficult than reading, if he cannot read a word, he should not be expected to spell it.

Writing (handwriting and composition) is challenging for dyslexic readers. Given Sam's penmanship difficulties, time limitations, and his facility on the computer, I recommended that he learn keyboarding. In addition, more than other children, dyslexic readers require and greatly benefit from being directly taught writing strategies and a structure to follow in constructing sentences and in developing paragraphs. The instruction in the basic skills of composition that Sam is receiving in the resource room is integrated with writing assignments from his social studies and science classes. Sam is gradually writing more of his compositions in his regular classroom. The next step is beginning the assignment in his regular classroom and reviewing it in the resource room. Once he is skilled in keyboarding, he'll purchase a portable mini-keyboard (AlphaSmart is a good one; see Chapter 23) that he can take from class to class.

Efforts in the resource room are also focused on ensuring that Sam's afternoons and evenings at home are productive. As mentioned earlier, in the resource room Sam reviews all his homework assignments to ensure that he has read each one correctly and knows what to do. In addition, each of Sam's textbooks is ordered as a book on tape or CD-ROM from Recording for the Blind and Dyslexic (see Chapter 23). Eventually his tape recorder and tapes will be kept at home where he will be able to reread his books as he follows along with the tape. I also recommended that Sam keep an extra set of textbooks at home; this allows a parent or tutor to follow along with Sam as he reads a passage aloud.

The keystone in this entire process is a system of constant seamless communication between his reading, resource room, and regular classroom teachers as well as between school and home. A formal plan for such communication has been set in place. As I have emphasized, home is a place for reinforcement of skills and for pleasure reading; Sam should not have to depend on tutors or his parents to teach him new skills. At the same time, since dyslexic students benefit from practice, I view partnerships between school and home as a positive means of extending learning. I encouraged such a collaboration for Sam's family.

His home reading reflects three specific goals. First, he must reinforce what he is learning in class by practicing reading school-based materials *aloud* to his parents or tutor. Second, Sam is encouraged to read silently for pleasure. These books are of high interest to him and at his reading level. A close linkage between the *Language!* reading materials and the Degrees of Reading Power (DRP) system (see Chapter 16) helps in matching Sam's interests with his reading ability. (The level of difficulty of all reading materials in *Language!* is automatically translated into a DRP unit; this in turn can be used to access literally thousands of books listed according to their DRP rating and topic.) Since Sam loves sports and enjoys playing in Little League, a list of books about baseball at his reading level can easily be generated. Third, time permitting, his parents read books to Sam that are above his current reading level, or he listens to them on tape or CD. In this way Sam maintains access to print materials that are at his intellectual level but above his reading level, and he gains new vocabulary words and new knowledge of the world that would otherwise be unavailable to him.

These home activities support his school instruction and help him develop fluency skills as well as the word and worldly knowledge critical for skilled reading. (These activities are not all carried out in the same evening, of course; I have prioritized their importance so that reading school-based materials aloud receives the highest priority.)

Sam's reading progress is continuously monitored. His mastery of the curriculum is tested regularly (at the end of every six lessons) with formal measures of oral reading fluency and reading comprehension. At the end of the school year Sam is given standardized reading tests to see how he is doing compared to others his age. For this purpose I use the Woodcock Reading Mastery Tests (WRMT), the Gray Oral Reading Tests (GORT), and the Test of Word Reading Efficiency (TOWRE). Approaches to teaching and measuring fluency in dyslexic children are discussed in Chapter 19.

The major work of learning should take place during school hours when the child is most alert, but a tutor can perform a valuable function in helping to reinforce a child's reading skills. She can help him practice reading aloud and apply his growing reading and writing skills to his homework assignments. Tutors can introduce children to study skills, especially ways to organize their time and their notebooks, which has long-term benefits. Sam's family wanted to have the additional support of an after-school tutor. I urged that her efforts and that of the school's reading specialist be closely coordinated; it is essential that they work together as a unified team. Under no circumstance should the tutor operate as a separate agent.

Nine months after Sam began the program, he had increased his reading scores by almost two years. Most important, he had come to think of himself as a reader; he no longer guessed wildly at unfamiliar words. If he stumbled over a word, in general he eventually pronounced the word correctly—an unheard-of event just a few months before. Even when he could not fully decode a new word, he made a reasonable attempt to do so; he used his knowledge of how letters represent sounds and his excellent vocabulary to figure it out. He raised his hand in class and was eager to be called on. He was focusing on reading words more fluently, learning how to pull apart long words and about Latin-based word origins so that he could read the new words that were constantly appearing in his social studies and science texts. Sam was benefiting greatly from previewing his textbook reading assignments, identifying and then practicing difficult words. He was returning home from school eager to read a passage aloud to his parents. Spelling was still difficult but was improving. He had just about mastered keyboarding skills and was now writing his compositions on the computer. This had relieved him of so much pressure that he could concentrate on content rather than on letter formation. He was delighted by his progress, as were his parents and his teachers. The teachers started adapting Sam's program for their other students with reading problems.

Successful programs like Sam's can be developed for any child. In doing so you must keep in mind that teaching a dyslexic child to read is based on the same principles used to teach any child to read. Since the neural systems responsible for transforming print into language may not be as responsive as in other children, however, *the instruction must be relentless and amplified in every way possible so that it penetrates and takes hold.* The ultimate goal is for the child to become an independent skilled reader. Along the way the aim is to build the neural systems responsible for reading—first, the slower left-side frontal and parieto-temporal systems that analyze each word, and then, if possible, the automatic fast-track word form system that allows the fluent reading that characterizes skilled readers.

Earlier I told you that an effective reading program is predicated on a three-prong approach involving reading intervention, integration of the intervention with regular schoolwork, and frequent monitoring of reading progress. The key lies, of course, with the intervention, and this deserves special mention.

Essentials of a Successful Reading Intervention

Several essentials make up a successful reading intervention. The first is program content, which I will discuss in detail in the next chapter. Here I want to focus on issues of implementation—when, how, by whom, and for how long the intervention is presented to the student. Often overlooked, these factors determine the ultimate success or failure of even the very best interventions. They reflect the components that were built into Sam's program, and you must ensure that each is made a part of your child's reading program.

Early intervention

Diagnosis is the essential first step in successfully teaching a dyslexic child to read—the earlier, the better. Because I have witnessed so many parents lose precious time by wanting to "wait a little longer" or to "give it time," I want to remind you that no amount of denial or rationalizing will change the situation; it only puts your child further behind and damages his self-esteem. A child needs help *before* he fails.

Children who receive help early can follow the same express pathway to reading as their classmates. Later-identified children miss out on essential practice. As you know by now, fluency comes about from repeatedly practicing the same word so that eventually its brain representation develops into a perfect replica. Poor readers receive the least amount of reading practice although they need it the most. They avoid reading, read less, and as a result fall progressively behind their classmates in the amount of printed words they have read and practiced. A dyslexic child who is not identified until he is in third grade or later is already thousands of unlearned words behind, a gap that he must close if he is ever to catch up with his peers. And so the best intervention is prevention in kindergarten or remediation beginning in first grade.

And happily, as said earlier, we have strong brain imaging evidence that scientifically based interventions can rewire a child's brain so that it is virtually indistinguishable from that of a child who has never had a reading problem. Early indicators are that the gains the children make tend to be maintained even after the special programs have been discontinued.

Intense instruction

Reading instruction for the dyslexic reader must be delivered with great intensity. This reflects the dyslexic child's requirement for more instruction, which is more finely calibrated and more explicit. Keep in mind that he is behind his classmates and must make more progress than they do if he is to catch up. He must make a leap; if not, he will remain behind.

Effective reading instruction is responsive to the child's unique needs, to his actions, and to his behavior. His teacher must know to slow down, to repeat, to speed up or change the pace, to find an alternative explanation, and to stop. This means that his teacher must interact with him often enough to be able to detect change and to adjust her instruction accordingly.

Optimally, a child who is struggling to read should be in a group of three and no larger than four students, and he should receive this specialized reading instruction at least four, and preferably five, days a week. A larger group or less time will greatly undermine the possibilities of success.

High-quality instruction

High-quality instruction is provided by a highly qualified teacher. As my colleague Louisa Moats often says, "Teaching reading *is* rocket science," and a teacher's knowledge of how children learn to read as well as her experience teaching a specific program will ultimately determine the success of even the best reading programs.

Recent studies highlight the difference that a teacher can make in the overall success or failure of a reading program. In one instance the same instructional method was used in two studies but with two different outcomes. According to the researcher who carried out both investigations, the study in which the program was most effective "employed highly skilled teachers who all had a number of years' experience teaching children with reading disabilities," while the other study "employed inexperienced teachers." This is a powerful argument for ensuring that anyone who takes on such a responsibility be a knowledgeable reading teacher or a teacher who has had recent training and experience in scientifically based methods for teaching reading. The primary job of teaching a dyslexic child to read should not be left to classroom aides, peer tutors, or teachers who do not possess the necessary knowledge or experience.

In another study, computers were used to teach reading-disabled children comprehension strategies. The children seemed to learn the specific approaches very well but did not use what they had learned. When their teacher was seated alongside them at the computer, the children applied the mastered strategy. When the children were alone at the computer, however, they did not apply the strategies they had been taught. So learning a strategy and using a strategy are not necessarily the same. Computers are not a substitute for a good teacher.

Teaching a dyslexic child to read is hard work. It is a highly interactive process rapidly resonating back and forth between teacher and child. Gaining the child's attention requires constant effort on the part of the teacher who must work diligently to involve the child, asking him questions or asking him to justify a response. ("Sam, I wonder why you would say that. Can you tell me?") Reading is extremely hard work for a dyslexic student, and a teacher's goal is to prevent him from drifting away and daydreaming. A teacher is constantly delivering the necessary knowledge while at the same time working hard to ensure that it is accompanied by a "hook" that she thinks will be meaningful to the child. She is constantly thinking about how to convey this information to the child.

Sufficient duration

One of the most common errors in teaching a dyslexic child to read is to withdraw prematurely the instruction that seems to be working. A child who is reading accurately but not fluently at grade level still requires intensive reading instruction. A child with a reading disability who is not identified early may require as much as 150 to 300 hours of intensive *instruction* (at least ninety minutes a day for most school days over a one-to-three-year period) if he is going to close the reading gap between himself and his peers. And, of course, the longer identification and effective reading instruction are delayed, the longer the child will require to catch up.

You can help ensure that your dyslexic child will learn to read by

- getting help early;
- maximizing instructional time with frequent sessions, small groups, and sufficient duration;
- insisting on qualified teachers;
- insisting on proven reading programs.

19

Teaching
the Dyslexic Child to Read

1. Learning to Read Words Accurately

Highly effective prevention and early intervention programs are now a reality. They are aimed at children between five and six years old, in kindergarten or first grade, who without such instruction are at high risk for developing reading difficulties. High-risk children are those who are likely to develop reading problems because of a family history of reading difficulties, their own early language problems, or low scores on a kindergarten screening test. Reading performance tends to be stable, so by the time a child is in first grade, his reading ability already strongly predicts later reading achievement. This makes it all the more remarkable that many of the new programs are so successful in altering the life course of an at-risk child's reading. According to G. Reid Lyon, who guides reading research at the National Institute of Child Health and Human Development (NICHD), widespread implementation of these scientifically proven prevention and early intervention programs will substantially reduce the number of children needing special education in higher grades. In one Tallahassee, Florida, elementary school where such a program was implemented, the percentage of struggling readers dropped eightfold—from 31.8 percent to 3.7 percent.

Common threads run through each of these programs. They follow the same template described earlier for teaching children to break the reading code. All children must master the same elements of reading to become literate. The process of mastering each of these steps is simply more difficult for the disabled reader. The essentials of an effective early intervention program are

- *Systematic* and *direct* instruction in:
  phonemic awareness—noticing, identifying, and manipulating
     the sounds of spoken language
  phonics—how letters and letter groups represent the sounds of
     spoken language
  sounding out words (decoding)
  spelling
  reading sight words
  vocabulary and concepts
  reading comprehension strategies
- *Practice* in applying these skills in reading and in writing
- *Fluency training*
- *Enriched language experiences:* listening to, talking about, and
telling stories

Powerful and proven reading programs incorporating these features are now bringing cutting-edge science directly into the classroom. There are a number of effective reading programs for children of all ages and at all levels of reading. My recommendations are for total "off-the-shelf" comprehensive programs rather than so-called eclectic ones that are stitched together by a child's teacher. Such eclectic approaches are untested and are essentially experiments that may or may not succeed. I would not want to take such a risk with my child; rather, I would want to stay with a proven, cohesive program that leaves nothing to chance.

If your child is at risk or struggling to learn to read, you must ask his teacher about the program she is using. If it is a recommended one, you are reassured: Your child is in good hands; he will learn to read. If not, discuss these programs with the teacher and suggest she consider using one for your child—or a comparable one that reflects the same principles.

All teachers want their students to learn to read, but many simply do not have a source of good, reliable information about effective research-based reading programs. Your role—indeed, your responsibility—as your child's chief advocate is to bring new and important information to your child's teacher and school. The tide has turned, given the findings of the National Reading Panel and the new Reading First legislation. Schools now have a mandate to provide evidence-based programs for their students. There is no other way.

I want to emphasize that each of these programs works. *The specific program chosen from among them is far less important than the provision of systematic, explicit instruction in phonemic awareness and phonics, and then teaching children how to apply this knowledge to reading and writing.* Specific programs are constantly changing, but the instructional principles remain the same.

Basically, there are two effective approaches to preventing reading difficulties; both are meant for young children who have early signs of reading problems. In one, a highly structured and comprehensive reading curriculum is provided to an entire class of at-risk children. An example of this approach is *Reading Mastery.*

Reading Mastery (www.sra4kids.com) is a highly structured reading program geared to children in grades kindergarten through six at high risk for reading problems. This program, based on an approach called Direct Instruction (DI), requires that teachers follow a highly scripted lesson plan, breaks down concepts into smaller subskills taught one by one, and does not permit children to move forward until they have mastered a particular concept. Some teachers are uncomfortable teaching such a tightly controlled program, feeling that it leaves no room for creativity or individualization. *Reading Mastery* is highly effective, however.

In the second approach, at-risk children receive a combination of the regular evidence-based reading instruction with their class plus an additional thirty-to-forty-five-minute period of supplemental reading instruction. The supplemental programs that I prefer are intense, highly focused on specific basic reading skills, and taught in small groups. They are not meant to be used as a child's total reading program. Examples of effective supplemental reading programs are *Proactive Beginning Reading, The Optimize Intervention Program,* and *The Read, Write & Type! Learning System.*

I want to give you an example of a supplemental program and how it might be used effectively. *Open Court Reading* (see Chapter 17) is an excellent classroom reading program aimed at typical readers. In addition to the daily class reading lesson, it provides for a flexible thirty-to-forty-five-minute period to be used with students who require more intensive instruction. Researchers have recently developed *Proactive Beginning Reading* (www.sra4kids.com), a more directed supplement to the original Open Court program and tailor-made to use with small groups of struggling readers during this extra period. Intended for first-grade students who are just beginning to slip behind, *Proactive Beginning Reading* provides the additional explanations and practice to keep a child on track. It is especially helpful in providing a boost to those children who are experiencing mild reading problems.

The Optimize Intervention Program (www.scottforesman.com), developed by University of Oregon researchers Ed Kame'enui and Deborah Simmons, is used with small groups of children in kindergarten and first grade as a supplement to their regular evidence-based reading instruction. Intended for children who require more intensive instruction in the foundational reading skills, *Optimize* provides thirty minutes of highly systematic activities to reinforce a child's skills in phonologic awareness, letter names and sounds, word reading, spelling, and simple sentence reading. In a recent study *Optimize* was highly effective in improving the reading skills of a group of the poorest functioning kindergartners. Afterward many were reading at levels comparable to their classmates who were always good readers.

The Read, Write & Type! Learning System (www.readwritetype. com) is helpful as a supplemental program in first grade classrooms, or it can be used as homework to reinforce basic phonologic skills. The program is multisensory: Children learn to associate a specific sound with a letter and a finger tap on the keyboard. As an added benefit, children become familiar with the computer keyboard at an early age. The program and the positive results obtained with it in an intervention program are further discussed on pages 282–283.

Today more than ever there is a strong likelihood that your at-risk child will be taught with such proven programs. This is because Reading First, the cornerstone of the "No Child Left Behind" legislation, allocates substantial funds to states *provided* they use research-based, effective reading programs in grades kindergarten through three.

There are also highly effective programs available for children who are older, have not had the benefits of these programs, and are still struggling to read. Figure 34 explains the kind of learning leap a child who is behind must make. There is not a minute to waste. Instruction must be highly efficient and highly effective. Beginning around second grade, regular reading programs no longer address the kinds of phonemic awareness and basic phonics skill instruction that your struggling reader requires. Furthermore, just like Sam, if he remains behind and in an ineffective reading program, he will not be able to handle the required reading in other subjects such as social studies and science.

The programs that follow are targeted to older elementary and middle school (or higher level) students who are one or two years behind grade level. Generally, they have failed to master the earliest reading skills but require faster-paced instruction and reading materials with topics and vocabulary geared to their age. The programs also include essential assessment measures, initially for diagnostic placement and later for monitoring ongoing progress, especially at important milestones such as the end of a unit. Among the best programs are *Language! A Literacy Intervention Curriculum* (www.language-usa.net); *READ 180* (www.scholastic.com); *Fast Track Reading Program* (www.wrightgroup.com); *High Point* (www.hampton-brown.com); and the *REACH System* (www.sra4kids.com). Each is targeted for disabled readers in grades four and above. *REACH*, based on the same Direct

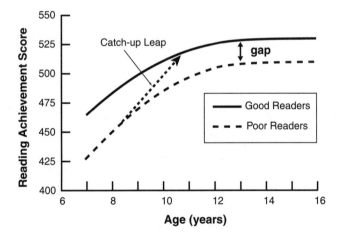

Figure 34. Closing the Reading Gap

To close the gap between his classmates (upper curve) and himself (lower curve), a dyslexic child must *accelerate* his pace of learning to read so that he leaps to a higher reading level. If he continues at the same pace he will not catch up to his classmates who are continuing to make progress.

Instruction approach mentioned earlier, represents a combination of three programs—*Corrective Reading, Reasoning and Writing,* and *Spelling Through Morphographs*—that in a cohesive way address all the reading-related needs of the struggling student. Especially beneficial is the addition of the spelling program for older struggling readers. Focused on learning to spell prefixes, suffixes, and word roots, it provides a strategy applicable to thousands of complex words while also teaching word meaning and improving reading. The above list is primarily reflective of programs or methods that were reviewed and found effective as part of the work of the National Reading Panel and subsequently adopted by the State of California. It is not meant to be inclusive of all effective reading programs.

Other programs aimed at older (and also younger) students do not represent as comprehensive a curriculum. They focus on teaching children how to sound out and identify words and how to spell them, along with practicing reading, but typically they are not linked to strong or systematic vocabulary, comprehension, or writing instruction. They are meant for small group instruction rather than whole classrooms. For example, you may hear reading programs referred to generically as Orton-Gillingham (after Dr. Samuel Orton and his associate, Anna Gillingham), an approach developed as a tutorial program for struggling readers. Orton-Gillingham is highly structured and systematic, tries to engage all the senses in learning about letters and sounds (a child taps each finger to his thumb as he sounds out a word), and typically is taught one-to-one or in small groups. There are many variations. One, the *Wilson Reading System* (www.wilsonlanguage.com), was developed for older elementary students through adults but is now available for younger children as well. Wilson concentrates on teaching phonemic awareness, decoding, spelling, and, to a lesser degree, comprehension, and has particularly good reading materials for older students. It provides students with many rules and may be especially appealing to brighter students who are highly verbal. Certified Wilson instructors are required to participate in an extensive professional development program.

Still another program, *Spell Read P.A.T. (Phonemic Analysis Training)* (www.spellread.com), is used with small groups of poor or at-risk readers from age five through adult. The program focuses on developing the child's ability to identify automatically the sounds of increasingly complex letter combinations and then to effortlessly apply this knowledge to reading and spelling words. Initial results support the program's effectiveness in improving reading accuracy, comprehension, and spelling.

There are also effective programs geared to students ready for the next step in reading, that is, figuring out how to approach longer or more complex words. Strategies for reading these complicated words are included in the *Benchmark School Word Identification/Vocabulary Development Program* and the *Benchmark Word Detectives Program* (www.benchmarkschool.org); the *Spelling Through Morphographs* component of *REACH*, which focuses on teaching prefixes and suffixes; and the *REWARDS* (*Reading Excellence: Word Attack and Rate Development Strategies*) program (www.sopriswest.com). These programs are particularly helpful for children who have learned how to decode small words but are stymied when they come across the multisyllabic words increasingly found in reading materials in third grade and above.

In contrast to these programs that teach children to focus on how the word *looks*, another type of reading program encourages children to learn about how the specific sounds are articulated and how each sound *feels*. This method, focusing directly on how phonemes are physically formed, is referred to as the *Lindamood Phoneme Sequencing Program* (LiPS) (www.lblp.com). In it children learn the *oral motor* characteristics of individual speech sounds. This means that they come to know how the different parts of their pronunciation machinery (that is, lips, tongue, and palate) work together to form each sound. Children are encouraged to study pictures of the position of the lips as various sounds are formed, and also to become familiar with their own lip motions as they form different sounds.

The National Reading Panel found this method effective, more so with first graders than with older children who had a reading disability. This program is labor intensive, and according to its developers, ideal instruction for those severely affected may require as many as four hours of work daily with a trained teacher, often a speech and language pathologist. Yet this program is often successful with those most strongly affected by dyslexia. Originally taught individually, LiPS has been adapted for small group instruction in school settings.

You will hear many claims of the superiority of one program over another. The good news is that the evidence-based programs are all highly effective and produce remarkably comparable results. According to the research, no one program is head and shoulders above the others.

While programs emphasize different components of reading, the evidence tells us that as long as they include the essential components outlined at the start of the chapter and are implemented by well-trained teachers with sufficient intensity and for the necessary duration, they are all effective.

2. Moving From Accuracy to Fluency

The ordinary reader becomes her own best reading teacher. She automatically compares each word she reads with its stored neural model. If it is a perfect match, she rapidly identifies the word. If her model is not quite an exact replica, she corrects it, and after a few readings, she has a perfect fit. That word becomes part of her internal dictionary of words read at a glance. A dyslexic reader, on the other hand, reads very little, which leads to faulty, inaccurate, or incomplete neural models of words. The "holes" are never filled in, and she never has the number of encounters reading the word correctly that is necessary in order to develop a stable, accurate representation. As a result, a dyslexic reader's internal lexicon is a mighty thin one.

Building Fluency: Training the Brain

As you know, fluency is elusive to the dyslexic reader but need not be. And so it is particularly urgent that the dyslexic child who has gained some degree of reading accuracy but still reads slowly and hesitantly receive ongoing fluency training. The goal is for your dyslexic child to become a fluent reader.

Earlier I reviewed the findings of the National Reading Panel concerning the most effective methods for developing fluency for all kinds of readers. Approaches that emphasize repeated oral reading with teacher feedback and guidance provide the strongest outcomes. Here I want to tell you about additional activities that might be especially helpful to the reader who is dyslexic. In general these depend on the principle of *overlearning,* which is just another way of saying that something becomes so ingrained and so automatic that it requires no active attention or conscious thought. Overlearning may be necessary for the development of automaticity in any area. It is the result of extensive repetition, drill, and practice. In his study of superior athletes over a decade and a half ago, educator B. S. Bloom found that those who developed into Olympians were the ones who had overlearned specific motor skills. The same is true of dance or music. Parents would not think of having their child miss hockey or clarinet practice. Yet the thought of saying to a child "You must now practice your reading aloud" does not come easily, in spite of the fact that in all likelihood it will have far greater impact on his future than either sports or music.

Fluency training is to be approached like any athletic endeavor. In this case we are going to concentrate on building highly stable, accurate neural models of words. Each fluency training session should require only minutes a day. Practice must be consistent and extend over a period of weeks and preferably months. Since fluency is built on accuracy, students must practice on materials that they can already decode. In practical terms this means that they must be able to read the passage they choose with a high degree of accuracy, making no more than one error for every twenty words read. Practice means rereading the same passage *at least* four times (of course, this need not be during the same practice session). Incentives should be built in. Students need to see tangible signs of their own improvement. Measuring fluency rates and then graphing the results, as we did for Sam, provides a hardworking student with visible evidence of his progress and strong motivation to keep practicing.

Overall, successful fluency training can be achieved through repeated oral reading of either entire passages or single words. Methods for repeated oral reading of passages with teacher feedback were described in Chapter 17, and here I want to tell you about the most effective way to practice reading single words. This is referred to as *speeded word training*, the goal of which is to make a child a really fast responder. In practice, a deadline is imposed on how quickly a word needs to be named, with shorter deadlines resulting in faster reading speeds. The goal is to bring naming times below one second per word so that the child names at least sixty words per minute. These can be single words on flash cards, or they can be rows of five or six words printed across a large card. There are many ways to practice reading individual words. As long as the guidelines in the previous paragraph are followed, you can improvise. As always, ask your child's teacher what words or letter combinations your child is working on; she will be able to provide you with the most appropriate words for practice. Graduated word lists (and easy-to-follow instructions) for speed drills can also be obtained from Oxton House Publishers (www.OxtonHouse.com).

The goal of speeded word repetition is to bind a word's critical features together so tightly that they become and function as a single unit—the prerequisites for becoming part of the automatic word form system for word identification. This accomplishes for dyslexic readers what other readers do through their efficient "self-teaching" mechanism. It is not surprising to learn that slow or poor readers appear to gain even more from repeated reading practice than do their more able reading peers.

Fluency Practice at School and at Home

I can think of no stronger impetus for fluency practice than this eloquent rendering of the impact of slow, disfluent reading on a student as described by Timothy Rasinski, who runs a reading clinic at Kent State University:

> Imagine yourself as a fifth-grade student who is assigned to read a twelve-page chapter in a social studies book in school. Imagine also that you are a disfluent or inefficient reader. You read at fifty-eight words per minute . . . or half the rate of your classmates. You begin reading as best you can. Like most students, you are well aware of what is happening around you. You are about halfway through the passage, and you notice that many of your classmates have finished reading—they are done and you still have six pages to read. What do you do? Do you pretend to have completed the assignment even though you haven't read or comprehended the entire passage? Or do you continue reading knowing that by doing so you will be broadcasting your lack of reading proficiency and making your classmates wait on you? Neither solution is palatable, yet the problem is all too common. . . . Even if an assignment were made for home reading, the sixty-minute reading assignment for most students would become two hours of reading for you.

Fortunately, such fluency problems can be successfully attacked, both at school and at home.

At School. Practicing fluency can start just as a child is beginning to read. Decodable texts are ideal for providing the kinds of repetitive practice he needs to be able to achieve success quickly in reading a small core of words. Such booklets are part of the *Open Court and Language!* reading programs recommended earlier or can be purchased (see page 221). Words should be practiced until they can be read fluently. As soon as this occurs, the child can begin reading a wider range of books and stories, providing him with the kinds of practice he requires in order to enlarge his reading vocabulary and build an increasing number of accurate word representations.

Once the student is able to read a core of words accurately, there are a number of effective ways to improve fluency. The key is to find enjoyable ways to encourage reading aloud. Having a child practice reading poetry is an excellent method for improving his fluency. Poems are usually short, they have rhyme, and they are tailor-made for reading quickly and with expression. Some teachers stage a "poetry party." The children select a poem and for the next several days practice reading the poem aloud over and over again. Then the day of the poetry party, lights are turned out and flashlights or lamps provide dimmed light and atmosphere. After sufficient practice even the most disabled readers seem to be able to read their poems with accuracy, smoothness, and expression. (See Chapter 16 for recommended books of poetry.)

Alternatively, many students enjoy and benefit from staging dramatic readings of a selection from a play script. They enjoy the drama that accompanies the repeated reading and are willing participants. Dramatic readings truly improve fluency. In one recent study, students participating in this approach—called Readers' Theatre—for a ten-week period made an entire year's gain in improving their reading rates. Students can face an audience or simply sit in a circle and read from a script. Readers' Theatre is successful with children beginning as early as second grade and continuing through high school.

Students also enjoy reading and rereading or singing songs or limericks. Lyrics to a song can be handed out to a class or to a small group for the song to be read or sung several days in a row. Song lyrics are particularly suitable for choral reading where the teacher first reads the words and then she and the students join together to read along as a group, rereading the lyrics four or even more times.

Older dyslexic students serve as wonderful reading tutors for younger students. Each student benefits from reading aloud; in addition, the dyslexic student gains a rare sense of satisfaction and accomplishment from being able to help someone read.

Daily fluency practice can be for as little as five or six minutes, as shown in a recent study by University of Florida researcher Cecil Mercer. Middle school students attending a special education program were asked to practice speeded oral reading of various sorts—letters, words, phrases, passages—for only six minutes each day but for extended periods of time ranging from six months to twenty-three months. The students made substantial gains both in their reading accuracy and in their fluency. This approach was particularly encouraging because the subjects were older students with severe reading difficulties, a group that is very difficult to remediate. *Great Leaps Reading*, the program responsible for bringing about these impressive gains, is available at www.greatleaps.com. It is well suited for use by teachers, tutors, and parents with children in kindergarten through high school.

At Home. Parents of dyslexic readers can also help improve their child's fluency. In a reading clinic at Kent State University, parents participate with their child in a method called *paired reading*—a variation of repeated oral reading. It requires only fifteen minutes an evening. Parents read a brief story or passage to their child, followed by the parent and child reading the same passage together a few times. Then the child alone reads the text back to the parent. Comparisons showed that children who read aloud with their parents made substantially larger gains in fluency.

Children can also practice fluency at home by using commercial programs developed specifically for this purpose. One, *Read Naturally* (www.readnaturally.com), follows the basic principles of effective fluency instruction: A student reads a story while listening to it on an audiotape or CD-ROM and then reads it aloud three or four times. Importantly, she times herself and graphs her fluency rate—both before practicing and again after—allowing her and you to monitor her progress. This program comes with twenty-four nonfiction stories for students reading at grade levels one through seven. It can also be used in the classroom.

An exciting new program, *ReadIt* (www.reading-assistant.com), developed by reading researcher Marilyn Adams at Soliloquy Learning, exploits the newest speech recognition technology to improve fluency in children in grades two through five. This ambitious program shares similarities with the program described above: A child listens to a story read to him on the computer (here, as the text is highlighted in time to the narrator's voice) and then reads aloud into a microphone. During this process, taking advantage of the high-tech software, the computer can help a child in several ways. It can monitor and keep track of his reading rate. If the child pauses and is stuck on a word, the computer on its own will pronounce that word for him; alternatively, the child can request the computer to pronounce a word or read an entire segment aloud for him. He can listen to a playback of his reading. He can also request written and spoken definitions for any word in the text or a list of all the words that gave him difficulty. There is a companion program, *Soliloquy Reading Assistant,* for use in the classroom. For both home and school programs children may select poetry, fiction, and nonfiction passages, including those from popular children's magazines such as *Spider* and *Ladybug.*

Both *Reading Naturally* and *ReadIt* allow children to practice reading independently and monitor their progress while at the same time providing parents (and teachers) with an ongoing record of the child's progress in developing fluency. I strongly recommend both programs. In addition, for those who want simple printed stories, sorted according to their grade level (grades 1 through 4.5), the Neuhaus Education Center produces *Practices for Developing Accuracy and Fluency* (neuhaus.org), a manual containing a set of thirty passages marked at the hundredth word. A child can read the passage at her grade level while a parent times how long she takes to read one hundred words and graphs her progress over time. Helpful information is included to guide parents in optimal use of these passages.

I urge parents of dyslexic children to make fluency training—repeated oral reading—their number one priority. Because it involves reinforcement rather than teaching a child a new concept, it is ideally suited for the home. Fluency training is something all parents can do for their child. It requires little time and minimal expertise, and it invariably works. You can read fiction, poetry, plays, and even single words or use commercial programs. In doing so you are training your child's brain and helping build the accurate word models and the word form reading system necessary for quick and accurate reading. There are very few activities for a dyslexic reader that provide as much improvement for the amount of time spent as does guided repeated oral reading.

Repeatedly reading a word correctly leads to the development of accurate neural representations. Activities that strengthen a child's vocabulary aid in building these brain models. In knowing a word's meaning, a child has already built part of the neural model for that word. And once a child has mastered one feature of the printed word (meaning), it becomes easier for him to join that feature with the others—the way the word sounds and the way it is spelled—and to add the word to his sight word vocabulary for reading.

Helping Older Children Become More Fluent

Older children bear the brunt of a lack of fluency. They are expected to read more and understand more, but they are held back by the incredible amount of effort and time that reading demands. It is not too late for them to benefit from carefully targeted fluency practice. The same principles described for younger children apply, but they are adapted to the needs and interests of older students.

Reading passages aloud is helpful to students of all ages, but older students have difficulty finding materials to read aloud that are suitable. To address this need, Mary E. Curtis, reading researcher at Lesley College in Boston, and Ann Marie Longo, director of the Boys Town Reading Center at Father Flanagan's Boys' Home in Nebraska, have compiled a book list for dyslexic high school students that includes the following:

Avi. *Something Upstairs* (New York: William Morrow, 1990).

Bennett, J. *Death Grip* (New York: Ballantine Books, 1993).

Cannon, A. *The Shadow Brothers* (New York: Delacorte Press, 1990).

Clark, M. *Freedom Crossing* (New York: Scholastic, 1991).

Crew, L. *Children of the River* (New York: Laurel Leaf, 1991).

Hayes, D. *The Trouble with Lemons* (New York: Fawcett Book Group, 1995).

Hesse, K. *Letters from Rifka* (New York: Penguin Putnam, 2001).

Hobbs, W. *Bearstone* (New York: Simon & Schuster, 1997).

Nixon, J. *A Place to Belong* (New York: Bantam Books, 1996).

O'Connor, J. *Blizzard (Survive!)* (New York: Grosset, 1994).

Paulsen, G. *Canyons* (New York: Bantam, 1991).

————. *The River* (New York: Bantam, 1995).

Rylant, C. *Fine White Dust* (New York: Simon & Schuster, 2000).

Taylor, M. *The Road to Memphis* (Upper Saddle River, N.J.: Prentice Hall, 1999).

Alternatively, students can make use of the DRP and Lexile systems for help in choosing interesting books at their reading level. Whatever the material, students should practice reading aloud passages that are relatively short, two hundred words or, preferably, less, yet long enough not to be easily memorized.

Older students also benefit from reading single words aloud, especially so-called irregular words. Around the fourth grade there is a tremendous surge in the proportion of words that are irregular, those that do not follow the regular rules for pronunciation and do not lend themselves to sounding out. Unless a child who is dyslexic is provided with specific practice targeted to these words (examples are *bough* and *though*), the child will suffer a setback. The sudden onslaught of such hard-to-decipher words may be one factor behind the well-known dip in reading performance that seems to occur around the fourth grade, colloquially referred to as "the fourth grade slump." Fortunately, more and more reading programs that are effective for older dyslexic readers are incorporating fluency exercises with these irregular words. For example, students in the upper-level units of the *Language!* program practice words such as *canoe, courage, promise, bouquet, cousin,* and *enough.* These words are likely to be found in reading materials meant for students in higher grades but must be learned and overlearned through repeated practice as part of fluency exercises. The word lists obtained from Oxton House Publishers mentioned earlier include more than one hundred irregular words.

Some older children may gain the most from practicing relevant words, words they will need in order to pursue their studies. Here I recommend the procedure that helped Sam so much: Students practice reading aloud words taken from their reading materials in different subjects, such as social studies and science. In practice, the student and his teacher or tutor preview reading assignments in those subject areas together, developing a list of words that the student needs to practice.

These words can be put on index cards or on the computer for practice reading aloud. Listening to the text on audiotape or CD while reading along is also helpful. Without such supports, assigning a dyslexic student reading in a textbook may only lead to frustration and disappointment.

As I noted for younger children, building a larger vocabulary also contributes to reading words fluently. For dyslexic readers, who benefit from more practice and more reinforcement, computer programs are helpful in supplementing vocabulary instruction. One program, called *Ultimate Word Attack,* is aimed at bolstering the vocabulary of that often difficult to reach group of students in middle and in high school. A particularly appealing feature of the program is that it permits the user to select the words to be practiced and to choose the speed of presentation, thereby both improving vocabulary and increasing fluency. There are specialized word lists in different areas including business, architecture, geography, law, literature, sports, science, medicine, and art. A particularly appealing feature for dyslexic readers is the availability of an audio CD-ROM with an abbreviated word list and definitions. *Ultimate Word Attack* (software by Davidson) can be found packaged as part of Excel@Middle School and Excel@High School produced by Knowledge Adventure (www.smartkidssoftware.com).

Lack of fluency in reading is often accompanied by a lack of fluency in speaking, that is, difficulty in quickly retrieving words, such as when a student is called upon in class to explain or describe a topic. Many of my students have found it extremely helpful to spend part of their study hall time working individually with a teacher (or at home with a tutor), reading, and then *talking through the content* of an assignment. Speaking and using the specific vocabulary relevant to a subject often help lubricate a student's retrieval processes and enable him to more readily access exactly what he wants to say. These strategies (previewing, reviewing, and talking through) are critically important for the dyslexic child if he is to participate more fully in the class and discussion periods.

One aspect of fluency that particularly impacts older students is the complex relationship between reading rate (fluency) and reading comprehension. As readers become more fluent, for example, they are also apt to comprehend better. It is important to remember, however, that until dyslexic readers achieve fluency, *they will increase their comprehension the more time they are given to read.* So make sure they are provided with that additional time for homework assignments and examinations.

Measuring Fluency

Almost as important as teaching fluency is measuring it. There are useful guidelines to help you judge a child's fluency relative to others his age. For children in lower grades the expected fluency rates for oral reading of passages are as follows:

Grade Level	Correct Words Read per Minute (CWPM)
Spring, first grade	40 to 60
Spring, second grade	80 to 100
Spring, third grade	100 to 120
Fourth grade and above	120 to 180

These rates are approximations to provide you with an expected range of oral fluency rates. A group of researchers at the University of Oregon has taken the next step and set specific thresholds for oral fluency rates in the early grades. Children scoring below the following levels are at high risk for reading failure: spring, first grade: 10 CWPM; spring, second grade: 50 CWPM; spring, third grade: 70 CWPM. Such children require urgent, intensive intervention with one of the programs mentioned at the beginning of this chapter.

To measure your child's fluency, select two or three paragraphs from materials he is assigned to read. Have him read the passages aloud to ensure that he can read them comfortably (nineteen out of twenty words read correctly). Next, instruct him to read as quickly and as accurately as he can and time him as he reads the passage aloud for one minute. Count the total number of words he reads. Timing can be tricky, so you might want to time him reading two or three passages and take an average in order to obtain a more reliable measurement. (It helps to make a copy of the passage he is reading so you can mark any words he misreads, omits, or hesitates over for more than three seconds before reading. If he makes an error and then self-corrects within three seconds, the word is considered correct.) Add up the number of errors he made while reading the passage. The correct words per minute (CWPM) score is the total number of words read minus the number of errors. As important as measuring a child's fluency rate is tracking (on a simple graph) his improvement, at least weekly, as he continues to practice. How to track fluency rates and provide expectations for weekly improvement are described below.

3. Answers to the Most Frequently Asked Questions

What is the best way to monitor my child's progress in a reading program?

Two complementary approaches, when combined, provide up-to-date monitoring of a child's rate of progress and his level of achievement in reading. One is called curriculum-based measurement (CBM) and relies on ongoing measurements of reading fluency (ideally, weekly; minimally, three times during a school year) using the child's classroom reading materials. This is meant to establish how fast he is acquiring new knowledge. The other method, which is not intended for very frequent administration, uses standardized reading tests and assesses reading performance periodically vis-à-vis his age-mates.

The curriculum-based approach, advanced by researchers Lynn and Douglas Fuchs at Vanderbilt University, measures how well a child has learned what he has been taught. His progress in meeting the demands of the reading program developed for him is graphed over time, so his growth or lack of growth is clearly visible. Progress in different areas of reading—including phonics, decoding nonsense words, reading real words, and reading passages aloud—can be measured. Earlier I discussed expected levels of fluency at different grades. CBM can be used to track fluency rates as an objective measure to identify if a child is responding to a particular instructional approach and, if necessary, to modify it. The rate of his reading growth is compared to norms that have been established for the amount of weekly growth expected at each grade level, beginning at grade one and extending through grade six. No one has to wait for the end of the school year to learn about a child's reading progress.

A child's *rate* of reading growth follows a distinct pattern: (1) growth is greatest in the early school years and lessens with each succeeding grade; (2) growth is most often at its maximum at the beginning of each school year and tapers off toward spring.

Using oral passage reading as an example, I have listed below the expected reading growth rates—how much (the number of words read correctly per minute) a child should be expected to *improve* each week. The important figure here is the amount of change—how many more words per minute a child can read correctly compared to the previous week. For each grade level, a lower number (referred to as "realistic") and a higher one (called "ambitious") are provided. The realistic number represents the amount of improvement observed for a typical child. The child who is experiencing reading difficulties, having fallen behind, has a lot more ground to cover, so he must make faster progress than his classmates. His goal is to achieve the ambitious rate of growth if he is to make a learning leap and catch up to his classmates.

Rate of Expected Weekly Reading Growth
(Increase in Correct Words Read per Minute)

Grade	Realistic	Ambitious
1	2.00	3.00
2	1.50	2.00
3	1.00	1.50
4	0.85	1.10
5	0.50	0.80
6	0.30	0.65

CBM is administered in the classroom. A child reads aloud a passage at her grade level, and each week she is assessed using a passage of equivalent difficulty. Her oral reading is timed for one minute; as she reads, her teacher follows along with a copy of the passage, using the scoring method described on page 277. The fluency score—the total number of words read per minute minus the number of errors—is calculated and charted. For example, a second grader's fluency (ambitious) rate should increase by two words each week; a fifth grader's growth should come close to one word per week. For this approach to work, a child must be reading at least at a mid–first grade level. It is important not to base any judgment on one or two weeks but, rather, to observe the child's progress over five, six, or more weeks. If she is on track, the program should be continued. If the observed reading growth is below the "ambitious" rate, however, the program needs to be modified.

DIBELS (see Chapter 15) is extremely useful for assessing a child's fluency in the early foundational reading skills. Accordingly, it is targeted for children from preschool through grade three. The goal is to identify those children who are not progressing and who may benefit from early intervention. DIBELS (or comparable surveillance) can benefit all beginning readers, especially those who are at risk for a reading disability or who are showing early signs of struggle.

The second approach to monitoring progress focuses on a child's absolute level of performance, at a fixed point in time, compared to his age or grade peers as measured by a standardized reading test such as the Woodcock Reading Mastery Test. These results are reported in percentile scores (for example, a nine-year-old boy who is reading at the 40th percentile is superior to 40 percent of all nine-year-old boys). They also may be reported as *standard scores,* which are adjusted so that 50 percent of the children score either below or above an average score of 100. This kind of standardized test is most often given at the end of the school year. The results establish at what level a child is reading and how he compares to other children of his own age, but they do not help determine how fast he is mastering specific reading skills. Keep in mind that both reading accuracy and reading fluency, as well as comprehension, must be assessed by these standardized measures. Otherwise, students who are accurate but read slowly and with great effort will be overlooked and not receive the required help.

All children do not respond in exactly the same manner to a program. Most important is the trajectory. A relatively flat line indicating little progress loudly proclaims the need for a change, just as a steep upward incline proudly trumpets rapid progress. Happily, new reading programs, like those I have recommended and those adhering to Reading First requirements, routinely build in ongoing monitoring.

Do the benefits of scientifically based programs last? Do the children become independent skilled readers?

Fluency is the critical marker for permanency. A fluent reader has formed permanent and perfect models of words in his automatic word form system for reading. The children most likely to develop fluency following an intervention are the boys and girls who receive proven early intervention and, optimally, prevention services in kindergarten or first grade. For children who are already experiencing reading problems, improvements are most likely to be maintained following the evidence-based programs I have recommended that are taught by a knowledgeable teacher, attended for a sufficient period of time, and provided with greater intensity (in an individual or small group setting). More intense interventions mean more exposure to print and more opportunities to practice reading words, the critical prerequisites to developing fluency.

When should a reading program be discontinued?

In general, when a child is just gaining momentum in reading is the time for an all-out push and never the time for an abrupt halt.

Simply teaching a child how to sound out words without providing him with practice in applying this skill to reading will likely result in a child who can sound out some words but has difficulty reading the many new words he comes across as he progresses in his studies. He will not be a fluent reader, and reading will remain effortful. Left alone, he will avoid reading. So this is the time to maintain the same level of intensity and quality of instruction while targeting fluency as well.

To repeat: A child should not be removed from an effective reading program until he is able to read words and passages *fluently* at his grade level. Fortunately, standardized tests such as the Test of Word Reading Efficiency (TOWRE) now make it possible to assess a child's efficiency in reading individual words, while other tests such as the Gray Oral Reading Tests-4 (GORT-4) measure his ability to read passages fluently aloud (see Chapter 13). The GORT-4 provides a standardized assessment of a child's oral reading accuracy, rate, and comprehension. A child may read isolated words efficiently but still struggle to read words when they are connected together in a passage—a much more demanding task. Request the results of your child's performance on both of these tests and discuss them with appropriate teachers before making any decision to remove him from a special reading program.

Has anyone evaluated the effectiveness of public school programs generally used to teach reading to dyslexic students?

Yes, and in general, public school programs for children with reading disability are failures. As it was for Sam, the designation *special education* per se is insufficient. Parents of a reading-disabled child must carefully examine the specifics of their child's reading intervention.

Special-education programs tend to stabilize the degree of reading failure rather than close the gap between a dyslexic student and his classmates. The evidence is overwhelming. One study that examined children's reading before and after they spent three years in a resource room as part of special education found no changes in word reading scores relative to their peers and a significant *decline* in their performance on measures of reading comprehension. Findings from another study echoed these results; fourth and fifth graders receiving special education showed virtually no change in their rate of reading growth compared to their rate of growth when attending regular classes previously. It is not surprising to learn, therefore, that researchers observing the daily activities in resource rooms confirmed that the reading programs the children were receiving lacked essential elements found in effective interventions, such as intensity and small size (groups were from five to nineteen children). Furthermore, there was minimal individualization even though the children varied widely in their reading skills. To make matters worse, since such children are pulled out of their regular classroom instruction, they often miss the language arts teaching taking place in their absence. The result is that the most needy students tend to receive the *least* reading and language instruction.

Studies examining "inclusion classrooms," where children receive special reading help within their own regular classes, show similar findings: Children demonstrate little change in their reading ability relative to their classmates. On the other hand, studies show that children receiving the new scientifically based programs made large and lasting reading gains, far surpassing their previous rate of growth. With the implementation of the Reading First legislation, I am optimistic that far fewer children will require special education and those who do will benefit from the scientifically based programs that I have recommended.

What is the role of the computer in teaching a dyslexic child to read?

To date, computers have had their greatest impact in reinforcing classroom teaching. Digitized books with synthetic speech, speech recognition software, and engaging graphics and animation provide potential support for effective reading programs. With talking books available on CD-ROM, for example, children can select either specific words or phrases or entire pages to be read aloud to them by the computer. For the time being, though, parents and teachers should be cautious about relying on highly promoted computer software as a *primary* source for teaching reading. However, there are some serious computer programs that are worth looking into.

The Read, Write & Type! Learning System produced by Talking Fingers (RWT), which was discussed earlier, provides systematic, explicit instruction in basic phonologic skills and emphasizes writing as a route to reading. Results with at-risk first graders are impressive in at least one study. Working in groups of three, children who received such computer support over the course of a school year significantly improved both their reading accuracy and their fluency. Using RWT, the researchers said, would result in only about 2 to 4 percent of children leaving first grade as poor readers.

RWT also demonstrates that as early as first grade, children can successfully learn keyboarding skills. These skills provide a foundation for other activities such as word processing. This is particularly important for dyslexic readers, many of whom have poor handwriting (and spelling) and "write" much better with a keyboard than a pencil.

Colorado researchers Barbara Wise and Richard Olson studied a group of children with reading disabilities in grades two through five who received part of their instruction via an individualized computer program. The results of this computer-based instruction administered in groups where the ratio of teacher to students was 1:3 were comparable with those obtained in other noncomputer studies where the ratio was 1:1. The intervention was relatively short-term, lasting only forty hours. Unfortunately, in this study, gains were not maintained when the children were tested one and two years later. The question remains as to whether more intensive or longer-duration computer-based instruction will result in the instruction taking hold after the intervention has ended.

In summing up the evidence about computer instruction, the National Reading Panel said, "It is extremely difficult to make specific instructional conclusions based on the small sample of experimental research available." The bottom line: The jury is still out on the efficacy of computer instruction to teach reading, although there is no question that it is an excellent practice tool.

How does my dyslexic child best learn content? What can I tell his teacher to facilitate his learning?

A dyslexic student's route to learning is through meaning; meaning provides a framework for remembering. More than for others, he must fully understand a topic; rote memory does not work well for him. Focus on concepts and real-life examples and experiences, and provide many opportunities for practice. In this top-down, big-picture approach, teach ideas first, establish categories for different groups of facts, and point out connections within and between categories. Look for opportunities for hands-on experiences; encourage visualization of concepts and facts mentioned in texts or during class discussions. Keep in mind that though it may take longer to acquire, knowledge gained through meaning is much more enduring than that obtained through rote memorization.

Motivation is critical to learning and can be strengthened by adhering to a few simple principles: First, any child, and particularly one who is dyslexic, needs to know that his teacher cares about him. Second, motivation is increased by a child's having a sense of control, such as a choice about assignments—which book he will read or what topic he will report on. Third, he needs some recognition of how hard he is working as well as tangible evidence that all his effort makes a difference; this can come in the form of improvement on a graph of his fluency rates or receiving a grade on the content of his written work rather than its form.

Are recordings and videos helpful?

There is an almost infinite variety of books and magazines on tape and CD-ROM provided by Recording for the Blind and Dyslexic (RFB&D), available at rfbd.org (more about this in Chapter 23). They allow a dyslexic child to follow along with classroom assignments that he cannot easily read. The same can be said of videotapes of novels or plays; viewing these first provides a schema or structure to which the child can attach details of the story. Once a child has viewed the video and grasped the gist of the story, he is often able to read a book that might otherwise have proved too difficult. Dyslexic children, in particular, do best when they have the big picture in mind—the full story and the individual characters. This is where the dyslexic reader can apply his conceptual abilities and his rich vocabulary to the context around a word and get to its meaning and pronunciation.

What books or stories can I read to a dyslexic child?

While a child is still struggling with reading, it helps to spend even as little as fifteen to twenty minutes each evening reading aloud to him; this can be either a story or a chapter of a book. *Hey! Listen to This: Stories to Read Aloud,* edited by Jim Trelease, includes a particularly enjoyable collection of stories for children aged five to nine (grades kindergarten to four). *Read All About It!* by the same author is intended for preteens and teens. Listening to stories will help a child retain his interest in reading and in books, and will expose him to the vocabulary and ideas he would be getting himself if he were reading. Keep in mind that a dyslexic child's ability to understand what he hears is often years ahead of his ability to read.

Are there any simple, more general strategies that a dyslexic child can use to help himself in his reading?

The most helpful overall strategy teaches a child what to do when he comes across an unknown or difficult word. As mentioned earlier, he is taught to look at the letters making up the word. In practice the child is encouraged to sound out as much of the word as he can, and then a little later he is taught to find a word that sounds like it and also makes sense in the context of the sentence. A teacher plays an important role in transferring this skill to the disabled reader. She first guides the child to read by blending the sounds or by analogy to a word he already knows, and then checking if its meaning is correct. With time and practice the child becomes increasingly independent in his ability to try out different strategies and to monitor his own reading. Once his support is taken away, it is always wise to make frequent checks to ensure that the child is continuing to apply his newly learned strategies.

For a struggling reader who cannot decipher many of the words on a line, the tendency is to lose one's place and end up on another line reading something that makes little sense. A child's simple habit of running his finger across the line of print as he reads keeps him from skipping words or lines. In general, for finger pointing to be effective, a child must be able to at least sound out the initial letter(s) as he reads aloud. When the child is older, he can use a ruler or other straight-edged object.

Does the "sea of strengths" factor into how a dyslexic child will respond to a reading intervention?

Once a child has broken the reading code and begins to encounter more complex words, the child's reasoning, and especially her verbal abilities, play an increasingly important role in determining how well she responds to reading instruction. While a child's overall cognitive ability may not influence her acquiring phoneme awareness or grasping phonics, her verbal and reasoning skills are likely to impact on how well she is able to transfer her phonetic skills to reading real words and to comprehending what she reads. A child with a deeper file box of vocabulary words, a larger storehouse of worldly knowledge, and sharper reasoning skills will be in a better position to identify an unfamiliar printed word, especially if it is in a story where she can use the context around the word to help figure it out.

Just as the phonologic weakness is amenable to effective interventions, the child's strengths can also be built up and fortified. Vocabularies can be enriched and worldly knowledge can be expanded. It is particularly important for a dyslexic child—who so relies on such knowledge and who is not able to obtain it as much from reading—to be provided with both explicit instruction in vocabulary (see Chapter 17 and also pages 274 and 276) and with the full range of life experiences such as trips to museums, travel, visual aids (maps and globes), educational videos and books on tape, family discussions, and the development of hobbies and special interests that will make words and the world come alive to her.

Do successful interventions affect only reading? Are there ripple effects extending to other areas?

Researchers have noticed improvements in other areas following exposure to effective reading programs. Children show impressive growth, for example, in their general language skills. In addition to the children's improved reading, this is thought to reflect the richness of the teacher-student verbal interchanges when children repeatedly are asked to think about what they read, to clarify, or to justify their responses. This increase is particularly impressive since children who are identified as having a reading disability often show a decline in their language skills during elementary and middle school. Performance on tests of memory and rapid naming increase, too.

What is the best approach to summer vacation time? Should a dyslexic child receive reading tutoring, or should he be allowed to have an entirely stress-free period?

Dyslexic children are at high risk for losing reading skills that are not continually practiced. They have not yet established permanent neural models of words, and so their word models remain fragile and unstable and may dissipate over a summer of disuse. I recommend that children receive some tutoring over the summer or read aloud regularly with a parent. If a child is severely behind, he should receive substantial tutoring (two hours, two to three mornings a week) in basic skills for much but not all of the summer. Local schools and universities often sponsor summer reading clinics that are worth looking into. Other readers who are more advanced but not yet fluent benefit greatly from practicing reading aloud. Reading aloud from books on a summer reading list and getting a jump-start on tackling the books to be read in the fall term are often extremely helpful. Before the spring term ends, try to obtain a reading list for next year's classes. Summer is a good time to order books on tape or to scan (digitize) books to be read when school resumes in the fall (see Chapter 23). But by all means allow your child to have some fun during the summer. Do not make school a never-ending year-round experience; having fun and spending time doing what he enjoys and is good at is essential, too.

Children and teenagers are not the only ones who struggle to read. Adults who are out of school still experience the consequences of dyslexia. And in the next chapter I will discuss the kinds of successful approaches and programs that help adults of all ages who have reading difficulties.

20

Helping Adults
Become Better Readers

There is no deadline or age limit for when a person can learn to read. Research attests to the plasticity of the human brain and its ability to reshape itself in mature adults as it does in children. There are many dyslexic adults who are out of school and working or in retirement who simply want to learn to read or have more focused goals related to their work or to pursuing a high school equivalency (General Education Development, or GED) diploma. Such adults face a serious challenge but one that can be met successfully.

Lack of literacy is a major national concern—almost one-quarter of adults in this country cannot read a simple passage such as a newspaper article and answer questions about it. Interestingly, surveys report that many limited readers perceive themselves as reading well and rarely having to ask for help. This may explain why only a small percentage of adults who have limited reading ability (less than 10 percent) are enrolled in adult literacy programs.

Any adult (no matter how old or young he is) who cannot read or who struggles to read should participate in a literacy program. It will turn his life around. Literacy skills are critical in providing options for training, jobs, and careers. In trade schools, for example, students are expected to read course manuals written at tenth grade levels or higher. In fact, in the coming years the vast majority of new jobs will require a twelfth grade reading level. The ability to read impacts the quality of everyday life. Printed materials we read every day require a surprisingly high level of reading: A Friendly's menu, instructions on an ATM, and the Internal Revenue Service EZ form are all written at a tenth grade level. To allow someone to enter adulthood and remain a very limited reader is to sentence him to second-class citizenry.

Adults with reading problems are a diverse group. At the most basic levels, some have a severe reading disability and received inadequate or no specialized reading help. Others were identified but received limited help. They learned to decode, perhaps, but did not receive the supervised reading practice necessary for fluency, so their reading skills are tenuous and they do not read for pleasure or information. Some of these students dropped out of school and are now aiming for a (GED) diploma.

Happily, highly effective programs for addressing such reading difficulties are capable of significantly improving a reader's skills, sometimes as much as the equivalent of three years of reading proficiency over the course of one year. More commonly the equivalent of at least one year's improvement is observed for each six months of instruction, depending on the intensity of instruction and the severity of the reading problem. And so while addressing the problem early is ideal, it is never too late to learn to read.

Just as for children, there has been a sea change in the approach to adults with reading problems, beginning with placement in the appropriate level. Rather than a global test of reading, more up-to-date literacy programs give adults a placement test to determine their exact level in different reading skills and to detect specific gaps in their reading development. While children who are poor readers have not learned the foundational skills, adults, in contrast, may have acquired a smattering of some skills while totally lacking others. And so placement testing is especially important for older disabled readers since each is invariably starting from a different point and typically shows an uneven and unpredictable pattern of reading skills. Keep in mind that the goal is to match the instruction as closely as possible with the adult's needs. Teachers (and adult students, too) tend to overestimate an adult's reading ability and are often shocked to see the results of the testing.

Ideally, the reading instruction is research-based, systematic, and delivered in small group settings. Adults in particular do well with group instruction (with a well-trained teacher). It's engaging, highly motivating, socializing, and effective. Adults benefit from learning from one another. Optimally, this instruction occurs four times a week, for one and a half to two hours per session. Some successful programs meet twice weekly but for longer periods, such as three hours each session. Consistency is critical since attendance is one of the few factors associated with better progress.

Adults are particularly sensitive to issues of consistency and duration of instruction. Adults work during the day or may have young children (the majority of students in adult reading programs are between sixteen and thirty), and it is often difficult to get to class more than twice a week. Long intervals between classes and lack of practice reading at home represent real barriers to more rapid progress. Adult students can expect to increase their reading one grade level for every one hundred or so hours of instruction; clearly, the more hours per week, the faster the improvement. So maximizing the amount of instructional time in class and, particularly, practice at home is very important.

For teaching adults, I recommend these: *Language!*, the *Wilson Reading System*, and *Starting Over*. All three programs are derived from the principles of the evidence-based Orton-Gillingham approach discussed in Chapter 19. *Language!* provides the broadest coverage, encompassing just about every aspect of language instruction while also managing to integrate nicely the different language components. As you now know, each of the units of study has been rated according to its level of reading difficulty and assigned a "readability" code based on the Degrees of Reading Power (DRP) formula. Once a student knows his reading level in *Language!* it is linked to a DRP score and to vast numbers of appropriate books. A student in the *Language!* program is now able to access ten thousand books in fifteen categories, including adventure, sports, science fiction, history, biography, science, and mystery. Without such a system, pinpointing a book's level of readability is often more difficult than you might think. Imagine how nice it is for an adult reader to be able to find a book that interests him and to know that he can read it. Although developed for teaching entire classes, *Language!* easily lends itself to small group instruction where it is likely to achieve even better results.

The *Wilson Reading System*, also discussed in Chapter 19, uses manipulatives (that is, cards with letters and a finger-tapping procedure) to teach phonics and word analysis skills systematically while stressing fluency, incorporating spelling, and providing engaging materials for adults to read. The program is designed to be taught in a one-to-one setting or in small groups. It typically requires one to three years to complete and is very well received by teachers and adult students. Another program, *Starting Over* (www.epsbooks.com), was developed primarily for mature men and women, particularly those attending adult basic education classes. Adults enter the program following an in-depth interview and assessment. They are introduced to the basic sound structure of language, including phonological awareness and letter-sound relationships; there is also instruction in handwriting, composition, spelling, vocabulary, and comprehension. While there are no texts or stories specifically associated with the program, teachers are encouraged to make use of all sorts of printed materials, including newspapers, dictionaries, and telephone books. Even the highest-level readers, who are reading at a fifth or sixth grade level, will require at least one year to develop into competent, independent readers; many students require about three years. In addition, adults wanting to practice their reading skills will find helpful a software program called *Lexia Reading SOS* (*Strategies for the Older Student*) (www.lexialearning.com). It follows the Orton-Gillingham method used by all three reading programs and provides practice in a wide range of reading skills that extend from letter-sound linkages to applying strategies for multisyllabic word analysis to learning the meanings of roots, prefixes, and suffixes. *Lexia* is intended as a supplement, not a total reading program.

In one very successful adult education program in Connecticut, Read to Succeed, students attend a two-hour session four evenings a week. Intensity is stressed; students may not miss more than thirteen days annually (in addition to a four-week vacation). Progress is often remarkable, with some adults achieving a twelfth grade (or higher) level of reading proficiency. Many students come with work-related concerns. Carmine Lombardi, for example, a talented forty-three-year-old appliance repairman, had to improve his reading skills when his company began using new computer technology. Today, repair work is based less on mechanical aptitude than on the ability to read. Most new washers and dryers are now manufactured with computer chips that provide detailed printouts of a machine's inner workings. As a result, all diagnostic work is based on the ability of the repairman to read and interpret schematics and other written information provided by the computer.

Although a high school graduate, Carmine was barely able to read.

With the support of his company he enrolled, attended classes diligently for three years, and is now reading at a high school level. Carmine can hardly contain his joy in describing how becoming a reader has changed his life. Not only has he received several promotions at work, but his everyday life has benefited in many ways as well. At a recent breakfast with his colleagues, an article in a local newspaper lying on the table caught his eye. Since it concerned a friend, he began reading it aloud. As he describes it, "Reading aloud in front of my colleagues [was] a very exciting thing for me to do. I called my wife to tell her about it." Now, for the first time in his life, on his own, he is able to read and select a birthday card for his wife, fill out medical record forms in a physician's office, and complete entry forms to participate in his beloved hobby of motocross racing. Previously he would go to the track, ask for an entry form, and with much embarrassment take it, fold it, place it in his pocket, and with head down quickly walk out the door, hoping that "none of the guys noticed." His wife would complete the form for him at home later. This has all changed; now he can "read any word." He continues to attend the night classes where he often teaches new tutors how to pronounce the sounds of different letter groups. In the future he envisions attending community college and taking courses in computer repair.

Another adult I came to know enrolled in a program in large part because she wanted to be able to read bedtime stories to her new granddaughter. Another student had longed to be able to read aloud in her Bible study class. Each succeeded in reaching her goal.

If you know someone who could benefit from further reading instruction, there are a number of things you can do to help. For example, there are more materials than ever for adults with limited reading skills, including a weekly newspaper, *News for You* (www.news-for-you. com), published by the New Readers Press, a division of Laubach Literacy International, and *Thumbprint Mysteries*, a collection of thirty easy-to-read books written in conjunction with the Mystery Writers of America, available from McGraw-Hill Contemporary Publishing (mhcontemporary.com). More and more libraries now have special collections of books that are of high interest to adults and can be read by those with lower-level reading skills; ask your local librarian about them. For details about joining a program or for more general information about literacy programs for adults, I suggest contacting the Literacy Directory at www.literacydirectory.org, telephoning your State Department of Education and asking for the adult education division, or visiting your local public library and asking for a state directory (some libraries also serve as sites for literacy programs).

I should add that the General Education Development (GED) diploma is meant for students who did not graduate from high school but want to pursue further education or jobs that require a high school diploma or its equivalent. Obtaining a diploma requires passing a rigorous examination. Revised in 2002, it covers five areas: reading, timed writing components, social studies, science, and mathematics. It calls for the reading skills and academic knowledge of someone who has passed the twelfth grade. Students preparing for the GED may enroll in literacy classes first to bring their reading levels up, and then register for practice classes focusing specifically on the components of the GED. Accommodations are granted for those who require extra time. For more information contact the official Web site of the GED Testing Service at www.gedtest.org.

Adult education teachers can often customize their instruction. A growing number of companies and unions are sponsoring such targeted reading instruction at the workplace itself. Participation is highly motivating; for example, instruction focused on the most common words found in work-related materials can allow a worker to function more easily at his job or help him move on to the next level, as Carmine did. These programs are short but intense, ranging from thirty to sixty hours over an eight-to-ten-week period. Tom Sticht, who developed highly successful literacy programs for the army in the 1970s, believes that such work-related programs are especially effective because of their relevancy to the person's life goals—a student quickly experiences tangible results, such as reading a cookbook if he wants to be a chef or a plumbing manual if he wants to repair pipes.

The stakes for literacy are higher than they've ever been. In our increasingly technical society it's all about print: instructional manuals for the workplace, for computers, for cars, for putting together children's toys; directions for travel or for work, for taking medications, for making up baby formulas, for safety, for voting; for messages via the mail, e-mail, the Internet, pager, and fax. Learning to read opens the door to a better, brighter future. Given the effective programs to teach reading at all levels of reading ability and at all ages, it is truly never too late to learn to read.

21

Choosing a School

For all parents, choosing the right school for their child is a high priority. This is even more so for a child with a reading disability. There are so many questions to be answered: Which school will have the best reading program? Does that school have equally strong history and science teachers? Will there be opportunities for pursuing your son's strengths in mathematics and for exploring his interest in photography as well as for dealing with his reading problem? Where will he be most appreciated and understood? What kind of children will his friends be? Does the school have a good sports program since he loves playing soccer?

Most parents I know prefer to have their child attend the local public school. But as I've said, the typical public school special education program does little to move a dyslexic child forward. Sam's experience illustrated that. On balance, public schools are generally slow to identify a reading problem, provide too little instruction, and, worst of all, often use unproven and incomplete programs taught by teachers who may know little about teaching reading.

On the other hand, there is much to be said for having a child remain in his local school. Public schools generally offer much more diversity than can be found in a private school setting. This diversity extends to the composition of the student body, to the possibilities for choice within the curriculum, and to the opportunities for participation in important nonacademic activities such as sports, music, and art. Public schools are also free.

It would not take much to vastly improve public school education for a child with a reading disability. Reform is occurring across the country. Schools can be opened up to new ideas, they can change, and they can successfully institute effective educational programs. Parents and teachers can use the information in this book together with the Report of the National Reading Panel to bring evidence-based reading instruction to every child's classroom. Particularly with the impetus of the Reading First legislation, evidence-based interventions will soon become a widespread reality for struggling readers, teachers will come to expect success from their reading-disabled students, and children will benefit enormously.

The availability of special education is by itself, of course, no guarantee that a child is receiving an appropriate education. Parents must always be vigilant to ensure that their child is receiving the most effective reading instruction, that it is integrated with his other academic subjects, and that his strengths are not overlooked.

There may be instances when it is in the best interests of the child for him to change schools. If you have tried a public school setting and (1) the school has provided a special reading program but your child is still lagging behind, or (2) after much effort the school still has not organized a coherent program and your child is falling behind, or (3) the constant battle to have the school provide promised services is adversely affecting your family, then serious consideration should be given to changing schools.

Selecting that new school represents a critical juncture for parents. Jack and Inez Johnson were at this point when they came to see me. Their son, Eddie, was the spitting image of his large, bearlike, ruddy-faced father. Eddie had begun his schooling in a private day school in a suburb of New York City. As is often the case, Jack and Inez had complex reasons for sending Eddie to private school. On the surface it seemed obvious that this was *the* school to go to if you were smart and your parents could afford it. His father longed to give Eddie the kind of education he never had.

Jack, the managing partner of a large law firm, knew what it was like to have reading problems. As a child and until this very day, reading was and is a struggle for him. At first Jack rejoiced in Eddie's advanced vocabulary and quickness at solving math problems, and his general brightness in the preschool years, and enrolled him in private school. Once there, Eddie was not the academic star his parents imagined he might be. Perhaps it was just a period of adjustment, they thought. He's a boy, and boys are slower to adjust. Knowing deep down what they could not outwardly admit, they set about creating a safety net for their son. They hired a tutor. Eddie went to school from eight to four; then after dinner he worked with his tutor or with one of his parents. The days were very long, and it was a losing battle: Eddie was in free fall, heading for the bottom of his class. The school itself was deaf to his needs. "He must buckle down and work harder," the headmistress told Eddie's parents. At age ten Eddie was seriously reading-disabled. He was facing daily what seemed to him an avalanche of new words, long, complicated, multisyllabic words; he could no longer get by with just memorization. The only saving grace was that Eddie was a star soccer player.

Worn down by their nightly homework sessions with Eddie and concerned about his increasingly gloomy persona, Jack and Inez came to the Yale Center. After discussing Eddie's evaluation and his needs for specialized reading instruction, we talked about school options: special education in a public school, another independent day school, or a school specializing in educating children with reading or other learning difficulties. We talked about the benefits and costs associated with each type of school.

Many parents turn to independent day schools because they find the local public schools wanting. Private schools offer smaller classes and potentially more opportunity for individualization. Discipline tends to be firmer, and the students have a greater chance of going on to college. Of course, like public schools, the day schools vary in quality. At their very best such schools can provide a constructive refuge for a child like Eddie. If the administration and faculty are willing, a small private school can provide the bricks and mortar of an effective program for improving reading. Relative smallness can also bring with it a sense of intimacy in getting to know the student and in providing him with a supportive network of encouragement throughout the school.

A growing number of nontraditional smaller private schools pride themselves on innovation and on serving the individual needs of each student. These boutique schools fill an important niche for parents because they incorporate in their programs cutting-edge educational research while developing the child's interests in diverse areas such as science, drama, art, and music. Such private schools are increasing in number, but in my experience, they are still the exception. For many children the options for private schooling are more likely to be country day schools or boarding schools. More often than not, these schools turn out to be a disaster for a child with a reading problem. In contrast to most public school settings, I have found that the children in private schools are more likely to be in lockstep with one another. Such schools pride themselves on uniformity, which often extends to the curriculum and to reading instruction. The lack of student diversity in this setting does not usually serve the interests of a student with a reading disability; the opportunities for innovation and for creating special programs are limited.

The experience of Kara Winsford at a school in Virginia illustrates the surprisingly icy climate that often greets children with dyslexia in private schools. As Kara's mother, Claire, told me, her daughter, who has a high IQ and an addiction to hard work, had to struggle continuously just to maintain barely passing grades. An evaluation conducted outside of the school revealed that Kara had dyslexia. The school's response was: "There is no such thing as dyslexia. She just has to work harder."

The school attempted no intervention and provided no specialized services. The school insisted Kara continue with the traditional course of study.

As Claire told me, "Kara's strengths can often obscure her weaknesses; you don't see her deficits easily or outwardly, but they take their toll." With unceasing effort Kara was able to pass her courses, though she desperately needed help. The teachers at the school were for the most part young and inexperienced, without much or often any professional training. As Claire put it, "These schools serve as a turnstile for young men and women who are often unclear about their future directions. These well-intentioned young teachers stay for a few years and then leave and go on with the course of their lives. Those who do stay often come to reflect—physically, morally, and educationally—the school's views on life itself." They feel comfortable with sameness and tradition, and are not about to question the school policies.

Oftentimes such reluctance to meet the instructional needs of a student with dyslexia reflects a school's own ignorance of reading disabilities and of the true nature of its student body. Given the high prevalence of reading difficulties, it is quite likely that there are at least two or more students with a reading impairment in each class at Kara's school. Such schools actively discourage children with learning disabilities from enrolling. It complicates things; all their graduates won't be symbols of a "flawless" education, the school's calling card.

In addition to failing to address the learning problems of many of their students, these schools often deny requests for modifications or accommodations to address a child's learning disability. Denial of a problem insulates a school from having to address it. And so, at these bastions of tradition, the newer, evidence-based reading interventions are generally not available; enriched language instruction as well as additional support for spelling and for writing are not provided. Parents who persist in requesting such modifications for their child are often treated in a demeaning manner. As Claire said to me, "If you persist in asking for these changes, your child will have to leave." In Kara's case, the school refused to allow her to identify herself as reading-disabled on her college application, and the school would not allow her to take her College Board tests with accommodations.

I doubt this is an isolated example. Still, there are private schools with quality reading programs. It is your job to assess the overall quality of the school in all its programs before enrolling your child. Moreover, if your child has already been identified as having a reading problem or you suspect one, proper testing and evaluation should be conducted before approaching any school. Identifying a problem and its nature better equips you to ask the right questions and find the best school.

As noted earlier, for the parent of a child who is dyslexic, attendance at a private school represents the belief that he will get more attention and a better education than possible in a public setting. But on another, perhaps deeper level, attendance at an independent school conveys acceptance and means the child is just like everybody else. Many parents worry that if their son or daughter attends a special school for children with reading disabilities, he or she will be removed from the mainstream of society and will not be able to participate as a full member. Society tends to view people with disabilities as not only different but as lesser individuals, often confusing a learning disability with mental slowness or retardation.

Parents like the Johnsons are often torn. Jack, having suffered both in school and in life from poor reading relative to his intellectual strengths, now wanted his son to have a better education, to be a reader. He was in favor of sending Eddie to a nearby day school for children with reading and other learning disabilities. On the other hand, the thought of Eddie attending some special school for dyslexic children frightened Inez. "Let him stay one more year at the school," she pleaded with her husband. "We'll work harder, get a better tutor. It will work out." She worried that the children at such a school would not be as bright and as sweet as Eddie. Going to a special school would mean giving up soccer, from which he gained so much positive feedback. She wanted to keep Eddie with his friends and allow him to continue playing soccer. He was so bright, she thought; surely reading would come. Jack, based on his own experience, believed that going to a special school would help Eddie develop a more positive view of himself. Inez believed that if their son were to attend such a school, his sense of self would be diminished; he would view himself as somehow defective.

The Johnsons made many inquiries, followed by visits to several schools in their area. They wavered and vacillated; they wanted so much to do what was best for Eddie. Finally, Eddie's parents settled on their priorities. The school should (1) be within commuting distance, (2) have a mixed student population rather than an entirely learning-disabled one, (3) offer a strong sports program in which their son could participate in interscholastic matches, and (4) already have in place or at least be willing to create a comprehensive educational program with an evidence-based reading intervention at its core. The Johnsons chose a setting that would emphasize Eddie's strengths—socialization with a nondisabled peer group and active participation in team sports—rather than his differences. They found a school that was primarily for typical learners but was also willing to accept a child who had a learning disability. The school's reading program was earnest and had several components that characterized evidence-based interventions; however, it was not clear if these parts would be sufficient to provide Eddie with the explicitness, practice, and intensity he required in order to become a skilled reader. We shall have to see how things progress.

There are also specialized schools for boys and girls with a reading disability. Like all schools, these vary in the quality of their instruction and in the makeup of their student body. The reader may be surprised to learn, as I was, that quite a number of highly accomplished college students spent part of their formative years at schools for children with dyslexia (in most instances two or three years). My own impression is that students with dyslexia who attend such schools are more likely to have an overall positive outcome than students who attend a traditional independent school. Schools of this type include the Eagle Hill School in Greenwich, Connecticut. I have observed classes there and met with faculty and students. Each time I visit, I come away wishing that every dyslexic boy and girl were able to experience the benefits of such a school. Although not every child succeeds totally, each child leaves with his dignity intact and a sense of competence.

To start with, a school like Eagle Hill is special because virtually all the children there, from the primary grades through high school, require help in reading; this ensures that reading-related educational needs serve as the central focus of the school's instructional program rather than being incidental or peripheral to it. There is no need to negotiate or to argue for the proper reading instruction; students receive evidence-based reading instruction that is provided with sufficient intensity and over the necessary duration. Teachers are highly knowledgeable and share a sense of camaraderie; the expectation is for success and not for failure. Faculty are encouraged to attend conferences and to keep abreast of new developments in the teaching of reading. Instruction is optimized: Children are taught in very small groups; learning language-related skills occupies a significant segment of the day; classes are coordinated around a specific theme or a child's needs; and new technologies are quickly adapted to serve the needs of the children. Each child's literacy needs and academic curriculum are fully integrated: Reading is related to writing, and writing is related to what the child is learning in literature or social studies. The science curriculum is not watered down, but difficult-to-pronounce words are reviewed before pages are assigned for reading. No child need fear that when he is called on, the class will laugh when he stumbles over words.

Early on at Eagle Hill students learn how to harness the power of the computer to help overcome their weaknesses and to allow their talents to emerge. After learning to type in the early grades, children actively use the computer for writing essays, taking notes, and generating outlines. For students who are dyslexic, committing details to memory and retrieving words can be particularly difficult and, as a result, standard oral presentations are avoided. But since these same students are often facile with the computer and quite creative, they are taught how to prepare computer PowerPoint presentations. They soon learn that they can deliver oral presentations more effectively by first making notes on the computer and then using these notes as a type of TelePrompTer as they are projected on a screen in front of the classroom. In preparing history reports or science projects, networked computer systems make it possible for the students to learn about and gain the benefits of working collaboratively with their partners.

Children also learn how to use the power of the computer to better organize themselves. For example, computers are used to deliver the homework assignments to children and to their parents, and then each student's completed homework is maintained in a separate computer file. In this way assignments are not lost or confused.

Although many parents, like Inez Johnson, shy away from such schools because they are fearful of its effects on their child's self-esteem, my opinion is that the result is often just the reverse. I believe that, even more than improvements in reading, the most important long-term benefit of being a student at such a school may well be its positive influence on a child's self-esteem. Building self-esteem is essential for later success. Attending a school where you are in the majority represents a very different kind of experience for boys and girls who are reading-disabled. They can relax. They no longer need to hide or cover up their learning problems. They also meet bright people like themselves. It is akin to looking in the mirror and liking what you see. Students are often pleasantly surprised to find others who share their experiences and concerns. They also learn that they do not have to like all people who have a reading disability; like everyone else, such individuals run the gamut of personalities and traits. Because these students are in a supportive environment, they can learn about and practice the self-advocacy skills they will need when they are in other settings. Typically, as I said, children spend two or three years at such a school and then either return to their local public school or to a nonspecialized private school. Explicit plans are made to help ensure that the child makes a successful transition.

Without the pressures often found at other places, children at schools like Eagle Hill have the opportunity to grow and to discover who they are. They develop a self-awareness of the full range of their skills, their strengths as well as their weaknesses. At the Windward School, for example, students participate in a course about learning disabilities and develop insights into their own characteristics as learners. Contrary to the view that enrollment at a special school is a sign of defeat, attendance at such a school may be the initial step in a student's pathway to success. In fact, one of the first dyslexic students I encountered at Yale had attended the Charles Armstrong School. A recent newsletter from this school highlights students who are National Merit finalists and who attend prestigious colleges. Such successes answer the question of how these students do in the "real world."

In truth, there is no one perfect school environment that will suit every child with a reading problem and his family. The perfect school does not exist; each school is going to have pluses and minuses. The key in selecting a school is to determine which school's profile best matches you and your child's priorities at a particular point in time. And your priorities will change as a child goes on in school. In grade one, for example, your priority may be for your child to learn to read; later on, when the child is in grade nine, the provision of accommodations such as extra time on exams and participation in a team sport may be most critical.

Once you have determined your priorities, it is important that you know not only about each type of school but about the specific schools you are considering. To help you collect and organize the relevant information, I have provided a list of steps to take and a checklist of questions to ask about each school under consideration. (Clearly, not every parent has to ask every question; you must choose the questions that are important to you and your child.) In addition, by reading through these questions you may learn about the range of possible programs and services that a school could potentially offer to your child.

Ask as many people as you can about the school.

Find out as much as you can about the school from friends and neighbors. Try to speak to parents whose children already attend or are graduates of the school. Parents whose children are no longer in the school but who have attended recently are usually the ones who are the most frank.

Visit the school.

Before deciding on any school, public or private, parents and then the child should visit. Ask yourself:

- What is the overall environment like?
- Do the children seem happy?
- Is there a sense of orderliness?
- Are the teachers and administrators open and friendly, and do they welcome questions?

Find out how the school views itself.

Most schools have a mission statement; find out what the school envisions as its goals.

- Does the school have a policy regarding children with disabilities?
- What proportion of children at the school have a learning disability?
- What has the school's experience been with such children?

Observe several classes in session.

Focus on the classes your child might attend. Imagine how he would react, socially and emotionally as well as educationally, to being in this group. During such a visit, force yourself to keep in mind your child as he is, as opposed to your imagined, idealized child. Spend as much time in the school as you can. It often takes a while to get a feel for a school, and your impression may change over the course of a day as you see more.

Learn about the students who attend the school.

- Is it diverse (socially, ethnically, educationally) or homogeneous?
- What is the most common reason students come to this school?
- How severe are the reading problems found among the students?
- What are their general abilities?
- What is the prevalence of serious behavior problems among the students?
- Do the children live nearby?
- How long does the average child remain at the school?
- Where do the children go after they leave the school?
- How many of the students go on to college, and which schools?

Learn about the school's academic curriculum and its reading program.

Once you have a general sense of the school and its students, ask about the instruction provided in reading and in other academic areas. Try to obtain specific answers about the bricks (the program's content) and mortar (the explicitness, intensity, and quality of the instruction) that make up the reading program. (You can refer to Chapter 18 to refresh yourself on the essential elements of an effective reading program.)

- What specific reading programs or methods are used, and are they evidence-based?
- Since effective programs teach children phonemic awareness and phonics, fluency, vocabulary, and reading comprehension, ask if these are elements of the program.
  - Are these elements taught systematically and explicitly?
  - Are decodable booklets used for beginning readers?
  - Do these children regularly read aloud under supervision?
  - How is fluency encouraged? Is it measured; if so, how regularly? (You can refer to Chapter 19 to refresh yourself about teaching fluency.)
  - What is done to promote the growth of a child's vocabulary?
  - Are specific comprehension strategies taught?
  - Is there a specific writing program?
  - How large are the classes?
  - How are the students grouped?
  - How is instruction individualized to fit each child's needs?
- What approach is taken with older students who are bright but cannot easily read texts in different subject areas?
  - How is reading instruction integrated with other academic work?
- Are there provisions for hands-on or experiential learning, that is, learning through doing?
- Are there opportunities for advanced work in art, math, or science?
- How is technology used? (While it is important to have the newest computers and software programs, it is even more important that computers do not take the place of teachers in providing first-line instruction.)
- Are students able to use a laptop computer for taking notes and for writing compositions in class?
  - How is a student's progress in reading tracked?
  - How is the information obtained from these tests used?
- Is there a formal course or ongoing support for developing organizational and study skills?
- How is a child helped to keep track of his daily homework and long-term assignments?
  - Are self-advocacy skills taught and practiced?

Find out about the school's attitude toward providing accommodations (such as extra time on tests).

- Is there a faculty member with expertise (or interest) who coordinates services for students with a reading disability?
- Are students provided with accommodations, and if so, what kinds?
- Does the school work with books on tape from Recording for the Blind and Dyslexic (see Chapter 23)?
- Are dyslexic students allowed extra time on their examinations?
- Can examinations be written on a computer?
- What is the policy concerning foreign languages, and are waivers granted?

Learn about the faculty.

- Are any of the teachers reading specialists?
- How available are the faculty for students who require extra help?
- Does the faculty in this regard have an open-door policy, specific office hours, or availability after school?
- Who is responsible for monitoring and tracking each child's progress?
- How does the faculty communicate and update one another on each child's progress?
- How are parents kept informed of their child's progress?
- How long have the teachers typically been at the school?

Learn about what extracurricular activities are offered.

- Are there team sports, and if so, which ones?
- Do the teams play in interscholastic leagues, and if so, which ones?
- What are the opportunities for exploration of other interests and skills?
- Is there an art program?
- Is there a photography program?
- Is there a drama program?
- Is there equipment and a studio for video recording?
- Is there a school radio station?

- Is there a music program?
- Is there a school orchestra or band?

At the risk of repetition, let me summarize the advantages and disadvantages associated with each choice of school.

Public schools

Public schools allow a child to interact with a diverse group of children and to participate in a range of local activities. They are convenient and free. On the downside, there is no evidence that most current special education reading programs in public schools close the gap. (As I have been indicating, this may be changing with the implementation of the new Reading First legislation, which provides financial incentives for schools to use evidence-based reading programs.) If your local school is willing to provide an evidence-based intervention (perhaps using Sam's program as a guide), to integrate your child's reading needs with the remainder of his academic subjects, and to regularly monitor his reading progress, it is certainly worth a try. As school systems and educators become aware of evidence-based interventions, schools should increase their receptivity to developing more effective reading programs. Six months or a semester represents a reasonable trial period. It is long enough to see positive results if they are going to occur and short enough not to inflict permanent harm on your child. Above all, don't wait any longer if you are troubled by the results. If you have the resources and your child is floundering, consider an alternate school.

Private independent schools

If you have your heart set on sending your child to an independent day school, it is important that you learn about the school's attitude toward children with reading problems. Explicitly ask the school how it addresses the needs of dyslexic children. Private schools generally do not offer specialized reading programs for such children. They vary in their understanding, and in the availability, of accommodations. They may offer advanced science or computer courses for those students who have the interest and the ability. Extracurricular activities and social activities are often a strength.

Specialized schools for children with dyslexia

If a child has a severe reading disability and his parents have the financial resources, there is no question that a specialized school should be seriously considered. In fact, these schools should also be given consideration for children with less severe reading disabilities—those who, like Kara, fall between the cracks. These children often struggle unnoticed and unassisted when they could benefit from the enrichment of their reading skills and the building of self-esteem that a specialized school offers. Here is a list of recommended schools of this type:

The Charles Armstrong School	Belmont, California
The Park Century School	Los Angeles, California
The Summit School	Los Angeles, California
The Prentice School	Santa Ana, California
The Eagle Hill School	Greenwich, Connecticut
The Eagle Hill-Southport School	Southport, Connecticut
The Forman School	Litchfield, Connecticut
The Vanguard School	Lake Wales, Florida
Atlanta Speech School	Atlanta, Georgia
The Schenck School	Atlanta Georgia
The Assets School	Honolulu, Hawaii
Brehm Preparatory	East Carbondale, Illinois
The Cove School	Northbrook, Illinois
Jemicy School	Owings Mills, Maryland
The Carroll School	Lincoln, Massachusetts
The Landmark School	Prides Crossing, Massachusetts
The Churchill School	St. Louis, Missouri
New Grange School	Trenton, New Jersey
The Kildonan School	Amenia, New York
The Churchill School	New York, New York
The Gow School	South Wales, New York
The Windward School	White Plains, New York
Marburn Academy	Columbus, Ohio
The Benchmark School	Media, Pennsylvania
The Hamilton School at Wheeler	Providence, Rhode Island
Trident Academy	Mt. Pleasant, South Carolina
The Greenwood School	Putney, Vermont
The Lab School of Washington	Washington, D.C.

In the final analysis, my advice is to acquire all the information you can and weigh all the factors—but also value your gut feeling. Your overall impression of the school is important and may provide a clue about intangibles that are difficult to characterize but may be extremely meaningful to you and your child. Schools can look very good on paper, but somehow not have the parts come together in a satisfactory way. Just because you can't easily put your gut feeling into words, do not dismiss it. Trust your instincts.

22

Protecting and Nourishing Your Child's Soul

In addition to providing the loving and nurturing that comes naturally with parenting, parents (and teachers, too) of children with reading problems should make their number one goal the preservation of their child's self-esteem. This is the area of greatest vulnerability for children who are dyslexic. Teachers and parents often hold high expectations for a child who is harboring a hidden disability and then are surprised, disappointed, or even angry when the child does not perform well in school. If he is accused often of not working hard enough, of not being motivated, or of not really being that smart after all, the child soon begins to doubt himself. The enormous effort and extraordinary perseverance he must expend just to keep up seems to have no payoff. That is why it is critical for parents, teachers, and, ultimately, the child to understand the nature of his reading problem in order to help him develop a positive sense of himself.

An unwavering commitment to the intrinsic value of a child with dyslexia is essential. Every child with a reading difficulty is invariably going to endure ups and downs in his school experiences. So, early on, each child needs to know that no matter what, he can always count on his parents for unconditional support. All dyslexics who have become successful by any account share in common the unfailing love and support of their parent(s) or, occasionally, a teacher or a spouse. Such supportive parents are always ready to be there for the child where and when he needs it—in seeking an accurate diagnosis and then an effective intervention; in helping to ensure that school is a positive experience; in exposing him to the world so that his reading difficulties do not prevent him from learning about it; and in reading with him and, perhaps, for him. They constantly remind their child of his value as a person.

There are a number of specific steps you can take to build your child's self-image. The first is to let him know the nature of his reading problem. Children are greatly relieved to learn why they have so much difficulty reading. There are certain facts you should share with a child when he first finds out he has dyslexia:

- Tell him that his difficulty has a name, *dyslexia.*
- Tell him dyslexia is a problem that intelligent people have with reading. You can actually use our model of the reading difficulty surrounded by a sea of strengths, appropriate to the child's age and level of understanding. Drawing it helps.
- Reassure him that dyslexia has nothing to do with how smart he is.
- Explain that his problem is caused by a difficulty in pulling apart the sounds of words; refer to them as *sticky sounds.*
- Tell him that words have sounds that come apart and that people with dyslexia have trouble pulling the sounds apart. Instead of hearing three sounds in a word, he may notice only one or two. You can use a set of blocks to make your point.
- Explain to him the kinds of problems that *sticky sounds* cause in sounding out words; confusing words that sound alike, such as *general* and *gentle;* reading aloud; and spelling as well as pronouncing words. You can tell him that some people often know the answer to a question but have a problem getting the right words out of their mouth.
- Reassure him that many children have this common problem and that it can be helped by the right teaching.
- Tell him that he will learn to read.
- Tell him about the many famous people who are smart, successful, and also dyslexic. Depending on his age and interests, these could include the late Nobel Prize–winning physicist Niels Bohr; the singer Jewel, the cartoonist of Dilbert, Scott Adams; the actor Tom Cruise; the playwright Wendy Wasserstein; the entrepreneur and founder of Virgin Airlines, Sir Richard Branson; the comedian Jay Leno; the economist

and financial expert Diane Swonk; the author of the popular children's book series "Captain Underpants," Dar Pilkey; and the rocket scientist (yes, rocket scientist) Kettler Griswold, who works on the NASA space program. Cite the stories of struggling dyslexics mentioned in this book, people who are now highly successful.

• Reassure him that his brain is normal, that there are no holes or defects in it.

• Explain to your child that the express route or highway to reading is blocked in dyslexia and that he has to take another route, the secondary, bumpier, and slower back roads. As a result, he can get to his destination, but it just takes him much longer.

After one of my patients, Phillip, shared his MRI with his third grade classmates and told them he had dyslexia, his teacher wrote me to say the children were curious about it and had the following questions (my responses follow):

What is dyslexia?
   Dyslexia means having a hard time learning to read.
When you have dyslexia will you always have it? Can it be made better?
   Children who have dyslexia can learn how to read. Sometimes it takes a while for reading to get better, but it always improves a lot.
How do you get dyslexia?
   Children get dyslexia just like they get brown or green eyes, or get to be short or tall—they are born with it.
Does dyslexia come from a virus?
   No. Dyslexia is not catching. You cannot get it from another person.
Why is it called such a funny name like dyslexia?
   The word "dyslexia" comes from the foreign (Latin) word "*dys,*" which means *difficult,* and the foreign (Greek) word "*lexia,*" which means *words;* the two parts add up to a *difficulty reading words.*

Your child may have other questions as well and you may want to tell him about a new interactive Web site, www.sparktop.org developed just for kids with dyslexia and other learning differences. This site answers questions children may have about learning, helps them recognize their strengths, encourages creativity, and connects them to other children like themselves.

Early on it is critical to help your child identify an interest or a hobby, an area in which he can have a positive experience, whether it be pure enjoyment or perhaps the ability to stand out or excel—an interest in fish or in rocks, a talent for baton twirling or juggling, skill in skating or swimming, a talent for acting or drawing, a propensity to understand science or computers, or a love of poetry or music. It doesn't matter what it is. For the writer John Irving it was his involvement and skill in wrestling that helped him endure particularly harsh experiences at school. Having an interest or athletic activity often means a child's life is not always negative or entirely about studying or catching up. It allows the child to see himself as a victor, as a competent individual who has mastery over a topic or an area. He gets to experience the feel of winning. You must encourage him to explore a range of possibilities—in school and after school, at the Y, in sports, in music, in art, in photography—and support his participation. Not every child falls in love with an activity immediately, so it is important to expose him to different possibilities and help get him through the initial rough spots when his first response may be to want to give up. Remember that stars are not born in most areas but are made after lots of practice and hard work. Praise should not be treated as a rationed item; be generous with your praise as long as it is honestly deserved. Your child will receive more than his share of criticism from the uninformed; you should see to it that he knows the soothing sounds of praise.

Encourage your child to view himself as a person who has something to say and whom people should respect. Discuss important decisions with him. These might involve issues that affect the entire family, such as where to vacation in the summer, or issues that are more personal to him. You might talk about a current events issue, such as a national, local, or school election, or about a movie or television show. Be patient and listen to him as he expresses himself. Take his comments seriously and respond to them. As he gets older, there will be many occasions when he needs to speak up and be an advocate for himself. Getting into the habit of speaking out and being heard is invaluable preparation for that. It is important for him to fully understand the nature of his reading problem and its implications so that as he goes on in school he can determine his needs for educational modifications or accommodations and feel comfortable in speaking up for himself. Role-playing with a parent, trusted teacher, or tutor can be helpful practice.

How you as a parent view your child is very important. If you feel that a diagnosis of dyslexia means that his future is doomed, he will come to feel that way, too. Having a diagnosis of dyslexia should not preclude a child from pursuing his dreams. Given adequate intelligence, skill, persistence, and support, a child who is dyslexic can pursue virtually any area that interests him. Men and women who are dyslexic have distinguished themselves in every area imaginable, including areas that the uninformed might not believe are possible for a person who is dyslexic: writing, law, medicine, science, and poetry. Children who are dyslexic should not be reflexively shunted onto a path of nonacademic ambition unless that is clearly their preference; they should at least be helped to understand that they have a much fuller range of options.

Many parents of children who are dyslexic have experienced reading problems themselves. If you have, tell your child about them and about how you felt when you were growing up. Allow him to see that people whom he admires are not perfect and are able to succeed in life.

Be aware that some of the behaviors of a child, such as procrastinating with regard to reading or studying for a test, may reflect anxiety associated with previous difficulties in reading or taking tests. If these begin to interfere with his daily functioning—that is, he always seems anxious, sad, or worried—it may be helpful to consult with a child psychiatrist or psychologist. Your pediatrician can provide you with an appropriate referral. A visit to a professional often helps you better manage a problem or prevents a more serious one.

Finally, don't patronize a child or lessen his expectations. Always treat him as a person with many dimensions, not simply as a person who has a reading problem. Let his strengths and not his weaknesses define him as a person.

23

Accommodations

Building a Bridge to Success

For a dyslexic reader, accommodations represent the bridge that connects him to his strengths and, in the process, allows him to reach his potential. By themselves accommodations do not produce success; they are the catalyst for success. Accommodations grow in importance as a dyslexic progresses in his schooling. As he advances, his strengths mature—in thinking, reasoning, vocabulary, and analytic skills; at the same time his academic challenges increase. Consequently, it becomes even more crucial for the dyslexic reader to access his strengths in order to bypass his phonologic weakness.

Far and away the most critical accommodation for the dyslexic reader is the provision of extra time. Dyslexia robs a person of time; accommodations return it. Studies carried out over the last two decades confirm a dyslexic reader's absolute "physiologic" need for extra time. For him additional time is obligatory, not optional. It is the dyslexic's unique constitution that makes it possible for extra time to exert a positive effect. For this kind of reader, learning capacity is intact; he simply needs time to access it.

Accumulating scientific evidence shows that good readers and dyslexic readers follow very different pathways to adult reading. For good readers the route is smooth, straight, and orderly: Their phonologic skills increase with age, they become more accurate and more automatic in their reading, and they identify words without any need to rely on context around the word. By fourth grade good readers are no longer using context to figure out a word. The dyslexic, however, encountering a bottleneck created by his phonologic weakness, must take an alternate, indirect, and demanding route. This secondary pathway will get him to the same destination, but it will take a lot longer. He learns to read accurately, but to achieve the same level of reading accuracy as his nondyslexic classmate, he must read much more slowly and with great effort. The automatic route to reading is unavailable to him. Consequently, if he is to identify many of the words on the page, he must pause and rely on the support of his higher-level thinking skills. He must survey the context and get to the word's meaning by this slower and more indirect pathway.

David Boies, a brilliant litigator, is dyslexic. He tries not to rely on notes in court because as a dyslexic he is not automatic in his reading. If he needed to refer to his notes, he would not be able to capture the words on paper instantly. He would need to take time. This is the imprint of a lack of automaticity in reading in this highly gifted man. That lack sometimes manifests itself in unexpected ways in others. John Irving, for example, finds it frustrating that in an airport he cannot rapidly locate his flight on the departure monitor, though he tries very hard.

> I look at that thing and I am the only one who is competitive about it. I think, God damn it, I'm going to find that city and flight and gate number before [my wife] Janet. And Janet's . . . not paying any attention to this. I'm just killing myself to find the flight to Dusseldorf or Paris or Helsinki. And Janet will look up and say, "Oh, it's B-9," like that. Instantly. I can't do that.

What his wife, an automatic reader, can do at a glance, Irving must do manually and therefore much more slowly.

Extra Time and the Need for Quiet

Brain imaging studies are providing us with a new level of understanding of the path that dyslexic readers must take. To review briefly, in these readers all features of the word have not been properly integrated, so they do not develop the automatic word form area. As a consequence, they must rely on other brain systems to figure out the word manually and get to its meaning. This process takes a much longer time. As mentioned earlier, the results of brain imaging studies of children and adults show qualitatively different brain activation patterns in dyslexic and nondyslexic readers. Instead of the intense activation observed in the back of the left side of the brain of good readers, there is a more diffuse activation pattern, and it is seen in the right hemisphere and front of the brain. An auxiliary team of neural systems is trying to take over for the disrupted primary reading system, and it requires extra time. Dyslexic adults who are able to achieve average levels of accuracy have to do so by resorting to these backup, slower, secondary neural routes to reading.

From these and other studies of students, older adults, and children we know that, as Maggie Bruck, a senior researcher at Johns Hopkins Medical School, said:

> The patterns of deficits that characterize dyslexic children are the very same patterns that characterize adults with these childhood histories. Despite the fact that many of the students have been educationally successful, and despite the fact that as adults they have increased their level of word recognition skills, these data suggest that the primary deficits have not dissipated. The mechanisms and the processes do not seem to change or to mature.

Observations in university students who are accurate but slow readers—in the United States, the United Kingdom, France, and Italy—indicate that the phonologic deficit and the neural disruption persist. As shown in Figure 35, if the dyslexic reader is going to decipher the print before him, he has to rely on higher-level sources of knowledge—vocabulary and reasoning—and slower, secondary neural pathways. The equation for adult readers who are dyslexic goes something like this: *Higher-level thinking skills + context + extra time = meaning.*

The bright dyslexic reader's reliance on context is both absolute and unique. Children who are poor readers but not dyslexic—for example, those who have across-the-board language difficulties—are generally not benefited by context. They do not possess the verbal skills, particularly the vocabulary and reasoning skills, necessary to help bootstrap the

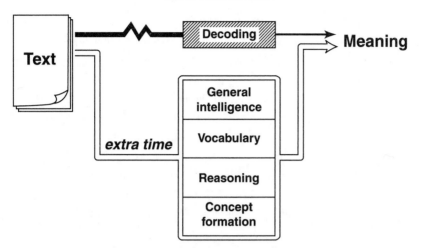

Figure 35. Using Context Takes Time

Since the direct route to meaning is not available to a dyslexic reader, he must apply his intelligence, vocabulary, and reasoning to the context around the unknown word in order to get to its meaning. This means taking a secondary reading pathway that requires extra time.

identification of unknown words. It is only the dyslexic who possesses a sea of strengths she can apply to the surrounding context to help figure out the mystery word.

Aided by their intellectual and verbal abilities, highly able dyslexic readers have the desire to go on to higher education, but they face the barrier of standardized tests, on which they perform poorly. They are particularly penalized by multiple-choice exams that typically provide sparse context, and time constraints. These tests are not a fair estimate of a dyslexic individual's grasp of knowledge.

Writers John Irving and Stephen J. Cannell both scored poorly on the verbal SAT. Renowned academic physicians Drs. Delos M. Cosgrove and Graeme Hammond scored so low on their Medical College Admissions Test (MCAT) that were it not for unique circumstances in each of their cases, neither would have been admitted to medical school. David Boies, the legal scholar Sylvia Law, and the financier Charles Schwab join the illustrious circle of highly gifted individuals whose performance on timed standardized tests underestimated their abilities—and almost kept each from pursuing and succeeding in his or her life's ambition.

Then there are the stories of everyday citizens. Hannah, a dyslexic born in a tiny community in the South, suffered through years of the all-too-familiar misdiagnosis and despair. When she turned eighteen at the end of her eleventh grade year, with her grades dreadful and no help in sight, Hannah dropped out of school. Still, she loved to think and to imagine, no matter what her reading skills. Once free of the burden of an ungiving school environment, she started working on a laptop computer and spent the next three years trying to become a writer. No longer stressed by having to handwrite her essays or race through her papers, she took pleasure in crafting her essays. Her confidence returned, and she set about earning her GED. A local community college, when apprised of the relevant facts, allowed her the accommodations she had been denied in public school (mainly extra time and a separate room for exams). In a remarkably short time she passed her examinations and was awarded her general education development (GED) degree.

When granted similar accommodations, Hannah scored very well on her ACT examination and was admitted to a small state college where she continued to receive accommodations and earned a perfect 4.0 average. Today, Hannah is pursuing a law degree at a prestigious school where she continues to receive accommodations.

As is typical for dyslexic readers, Hannah still requires extra time and a separate room for her testing. Since her reading is quite fragile, she continues to require a quiet room of her own so that she can focus her full attention on the task at hand. To ensure quiet, she uses earplugs during testing. Any noise or distraction will likely disrupt her reading, siphon her attention away from reading, and interfere with her performance on the test. These accommodations are hardly onerous on any school, and every dyslexic student should have access to them.

Satisfying the Goals of a Foreign Language Requirement

As I have already mentioned, students who are dyslexic struggle with foreign languages. Since these students have yet to master the basic phonology of the language they have been immersed in since birth, they are hardly likely to become proficient in a new language when they are young adults. In secondary schools students can and often do slip by through rote memorization, diligence, and pleasant personalities, receiving passing grades without having the slightest ability to converse in that language. But in college, students are expected to become proficient in a language, able to converse in it and read its literature.

Sometimes students realize the futility of their quest and request a partial waiver of the foreign language proficiency requirement. Alternatively, an experienced instructor may be the first to appreciate the depth of a student's difficulties and recommend a waiver. At Yale, after careful review, a partial waiver may be granted with the stipulation that the student is expected to take six course credits in the study of the culture, history, politics, or literature of any specific non-English-speaking culture or society. This model policy reaffirms the importance that the university places on the foreign language requirement and its desire to have students meet the spirit of the requirement rather than solely passing a course. This is a very useful and proper accommodation. Furthermore, it prevents needless suffering and waste of a student's time and energy while allowing him to focus on courses that he has a real chance of mastering.

Recorded Texts

In the spring of 2000, Seth Burstein, a Yale freshman, was awarded the Recording for the Blind and Dyslexic (RFB&D) Marion Huber Learning Through Listening Award at a ceremony held at the Essex House in New York City. Seth, who is dyslexic, endured years of struggle until he heard about RFB&D as he began high school and ordered tapes of his course textbooks. The recorded books soon became a positive force in Seth's life.

> I could remember just about everything I heard, but read too slowly to keep up, and so much effort was put into trying to get the words out that I had little comprehension afterwards. Once I began the tapes, everything changed. I was able to read along with the book at my leisure, absorb nearly everything I was reading, and no longer be reliant on my parents to read to me. I started to feel much better about myself. I really was learning the material, and I no longer made excuses to avoid doing my work because it made me feel bad. The tapes have changed my life. For the first time ever, I got straight A's.

Beyond schoolwork, dyslexia tears at the very independence of the maturing adolescent. Having his texts on tape can mitigate that. As another dyslexic student said, "What it means when you can't read for yourself is that you have to totally rely on your parents and your friends who do it at their convenience."

Parents and students should contact RFB&D of Princeton, New Jersey, as soon as a reading difficulty is detected. The recordings can be a student's passport to the world of the reader. Listening to books on tape or CD-ROM allows the student to participate in courses and study at his level of understanding rather than be held back by his slow reading. Furthermore, tapes introduce him to vocabulary words that he may not have encountered in his otherwise limited reading. Listening and following along improves reading itself and allows a student to actively dig into his reading by underlining, taking notes, and highlighting—important reinforcement activities that were not even considered when he was totally focused on deciphering the words on the page.

RFB&D's library contains more than ninety thousand books on a wide range of subjects including science, literature, history, and women's studies, and extends across all academic levels, from kindergarten through graduate and professional school. If a particular book or text has not already been recorded, RFB&D will record it on request. If it is a new textbook, it may need to be given to a reader to be taped, so try to obtain a book list as early as possible, ideally before the school year or semester begins.

Joining RFB&D involves completing a membership application and obtaining a signature from a professional in the field of disability services. RFB&D can be reached at its Web site, www.rfbd.org.

Currently, RFB&D is making textbooks available in a digital audio format on CD-ROM through the conversion of its existing analog library and by digital mastering of new titles. Happily, this new digitized format, called AudioPlus, still presents the natural human voice rather than a synthetic one. The versatility of having digitized books on CD-ROMs means that the reader can instantly go to the exact chapter, page, or section that he wants to read or needs to reread and listen to it on his home computer. With the new digital format, the recordings have true portability; a student can also listen to a page or a chapter on his portable CD-ROM player as he rides the bus or jogs. According to plans, the recordings may soon be accessed over the Internet. (See pages 324–325 for additional options for digitizing books.)

And so for the dyslexic student, building a bridge to success requires three basic ingredients: (1) extra time and a quiet separate room for examinations, (2) some form of waiver of the foreign language requirement, and (3) recorded texts for listening. These are all passive accommodations; rather than giving something to the dyslexic, they provide a bridge that allows his strengths to emerge and his potential to express itself. In addition to these three, there are other useful accommodations: alternate testing formats (short essays, oral reports, projects); recording lectures; and the use of a laptop in class and for tests. Dyslexic students also benefit from materials that provide visualization (figures, graphs, illustrations) to accompany print; courses and grading that emphasize concepts versus isolated details, content versus form; and the use of advanced computer technology (see pages 324–327).

To offer practical guidance for integrating these and other accommodations into a student's educational program, I am going to focus on Andrew and Gregory, and on the plans I developed for each of them.

From Theory to Practice

Andrew's Plan (High School and College)

Andrew Bennett was fifteen years old and about to enter his freshman year of high school. After he was evaluated at the Yale Center and diagnosed as dyslexic, I met with Andrew and his parents and explained the diagnosis. For adolescents like Andrew who will soon be expected to function independently while attending college, it is particularly important to understand at a very basic level what dyslexia is and how it might affect his everyday life. Then Andrew would be better equipped to figure out how to deal with it in a range of situations. He gains autonomy and in the process becomes a powerful advocate for his own needs.

I gave Andrew the following summary outlining the predictable consequences of dyslexia and the most appropriate accommodations for each. Because students who are dyslexic learn best by first understanding the big picture, I began by providing Andrew with a conceptual framework that summarized the overall rationale and goals of the plan.

Understand How You Learn: Your Strengths and Your Weaknesses

Visualize an encapsulated, circumscribed phonologic weakness surrounded by a soaring sea of strengths (excellent reasoning skills, vocabulary, the ability to understand concepts; see Figure 11, page 58).

Remember the Goal: Maximize Your Strengths, Minimize Your Weakness

Your plan is based on understanding that dyslexia is a language-based problem that affects reading, writing, and speaking. Here are the five basic consequences of dyslexia for you and what you should do about each.

1. Reading Is Slow and Laborious

Request extra time on examinations. Extra time on examinations is a necessity. The amount of time cannot be determined from testing but should be based on your own experience. The first time you request this accommodation, request double time. Based on how well this timing works for you, you can request more or less time on subsequent occasions. Since your decoding skills are not yet automatic, it takes you longer to read each word. In addition, many bright dyslexics like yourself use the context of a paragraph to help identify a word they cannot decode. For example, you may not be able to read a specific word in a paragraph but often you can read enough of the surrounding words to get the point of the selection. This allows you to fill in what the unknown word probably means even if you can't pronounce it. This rather indirect route to word meaning takes extra time. You absolutely need this extra time if you are to show what you really know. Never feel guilty about requesting extra time. A dyslexic needs extra time the same way a diabetic requires insulin. A quiet, separate room and earplugs help minimize distractions and allow you to concentrate as you read the test questions. So, although you read words slowly, your comprehension is at a high level because you can apply your skills in vocabulary and thinking to figure out the meaning of a passage.

Avoid taking too many courses with large volumes of reading. You should limit yourself to no more than two "reading" courses per semester; if necessary, take a fifth year of high school (and, later, college). When you begin college, try to take a reduced course load the first semester (or even the first year) until you adjust to the academic and other demands of university life.

Pace yourself when you read. Read for twenty minutes, take a break, exercise, and then return to your reading. Since your reading is fragile, read in a quiet room. Listening to background music such as jazz or classical—as long as it does not have lyrics—helps to block out or mask any distractions.

Many students do not know how to get the most information out of a passage they are assigned to read—they focus on all the details and remember few—but there is an approach that has worked for many students. It encourages *active* reading, which is the basis of remembering what you have read. This approach is called SQ3R; each letter stands for a process that will help in your reading:

S—*survey.* Look over the chapter before you read it. Look at the title and subheadings of each section, and read the introduction and the summary at the end. It helps to know what to expect from your reading; this puts you into a mind-set for receiving the information.

Q—*question.* Change the headings into questions and then let these questions guide your reading. For example, if the section heading in a biology textbook is "Functions of the Stomach," change that into "What are the functions of the stomach?"

R—*read.* Read the text to search for answers to the questions you have created. Highlighting or underlining the key sentences helps you recall the information. Taking *brief* notes on the highlights of each section will also help you remember the important points.

R—*recite.* Say your answers out loud.

R—*review.* After completing SQ3R for a section, go over the main points of your highlighted sections or your notes by reciting the information out loud and making sure you are correct.

This very simple process will help you organize your reading and gain more from it. Dyslexic students frequently find that taking short notes on the computer is very helpful in their studying. In fact, many distill things even more, taking notes on their notes until they are left with a very small amount of notes. Rewriting the notes is helpful in remembering and also creates a concise, abbreviated set of information from which to study for a future examination.

Active learning along with *repetition and practice* are the keys to remembering. Actively engaging with the material by highlighting, underlining, and even enlarging the print, if it is on a computer, are all helpful in making the material salient for you. Explaining or rephrasing specific ideas or concepts aloud and also reading your notes aloud over and over again will help you keep information in your memory and be able to retrieve it when needed. Visualizing what you read may be especially helpful to you. Creating an exaggerated or ridiculous visual image, or any image that is meaningful to you in some way, will be remembered more easily.

Obtain books on tape or in digitized form. Obtain recorded versions of your textbooks from Recording for the Blind and Dyslexic. Ask your instructor for a book list *before* the start of the semester so that you can be sure of having the recording in time for class. Listen to the recording as you read the book. Hearing and seeing the words will help you pronounce and remember difficult words. Listen actively; for example, you can highlight and underline important parts as you read along. Use this source for pleasure reading as well. This way you can get to enjoy the stories and literature you might not read in their printed form. Magazines are also available.

As an alternative, you might consider the Kurzweil 3000 (Kurzweil Education Systems, www.kurzweiledu.com) or WYNN 3.1 (What You Need Now; www.freedomscientific.com), software programs that will convert scanned printed material into a computer text file that can be read aloud by your computer. The system requires certain hardware (a scanner) plus the specialized Kurzweil or WYNN software to be installed in your computer. (Kurzweil will run on either a PC or Mac; WYNN on a PC.) Scanners are relatively inexpensive, and many schools own one. Scanning the lengthy textbook chapters takes quite a while, but once the text is digitized, there are many options available to help you in your reading. The software reads the text aloud for you (you can select the rate); it highlights each section in color as it is read; and it features a second color to highlight each word as the computer reads it, helping you read along or take notes. You can also enlarge the print, change the font style, increase the white space between lines, and move the text around. A search function allows you to locate a particular word within the text rapidly. Specific sections of a text can be "clipped out" and saved as a separate text file. In addition, these programs provide bookmarks, dictionary functions, voice notes (you can dictate short notes to be attached to specific text sections and play them back when needed), spell checkers, and they will create an outline from any text. They also link up to and read Web-based e-mails and other Internet text. Hardware requirements include a PC, a Pentium IV or faster processor, 256 megabytes of memory, a 120–150-megabyte hard disk, and a high-quality sound card. This software can also be adapted for use with a Mac, mainly with the addition of *Virtual PC with Windows* from Connectix (connectix.com).

Alternately, digitized text (also called e-text) can sometimes be accessed online via Bookshare.org and then linked to the Kurzweil or WYNN software and read aloud for you.

There is a continuing stream of computer products that can help you via speech recognition, spell checking, and voice feedback. Speech recognition software such as *NaturallySpeaking* (ScanSoft, PC only, www.scansoft.com), *ViaVoice* (PC and Mac, www-3.ibm.com/software/speech), and *iListen* (MacSpeech, www.macspeech.com) allows you to dictate into a headset microphone, and your speech is automatically converted into print that is visible on your computer screen. This requires you to train the program to recognize your voice. Such programs work much better for people who speak clearly; they are not magic and will not turn mumblings into erudite essays. A complementary software program, KeyStone *ScreenSpeaker* (www.keyspell.com), permits a student to listen to what the computer has just transcribed from his voice dictation. Thus, *ScreenSpeaker* used in conjunction with *NaturallySpeaking* will read aloud back to the student what *NaturallySpeaking* has transcribed. So with this system a student can dictate an essay, have it transcribed into print, and then listen as it is read back to him. This allows him to refine his essay and correct any spelling errors or homophone confusions (see below).

Speech recognition programs require the same topflight computer hardware that the Kurzweil and WYNN systems demand. Speech recognition programs can be complemented by still other software programs such as *WordSmith* (www.textHELP.com) or *Co:Writer* 4000 (DonJohnston.com), which reads aloud and pronounces words that you have typed, making sure you typed the word you intended. An especially welcome feature is homonym support provided by *WordSmith*. In this program the computer will read aloud whatever word you have written and provide a definition so that if you wrote, "I want to *heel* the sick," it will read aloud the definition of *heel* and provide the spelling and definition of other like-sounding words. Once you see and hear the word *heal* read aloud with its definition, you can correct your spelling. WordSmith and *Co:Writer* 4000 also help to formulate complete sentences by predicting what common words should logically come after the first few words you type. This feature can be helpful in developing essays and writing reports.

Computer aids are also available from Franklin Electronic Publishers (www.franklin.com), which is known for handheld products, including spell checkers and homonym checkers. For example, the Speaking Spelling Ace will pronounce and define a word that you type in. Software programs such as *Home Page Reader* (www-3.ibm.com/able/hpr.html) and *eReader* (CAST.org) will read the text on Web pages. Of course, much of the information on these pages is in the form of graphics, cartoons, or other nontext forms, which cannot be read by these programs.

All of these sophisticated tools require understanding, guidance, time, and practice. For these and other new products that come on the market, it is helpful to locate someone who can give you expert advice. Computer products for education require care and fine-tuning. Computer consultants charge for their services, but they help ensure that your new program will be used to its fullest capabilities. Schools, computer stores, and your state's Department of Vocational Rehabilitation are knowledgeable and can refer you to the most helpful computer consultants in your community. Similarly, if sophisticated technology is to be used effectively within a school setting, the staff must be fully trained in its implementation. If the staff is uncomfortable with it or doesn't understand how to run it, even the most promising technology will lie unused.

Find alternatives to reading the originals. If you have to read a book for a literature class, you might try to first find an alternative version; for example, Shakespeare's *Hamlet* and Theodore Dreiser's *An American Tragedy* have been made into movies.* A very useful Web site for movies is www.imdb.com; it provides a complete catalogue of just about every film ever made so that you can check to see if an assigned book has been made into a movie. Watching the movie version as a preliminary to reading the novel introduces you to the plot and the names of characters and places, making it easier to then read the book.

Both Charles Schwab and David Boies told me that they learned a great deal from Classic Comics when they were younger. In a similar way you can read a series of books called Streamlined Shakespeare, which features works of Shakespeare rewritten so that someone reading at a fourth-grade level and up will be comfortable; there is also Cornerstone Classics, which includes *Great Expectations* and *Gulliver's Travels* writ-

---

* The most famous movie version of *An American Tragedy* is called *A Place in the Sun.*

ten at a third- to fourth-grade reading level. Both of these series are available from High Noon Books, a division of Academic Therapy publications (www.academictherapy.com). Or you can listen to audio books; these books can be downloaded from the Internet to your personal digital assistant (PDA) such as Palm, or MP3 player, or burned to a CD. A company called Audible (audible.com) provides this service on a subscription basis. Newspapers, magazines, and public radio shows such as "All Things Considered" or "Car Talk" are also available.

Even if you don't read a lot, there are alternative ways to get information and to learn about the world. Watch the news on television, listen to it on the radio, and visit museums. In museums you can rent audio guides and listen to minilectures as you walk around. If it works for you, television, movies, and comic books are acceptable and even encouraged.

Preview reading to identify words you can't pronounce. If you can't pronounce a word, chances are you won't recognize it in a textbook or in a lecture the following day. Obtain a pocket dictionary and take it with you everywhere. Get in the habit of looking up words, especially their pronunciation. Pronouncing the word out loud helps you get it into its phonologic form, a route to a word's meaning. This is particularly important in courses such as biology and chemistry where complex new words often appear (such as *oxidative phosphorylation*). New assistive technology like the Quicktionary Reading Pen II (www.wizcomtech.com) can help you. This computerized pen first scans a troublesome word in the text and then displays it in a reasonable-sized window on the pen; it can read the word aloud and define it for you. Both Kurzweil and WYNN software will develop a cumulative list of words that gave you difficulty so that you can review them later. The American Heritage Dictionary on CD-ROM will also pronounce words that are giving you a problem, as will the Encarta World English Dictionary, which is available free online.

Talk through the material with your teacher or a tutor on a one-to-one basis. Since you have trouble getting information from printed material, you will benefit from meeting with your teacher or a tutor and talking through the material. This usually works best after you have read the required pages. An active, one-to-one oral interchange will help you get at the concepts and remember them. Using new terms in such a dialogue allows you to get to know unfamiliar words and to recognize each one more easily the next time you see it in print or hear it in a lecture.

You will remember what you have *heard* much better than material you have *read*. In addition, try to join a study group when preparing for a test. Talking through the material and listening to the group often helps much more than sitting alone in your room trying to read volumes of material.

Avoid multiple-choice tests; instead, request tests that are based on short essays. You use context to get at words you cannot decode. Multiple-choice tests do not provide enough context to help you get to the meaning of difficult-to-decode words. Short essays (or oral presentations) are the best test format for you; they allow you to demonstrate the true level of your knowledge.

Avoid speed-reading classes. They will not benefit you or any other dyslexic reader. Don't waste your time.

2. There is a basic problem in language.

Obtain a waiver from foreign language requirements. Remember, dyslexia reflects a deficit in your most basic level of language processing: getting to the sound structure of words. Given your problems with learning your own native language, you will invariably experience even more difficulty in acquiring proficiency in a foreign language. The goal of studying a foreign language is to learn about another culture. Request a partial waiver and substitute instead a course (or an independent project) on the culture of another country. Many colleges now accept students who have substituted culture for language courses and allow students to obtain partial waivers at the postsecondary level.

Visualize the material. Visual imagery and visual study guides can be especially helpful to you. You will learn best when you can picture what is on a page or are able to convert the printed information into a visual format such as a chart or graphic. *Inspiration V6* (www.inspiration.com) software helps you organize your ideas visually; with it you can create flowcharts, idea maps, tree charts, diagrams, and outlines.

Do not allow language problems to influence performance in other academic areas. You may have problems on tests simply because of a language problem: You cannot read the questions or instructions. Having the problem read to you or listening to a tape-recorded exam can be very helpful in ensuring that a test really measures your knowledge and not your reading skills. This is often the case when it comes to math word problems.

3. Handwriting is laborious and barely legible.

Get a laptop computer.   Because you have trouble forming letters and words, you often write very slowly and illegibly. The best cure for this is word processing. Purchase a laptop (notebook) computer and take it everywhere you go. Use the computer for notetaking if the instructor speaks at a reasonable speed (otherwise, see below) and to write assignments. Always try to write your essays and tests on the computer. This will free you from the labor of writing by hand and help you focus on the content of your written work. You can cut down on cost by using an AlphaSmart 3000 (www.alphasmart.com), a small, light, relatively inexpensive keyboard that has a small window that allows you to see several lines of text. With the AlphaSmart you can type notes in class and write essays; it stores whatever you write and links to just about all word processing software so that once you are home, you can download whatever you have written in school. Or if you already own a Palm OS handheld device, you can purchase a small collapsible keyboard that links to it and is useful for taking notes in class.

For taking notes from a book, the QuickLink Pen (wizcomtech.com) will scan sentences that you can download later on your computer.

Borrow someone else's lecture notes.   Since you have trouble retrieving phonemes and writing them down as you listen to a lecture, make arrangements to obtain either your teacher's notes or those of a classmate and photocopy them. During class just jot down the most important points and get the rest from someone else's notes.

Record lectures.   Record lectures on a pocket-size digital recorder. Such machines are helpful as a backup in order to clarify specific points. If you listen just prior to going to sleep, it will help you remember things.

Record your own essays.   It is often helpful to make a recording of an essay you are trying to compose. You can transcribe the essay with the assistance of a peer, an aide, or a teacher. Recorded essays can sometimes be substituted for written essays. Of course, if you are able to use speech recognition software easily, you can first record and listen to your essay, then modify it while producing a hard copy at the same time.

Your written work should be graded on content rather than on form, especially spelling. Like many dyslexic readers, you conceptualize at a very high level, but as a result of a phonologic weakness, you experience difficulty with handwriting and spelling. The same difficulties decoding words (going from letters to sound) show up when you try to carry out the reverse process, spelling, which relies on encoding sounds and transforming them into letters. Because you are often unable to store the exact model of a written word (that is, its spelling), you will also confuse homonyms. You will not notice that you wrote "heal" for "heel" or "sail" for "sale." For these reasons I recommend that you have someone proofread your written work. Spell checkers are a great help, too, as are the software products mentioned earlier in this chapter.

4. Giving oral responses "on the spot" is slow and labored.

The same phonologic weakness that affects your reading can also affect your ability to come up with spoken words quickly. Oral language, too, depends on phonologic ability. You must go into your internal dictionary, select the appropriate phonemes, put them in the correct order, and then express the word. This explains why you may often jumble parts of words so that they come out in the wrong sequence. You may recognize these signs in yourself:

- You have trouble giving oral response quickly.
- You mispronounce words or phrases.
- You have trouble finding the correct word, often talking around a topic.
- You have a problem reading aloud.
- People say you tend to use imprecise words such as "like," "stuff," "thing," "you know."
- You tend to confuse words that sound alike.

If you have these difficulties, it explains why you cannot come up with the exact answer when called upon in class even when you know the answer. Once you understand the basis for your problem with answering oral questions quickly, you can take steps to remedy the situation. Your teacher is an important partner in this; you must explain to her that your dyslexia impacts how you respond in class. Share these suggestions with your teacher (I've also included the reasons for each suggestion, which you might want to copy and give her):

Give prepared short oral reports rather than instant oral responses in class.   As a dyslexic you have difficulty retrieving words instantly, but given time, you can prepare and deliver excellent oral reports. Computers can help enormously in organizing and delivering such presentations. Learn to use *PowerPoint* (Microsoft) software to prepare reports. This allows you to take advantage of your strong visual and thinking skills as well as use the slides as an aid during the presentation. You will also practice at home, of course. Preparing a *PowerPoint* presentation (or simply making an outline on the computer) is also an excellent exercise in organizing large amounts of material and learning how to select the most salient points. *Inspiration,* a software program mentioned earlier, is ideally suited for people like you who are visually oriented, and it can be an enormous help in organizing your thoughts in preparation for a class presentation. The software that generates graphic displays also creates traditional text outlines of the same information. You can even switch back and forth between your diagram and your text outline as you modify and refine each one. Using the computer in this way gives you an opportunity to demonstrate your strengths and obtain positive feedback in front of your classmates. It's also an enjoyable way to learn the importance of preparation.

Phonologic slips should not be mistakenly interpreted as a lack of knowledge.   If your oral response sounds off the mark, your teacher should consider that it may be a phonologic error and allow you to explain. Dyslexics often have difficulty finding the precise or specific word. You should be asked to elaborate or more fully describe what you are trying to say. Tell your teacher, "I misspoke. Let me explain what I mean."

5. Learning is by a top-down approach, going from meaning to facts.

Select courses where the emphasis is on concepts, not on details. You will do much better in courses where the emphasis is on your strengths—understanding broad concepts and ideas, using reasoning and analytic skills—rather than on memorizing isolated bits of information. Rote memory (memorizing exact dates and places) requires strong phonologic abilities. *You* are best at remembering information that is attached to meaning. Before selecting a course, find out if you are expected to memorize specific facts or instead can demonstrate your knowledge through projects and reports. The latter are much better for you. Before the course begins, don't be afraid to discuss with your instructor how you will be evaluated. Be your own advocate; explain what you need and why.

Andrew and his parents met with the principal of his high school and presented him with the results of my evaluation and recommendations. They were pleasantly surprised by his positive reaction. He seemed relieved. We had given him a plan of action. The new information produced a significant turnaround for Andrew at school. Andrew as well as his teachers were surprised and pleased at what a difference extra time and a quiet room made in his test performance. Some of his teachers now offered to provide Andrew with copies of their own lecture notes for him to preview before class, and his classroom contributions improved significantly. He is substituting a course in French culture as a partial waiver of the foreign language requirement. He has purchased a laptop computer and is amazed at how helpful word processing is to him. Seeing Andrew use his laptop in class has resulted in several of his nondyslexic classmates purchasing computers for themselves as well. Andrew is pleased because it makes him stand out less. Like many other dyslexics, more than anything Andrew wants to appear like everyone else and not be noticed.

On his last visit Andrew reported that things were going quite well. He was happy, and for the first time in many years his parents could feel optimistic about his future.

Gregory's Plan (Medical School)

You already know about Gregory, the bright young man whom I wrote about in *Scientific American*. He was experiencing frustration in medical school and knew it didn't have to be that way. I met the dean of student affairs at Gregory's medical school and told him that a few critical steps would make a significant difference. Operationally, this meant that teachers had to recognize and attempt to accommodate rather than penalize Gregory.

In words that will now be familiar to you, I told the dean that a dyslexic like Gregory cannot provide instant answers, but he can learn—and learn very well—if given the opportunity to do so. I said it was important to separate the learning process from the evaluative process. During clinical clerkships, for example, a first attempt or response is often regarded as the final evaluation. But Gregory had to be given an opportunity to learn without fear: If he responded hesitantly or incorrectly on the first try, it would not be taken as an indication of a failure to learn. His evaluation must not confuse oral language facility with ability. Accordingly, Gregory must be evaluated on the basis of his knowledge and reasoning skills, not his glibness or speed of verbal response.

I said that for each course Gregory needed to meet regularly with someone knowledgeable with whom he could preview and talk through the content materials. This would help overcome Gregory's problem with rapidly retrieving words. Faculty members, fellows, senior residents, or even retired faculty members have served effectively in this capacity. I said it was critical that this individual *not* be part of the evaluative process.

I also said it would make a real difference if there was someone who would function as a faculty advocate or mentor to Gregory, someone who would represent his needs to the clinical course directors. Such a person should be a member of the academic faculty who carries the authority and respect of the institution, has an understanding of the nature and consequences of dyslexia, and is genuinely supportive. Having a respected faculty member run interference for the student makes a world of difference; otherwise, the student may say the same things, but with little effect.

Finally, I said the evaluative process must be a reflection of Gregory's ability and not a measure of his disability. I told the dean about how unfair multiple-choice examinations were for Gregory and why. This had been demonstrated during Gregory's obstetrics/gynecology rotation. During the six weeks of this course, his performance was observed around the clock by a range of attendings and team members; the consensus was that he performed at an honors level. At the end of the rotation he was given two oral examinations by senior faculty; on one examination he rated an honors grade, on the other a high honors. In stark contrast, he failed the multiple-choice written examination, a result he had anticipated and spoken about with the course director. The extreme disparity between his performance on the wards and on the oral examination, in contrast to the multiple-choice examination, speaks for itself and clearly documents the inappropriateness of this type of examination to measure Gregory's knowledge.

A dyslexic medical student like Gregory who has had to adapt to and successfully cope with a chronic disability for virtually his entire school career clearly has a great deal to offer as a physician, including many of the most meaningful yet least teachable qualities: compassion, empathy, and sensitivity, as well as intelligence and motivation. With the kind of support and understanding I indicated, Gregory could not only survive, he would thrive.

Most of my recommendations were adopted. Gregory is now completing his residency.

Change starts small. The days when accommodations didn't exist for dyslexic children are over. And there are signs that the denying of accommodations will soon be a thing of the past. In Oregon, after prolonged efforts, students with dyslexia will now be able to use word processors with spell checkers on high-stakes exams. In addition, as needed, they are permitted to recite their answers orally, to have the test read to them, and to be given additional time to answer the questions. Many believe that this enlightened policy sets a standard for protecting the rights of children who are learning-disabled and for ensuring that it is their abilities rather than their disability that is tested.

Our new level of understanding of dyslexia (and learning) and of the importance of accommodations is now being transformed—through the requests of individual students, through the insights of perceptive teachers, and through changes in public policy—into real and lasting changes in educational practices and policies. The scientific basis of, the urgent need for, and the life-transforming difference made by the provision of accommodations have been proven and are rapidly taking root in classrooms throughout the country. As a result of these much-needed adaptations, dyslexic students will now have the opportunity to develop their full potential. Not only will the individuals benefit, but society as a whole too.

Answers to the Most Frequently Asked Questions

How is dyslexia identified in college and graduate students?

Dyslexia is a clinical diagnosis; it must be made by a clinician who knows the student and who is able to thoughtfully synthesize the pertinent historical information, clinical observations, and results of relevant testing. The diagnosis is based on a pattern of findings; it should never be made or ruled out on the basis of an isolated test result. Tests are just proxies; a person's lifelong history and the reality of how that individual reads aloud are the best measures of dyslexia in an accomplished adult.

The hallmark of dyslexia is unexpected difficulties in phonology and reading in relation to the person's other cognitive and academic abilities. In college (and beyond), the most valid approach relies on the person's accomplishments, such as his academic performance (outstanding grades in math, philosophy, or chemistry); educational status (attendance at or a graduate of a competitive college, graduate, or professional school); or professional status (an attorney, physician, writer, engineer, or successful businesswoman). Within this context a college student, a law school graduate, or a physician who reads slowly and with great effort is manifesting an unexpected difficulty in reading. (The use and misuse of IQ testing is discussed in Chapter 11; it is important to keep in mind that by young adulthood the influence of a reading disability may have artificially depressed the IQ score.)

Reading accuracy should not be used as a measure of reading proficiency in a bright, educated adult. By adolescence a student who is dyslexic will improve his ability to read words accurately so that measures of word accuracy are expected to be in the so-called average range. Consequently, the finding of average word reading skills in an educated adult dyslexic is not very helpful in determining if he is experiencing difficulty in reading. Scientific evidence shows that adults with childhood histories of dyslexia who appear to be able to identify words accurately are reading those same words differently from others; they are reading them more slowly and using different brain systems.

Lack of fluency is the only true index of dyslexia in a bright adult. How the person reads *aloud* is the critical measure of fluency: Does he stumble over words or hesitate, mispronounce, omit, or add words as he reads? In addition, timing a person's speed during silent reading or, alternatively, having the person read silently under timed and untimed conditions and then answer questions about the passage may provide some indication of how fluently that individual is able to read.

Are there other problems that could be confused with dyslexia?

In a bright postsecondary school student or in an accomplished adult, very few problems can reasonably be confused with dyslexia. If the pattern I have outlined in this book has been established in someone, she is dyslexic. Only dyslexia produces the clinical syndrome characterized by the paradoxical pairing of a phonologic weakness and higher-level cognitive strengths expressing themselves throughout the person's life. If a person has a history of phonologically based speaking, reading, and spelling difficulties going back to her childhood and now reads very slowly despite signs of her cognitive strengths—that person is dyslexic.

Sometimes ADHD is confused with dyslexia; it shouldn't be. As you know, dyslexia reflects difficulty getting to the basic sounds of language; ADHD reflects problems with the modulation of attention and activity. The symptoms, the neurobiology, and the effective treatments differ. At times, however, a person who is dyslexic may appear not to be paying attention to her reading because it is so demanding for her to decipher the words on the page. And so it's not that she has a primary attention problem but, rather, that reading for her requires an unusual outlay of attention.

What is the best way to establish how much extra time is needed for an exam by a person who is dyslexic?

The only valid gauge is the person's own life experience. There is absolutely no test that can provide this information. Each accomplished dyslexic has developed her own route around her phonologic deficit; the specific strategies or alternate pathways that she has perfected over the years and found to work for her will determine how much extra time she requires.

How often should a person be tested?

Dyslexia is a chronic condition; it is not outgrown. Once a student has been identified as dyslexic and has received accommodations, there is no logical reason to believe that there will come a time when he will not require this accommodation (for timed tests) in order to access his cognitive strengths. As mentioned earlier, scientific studies have clearly demonstrated that the thread of the phonologic deficit persists throughout a person's life. Imaging studies demonstrate that even so-called compensated dyslexic students continue to call upon secondary (nonautomatic) neural routes and to read more slowly than their peers. There is absolutely no evidence to indicate that a person who is dyslexic as an adult somehow metamorphoses into a person who is a fluent reader and uses traditional primary brain systems for reading. Lacking this evidence, requests for repeated assessment are without reason. There is no evidence of benefit from asking students past high school to go through the expense and the psychological trauma—and the potential for misinterpretation—of a new series of evaluations.

In this context, many believe that the request for frequent testing of the dyslexic once he has completed high school represents an artificial barrier raised to discourage students from applying for accommodations. The requirement for additional time for a dyslexic reader is so fundamental that there is no tenable counterargument; there is no plausible rationale for believing that a person who is dyslexic will no longer require extra time.

Do accommodations pose an unfair advantage?

Researchers have compared the performance of learning-disabled and non-learning-disabled college students on timed and untimed standardized tests. The results were consistent: Only students diagnosed as learning-disabled actually showed a significant improvement in test scores with additional time.

Those who worry about the "advantage" of extra time for a person who is dyslexic fail to appreciate that even with additional time he will continue to feel rushed. Extra time is not an advantage, it is an attempt to level the playing field. Even with the additional time, a slow reader will continue to feel at least the same or more time pressure compared to the ordinary reader.

Do people fake dyslexia just to get the "perks" associated with it?

The belief that somehow many parents, particularly middle-income parents living in the suburbs, are seeking a diagnosis of a learning disability to gain some imagined advantage for their child is an insidious, unfounded, and malicious rumor. These rumors poison the atmosphere and create a backlash that is harmful to children who are struggling to learn and to their parents who are struggling to understand and help them.

Recently, a blue-ribbon panel concluded that rather than overidentification of suburban students as dyslexic, the problem was the relative underidentification of disadvantaged children, especially minority children. The panel strongly urged that the major testing agencies make proactive efforts to inform these disadvantaged reading-disabled students of their rights to testing accommodations.

How early should accommodations begin?

Once a child is expected to write, to complete time-consuming class or homework assignments, and to take standardized tests, consideration should be given to providing accommodations. By second or third grade, children struggling to read can be introduced to Recording for the Blind and Dyslexic and to learning to type on the computer. Teachers should be instructed to grade a dyslexic student's essays on the basis of her creative writing and not her spelling. If homework seems to go on for hours, the student should be allowed to reduce her assignment, such as completing every other question. Reducing the time required for completing assignments is critical; it is demoralizing and self-defeating for a student in third or fourth grade to spend hour after hour struggling to complete her work at home.

Children who are dyslexic require additional time for tests. This is especially important for high-stakes standardized tests that often represent the gatekeeper for admission to specialized programs or schools and, increasingly, for promotion and graduation.

In providing accommodations, a child's dignity and sense of privacy must be considered. Frequently there are several children in a class whose reading difficulties necessitate accommodations. Providing accommodations most sensibly and most effectively should become part of the planning discussions routinely held within each school, and not carried out as a spur-of-the-moment and sometimes thoughtless gesture.

Is there a downside to requesting accommodations?

Because of the stigma and the misunderstanding associated with the diagnosis of dyslexia, most adults and children prefer to keep their dyslexia private. Requesting accommodations almost always means exposing a child's or young adult's imperfections publicly. The student who is dyslexic and who relies on accommodations can begin to doubt herself and to question her own need for accommodations. But while at one level these feelings do become etched into a person's sense of herself, at another level most dyslexics are able to develop an appreciation of their own unique qualities.

At the same time it is possible to provide accommodations while maintaining anonymity. A program developed at Yale Law School can serve as a model for other schools. Details can be obtained from the Yale University Resource Office on Disabilities.

The practice of flagging the scores of tests taken with accommodations has been distressing to many students with disabilities. While the purpose of the accommodation is to place those with disabilities on a par with others taking the test, the asterisk placed next to the score telegraphs to all who see it that the test taker has a disability. The evidence is strong that once an admission committee sees the asterisk, the tendency is "to place that applicant's file on the bottom of the pile." The asterisk identifies the applicant as having an exceptionality and his scores as ones the testing organization cannot validate. A civil rights law group, Disability Rights Advocates (DRA), filed a lawsuit on behalf of a physically disabled man, Mark Breimhorst. He charged that the Educational Testing Service's (ETS) policy of flagging accommodated test scores with the notation "Scores Obtained Under Special Conditions" violated state (California) and federal antidiscrimination laws, "stigmatizing disabled students with a kind of scarlet letter." The judge hearing the case ruled that the tests should "equally measure the skills of disabled and nondisabled test-takers," and then there would be no need to flag these scores. In a settlement reached between the civil rights group and ETS, the testing organization agreed to stop flagging the test scores of individuals with physical and learning disabilities who take these tests with accommodations. Initially, the new policy applied to the Graduate Record Exam (GRE), the Graduate Management Admissions Test (GMAT), the Test of English as a Foreign Language (TOEFL), and Praxis, a test for teachers. A blue-ribbon panel was named to reexamine flagging and make recommendations for the major standardized test, the SAT I. On July 15, 2002, the panel released its findings: "The majority position of the Panel was to discontinue the practice of flagging the SAT I based on scientific, psychometric, and social evidence." I served on the panel and joined in the majority opinion that noted the "compelling" evidence against flagging.

How does the need for accommodations on exams impact the kinds of work the person who is dyslexic will be able to do once he is out of school? Will he be able to "do the job"?

I want to emphasize that most dyslexics can succeed on the job. It is the artificial barrier presented by multiple-choice tests that is the problem. Dyslexics generally do not have a problem practicing medicine or law or engineering or writing novels or plays—if they can survive the hurdle of the multiple-choice test. These tests tap their weakness and yet at the same time are often the gateway to future opportunity.

Having said this, the person who is dyslexic will be relatively more successful at some occupations than others. Ironically, the jobs with which he will have difficulties tend to be entry-level ones involving dependence on lower-level skills, with very little requirement for higher-level thinking abilities. A person who is dyslexic would not enjoy work entirely centered on clerical or filing duties.

In law, the ability to read quickly or to carry out rote, mechanical skills is often confused with the ability to think and reason. Early on, few would have predicted that David Boies, who did not learn to read until third grade, would become the leader of a field that seems to be so dependent on reading. Yet Boies's life experience reinforces the dictum that it is not how fast you read but how well you *think* that counts. Boies's approach is to skim through the text until he recognizes what is important; then he slows down, homes in on this material, and carefully reads the critical facts. He has an uncanny ability to grasp exactly what is important; once he has set his sights on the most meaningful target for further analysis, he can concentrate on this much-reduced volume of material and carefully analyze it.

Earlier I mentioned dyslexic physicians, including surgeons, who have thrived. What flies in the face of so much that we assume to be related to surgical expertise is that some of the most renowned surgeons failed anatomy in medical school. One of those surgeons told me that anatomy is not related to surgical skill. "It actually has little to do with the practice of surgery," he told me. "Performance in an anatomy course has more to do with the ability to rotely memorize the names of assorted bodily parts." Most surgeons are in agreement that "surgery has to do with thinking, with knowing what to do and not with knowing the names of particular structures." It is hoped this information will caution medical educators to be more thoughtful in their career counseling; they should not assume that dyslexic medical students who have trouble with anatomy cannot become outstanding surgeons.

Slow-reading lawyers, poor-spelling writers, and surgeons who failed anatomy in medical school—they all flout conventional wisdom. From these individuals we learn that reading slowly tells nothing about the ability to comprehend, that poor spelling has little to do with one's ability to write creatively, and that an inability to memorize the names of anatomical structures does not portend one's skills in operating on those same bodily parts. Most would have counseled each one of them against pursuing the career of his dreams in which he has found such fulfillment. I hope that educators and parents alike will encourage children who are dyslexic to pursue their dreams.

What is the role of multiple-choice standardized tests in assessing people who are dyslexic?

Under scrutiny these ubiquitous and influential tests do not seem to hold up very well. Many of our assumptions concerning the tests and their predictive value turn out to be questionable. The imbalance between their power and their flawed nature are particularly harmful to those who are dyslexic. These tests measure the rapid retrieval of rote facts, which taps directly into the dyslexic's phonologic weakness, while they are mostly unable to measure what may be his strongest assets, namely, his ability to reason, to think abstractly, to see the big picture, and to think out of the box. These are the kinds of creative abilities that tend to reflect the dyslexic's sea of strengths, the kinds of cognitive skills in which the dyslexic might score in the 99th percentile—were they measurable by a simple test. And so multiple-choice standardized tests represent another kind of paradox for the dyslexic: They telegraph his lower-level weaknesses while they obscure and keep hidden his talents.

High school SATs add surprisingly little over and above high school grades as predictors of college performance. At the next level, the Law School Admissions Tests (LSAT) are not proving to be especially strong predictors of law school performance. One judge proposed that law schools "relax or even eliminate reliance on the LSAT." As reported in the *Wall Street Journal*, the judge wrote that the test "does not predict

341

success in the legal profession at all. . . . One must wonder why the law school concerns itself at all with an applicant's LSAT score."

The United States Medical Licensing Examination is now being criticized, often by those such as Dr. Stephen Smith, associate dean of student affairs at Brown University School of Medicine, and Dr. Graeme Hammond, professor of surgery at Yale University School of Medicine, both of whom have served on the National Board of Medical Examiners and participated in the test-making process. According to Dr. Hammond, "I shudder when I think about how those questions were constructed. . . . I believe that the time has come to get rid of these examinations which test the ability to take multiple-choice tests and little more."

The Future: A Time for Hope

I am optimistic about the future for those with dyslexia. Science, morality, and the law are converging to provide the rationale, the societal good, and the legal grounds to support the provision of accommodations to students who are dyslexic. More and more, learned groups are beginning to question the role of these tests. Most recently, Richard C. Atkinson, president of the University of California, proposed "an *end* to the use of SAT's as a requirement for admission to the state university system . . . one of the largest and most prestigious." Atkinson indicated that "he would like to move away from numerical measurements of student aptitude and encourage a more 'holistic' approach to evaluating candidates."

As for higher levels of education, a comprehensive study published in the *Journal of the American Medical Association* (JAMA) suggests that a nontraditional approach to medical school admissions produces physicians whose postgraduate training and career experiences are indistinguishable from those selected through more usual procedures. In this study carried out at the University of California at Davis, the researchers were interested in the consequences of an admissions process in which special consideration was given to a range of factors considered important in choosing future physicians. The goal was to select the "best" applicants but not to be bound by the traditional criteria of grade point averages (GPA) and medical school admissions test (MCAT) scores. Students who scored poorly on standardized tests but who demonstrated other, more difficult-to-measure qualities were eligible for consideration by the admissions committee. In this study, which extended from 1968 through 1987, approximately 350 students were admitted by special consideration criteria; 67 percent did not meet the minimum standardized test criterion set by the school for admission, while a smaller number of students did not meet the minimum undergraduate GPA.

The admissions committee was able to disregard the results of standardized tests and to select students who went on to successful completion of medical school and residencies. By the time they were residents and in practice, the special group was indistinguishable from their higher-scoring classmates.

As a *JAMA* editorial said:

> Applicants who qualified for the special admissions programs because their Medical College Admissions Test (MCAT) scores and GPAs were *below* the "minimum" established for regular admission had excellent outcomes that were comparable to those admitted in the usual way. The students with higher MCAT scores and GPAs were not significantly more likely to graduate, complete residency successfully, become licensed, attain board certification, or enter the full range of career opportunities (including academic medicine) than were the students admitted under the special admission program. If the highest MCAT scores and GPAs are not predictive of these outcomes, they are not meaningful admissions factors.

The failure of numerical scores to differentiate between who will and who will not become a good doctor substantially increases the work of the admissions committee members; they will clearly need to rely on other, hopefully more valid criteria.

And so there is accumulating evidence—in undergraduate admissions, in graduate school, and now in law and in medical school—that reliance on standardized test scores as reliable predictors of future performance is not fulfilling its promise. Such scores may not select the best students and in fact may be keeping out those students who have the ability not only to successfully graduate but to contribute in unique ways to their profession.

The importance of the more intangible qualities—of getting beyond the facts—is of more than theoretical interest. These are the kinds of qualities that impact our daily lives, that can make the difference between a good scientist, physician, lawyer, artist, or writer—and a great one. It's really all about the difference between relying on an accumulation of facts and thinking on a higher plane. And this is why we must not abandon the future and the selection of the next generation's leaders to how well they can score on mechanical standardized tests. We must take in all the information about a person, the kinds of data that are not subject to easy reduction. Creativity is too large and too far-ranging to be fit into the narrow confines of a bubble response to a multiple-choice question.

Epilogue

A Person Like That . . .

Not long ago at a dinner party a professor at my table was speaking about dyslexia. "Now dyslexics want to go to law school," he said. "Can you imagine: a person like *that* as your lawyer?" I smiled at him as I replied, "I would consider it fortunate to have David Boies as my lawyer. Yes, a person like *that*."

My misguided dinner companion hadn't yet grasped that children who struggle with dyslexia in school often go on to excel in life. Apropos, I want to end this book by introducing you to a group of dyslexics who are successful by anyone's standards. As children, these people struggled to read, could not spell, were laughed at when they read aloud in class, rarely finished a book, failed foreign languages, and fared miserably on standardized tests. For all people like *that*, success is within their grasp.

John Irving

When John Irving was a student at Phillips Exeter Academy, a New England prep school, he demonstrated glimmers of talent only to those few who were able to appreciate it. He was a C– student in English with an SAT verbal score of 475. Later, of course, he became the best-selling author of *The World According to Garp* and *The Cider House Rules,* and an Academy Award–winning screenwriter. As Irving tells it:

> I simply accepted the conventional wisdom of the day—I was a struggling student; therefore, I was stupid.
>
> I needed five years to pass the three-year foreign language requirement. . . . I passed Latin I with a D, and flunked Latin II; then I switched to Spanish, which I barely survived. . . .
>
> It wasn't until my younger son, Brendan, was diagnosed as slightly dyslexic that I realized how I had been given the shaft. His teachers said that Brendan comprehended everything he read but that he didn't comprehend a text as quickly as his peers; they said that he could express himself as well as, or actually better than, his peers but that it took him longer to organize his thoughts on paper. This sounded familiar to me. As a child, Brendan read with his finger following the sentence—as I read, as I *still* read. Unless I've written it, I read whatever "it" is very slowly—and with my finger.
>
> I wasn't diagnosed as dyslexic at Exeter; I was seen as just plain stupid. I failed a spelling test and was put in a remedial spelling class; because I couldn't learn how to spell—I *still* can't spell!—I was advised to see the school *psychiatrist!* This advice made no sense to me then—it makes no sense to me now—but if you were a poor student at Exeter, you would develop such a lasting sense of your own inferiority that you'd probably be in need of a psychiatrist one day.
>
> I wish I'd known, when I was a student at Exeter, that there was a word for what made being a student so hard for me; I wish I could have said to my friends that I was dyslexic. Instead, I kept quiet, or—to my closest friends—I made bad jokes about how stupid I was. Brendan knows he's not stupid; he knows he's the same kind of student I was.

It was painful to Irving that people didn't acknowledge how hard he was trying.

> My only anger was at people who presumed that I was lazy—because I was working harder than anybody else. I had at least

one teacher each year who thought that there was nothing the matter with me except that I was lazy.

And it was not academics but athletics—wrestling—that was Irving's salvation. Whatever satisfaction he was not receiving in the classroom, he was achieving on the wrestling mat.

My wrestling coach, Ted Seabrooke, kept me in school; he gave me enough confidence in myself—through wrestling—that I was able to take a daily beating in my classes and keep coming back for more. An ironic blessing of my having to repeat my senior year at Exeter was that I finally got to be captain of the wrestling team—my sole distinction, my only honor, in five years at the academy.

Writing was not automatic for Irving. He had to learn how to make it work:

To do anything really well, you have to overextend yourself. In my case, I learned that I just had to pay twice as much attention. I came to appreciate that in doing something over and over again, something that was never natural becomes almost second nature. You learn that you have the capacity for that, and that it doesn't come overnight.

How has dyslexia influenced his writing?

It's become an advantage. In writing a novel, it doesn't hurt any-body to have to go slowly. It doesn't hurt anyone as a writer to have to go over something again and again.

One reason I have confidence in writing the kind of novels I write is that I have confidence in my stamina to go over some-thing again and again no matter how difficult it is—whether it is for the fourth or fifth or eighth time. It's an ability to push myself and not to be lazy. This is something I would ascribe to the diffi-culties I had to overcome at an early age.

How does Irving, a poor reader, read the voluminous number of pages he produces?

> I read slowly and I reread a lot. I read a paragraph, and if I'm not 100 percent concentrating on what I'm reading or if I'm the slightest bit tired, I have a problem. And from that, too, I have learned that if you have to concentrate twice as hard as somebody else, you get twice as tired—twice as soon. And so when I am a little bit tired, the difference is enormous.
>
> I also had to practice. I am actually a very good reader of my own work. But I think that comes from my practice of reading my work aloud and understanding the cadence with which it's written. I read my own work aloud as I write it or I say it aloud as I write it. And, in fact, when I am writing in my office at home, people walking by always think I'm on the phone.
>
> I also use my finger, as I did when I was a student. Especially when I'm tired or when the print is a little too small, I just keep my finger on it. And when I do public readings, I never take my finger off where I am.

One could not ask for a more classical description of how a very bright person who is dyslexic reads or the usefulness of reading aloud.

The spelling demon continues to plague Irving today.

> The dictionary, a very large dictionary, is 180 degrees behind me so that all I have to do is swivel my chair when I turn to it. It's open all the time. And I use it all the time. And probably once or twice a week I buzz my assistant or my wife, Janet, because I'm so far off in the spelling of a word that I can't find the damn thing in the dictionary.

Time impacted Irving's studies and also his performance on standardized tests:

> The colleges that admitted me out of Exeter all cited my writing sample and a couple of recommendations from teachers who said decent things about my capacity to write. I certainly would

have had nowhere to go if I had only been judged on my standardized test scores.

Life was better for Irving as his education progressed. Graduate school was the best, for it was more specialized.

When I got to graduate school at Iowa in creative writing, I was taking one literature course. I could concentrate on one thing for three or four or five hours instead of doing something for an hour and putting it aside and doing something that was completely different for an hour.

As a beginning student you have to move at someone else's pace. You don't have the luxury of concentrating and delving deeper and deeper into one subject.

When you are a graduate student, you have the freedom to set your own pace and to develop an expertise in whatever area interests you. Today, as an adult, Irving still requires lots of time to do his work, but he can now plan his own schedule and use as much time as he requires to do his writing.

Irving's problems with rote memory do not reflect a general memory problem. He has a "wonderful" memory when it comes to remembering the most complex information—as long as it has a meaningful connection. While he cannot remember telephone numbers (which are random numbers), he can recall the most arcane bits and pieces of his novel because they are part of a network of information that forms a meaningful whole. "My interpretation of myself when I was in my late teens was that I had a lousy memory," he says. "I've since discovered that I have a very good memory because to write a long, complicated, plot-driven novel, you need to have a wonderful memory."

And while he is capable of reading and understanding the most complicated of narratives, he is almost incapable of reading instructions.

Everything—a child's toy, an alarm clock—comes with instructions and things need to be assembled. I can't understand them. Whenever there's reading—when there are toys at Christmas time, for instance—my father-in-law or my wife does it. I can't put things together. I get halfway into the project, and I feel that

I'm back in the world of multiple choice again. I don't get it. I try very hard to understand instructions, but I simply can't.

Irving has ridden the roller coaster of life that you experience as a dyslexic and has been deeply affected by the experience. As a parent he is also extremely sensitive to the needs of children who are dyslexic.

I think the burden on parents and on teachers, when they see that the task of reading is a challenge, is to make learning as much fun as it can be. They have to find ways to reward the child constantly. And you have to not lower your expectations for that child. You have to keep up your belief in the child and maintain your vision of his future.

I had difficulty in school. But I had around me my parents and my coach to give me support and to recognize that I needed to have more and more confidence in myself, because I wasn't getting it from school. And so the harder you have to work at anything, the more important it is that you have somebody telling you you're doing a good job. You need somebody who is giving you a lot of encouragement, a lot of support; someone who knows how hard you're working.

I think that the unforgivable thing that parents and teachers do is to think or to imply that because their kids are struggling, that they're lazy or that they're not trying hard enough. Actually, having to go through something that's a struggle, even at a young age, can be a very positive experience for you—if you're being supported and constantly told that you're doing a good job. I am a believer in telling kids that they're great kids, that you know how hard they're working—you can't overdo that. And, finally, you have to help the child imagine that he can be a success and to sustain that vision of himself. My very first wrestling coach used to say that before you could beat someone better than you, you had to be able to imagine you could be a winner. You had to believe you could do it. It sounds like coach-speak on the one hand, but on the other hand, it's very true.

Epilogue

Wendy Wasserstein

"I won a Pulitzer Prize for playwrighting, and I grew up having trouble reading," said Wendy Wasserstein.

An accomplished comedic and satirical playwright, Wasserstein's credits include *The Heidi Chronicles,* which, in addition to the 1989 Pulitzer Prize, won the New York Drama Critics Circle Award, the Outer Critics Circle Award, and the Tony Award. To many she is the epitome of the literate, urbane New Yorker.

She is also dyslexic. Although the term *dyslexia* wasn't used at the Flatbush Yeshiva school she attended in Brooklyn, she knew she had a reading problem and tried to adapt. It was especially confusing having to learn Hebrew and English at the same time. Told to "read this," Wendy would often pretend to turn the pages at such a quick rate that her teachers would comment, "You read so fast."

In truth, Wendy struggled to read and read very slowly. While speed-reading classes at a local university were not helpful, a transfer in the fifth grade to the progressive Brooklyn Ethical Culture School allowed Wendy's intellect to find expression through other routes. There, her interest in the arts, especially the theater and art history, flourished. She was drawn to plays.

> I figured out they're short, they're also printed large, and there's a lot of white space on the page. And you can go (as I used to do) to the Library of Performing Arts and read and listen to them at the same time. And later, reading the plays again, you can hear the voices of those people.

Wasserstein's spelling always brought down the grades of her compositions.

> The joy of my life was when I figured out I could have a typist— even when I didn't really have money to pay someone to type my work. I can't tell you what that's like. It changed my life. Before that, in high school, in playwrighting, I would get an A for content, a D for form, and then they would grade them together and give me a C.

For Wasserstein, as for Irving, things got better as she went further in school and "started concentrating on things I could do." A wonderful teacher, Professor Leonard Berkman at Smith College, helped Wasserstein believe she could be a playwright. Using herself as an example, she urges dyslexic students not to allow themselves to be categorized or to fall into stereotypes. Just because you are not a skilled reader doesn't mean you can't be a writer. Even today, reading takes her a long time, she says.

Wasserstein is fascinated by people for whom reading comes easily, and she loves libraries.

> I write in libraries, almost because I have the sense of wonder about all these other people who sit and read. I have an awe of people who really read. My closest friends in the world are steeped in reading. They talk to me about reading.

Reading continues to be "energy-draining" for her, and she requires quiet in order to concentrate. "I can't read while there are other people in the room. There isn't a chance in hell that I would be the summer guest who shows up with a book for a weekend and happens to read it while everyone's screaming."

As a dyslexic reader, the print and the appearance of the page are very important to her. "I'm not going to be able to read a book with small print or a lot of print. It helps if it has really dark print." And although she does not read a lot, "if I do read, I read thoroughly." She will likely finish a book "if it's an important book to me. But it takes concentration and time." For Wasserstein, reading books "so slowly and so thoroughly" has its advantages, too. "If I read it, I remember it." This is a significant benefit in her work of adapting stories and books for movies and television.

Wasserstein also makes this acute observation for today's child with dyslexia:

> There are many ways to learn, and you can learn things by not reading. There has to be pleasure in learning; there have to be creative outlets. At the progressive school I went to there was dance and theater. Genuine learning can also take place through talking and through storytelling. In some ways being dyslexic is a gift, because you think less linearly. And you have to know it's okay to think out of the box.

Stephen J. Cannell

Stephen J. Cannell, a novelist and an Emmy Award–winning writer of such television hits as *The Rockford Files* and *The A-Team,* is dyslexic. For him, too, school was a nightmare:

> I couldn't spell, my handwriting was sloppy, I tended to print rather than do cursive, and I was a slow reader. I was terrible at reading out loud. Terrible. I was not able to keep up with my class, and finally I was kept back in fourth grade. Then I was told I couldn't stay at that private school.
>
> Then in tenth grade I went to Choate and flunked out. I was the goat of the class. I finally graduated from a different school at the bottom of my class.

As resilient as he is, Cannell was devastated by these experiences: "I always felt I was the dumbest one in school." He understands the lasting impact of such experiences: "The real fear that I have for dyslexic people is not that they have to struggle with jumbled print or that they can't spell, but that they will quit on themselves before they get out of school."

Especially traumatic to Cannell were the terrible misjudgments of his abilities, particularly his potential as a writer. "I couldn't spell, and that meant to them I couldn't write." And just as an inability to spell some words impacted John Irving and Wendy Wasserstein, misspellings also constricted Cannell's writing. He recalls that "even the words I thought I could spell I couldn't spell. By the time I got to college, I would only use the words I could spell, so I wouldn't use all the words in my vocabulary. That limited my ability to write a good essay."

And again, like Irving and Wasserstein, life got much better for Cannell when he was an adult.

> One of my great joys is that I've won the most distinguished alumni award from the four schools that flunked me out. Of course, they had a certain way of judging people, and I didn't fit that mold. All my talents were hidden below the surface. They couldn't see my creative thought processes. They couldn't see my imagination. They couldn't see the way I could get lost in a story. They would call that daydreaming.

Cannell is ambivalent about private schools. He knows their small class size and curriculum hold the promise of a good education, but he wishes they were more understanding and more flexible, especially toward students who are dyslexic, like his children:

> They were going to throw my son out. He was only in the fourth grade, and he was trying so hard to stay with his class. My wife, Marcia, and I went to talk to the headmistress of the school. I was trying to explain dyslexia and his trouble spelling.
>
> She looked at me and said, "Oh, Mr. Cannell, you know if he really tried he could do it." And it was then that we realized, Here's somebody who was always a good student; things like that were never a problem for that woman. For her, effort was always related to outcome—if you studied more you did better. And so you run up against certain people whose life experience blinds them to the needs of a kid who can't give you the months of the year in order or can't spell. . . . It's the kid isn't trying.
>
> The headmistress is incapable of understanding that for someone with dyslexia you can study until you are blue in the face and you still will not read quicker, pronounce all words correctly, or spell better. The idea that someone just can't do certain things is foreign to some people. So I said to her, "You know, you could write a novel if you tried, if you really tried."

Football saved Cannell. It functioned as a respite, an interim support that perhaps got him through high school. As a running back he set high school football records that still stand, and so he could at least—each Sunday morning—read good things about himself in the local newspaper. But if sports gave him self-esteem, it was a special teacher, Ralph Salisbury, who finally saw the talent that had remained hidden throughout his previous twelve or so years of schooling. A grateful Cannell describes what this teacher meant to him: "Ralph was the first instructor I ever had in my entire academic career who said to me, 'It isn't important to me whether you can't spell. I'm interested in your ideas. I'm a creative writing instructor, not a spelling teacher.'"

Cannell is eager for people to understand what Salisbury clearly understood—that writing and spelling are not related, and also that writing and dyslexia are not related. "*Writing has nothing to do with dyslexia. Spelling has something to do with it,*" he stresses. He is often asked how someone who is dyslexic can choose writing as his career: "We [dyslexics] are very good with abstract thought. And that's the key in writing," he says. You can feel the excitement as he describes how his outline—what he refers to as "the cerebral part"—allows "the more visceral part" of his writing to come out:

> Everything I write I see; it's really a written picture. It's like I'm in the scene with the characters. I see it like it was a movie. And I will often describe it the way my imagination is picking it up. For dialogue, I'm everyone in the scene, and I say my lines of dialogue. And so my outline gives structure, it frees me to be all these people, to have a party with my characters.

For Cannell it is the *image* that drives the writing. He can use words to paint the picture that he sees in his imagination. Words are the servants of the visual images. They are the tools but not the creators of the images that he writes about.

Cannell does not allow his difficulties sounding out words to deter him:

> I sound out new words incorrectly. In my mind it sounds differently. I do that with names of characters when I'm reading a novel. And then I hear the name pronounced by the author and I go, Oh, it's Alicia and not Alice. When I am writing, I just don't let it get to me. I just figure that it isn't a strength. My strength is in abstract thought.

Cannell shares the view that dyslexia also confers some advantages: "I don't have writer's block because writer's block is caused by the desire to be perfect. And as a dyslexic you know you're not going to be perfect." Furthermore, knowing his imperfections has taught Cannell to be very careful as a writer. For example, he deals with scientific terms by making sure he copies each word exactly right, rechecking it again and again. He says, "When you know your limitations, you are extra careful. People who are dyslexic are not going to make the mistakes. I have a self-check, safety mechanism built in; I'm humble enough to double-check everything I do."

What advice does Cannell have for parents of children who are dyslexic?

Parents have to create victories whenever they can, whether it's music, sports, or art. You want your dyslexic child to be able to say, "Yeah, reading's hard, but I have these other things that I can do."

If a child is struggling in reading and succeeding in football, you can't take football away from him. He can't spend his entire life studying. You have to recognize the total child, you can't just attend to—or neglect—any part of that child. You have to build up and acknowledge those strengths. That's what will carry him through all those difficult times. I know it. I have lived it.

And what does he think is most helpful for children as they get older?

I think untimed tests for dyslexics are really critical. They can mean the difference between a child's reaching his potential and realizing his dreams—or not. They are everything to a dyslexic child. I read very slowly. I know that extra time can make a difference for children and young adults.

Dyslexia may be very difficult for a child in school, but it may also be a great gift. That's the way it has to be viewed. Because once you get out of school, you will see that this world needs abstract thought and creativity desperately. Anyone can ply equations and formulas and memorize details, but it is the rare person who comes up with a new question or a new insight.

The ranks of dyslexic writers also include John Cheever, Fanny Flagg, Richard Ford, and John Grisham.

Charles Schwab

Charles Schwab, who revolutionized the financial services business, is also dyslexic.

As a child, schoolwork never came easily for me. Reading and writing were particularly difficult, though I was pretty good at math. Though I didn't know why at the time, I had to work three times as hard as other kids to accomplish the same thing.

I flunked English at Stanford not once but twice. I couldn't write a composition. I couldn't finish a book. I never read a novel. I struggled in French. I had taken Latin in high school, so I could memorize the things that were very logical and consistent, it was almost a math kind of thing.

His comment, "I couldn't read aloud that well, but I could talk and solve problems pretty well," captures both his difficulties and his sea of strengths. And it was these strengths that helped get him through school:

I had this outgoing personality. I was confident, and that kept me going. In some ways I just conned my way through. I had good leadership skills, I had good ways with people.

I also had strengths in thinking. I was great at conceptualizing. I was naturally good in science and math, as I said. And maybe the creative part of my brain was being used for imagining and for problem solving. From the earliest part of my life I can remember thinking that I could solve almost anything if I just thought about it. But I never pushed it, because I was so poor at English.

Even though I couldn't read quickly, I could imagine things much faster than some other people who were stuck thinking sequentially. That helped me in solving complex business problems. I could visualize how things would look at the end of the tunnel.

He had a strategy to get around his excruciatingly slow reading.

I always used, wherever I could, the abbreviated kinds of books, the ones that would give me a five-page synopsis. I learned about Classic Comics back in elementary school. And so as a student I relied on these comic books to "read" such assignments as *A Tale of Two Cities* and *Ivanhoe.*

Sports were very important to Schwab, too. "I had very poor SATs, and I would never have been admitted to Stanford on the basis of those. Fortunately, I was very good at golf."

Schwab knows firsthand about the impact of dyslexia on a child when he must read aloud in front of his classmates who laugh, and "the kid just dies a thousand deaths." Schwab's greatest concern is the child's self-esteem and the impact of dyslexia on children and families. He has never forgotten the overwhelming helplessness he and his wife, Helen, felt when one of their own children first experienced what was eventually recognized as dyslexia. As so often happens, the diagnosis in his child led to the diagnosis of dyslexia in himself. He later established Schwab Learning, a program of the Charles and Helen Schwab Foundation to provide parents with the kinds of services and support he and his wife wished they'd had.

He wants to prevent the pain that is so much a part of the struggle to read.

> Some of the kids feel as if they're really stupid. If there is anything I'd want them to know, it is that they're not stupid. They just learn differently. Once they understand that, they can feel better about themselves.

Schwab demonstrates his ability to get to the heart of an issue when he describes the rationale for providing accommodations to students who are dyslexic. It is the best summary I have come across:

> What you're trying to do is convey knowledge to these kids; it's not about trying to trick them out of success.

Most of all, Schwab wants to encourage dyslexic men and women to pursue their dreams:

> People who have a passion and have shown they can do the work should be encouraged to go on to the next level. With their passion, intellect, and compassion, they may be among the best lawyers and doctors.
>
> The important thing is to allow a person to focus on something he has a passion for. The more you focus on something, the more successful you are at it.
>
> I'm still a very slow reader of most things. I spend a lot of time on one subject, business, which is pretty boring to some people, but not to me. *The Wall Street Journal* is one thing I know like

the back of my hand, because I immerse myself in it every day, and I know the language of business pretty well now, thank God. But when I go on vacation, I'll be packing along a copy of [James Clavell's] *Shogun*, which is pretty tattered, and for the tenth time I'll try to get through part of it. I'm still working on it, and it may take me another ten years to get through it all.

Charles Schwab credits dyslexia for the kind of visionary thinking that led to his own business success. He is one of an ever-growing list of businessmen and businesswomen who are dyslexic: Sir Richard Branson, founder of Virgin Enterprises; John Chambers, CEO of Cisco Systems; William Hewlett, cofounder of Hewlett-Packard; Ken Kilroy, president of the Davis Companies; Craig McCaw, CEO and founder of Cellular One; Paul J. Orfalea, founder of Kinko's; Ingvar Kamprad, founder of IKEA; Diane Swonk, chief economist at Bank One; and Ted Turner, founder of Turner Broadcasting.

Graeme Hammond

Graeme Hammond is one of an elite group of surgeons actively engaged in cutting-edge research while maintaining a busy operating schedule. A cardiothoracic surgeon, he is now focused on transplantation, specifically on developing methods for xenograft, transplanting tissues or organs from one species to another. If successful, this line of research could dramatically alter the landscape in tissue transplantation and bring new hope to the thousands of men and women waiting on transplant lists.

Hammond came within a hairsbreadth of not gaining entry to medical school. His difficulties in reading were obvious in grade school.

In the first few years, I knew I couldn't read. I couldn't read a single thing. The teacher would look at me when my turn came to read aloud and try to help me. It was terrible. I would take it out on the book. I'd take my pencil and grind it into these words that didn't make any sense to me. I'd start beating on the books because I couldn't read the words.

Finally, his parents took him to the ultimate diagnostician of his time, Dr. Samuel Orton, who confirmed that the young boy was dyslexic. Hammond began taking reading lessons, but they were provided haphazardly and were not very effective. It would be years before he was able to read his first book, *Mr. Popper's Penguins,* in eighth grade.

> It felt good. I was proud of myself. I couldn't believe it. It wasn't a very thick book, but I actually read it—I got from one cover to the other without ever throwing it down or slamming it down or having a temper tantrum.

Once he was in high school, the necessity to complete a foreign language requirement almost prevented his graduation. "Foreign languages killed me in high school," he recalls. "It took me four years to get through two years of Spanish. That's one of the reasons I was eighty-second out of eighty-eight when I graduated."

Hammond began at Hobart College, experienced difficulties, and dropped out. Then he was drafted into the army (it was during the Korean War), which turned out to be a very positive life-changing experience for him. In the army he experienced success and gained a sense of self-competence. After his discharge he was eager to give college one more try. Always an excellent student in science, he now found that he had a particular knack for the physical sciences and planned to become a geologist.

> But then I had an interview in the geology department at Yale. The interviewer came down on me very, very sternly about the need to master two languages to get a Ph.D. So I just said, No. That's not for me. And that's why I applied to medical school. I didn't need any foreign languages for medical school, and I knew I could handle the science.

Hammond found that as he progressed, learning medicine in depth, medical school got "better and better every year. Finally, in my last year, I was one of the top ten students of my class."

Following graduation he was accepted for a surgical residency at Massachusetts General Hospital and then for a faculty position at Yale. Hammond, as judged by his mentors—senior surgeons at both Harvard and Yale—had what it takes to be a top-tier surgeon. However, while Hammond could exercise superior judgment, operate with a sure hand,

and in every way more than meet the day-to-day demands of surgery, passing the National Board of Medical Examiners Licensing Examination was another matter. To him this seemed more about test-taking skills than about knowledge. But these tests almost curtailed his career:

> I have always been a slow reader and did poorly on these kinds of tests. And when I was a fourth-year medical student, I absolutely could not pass the national boards. I still have not passed them. And so I had to come through the back door. And the back door for the national boards was the state boards, which consisted of questions to be answered in essay form, not multiple choice. I have no problem with these, and so I took the New York State boards and sailed through them. And when I was a resident at Mass. General Hospital, the Massachusetts boards accepted the New York State boards. They never knew I hadn't passed my national boards. Subsequently, I was on the National Board of Medical Examiners and have a diploma hanging on my wall from them thanking me for being on their board for so long. But ironically I never passed their boards.

After he learned surgery during a rigorous residency, he was faced with another multiple-choice test before he could go on with his career.

> I had a terrible time with Part I of the surgical boards; that's the written part. And they are just like the national boards. I flunked that flat. And I had to take a course in Chicago, not to learn surgery but to learn how to answer these questions. After that I passed the boards.

The second part of the surgical boards was an oral examination. "I just sailed through the oral part," he said. "Surgery is judgment. And this is something that isn't tested in the written test in surgery, only in the orals."

As much as dyslexia has frustrated him, he, like others, believes that dyslexia is responsible for the qualities that ultimately led to his success:

> For me it's been a blessing in disguise. This difficulty reading gave me a tremendous amount of perseverance; my whole life is about striving because I've had so many roadblocks put in my

way. I see a lot of surgeons who do everything well, yet they never ever question. They've never been forced to try another way to find an answer to a problem. In my own case, I had developed the ability to look for other ways of doing things.

And just as John Irving was particularly offended by accusations of not trying hard enough, Hammond was similarly wounded by accusations of laziness when he was young, and that rankles to this day. In fact, in 1998, when he saw me on *The Lehrer News Hour* talking about the functional disruption in the neural systems of readers who are dyslexic, he knew he had found what he had been searching for:

> That's it, I said to myself. They've found it. They've found the problem. These images meant I could point to something tangible as the cause of my problem. I was very emotional when I saw that. It was fantastic. I would now be able to say to all those critics, I was right. You were wrong.

Delos M. Cosgrove

Dr. Delos M. (Toby) Cosgrove, chairman of the department of thoracic and cardiovascular surgery at the Cleveland Clinic, is dyslexic. He is renowned in the field of heart valve repair, in which he has worked tirelessly to make cardiac procedures safer and more effective. Known for his innovation and creativity, his eighteen patents for cardiac procedures have helped solve many problems encountered in valvular surgery.

Cosgrove struggled to learn to read throughout his early schooling. In college, French was "almost the end of me as I worked my butt off to obtain three D–'s and a D in remedial French." Reading, writing a paper, or giving a talk remained "big problems." For young Toby, college meant nonstop work. "All I did was study, even on weekends. While everyone else was partying or going to the movies or sports events, I packed my suitcase and left campus for home where I studied all weekend."

Reflecting his reading difficulties, standardized testing was a disaster for him, including the MCATs (Medical College Admission Test), and it seemed doubtful that Cosgrove would ever fulfill his dream of becoming a doctor. In fact, he was accepted at only one of the thirteen medical schools to which he applied. The University of Virginia Medical School was eager to admit students from his college, Williams, and so his admission was expedited. As a medical student Cosgrove received "the first A of my life" in surgery. He was already a physician and completing his surgical residency when he was drafted into the Air Force. Between 1968 and 1969 he served as chief of the United States Air Force Casualty Staging Flight at Da Nang, Vietnam, and was awarded the Bronze Star. Following his military service he was accepted into a residency in surgery at Massachusetts General Hospital in Boston, the same residency program that Graeme Hammond had completed several years earlier.

During his career Cosgrove has served on the editorial board of just about every major cardiothoracic surgery journal. Yet he continues to experience reminders of his dyslexia. These reminders do not come when he is in the midst of his professional work but emerge during other times.

> Four or five times each day I completely stop a patient's heart from beating for one to two hours, perform some type of surgical intervention, and attempt to restart the heart. In each case there is a moment of tension while I wait to see if the heart will start beating. As tense as this is, I know I am in control and can deal with any contingency that may arise.
>
> After the surgery is completed, it's a different matter. When I pick up the telephone to call the patient's family waiting in the lounge, I am often unable to pronounce the patient's family name.

Family names are the equivalent of nonsense words, and chances are that a dyslexic has not previously encountered many of the names. As a result, he has not memorized their pronunciation and is unable to pronounce the names correctly.

Cosgrove sees failure as the starting point for a process of learning and discovery. Even after being rejected by twelve of thirteen medical schools, being told he was the worst resident in his class at Massachusetts General Hospital, and being strongly advised not to go into cardiothoracic surgery, he did not give up, nor did he lose sight of his dream. By now Cosgrove has been offered the position of chair of surgery at just about every one of the schools that rejected him. Yes, he turned them down.

Hammond and Cosgrove follow in the footsteps of many renowned physicians, past and current, who are dyslexic, including Harvey Cushing, who founded modern neurosurgery and was awarded a Pulitzer Prize for his biography of Sir William Osler.

Gaston Caperton

Early in Gaston Caperton's career he transformed a small local insurance agency into the tenth largest privately owned bank and mortgage company in the United States. When he took office as governor, the state was on the verge of bankruptcy; a decade later, West Virginia was named "the most improved state in the nation" by *Financial World* magazine. Currently, he is CEO and president of the College Board.

School was a struggle for young Gaston. He remembers spending "so many summers being tutored, it seemed as if I was always going to a tutor." He attended a private school and after "flunking three out of five courses" was able to remain in school only because of his father's strong encouragement. After studying all summer long, he passed his re-exams. His grades improved and at the end of the next semester, during a school assembly, it was announced that he had made the school honor roll. As he was walking out of the assembly, one of the teachers said to him, "If Gaston Caperton can do it, anyone in the school can." As I spoke with Caperton, he commented, "While it seemed like a funny statement at the time, when I look back, it certainly wasn't a statement of encouragement." Dealing with his reading, spelling, and foreign language problems, it was difficult for Caperton to think of himself as smart. Although he was the quarterback of his junior high school football team, for example, he was not permitted to call the plays. Rather, this responsibility was given to a halfback who received straight As. He progressed in high school, so that he not only played quarterback, but also called the plays. In college he majored in business. "I worked hard to get a C; I had to work a lot harder than most people." Caperton was able to maintain his sense of self-worth, mainly, he believes, because his parents viewed him as smart and maintained high expectations for him.

This combination of high expectations and hard work has been key to his success and has influenced everything he has done in his life; he sees it as a solution to most problems. Moreover, he believes that having to struggle early on can help develop strength and resiliency. Using himself as an example, he explains that as he learned to read, he also began to learn more about himself and his strengths. As a result, he developed a self-confidence and a "can-do" attitude that has remained a powerful force in his life.

As an adult Caperton felt a need to better understand the nature of his reading problem, so he went to a doctor in West Virginia who Caperton, as governor, had honored for his work with learning disabilities. The physician told Caperton he could administer "a lot of tests," but he already knew what was wrong.

"You had trouble reading," he said. "You did terrible in foreign languages. You still can't spell."

Caperton responded yes to each statement. The physician continued: "You're not very good at remembering names, are you?"

The governor responded, "No, terrible at it."

"You're very intuitive. You're sitting in a room and there's a complicated problem that people are talking about and asking what the solution should be—and you get it twice as fast as anybody else."

Caperton said yes.

"You are dyslexic. Fortunately, you have a good brain. It just processes things differently."

For the governor, it was as if a great weight had been lifted.

Today, he is a prolific reader and it is his favorite pastime. And yet there are reminders of his dyslexia as he goes about his daily activities. He gives many speeches; most are given from notes and not read word for word because reading out loud is still difficult. And yet he believes that dyslexia is a "tremendous asset," one that has made him more intuitive, a more original thinker, and more creative. He believes as a result of dyslexia he has also developed more compassion and a better understanding of other people.

After reading these stories, no one should ever doubt "a person like *that*" can be a winner in any field in which he or she has an interest and talent. These are stories of triumph—over innate difficulties as well as those created by misunderstandings, misjudgments, and stereotyped views of what constitutes real ability or talent. For these dyslexics and for thousands of others, the obstacle to success is often not their inherent physiologic weakness but the misguided perceptions of others, those who believe that for dyslexics spelling has something to do with creative writing, that slow reading is incompatible with sharp thinking, that scores on standardized tests predict performance in real life. Each of these remarkably talented individuals we've just met almost didn't realize his or her dream. Each was made to feel stupid or incapable. So-called experts erected barriers and gave bad advice. And yet each ultimately triumphed, viewing dyslexia as a gift more than a burden. As Sir Richard Branson said during an appearance on *The Charlie Rose Show,* "If I hadn't been dyslexic, I would never have done it."

Dyslexics think differently. They are intuitive and excel at problem solving, seeing the big picture, and simplifying. They feast on visualizing, abstract thinking, and thinking out of the box. They are poor rote reciters but inspired visionaries. Adult dyslexics are tough: Having struggled, they are used to adversity; hard work and perseverance now come naturally. Having experienced failure, they are fearless, undaunted by setbacks. Repetition and practice are a way of life. Each person I've focused on was rescued by a special person—a parent or a teacher—who saw the raw talent and nurtured it in the midst of all the naysayers. The feeling of hope was sustained by the taste of success in sports, the arts, or some other activity. Yes, the symptoms of dyslexia persist, but they needn't interfere with success.

Success is waiting for your child, and now you know what to do to help him achieve it. You don't have to rely on chance. You know how to identify a problem early and how to get the right help to ensure that it is your child's strengths and not the misperceptions of others that ultimately define him. You know what is possible and how to nourish it: Children blossom with reward and praise, and flourish because of high expectations. Above all you must maintain your belief in your child, provide unconditional support for him, and hold true to a vision of his future. The rewards will be great.

Today, each dyslexic child is free to develop his talents and to pursue his dreams—and to know he will succeed. Dyslexia *can* be overcome.

Notes

Chapter 2: The Historical Roots of Dyslexia

13 "He has always been": W. Pringle Morgan, "A Case of Congenital Word Blindness," *The British Medical Journal* (1896): p. 1378.

14 What is perhaps the earliest: A good discussion of the earliest reports of acquired reading problems can be found in Arthur L. Benton and Robert J. Joynt, "Early Descriptions of Aphasia," *Archives of Neurology* 3 (August 1960): 109/205–126/222.

14 When the patient: Sir William Broadbent, "Cerebral Mechanisms of Speech and Thought," *Transactions of the Royal Chirigal Society* 55 (1872): 145–94.

14 Although Broadbent's contribution: Dr. Adolf Kussmaul, *Die Storungen der Spache* (Leipzig, Germany: Verlag Von F.C.W. Vogel, 1877).

15 If the disruption was only partial: In R. Berlin, *"Eine besondre Art der Wortblind-heit"* (Weisbaden, Germany: Verlag von J. F. Bergmann, 1887), as quoted by James Hinshelwood, M.D., in "A Case of Dyslexia: A Peculiar Form of Word-Blindness," *The Lancet* 2 (November 21, 1896): 1451–54.

15 "Reading of printed and written": Ibid.

16 "He could not read": J. Hinshelwood, M.D., "Word-Blindness and Visual Memory," *The Lancet* (December 21, 1895): 1564–70.

18 "He had such an excellent": J. Hinshelwood, M.D., "Congenital Word-Blindness," *The Lancet* (1900): 1506–08. All quotations describing both Case 1 and 2 are from this early article by Hinshelwood.

19 One was a ten-year-old girl: J. Hinshelwood, "Congenital Word-Blindness, with Reports of Two Cases," *Ophthalmic Review* 11 (1902): 91–99. All quotations on this page are from this 1902 paper.

20 "I had little doubt": Ibid.

20 Both Hinshelwood's and Morgan's: Binet was first commissioned by the French government to develop a test in 1903: he did not publish his methods until 1905. A. M. Binet and T. Simon, "Methodes nouvelles pour le diagnostic du niveau intel-lectuel des anormaux," *L'année Psychologique* 11 (1905): 191–224.

21 "were frequently overlooked": Quoted in discussion following J. H. Fisher's article, "Congenital Word-Blindness (Inability to Learn to Read)," *Transactions of the Oph-thalmological Society of the United Kingdom* 30 (1910): 216–25. In addition to his

clinical position at the ophthalmic hospital, Dr. Treacher Collins was also a professor at the Royal College of Surgeons.

21 "The father . . . who is": In J. Lange, "Agnosia and Apraxia," as quoted in J. W.
Brown (ed.), *Agnosia and Apraxia: Selected Papers of Liepman, Lange, and Potzl*
(Hillsdale, N.J.: Lawrence Erlbaum Associates, 1988), p. 85.

21 "It is a matter of": J. Hinshelwood, "Congenital Word-Blindness, with Reports of
Two Cases," *Ophthalmic Review* 11 (1902): 91–99.

22 "In these days": J. Hinshelwood, "A Case of Congenital Word-Blindness," *The Ophthalmoscope* 2 (1904): 399–405.

22 "On my advice": J. Hinshelwood, "Congenital Word-Blindness, with Reports of Two
Cases," *Ophthalmic Review* 11 (1902): 91–99.

23 "I advised them to": J. Hinshelwood, "A Case of Congenital Word-Blindness," *The
Ophthalmoscope* 2 (1904): 399–405.

23 "The detection of congenital": E. Nettleship, "Cases of Congenital Word-Blindness
(Inability to Learn to Read)," *Ophthamic Review* 20 (1901): 61–67.

23 Here the first report: E. Bosworth McCready reviews the number of reported cases
of congenital word-blindness in "Congenital Word-Blindness as a Cause of Backwardness in School Children. Report of a Case Associated with Stuttering," *Pennsylvania Medical Journal* 13 (1910): 278–284. The cases from the United States are
described by E. Jackson in "Developmental Alexia (Congenital Word-Blindness),"
American Journal of the Medical Sciences 131 (1906): 843–49.

24 "While the majority of cases": E. Bosworth McCready, "Congenital Word-Blindness
as a Cause of Backwardness in School Children. Report of a Case Associated with
Stuttering," in *Pennsylvania Medical Journal* 13 (1910): 278–84.

24 He describes one man: E. Bosworth McCready, "Defects in the Zone of Language
(Word-Deafness and Word-Blindness) and Their Influence in Education and
Behavior," in *American Journal of Psychiatry* 6 (old series 83, 267–277 (1926–27).

Chapter 3: The Big Picture

25 On August 17, 1987: the Interagency Committee on Learning Disabilities (ICLD)
was mandated by the Health Research Extension Act of 1985 (P.L. 99–158), and its
establishment was announced in the *Federal Register* on March 11, 1986, by the
National Institutes of Health (NIH).

25 After a comprehensive investigation: Interagency Committee on Learning Disabilities, *Learning Disabilities: A Report to the U.S. Congress* (Washington, D.C., U.S.
Government Printing Office, 1987).

27 "Classification is the art of carving" R. E. Kendell, *The Role of Diagnosis in Psychiatry* (Oxford, England: Blackwell Scientific Publications, 1975), p. 65.

28 Evidence from the Connecticut study: Sally Shaywitz et al., "Evidence that Dyslexia
May Represent the Lower Tail of a Normal Distribution of Reading Ability," *New
England Journal of Medicine* 326, 145–50; P. A. Silva, R. McGee, and S. Williams,
"Some Characteristics of 9-Year-Old Boys with General Reading Backwardness or
Specific Reading Retardation, *Journal of Child Psychology and Psychiatry* 26

(1985): 407–21; B. Rodgers, "The Identification and Prevalence of Specific Reading Retardation," *British Journal of Educational Psychology* 53 (1983): 369–73.

28 "The notion of dyslexia": Ibid., p. 149.

29 "No one would accuse": Kerri Schwalbe's story appeared in *Newsweek* magazine, February 3, 1992, p. 57.

29 According to U.S. Department of Education Statistics: Prevalence data is based on the *18th Annual Report to Congress on the Implementation of the Individuals with Disabilities Education Act* of the U.S. Department of Education for the 1994–95 school year and J. W. Lerner, "Educational Interventions in Learning Disabilities," *Journal of the American Academy of Child and Adolescent Psychiatry* 28 (1989): 326–31.

29 National Assessment of Educational Progess (NAEP): From National Education Goals Panel, U.S. Department of Education: *Reading Achievement State by State, 1999.* Washington, D.C.: U.S. Government Printing Office, 1999.

30 Seventy-eight percent: The National Assessment Governing Board of the National Assessment of Educational Progress adopted three achievement levels—basic, proficient, and advanced—and set its performance standard at the proficient or advanced levels. Proficient is defined as reflecting "a consensus that students reaching this level have demonstrated competency over challenging subject matter and are well prepared for the next level of schooling." Basic levels reflect reading "below proficient . . . partial mastery of knowledge and skills that are fundamental for proficient work." *(Reading Achievement State by State, 1999,* p. 131).

30 as many as 38 percent: P. L. Donahue, K. E. Voekl, J. R. Campbell, and J. Mazzeo, *The NAEP 1998 Reading Report Card for the Nation,* NCES, 1999–459 (Washington, D.C.: U.S. Department of Education, Office of Educational Research and Improvement, National Center for Educational Statistics, 1999).

30 "The educational careers of": C. E. Snow, M. S. Burns, and P. Griffin (eds.), *Preventing Reading Difficulties in Children* (Washington, D.C.: National Academy Press, 1998), p. 98.

30 The Connecticut study: S. E. Shaywitz and B. A. Shaywitz, "Unlocking Learning Disabilities: The Neurological Basis," in S. C. Cramer and W. Ellis (eds.), *Learning Disabilities: Lifelong Issues* (Baltimore, Md.: Paul H. Brookes, 1996); S. E. Shaywitz, J. M. Fletcher, and B. A. Shaywitz, "Issues in the Definition and Classification of Attention Deficit Disorder," *Topics in Language Disorders* 14 (1994): 1–25; Interagency Committee on Learning Disabilities, *Learning Disabilities: A Report to the U.S. Congress* (Washington, D.C.: Government Printing Office, 1987).

30 We found that less than: S. E. Shaywitz, unpublished data.

30 Dyslexic children are generally: G. R. Lyon et al., "Rethinking Learning Disabilities," in C. E. Finn, Jr., R.A.J. Rotherham, and C. R. Hokanson, Jr. (eds.), *Rethinking Special Education for a New Century* (Washington, D.C.: Thomas B. Fordham Foundation and Progressive Policy Institute, 2001), pp. 259–87.

31 The high prevalence of reading difficulties: See H. W. Stevenson et al., "Reading Disabilities: The Case of Chinese, Japanese, and English," *Child Development* 53 (1982): 1164–81; Takehiko Hirose and Takeshi Hatta, "Reading Disabilities in Modern Japanese Children, *Journal of Research in Reading* 11 (1988): 152–60; Jun

Yamada and Adam Banks, "Evidence for and Characteristics of Dyslexia Among Japanese Children," *Annals of Dyslexia* 44 (1994): 105–19; L. Ganshow and T. R. Miles, "Dyslexia Across the World," *Perspectives* (Newsletter of the International Dyslexia Association) 26 (2000): 12–35.

31 In 1996 my article: S. Shaywitz, "Dyslexia," *Scientific American* 275 (1996): 98–104.

31 The diagnosis of dyslexia: See S. E. Shaywitz et al., "Prevalence of Reading Disability in Boys and Girls: Results of the Connecticut Longitudinal Study," Journal of the American Medical Association 264 (1990): 998–1002. In this study the identification of research-identified subjects was based on the *Connecticut Guidelines for the Identification and Education of Students with Learning Disabilities* (Hartford: Connecticut State Department of Education, 1983).

33 Here, too, we were able to use data: D. J. Francis et al., "The Measurement of Change: Assessing Behavior over Time and Within a Developmental Context," in G. R. Lyon (ed.), *Frames of Reference for the Assessment of Learning Disabilities: New Views on Measurement Issues* (Baltimore, Md.: Paul H. Brookes, 1994).

34 Our investigation of the so-called Matthew effect: B. A. Shaywitz et al., "A Matthew Effect for IQ but Not for Reading: Results From a Longitudinal Study," *Reading Research Quarterly* 30 (1995): 894–906.

34 "To all those who have": Matthew 13:12 (see also 25:29), *The New Oxford Annotated Bible,* New Revised Standard Version (New York: Oxford University Press, 1991).

Chapter 4: Why Some Smart People Can't Read

38 Gregory: Gregory's story appeared in "Dyslexia," *Scientific American* 275 (1996): 98–104.

40 Understanding that dyslexia: Evidence that the difficulty in dyslexia is within the language system is based on findings described by J. Torgesen, R. Wagner, and C. Rashotte in "Longitudinal Studies of Phonological Processing and Reading," *Journal of Educational Psychology* 27 (1994): 276–86, and in J. Fletcher et al., "Cognitive Profiles of Reading Disability: Comparisons of Discrepancy and Low Achievement Definitions," *Journal of Educational Psychology* 86 (1994): 6–23.

40 Think of the language system: Explanations of the modular system can be found in D. Shankweiler and S. Crane, "Language Mechanisms and Reading Disorder: A Modular Approach," *Cognition* 24 (1986): 139–68, and J. A. Fodor, *The Modularity of Mind* (Cambridge, Mass.: MIT Press, 1983).

Chapter 5: Everyone Speaks, but Not Everyone Reads

45 As linguists: Steven Pinker, *The Language Instinct* (New York: William Morrow, 1994).

45 John DeFrancis, professor emeritus: John DeFrancis, *Visible Speech* (Honolulu: University of Hawaii Press, 1989).

46 In 1989 linguist William Abler: William Abler, "On the Particulate Principle of Self-Defining Systems," *Journal of Social and Biological Structures* 12 (1989): 1–13.

47 A speaker can generate phonemes: A. Liberman, "How Theories in Speech Affect Research in Reading and Writing," in B. Blachman (ed.), *Foundations of Reading Acquisition and Dyslexia: Implications for Dyslexia* (Mahwah, N.J.: Lawrence Erlbaum Associates, 1997).

50 "Writing is not language": Leonard Bloomfield, *Language* (New York: Holt, Rinehart and Winston, 1933), p. 21.

54 By age six: I. Liberman et al., "Explicit Syllable and Phoneme Segmentation in the Young Child," *Experimental Care Psychology* 18 (1974): 201–12.

55 In the 1980s: L. Bradley and P. Bryant, "Categorizing Sounds and Learning to Read—a Causal Connection," *Nature* 301 (1983): 419–21.

55 In the 1990s: J. M. Fletcher et al., "Cognitive Profiles of Reading Disability: Comparisons of Discrepancy and Low Achievement Definitions," *Journal of Educational Psychology* 86 (1994): 6–23. See also K. E. Stanovich and L. S. Siegel, "Phenotypic Performance Profile of Children with Reading Disabilities: A Regression-Based Test of the Phonological-Core Variable-Difference Model," *Journal of Education Psychology* 86 (1994): 24–53.

55 One type of test: J. Rosner, Test of Auditory Analysis Skills (Novato, Calif.: Academic Therapy Publications, 1975).

55 When we gave this: S. Shaywitz et al., "Persistence of Dyslexia: The Connecticut Longitudinal Study at Adolescence," *Pediatrics* 104 (1999): 1351–59.

56 Ten years ago: R. Katz, "Phonological Deficiencies in Children with Reading Disability: Evidence from an Object-Naming Task" (Ph.D. diss., University of Connecticut, 1982).

Chapter 6: Reading the Brain

59 The earliest conceptions of the mind: The Age of Pyramids and other early conceptualizations of the mind are discussed in Stanley Finger, *Origins of Neuroscience* (New York: Oxford University Press, 1994), p. 8.

60 Ancient Chinese medicine: Ibid., p. 12. Zang Fu has been traced to the Period of Contending States (475–221 B.C.).

60 "The heart is hottest": C. G. Gross, "Aristotle on the Brain," *The Neuroscientist* 1 (1995): 245–50. The quote is on page 248.

60 Most influential were: Galen's early physician-scientist views of the importance of the brain can be found in Stanley Finger, *Origins of Neuroscience* (New York: Oxford University Press, 1994), p. 18.

62 The doctrine that came: From S. Zola-Morgan, "Localization of Brain Function: The Legacy of Franz Joseph Gall (1758–1828), *Annual Review of Neuroscience* 18 (1995): 359–83.

63 He localized "carnivorous instinct . . .": Ibid., p. 374.

64 It was just such a circumstance: Localization of expressive language, including the derivation of the term "aphasia," occurred around 1861–65. See Stanley Finger, *Origins of Neuroscience* (New York: Oxford University Press, 1994), p. 379.

65 Following a stroke: Ibid.

65 Although perceptive physicians: Ibid., pp. 372–73. Finger discusses attempts to disentangle loss of speech from loss of movement of the tongue.

67 To pinpoint a site: Ibid., p. 393.

68 In the late 1970s: The first report of an examination of the brain of a person with dyslexia was W. E. Drake, "Clinical and Pathological Findings in a Child with a Developmental Learning Disability," *Journal of Learning Disabilities* 1 (1968): 9–25. For further discussion of dyslexia brain bank studies, see A. Galaburda et al., "Developmental Dyslexia: Four Consecutive Patients with Cortical Anomalies," *Annals of Neurology* 18 (1985): 222–23.

68 These abnormalities coincided: N. Geschwind, "Disconnexion Syndromes in Animals and Man," *Brain* 88 (1965): 237–94.

68 Using CT and, later: See A. B. Wolbarst, *Looking Within* (Berkeley: University of California Press, 1999), for user-friendly discussions of various imaging modalities.

69 "These facts seem to indicate": C. S. Roy and C. S. Sherrington, "On the Regulation of the Blood-Supply of the brain," *Journal of Physiology* 1 (1890): 85.

69 "It is, therefore, clear": Louis Sokoloff, "Relationships Among Local Functional Activity, Energy Metabolism, and Blood Flow from the Central Nervous System," *Federation Proceedings* 40 (1981): 2311–16, quote on p. 2315.

Chapter 7: The Working Brain Reads

76 To begin we recruited: Reported in B. A. Shaywitz et al., "Sex Differences in the Functional Organization of the Brain for Language," *Nature* 373 (1995): 607–09. The finding of a sex difference in the organization of the brain for language has been replicated by other investigators. See J. Jaeger et al., "Sex Differences in Brain Regions Activated by Grammatical and Reading Tasks," *Neuroreport* 9 (1998): 2803–07; and K. Kansaku et al., "Sex Differences in Lateralization Revealed in the Posterior Language Areas," *Cerebral Cortex* 10 (2000): 866–72.

78 These studies began: Our first study, with adults as subjects, was reported by S. E. Shaywitz et al. in *Proceedings of the National Academy of Science* 95 (1998): 2636–41. The subjects were thirty-two good readers (sixteen men and sixteen women) and twenty-nine dyslexic readers (fourteen men and fifteen women). The latter group had a lifelong history of reading problems; their reading average was in the sixteenth percentile on a standard test of nonword reading, compared to the seventy-sixth percentile for nonimpaired men and women.

78 As they read: Discussed in B. A. Shaywitz et al., "Disruption of Posterior Brain Systems for Reading in Children with Developmental Dyslexia," *Biological Psychiatry* 52 (2002): 101–10.

79 As early as 1891: J. Dejerine, "Sur un cas de cécité verbale avec agraphie, suivi d'au-

topsie," *C. R. Société du Biologie* 43 (1891): 197–201; and see his "Contribution à l'étude anatomopathologique et clinique des differentes varieties de cécité ver-bale," *Memoires de la Société de Biologie* 4 (1892): 61–90.

79   It responds very rapidly: C. Price, C. Moore, and R.S.J. Frackowiak, "The Effect of Varying Stimulus Rates and Duration of Brain Activity During Reading," *Neuroim-age* 3 (1996): 40–52.

79   Not surprisingly, the occipito-temporal: Disruptions of the word form area are explored in J. Dejerine, "Sur un cas de cécité verbale avec agraphie, suivi d'autop-sie," *C. R. Société du Biologie* 43 (1891): 197–201; and see his "Contribution à l'é-tude anatomopathologique et clinique des differentes varieties de cécité verbale," *Memoires de la Société de Biologie* 4 (1892): 61–90. See also French neurologist Laurent Cohen et al. "The Visual Word Form Area: Spatial and Temporal Charac-terization of an Initial Stage of Reading in Normal Subjects and Posterior Split Brain Patients," *Brain* 123 (2000): 291–307.

80   Figure 23 is from Dehaene, S., et al. "Cerebral mechanisms of word masking and unconscious repetition priming," *Nature Neuroscience* 4 (2001): 752–58.

81   One means of compensating: Discussed in B. A. Shaywitz et al., "Disruption of Pos-terior Brain Systems for Reading in Children with Developmental Dyslexia," *Bio-logical Psychiatry* 52 (2002): 101–10.

82   This signature seems to be universal: A worldwide community of scientists has con-tributed to our understanding of the neural circuitry in reading and the nature of the disruption in dyslexic readers. These data are consistent with functional brain imaging studies that show a failure of left hemisphere posterior brain systems to function properly in adult dyslexic readers while they perform reading tasks. The data are found in the following studies: N. Brunswick et al., "Explicit and Implicit Processing of Words and Pseudowords by Adult Developmental Dyslexics: A Search for Wernicke's *Wortschatz*," *Brain* 122 (1999): 1901–17; E. Paulesu et al., "Dyslexia: Cultural Diversity and Biological Unity," *Science* 291 (2001): 2165–67; J. M. Rumsey et al., "Failure to Activate the Left Temporoparietal Cortex in Dyslexia," *Archives of Neurology* 49 (1992): 527–34; R. Salmelin et al., "Impaired Visual Word Processing in Dyslexia Revealed with Magnetoencephalography," *Annals of Neurology* 40 (1996): 157–62; A. Seki et al., "A Functional Magnetic Res-onance Imaging Study During Sentence Reading in Japanese Dyslexic Children," *Brain & Development* 23 (2001): 312–16; S. E. Shaywitz et al., "Functional Disrup-tion in the Organization of the Brain for Reading in Dyslexia," *Proceedings of the National Academy of Science* 95 (1998): 2535–41; P. G. Simos et al., "Cerebral Mechanisms Involved in Word Reading in Dyslexic Children: A Magnetic Source Imaging Approach," *Cerebral Cortex* 10 (2000): 809–16; E. Temple et al., "Dis-rupted Neural Responses to Phonological and Orthographic Processing in Dyslexic Children: An fMRI Study," *NeuroReport* 12 (2000): 299–307.

82   Even high-achieving university students: Disruption present in bright dyslexic stu-dents is shown in E. Paulesu et al., "Dyslexia: Cultural Diversity and Biological Unity," *Science* 291 (2001): 2165–67.

83   Figure 26: Ibid.

84   Having identified the neural components: A helpful discussion of hypothesized

modes of neural interaction can be found in P. M. Churchland, *The Engine of Reason, the Seat of the Soul* (Cambridge: MIT Press, 1995), pp. 11–15. For discussion of functional connectivity, see K. J. Friston, "Functional and Effective Connectivity in Neuroimaging: A Synthesis," *Human Brain Mapping* 2 (1994): 56–78.

85 For example, imaging studies: In S. Shaywitz et al., "Neural Systems for Compensation and Persistence: Young Adult Outcome of Childhood Reading Disability," *Biological Psychiatry* (in press).

85 One of the most exciting applications: B. Shaywitz et al., "Development of Left Occipito-Temporal Systems for Skilled Reading Following a Phonologically-Based Intervention in Children." Abstract. To be presented at the Organization for Human Brain Mapping Annual Meeting, New York, June, 2003. A growing number of investigators are reporting the influence of reading interventions on brain organization. These include T. Richards et al., "Effects of a phonologically driven treatment for dyslexia on lactate levels measured by proton MRI spectroscopic imaging," *American Journal of Neuroradiology* 21 (2000): 916–22; P. Simos et al., "Dyslexia-specific brain activation profile becomes normal following successful remedial training," *Neurology* 58 (2002): 1203–13; and E. Temple et al., "Disruption of the neural response to rapid acoustic stimuli in dyslexia: evidence from functional MRI," *Proceedings of the National Academy of Science* 97 (2000): 13907–12.

Chapter 8: Early Clues to Dyslexia

95 In England, researchers asked: P. E. Bryant et al., "Nursery Rhymes, Phonological Skills and Reading," *Journal of Child Language* 16 (1989): 407–28.

96 Each child was asked: L. Bradley and P. E. Bryant, "Difficulties in Auditory Organization as a Possible Cause of Reading Backwardness," *Nature* 271 (1978): 746–47.

98 Dyslexia runs in families: Replicated studies of affected families (especially of twins) have identified chromosomes 2, 3, 6, 15, and 18 as associated with dyslexia. These studies and their findings are discussed in R. K. Olson, "Genes, Environment and Reading Disabilities," in R.J. Sternberg and L. Spear-Swerling (eds.), *Perspectives on Learning Disabilities* (Boulder, Colo.: Westview Press, 1999); S. E. Fisher and J. C. DeFries, "Developmental Dyslexia: Genetic Dissection of a Complex Cognitive Trait," *Nature Reviews Neuroscience* 30 (2002): 767–780; B. Pennington and J. Gilger, "How Is Dyslexia Transmitted?" in C. H. Chase, G. D. Rosen, and G. Sherman (eds.), *Developmental Dyslexia* (Timonium, Md.: York Press, 1996); and H. S. Scarborough, "Early Identification of Children at Risk for Reading Disabilities: Phonological Awareness and Some Other Promising Predictions," in B. K. Shapiro, P. J. Accordo, and A. J. Capute, *Specific Reading Disability* (Timonium, Md.: York Press, 1998).

100 In being alert to clues: F. R. Vellutino, "Dyslexia," *Scientific American* 256 (1987): 34–41.

101 Whatever subgroups of children: R. D. Morris et al., "Subtypes of Reading Disability: Variability Around a Phonological Core," *Journal of Educational Psychology* 90 (1998): 347–73. See also M. Wolf and P. G. Bowers, "The Double-Deficit Hypothe-

sis for the Developmental Dyslexias," *Journal of Educational Psychology* 91 (1999): 415–38.

Chapter 9: Later Clues to Dyslexia

102 When a child first begins: U. Frith, "Beneath the Surface of Developmental Dyslexia," in K. Patterson, J. Marshall, and M. Coltheart (eds.), *Surface Dyslexia* (Hillsdale, N.J.: Erlbaum, 1985), pp. 301–30.

102 These very young children: P. Maisonheimer, P. Drum, and L. Ehri, "Does Environmental Print Identification Lead Children into Word Reading?" *Journal of Reading Behavior* 16 (1984): 363–67.

102 Children can memorize: W. Nagy and P. Herman, "Breadth and Depth of Vocabulary Knowledge: Implications for Acquisition and Instruction," in M. McKeown and M. Curtis (eds.), *The Nature of Vocabulary Acquisition* (Hillsdale, N.J.: Erlbaum, 1987), pp. 19–35.

103 If a child knows: L. C. Ehri and L. S. Wilce, "Movement into Reading: Is the First Stage of Printed Word Learning Visual or Phonetic?" *Reading Research Quarterly* 20 (1985): 163–79.

103 Such children might read: For research on the tendency to confuse words that have some similar letters but no phonologic similarities, see M. Stuart, "Factors Influencing Word Recognition in Pre-reading Children," *British Journal of Psychology* 81 (1990): 135–46, and M. Stuart and M. Coltheart, "Does Reading Develop in a Sequence of Stages?" *Cognition* 30 (1988): 139–81.

104 The beauty of this process: G. Lukatela and M. T. Turvey, "Visual Lexical Access Is Initially Phonological: Evidence from Phonological Priming by Homophones and Pseudohomophones," *Journal of Experimental Psychology* 123 (1994): 331–53.

105 Studies in which the eye movements: K. Rayner and A. Pollatsek, *The Psychology of Reading* (Englewood Cliffs, N.J.: Prentice-Hall, 1989).

105 In the primary grades: J. B. Carroll, P. Davies, and B. Richman, *The American Heritage Word Frequency Book* (Boston: Houghton Mifflin, 1971).

105 Reading comprehension develops: T. G. Sticht et al., *Auding and Reading: A Developmental Model* (Alexandria, Va.: Human Resources Research Organization, 1974).

106 A child learns about seven: M. A. Just and P. A. Carpenter, *The Psychology of Reading and Language Comprehension* (Boston: Allyn and Bacon, 1987); W. E. Nagy and P. A. Herman, "Breadth and Depth of Vocabulary Knowledge: Implications for Acquisition and Instruction," in M. McKeown and M. Curtis (eds.), *The Nature of Vocabulary Acquisition* (Hillsdale, N.J.: Erlbaum, 1987), pp. 19–35.

106 Books offer almost three times: A. E. Cunningham and K. E. Stanovich, "What Reading Does for the Mind," *American Educator* 22 (1998): 8–15.

106 Children's books, too, "have 50 percent more . . .": Ibid., p. 10.

106 As shown in Figure 29: This figure is based on R. O. Anderson, P. T. Wilson, and I. G. Fielding, "Growth in Reading and How Children Spend Their Time Outside of School," *Reading Research Quarterly* 23 (1988): 285–303.

108 A Guide to the Development: These markers are adapted from C. E. Snow, M. S.

Burns, and P. Griffin (eds.), *Preventing Reading Difficulties in Young Children* (Washington, D.C.: National Academy Press, 1998), pp. 80–83. See also L. C. Moats, *Speech to Print* (Baltimore, Md.: Paul H. Brookes, 2000).

113 As your child progresses: Center for the Future of Teaching and Learning, "Thirty Years of NICHD Research: What We Now Know About How Children Learn to Read," *Effective School Practices* 15 (Summer 1996): 33.

118 "By focusing on a single domain": R. P. Fink, "Literacy Development in Successful Men and Women with Dyslexia," *Annals of Dyslexia* 48 (1998): 325.

118 "Even today, when": Ibid., p. 324.

118 "When you're immersed": Ibid., p. 327.

Chapter 10: Should My Child Be Evaluated for Dyslexia?

121 "To the extent that we allow": J. K. Torgesen, "Catch Them Before They Fall: Identification and Assessment to Prevent Reading Failure in Young Children," *American Educator* 22 (1998): 32–39, quote on p. 32.

121 Without identification and proven: The persistence of poor reading was demonstrated in the Connecticut Longitudinal Study sample in B. A. Shaywitz et al., "A Matthew Effect for IQ but Not for Reading: Results from a Longitudinal Study," *Reading Research Quarterly* 30 (1995): 894–906, and also in S. E. Shaywitz et al., "Persistence of Dyslexia: The Connecticut Longitudinal Study at Adolescence," *Pediatrics* 104 (1999): 1351–59.

Chapter 11: Diagnosing Dyslexia in the School-Age Child

132 The diagnosis of dyslexia: This is discussed in S. Shaywitz, "Dyslexia," *The New England Journal of Medicine* 333 (1998): 307–12.

133 Ashley, for example, was asked: Words cited appear in J. K. Torgesen, "Assessment and Instruction for Phonemic Awareness and Work Recognition Skills," in H. W. Catts and A. G. Kamhi (eds.), *Language and Reading Disabilities* (Needham Heights, Mass.: Allyn & Bacon, 1999), pp. 128–53. The authors indicate that these words originally appeared as part of the Woodcock Reading Mastery Test, Revised by R. W. Woodcock (Circle Pines, Minn.: American Guidance Service, 1987).

134 The Woodcock-Johnson III: R. W. Woodcock, K. S. McGrew, and N. Mather Woodcock-Johnson III (Itasca, Ill.: Riverside, 2001); R. W. Woodcock, Woodcock Reading Mastery Tests, Revised/Normative Update (Circle Pines, Minn.: American Guidance Service, 1987, content; 1998, norms); J. L. Weiderholt and B. R. Bryant, Gray Oral Reading Tests-4: (Austin, Tex.: PRO-ED, 2001); J. K. Torgesen, R. K. Wagner, and C. Rashotte, Test of Word Reading Efficiency (Austin, Tex.: PRO-ED, 1999); S. C. Larsen, E. D. Hammill, and L. C. Moats, Test of Written Spelling-4 (San Antonio, Tex.: Psychological Corporation, 1999); G. Wilkinson, Wide Range Achievement Test-3 (Austin, Tex.: PRO-ED, 1994); Wechsler Individual Achievement Test-II: (San Antonio, Tex.: Psychological Corporation, 2001).

136 As Richard Pryor said: Ascribed to Richard Pryor by Robert McTeer, president of the Federal Reserve Bank of Dallas, in his address before the Cato Institute Conference, "Monetary Policy in the New Economy," Washington, D.C., October 19, 2000.

137 There is an emerging consensus: The limitations of sole reliance on the discrepancy between IQ and reading achievement for the identification of children as reading-disabled is discussed in K. K. Stuebing et al., "Validity of IQ-Discrepancy Classifications of Reading Disabilities: A Meta-Analysis" *American Educational Research Journal* 39 (2002): 469–518.

137 Now that the central role: Demonstrated by K. E. Stanovich and L. S. Siegel in "Phenotypic Performance Profile of Children with Reading Disabilities: A Regression-Based Test of the Phonological–Core Variable–Difference Model," *Journal of Educational Psychology* 86 (1994): 24–53, and by J. M. Fletcher et al., "Cognitive Profiles of Reading Disability: Comparisons of Discrepancy and Low Achievement Definitions," *Journal of Educational Psychology* 86 (1994): 6–23.

137 The Comprehensive Test of Phonological Processing: R. K. Wagner, J. K. Torgesen, and C. A. Rashotte (Austin, Tex.: PRO-ED, 1999).

138 In the most commonly used test: L. M. Dunn, L. M. Dunn, G. J. Robertson, and J. L. Eisenberg, Peabody Picture Vocabulary Test, 3rd ed. (Circle Pines, Minn: American Guidance Service, 1997). The Boston Naming Test, 3rd ed., is part of the Boston Diagnostic Aphasia Examination by H. Goodglass, E. Kaplan, and B. Barresi (San Antonio, Tex.: Psychological Corporation, 2000).

139 But there is no single test: The differential diagnosis of dyslexia is further discussed in S. Shaywitz, "Current Concepts: Dyslexia," *New England Journal of Medicine* 338 (1998): 307–12.

141 At one time it was thought: J. L. Paradise et al., "Effect of Early or Delayed Insertion of Tympanostomy Tubes for Persistent Otitis Media on Developmental Outcomes at the Age of Two Years," *New England Journal of Medicine* 344 (2001): 1179–87.

141 Many people confuse: B. Shaywitz et al., "Cognitive Profiles of Reading Disability: Interrelationships Between Reading Disability and Attention Deficit/Hyperactivity Disorder," *Child Neuropsychology* 1 (1995): 170–86; *Diagnostic and Statistical Manual of Mental Disorders,* 4th ed. (Washington, D.C.: American Psychiatric Association, 1994); S. E. Shaywitz, J. M. Fletcher, and B. A. Shaywitz, "Issues in the Definition and Classification of Attention Deficit Disorder," *Topics in Language Disorders* 14 (1994): 1–25.

Chapter 12: Identifying the At-Risk Child

142 Kindergarten screening has become: J. K. Torgesen, "Catch Them Before They Fall: Identification and Assessment to Prevent Reading Failure in Young Children," *American Educator* 22 (1998): 32–39. This article presents a concise summary of issues related to kindergarten screening and early identification of reading difficulties.

143 Children's phonologic abilities follow: Phonologic skills and their assessment are discussed in: J. K. Torgesen and P. G. Mathes, *A Basic Guide to Understanding,*

Assessing and Teaching Phonological Awareness (Austin, Tex.: PRO-ED, 2000), and also in C. E. Snow, M. S. Burns, and P. Griffin (eds.), *Preventing Reading Difficulties in Young Children* (Washington, D.C.: National Academy Press, 1998). The different types of phonologic abilities are discussed in R. K. Wagner and J. K. Torgesen, "Nature of Phonological Processes and Its Causal Role in the Acquisition of Reading Skills," *Psychological Bulletin* 101 (1987): 192–212.

144 As the accompanying graph demonstrates: This graph (Figure 30) is from J. K. Torgesen, "Assessment and Instruction for Phonemic Awareness and Word Recognition Skills," in H. W. Catts and A. G. Kamhi, *Language and Reading Disabilities* (Boston: Allyn & Bacon, 1999), p. 131.

146 *Tests to Evaluate:* Adapted from J. K. Torgesen and P. G. Mathes, *A Basic Guide to Understanding, Assessing and Teaching Phonological Awareness* (Austin: PRO-ED, 2000).

147 Emerging data suggest: In addition to the sources noted above, there is H. S. Scarborough, "Early Identification of Children at Risk for Reading Disabilities," in B. K. Shapiro, P. J. Accardo, and A. J. Capute (eds.), *Specific Reading Disability* (Timonium, Md.: York Press, 1998), pp. 75–119.

147 Teachers are also critical: J. K. Torgesen et al., "Intensive Remedial Instruction for Children with Severe Reading Disabilities: Immediate and Long-term Outcomes from Two Instructional Approaches," *Journal of Learning Disabilities* 34 (2001): 33–58. Torgesen found that teacher assessment of attention and behavior was among the highest predictors of long-term growth in reading skills. The Multigrade Inventory for Teachers (MIT) was developed for the Connecticut Longitudinal Study to capture the valuable observations of the classroom teacher. Its development and use are described in M. E. Agronin et al., "The Multigrade Inventory for Teachers (MIT): Scale Development, Reliability, and Validity of an Instrument to Assess Children with Attentional Deficits and Learning Disabilities," in S. E. Shaywitz and B. A. Shaywitz (eds.), *Attention Deficit Disorder Comes of Age: Toward the Twenty-first Century* (Austin, Tex.: PRO-ED, 1992): 89–116; and J. M. Holahan et al., "Developmental Trends in Teacher Perceptions of Student Cognitive and Behavioral Status as Measured by the Multigrade Inventory for Teachers: Evidence from a Longitudinal Study," in D. M. Molfese and V. J. Molfese (eds.), *Developmental Variations in Learning: Applications to Social, Executive Function, Language, and Reading Skills* (Mahwah, N.J.: Erlbaum, 2002): 23–55.

147 Interestingly, IQ tests: The relationship between measures of IQ and reading is complex. Early on, individual differences within the typical IQ range are not as strong predictors of growth in word reading skills or response to intervention as are measures of phonemic awareness. However, as children progress, IQ, especially verbal ability, becomes more tightly linked to reading comprehension. These issues are discussed in J. K. Torgesen et al., "Preventing Reading Failure in Young Children with Phonological Processing Disabilities: Group and Individual Responses to Instruction," *Journal of Educational Psychology* 91 (1999): 579–93; J. K. Torgesen, "Phonologically-Based Reading Disabilities: Toward a Coherent Theory of One Kind of Learning Disability," in R. Sternberg and L. Spear-Swerling (eds.), *Perspectives on Learning Disabilities* (Boulder, Colo: Westview Press, 1999): pp. 106–35;

B. W. Wise, J. Ring, and R. Olson, "Training Phonological Awareness with and Without Explicit Attention to Articulation, *Journal of Experimental Child Psychology* 72 (1999): 271–304; and M. J. Snowling, *Dyslexia* (Oxford, England: Blackwell, 2000).

149 If his testing indicates: Compelling data regarding delayed kindergarten entry are presented by F. Morrison, E. Griffith, and D. Alberts in "Nature-Nurture in the Classroom: Entrance Age, School Readiness, and Learning in Children, *Developmental Psychology* 33 (1997): 254–62, and in F. Morrison, L. Smith, and M. Dow-Ehrenberger, "Education and Cognitive Development: A Natural Experiment, *Developmental Psychology* 31 (1995): 789–99. These are discussed by V. W. Berninger in *Guides for Intervention: Reading and Writing* (San Antonio, Tex.: Psychological Corporation, 1998), pp. 30–31.

Chapter 13: Diagnosing Bright Young Adults

153 In 1996, in celebration: S. E. Shaywitz, "Dyslexia," *Scientific American* 275 (1996): 98–104.

154 Numerous studies conducted: S. Shaywitz et al., "Persistence of Dyslexia: The Connecticut Longitudinal Study at Adolescence," *Pediatrics* 104 (1999): 1351–59; M. Bruck, "Persistence of Dyslexics' Phonological Awareness Deficits," *Developmental Psychology* 28 (5) (1992): 874–86; R. Felton, C. Naylor, and F. Wood, "Neuropsychological Profile of Adult Dyslexics," *Brain and Language* 39 (1990): 485–97; and R. Davidson and J. Strucker, "Patterns of Word Recognition Error Among Adult Basic Education Students," *Scientific Studies of Reading* (2002): 299–316.

154 The implication of all this: M. Bruck, "Persistence of Dyslexics' Phonological Awareness Deficits," *Developmental Psychology* 28(5), (1992): 874–86.

154 Researchers discovered: In addition to the above citations, see also D. Lefly and B. Pennington, "Spelling Errors and Reading Fluency in Compensated Dyslexics," *Annals of Dyslexia* 41 (1991): 143–62.

155 College students with histories: M. Bruck, "Word-Recognition Skills of Adults with Childhood Diagnoses of Dyslexia," *Developmental Psychology* 26 (1990): 439–54.

155 Studies have confirmed: E. Paulesu et al., "Dyslexia—Cultural Diversity and Biological Unity," *Science* 291 (2001): 2165–67.

163 Observing a person read: J. I. Brown, V. V. Fishco, and G. Hanna, Nelson-Denny Reading Test (Chicago: Riverside, 1993); GORT-4 (Gray Oral Reading Tests) (Austin: PRO-ED, 2001). Also see notes for pages 146–47 of Chapter 12.

164 In a legal case: On August 15, 1997, U.S. District Judge Patti Saris issued her much-awaited *Findings of fact, conclusions of law and order of judgment in the case of Guckenberger v. Boston University,* 974 F. Supp. 106 (D. Mass, 1997).

Chapter 14: All Children Can Be Taught to Read

173 There is now evidence: J. K. Torgesen, "The Prevention of Reading Difficulties," *Journal of School Psychology* 40 (2002): 7–26.

174 For the first time: Report of the National Reading Panel, "Teaching Children to Read: An Evidence-Based Assessment of the Scientific Research Literature and Its Implications for Reading Instruction" (Washington, D.C.: U.S. Department of Health and Human Services, Public Health Service, National Institutes of Health, National Institute of Child Health and Human Development, 2000). The report is available on the panel's Web site, http://www.nationalreadingpanel.org, or at http://www.nichd.gov. The report is available in its entirety or as an abbreviated (thirty-three-page) executive summary.

175 The findings of the panel: The legislation is the No Child Left Behind Act of 2001, Pub. L. No. 107-110, 115 Stat. 1425 (2002). Reading First is one element of this law.

Chapter 15: Helping Your Child Break the Reading Code

178 You can help sensitize: While the focus in this chapter is on the kindergarten child, I want to remind each parent that getting a child ready to read begins early. Very young children, even babies, benefit from hearing songs and being read to. Reading stories aloud is one of the most important things a parent can do for a young child. One highly successful early literacy program, the Reach Out & Read Program, started by two Boston pediatricians, Barry Zuckerman and Perri Klass, starts building a foundation for reading in young infants. At each routine health visit, each child age six months to five years receives age-appropriate books and his parent receives a "prescription" to read aloud to the child. Being read to builds vocabulary, curiosity, knowledge, and a desire to want to learn to read.

178 One richly illustrated rhyming book: Kevin Lewis and Daniel Kirk, *Chugga-Chugga Choo-Choo* (New York: Hyperion, 1999).

179 Here is a list: The list of rhyming books reflects suggestions by Bunnie Yesner, former chief librarian at the Beecher Elementary School in Woodbridge, Connecticut, and Hallie K. Yopp, who teaches courses in reading and language arts education at California State University in Fullerton, California.

181 First, she says, "Read the story": H. K. Yopp, "Read-Aloud Books for Developing Phonemic Awareness: An Annotated Bibliography," *The Reading Teacher* 48 (1995): 538–43.

181 I've chosen one: Seuss, Dr., *One Fish Two Fish Red Fish Blue Fish* (New York: Random House, 2001).

181 Or some children: L. Bemelmans, *Madeline* (New York: Penguin Putnam, 2000).

182 Most reading programs: Suggestions for these activities can be found in M. J. Adams et al., *Phonemic Awareness in Young Children: A Classroom Curriculum* (Baltimore, Md.: Paul H. Brookes, 1998).

184 Interestingly, most kindergartners: J. K. Uhry and L. C. Ehri, "Ease of Segmenting Two- and Three-Phoneme Words in Kindergarten," *Journal of Educational Psychology* 91 (1999): 594–603.

188 New brain imaging technology: Expertise depends on practice, elegantly demonstrated by T. Elbert et al. in "Increased Cortical Representation of the Fingers of the Left Hand in String Players," *Science* 270 (1995): 305–07.

189 The 2002 Olympic bronze medal: Timothy Goebel said this in response to a question from Katie Couric about "he did it" in an interview on the *Today Show* on February 15, 2002.

192 To get started: The list of recommended books for emerging readers was compiled by head children's librarian Mary Schumacher and the Children's Services Department of the Middle Country Public Library, Centereach, Long Island, New York. Their help is gratefully acknowledged.

194 A relatively new approach: R. A. Kaminski and R. H. Good III, "Assessing Early Literacy Skills in a Problem-Solving Model: Dynamic Indicators of Basic Early Literacy Skills," in M. R. Shinn (ed.), *Advanced Applications of Curriculum-Based Measurements* (New York: Guilford, 1998): 113–42.

195 Above all: Problems associated with retention are discussed in V. W. Beminger, *Guidelines for Intervention* (San Antonio, Tex.: The Psychological Corporation, 1998).

Chapter 16: Helping Your Child Become a Reader

198 The most successful: The following books are good general resources for background information on how children learn to read: M. J. Adams, *Beginning to Read* (Cambridge, Mass.: MIT Press, 1990); Committee on the Prevention of Reading Difficulties in Young Children, *Preventing Reading Difficulties in Young Children* (Washington, D.C.: National Academy Press, 1998); J. R. Birsh (ed.), *Multisensory Teaching of Basic Language Skills* (Baltimore, Md.: Paul H. Brookes, 1999); L. C. Moats, *Speech to Print* (Baltimore, Md.: Brookes, 2000).

200 The National Reading Panel: Report of the National Panel, *Teaching Children to Read,* 2000. See the notes for Chapter 14 for more detailed information, including ordering copies of the report.

200 One suggested sequence: D. W. Carnine, J. Silbert, and E. J. Kammeenui, Direct Instruction Reading (Upper Saddle River, N. J.: Prentice-Hall, 1997).

204 According to the National Reading Panel: The newest edition of Jolly Phonics by S. Lloyd, which is marketed in the United States, is called *The Phonics Handbook: A Handbook for Teaching Reading, Writing and Spelling,* 3rd ed. (Essex, England: Jolly Learning Ltd., 1998).

204 "To develop their understanding": Ibid., p. 21.

204 "When two vowels go walking": Ibid., p. 22.

204 Another engaging and helpful: L. Wendon, *Letterland* (Enfield, N.H.: Letterland International Ltd., 1992)

205 A child *learns to read:* J. Chall, *Stages of Reading Development* (New York: McGraw-Hill, 1983).

207 Knowing the etymology: Marcia K. Henry has written about using the knowledge of word origins as a strategy to help reading and spelling in *Words: Integrated Decoding and Spelling Instruction Based on Word Origin and Word Structure* (Austin, Tex.: PRO-ED, 1990); also M. K. Henry and N. C. Redding, *Patterns for Success in*

Reading and Spelling (Austin, Tex.: PRO-ED, 1996). These are good resources and offer practical instructional activities.

208 They are published: Curriculum Development and Supplemental Materials Commission, *Reading/Language Arts Framework for California Public Schools: Kindergarten Through Grade Twelve* (Sacramento: California Department of Education, 1999). This is available from the Sales Office, CDF Press, California Department of Education, P. O. Box 271, Sacramento, CA 95812-0271 or by calling 1-800-995-4099.

217 The prefixes: Based on T. G. White, J. Sowell, and A. Yanagihara, "Teaching Elementary Students to Use Word-Part Clues," *The Reading Teacher* 42 (1989), pp. 302–308.

219 Here is a list: The list is based on *The American Heritage Word Frequency Book,* J. B. Carroll, P. Davies, and B. Richman (Boston: Houghton-Mifflin, 1971).

221 A good series to start: The "Bob Books" series is published by Scholastic Books, Inc. (www.bobbooks.com). The "Books to Remember" collection is published by Flyleaf Publishing (www.flyleafpublishing.com).

222 One, the Degrees of Reading Power: Degrees of Reading Power is available from TASA, 4 Hardscrabble Heights, Brewster, New York 10509.

223 Another program called: The Lexile Framework is available from 2327 Engelert Drive, Suite 300, Research Triangle Park, NC 27713. Parents and others can access the Lexile Framework at www.lexile.com.

223 For discovering a book's level: *Children's Books in Print* (Bowker, 2002–2003), is published by Bowker, New Providence, N.J., and revised annually.

224 Here is a list: This list was compiled with the assistance of Bunnie Yesner of Woodbridge, Connecticut, and Mary Schumacher and the Children's Services Department of the Middle Country Public Library, Centereach, Long Island, New York.

Chapter 17: Helping Your Child Become a Skilled Reader

231 The National Assessment of Educational Progress: G. S. Pinnell et al., *Listening to Children Read Aloud* (Washington, D.C.: Office of Educational Research and Improvement, U.S. Department of Education, 1995).

232 When the National Reading Panel: Report of the National Reading Panel, "Teaching Children to Read: An Evidence-Based Assessment of the Scientific Research Literature and Its Implications for Reading Instruction" (Washington, D.C.: U.S. Department of Health and Human Services, Public Health Service, National Institutes of Health, National Institute of Child Health and Human Development, 2000).

233 From its extensive review: Ibid., pp. 3–20.

234 Thus, as a child matures: Dr. Seuss, *The Cat in the Hat* (New York: Random House, 1976); M. W. Brown, *Goodnight Moon* (New York: Harper Collins, 1991); S. Hoff, *Danny and the Dinosaur* (New York: Harper Collins Children's Books, 1978); A. Benarde, *The Pumpkin Smasher* (New York: Walker and Co., 1972); E. Raskin, *The Westing Game* (New York: Viking Penguin, 1997).

234 Reading should always be encouraged: What differentiates the NRP findings about silent reading and commonly held assumptions about the benefits of simply reading to oneself reflects the difference between true experimental data and correlational findings. The NRP examined specific reading programs that encourage children to read and analyzed the data obtained before and after to determine if reading more on his own improved a child's reading performance. This type of study where reading performance is measured *before* an intervention and then *after* is the *only* way to determine cause and effect. Other types of research studies—for example, those referred to as correlational, where the relationship between two topics such as reading performance and the amount of independent reading are correlated—can only indicate if there is a relationship but not cause and effect. Many studies have shown that there is a strong correlation between how much a child reads and how well he reads; poor readers tend to read very little while good readers devour books. However, these studies tell us nothing of the nature of the relationship. We do not know if it is because the more you read, the better you will read, or if the better you read, the more you will want to read, or if reading proficiency and amount of reading are both the end result of a third unknown factor that affects each. After reviewing the experimental cause and effect data, the panel concluded that "at this time it would be unreasonable to conclude that research shows that encouraging [silent] reading has a beneficial impact on reading achievement" (page 3-28). Although some studies suggest that children benefit from voluntary reading, overall we are still lacking definitive proof that reading on your own leads to better reading. For example, one study examined children's reading performance before and after a sixty-hour program of independent summer reading. The researchers found that this group of third to sixth graders did not show any change in their reading achievement after six weeks of the program.

235 I am pleased that: The Reading First program is a component of the No Child Left Behind Act of 2001, Pub. L. No. 107-110, 115 Stat. 1425 (2002).

236 Vocabulary instruction: I. L. Beck, M. G. McKeown, and L. Kucan, *Bringing Words to Life: Robust Vocabulary Instruction* (New York: Guilford, 2002), is an excellent additional resource for teaching vocabulary.

237 In one approach: This example of teaching vocabulary using the strategy of semantic mapping appeared in W. E. Nagy, *Teaching Vocabulary to Improve Reading Comprehension* (Newark, Del.: International Reading Association, 1988), based on a semantic map from D. Little and C. Suhor, *Prereading-Jargon and Shoptalk,* an unpublished manuscript.

238 In one highly successful program: Word Wizard and other activities for enhancing vocabulary learning are described by I. L. Beck, M. G. McKeown, and R. C. Omanson, "The Effects and Uses of Diverse Vocabulary Instructional Techniques," in M. G. McKeown and M. E. Curtis (eds.), *The Nature of Vocabulary Acquisition* (Hillsdale, N.J.: Erlbaum, 1997), pp. 147–63.

239 Everything is fair game: Use of the Alfred, Lord Tennyson poem "Flower in the Crannied Wall" to define "cranny" appeared in W. E. Nagy, *Teaching Vocabulary to Improve Reading Comprehension* (Newark, Del.: International Reading Association, 1988), p. 37.

239 Here are the most common ones: The list of most common prefixes is from T. G.

White, J. Sowell, and A. Yanagihara, "Teaching Elementary Students to Use Word-Part Clues," in *The Reading Teacher* 42 (1989): 302–308.

241 A recent study: K. Cain, "Story Knowledge and Comprehension Skills," in K. Comold and J. Oakhill (eds.), Reading Comprehension Difficulties: Processes and Intervention (Mahwah, N. J.: Lawrence Erlbaum Associates, 1997), pp. 167–192.

242 Consider *The Story About Ping:* This book was written by Marjorie Flack and illustrated by Kurt Wiese (New York: Penguin Putnam, 2000).

245 Here is a summary: Activities adapted from findings reported in the Comprehension section of the Report of the National Reading Panel, "Teaching Children to Read: An Evidence-Based Assessment of the Scientific Research Literature and Its Implications for Reading Instruction" (Washington, D.C.: U.S. Department of Health and Human Services, Public Health Service, National Institutes of Health, National Institute of Child Health and Human Development, 2000).

Chapter 18: Sam's Program

252 She and I reviewed: J. F. Greene, *Language! A Literacy Intervention Curriculum* (Longmont, Col.: Sopris West, 2002); www.language-usa.net.

255 For this purpose: R. W. Woodcock, Woodcock Reading Mastery Test, Revised/Normative Update (Circle Pines, Minn.: American Guidance Service, 1987, content; 1998, norms); J. L. Weiderholt and B. R. Bryant, Gray Oral Reading Tests—4 (Austin: PRO-ED, 2001); J. K. Torgesen, R. K. Wagner, and C. Rashotte, Test of Word Reading Efficiency (Austin, Tex.: PRO-ED, 1999).

257 Children who receive help early: J. Torgesen has demonstrated that high-quality reading instruction provided early on to at-risk children allows them to become accurate and fluent readers. One study, in which children participated in a reading intervention program from kindergarten through second grade is discussed in J. K. Torgesen et al., "Preventing Reading Failure in Young Children with Phonological Processing Disabilities," *Journal of Educational Psychology* 91 (1999): 579–93. In another, the intervention was provided during the first grade year; J. K. Torgesen et al., "The Effectiveness of Teacher-Supported Computer-Assisted Instruction in Preventing Reading Problems in Young Children: A Comparison of Two Methods," an unpublished manuscript.

257 Poor readers receive the least: Many studies have documented the gap between good and poor readers in the amount of reading practice. As noted earlier, the very best readers may read one million or so words a year, average readers about three hundred thousand, and poor readers about one hundred thousand or less. R. C. Anderson, P. T. Wilson, and I. G. Fielding, "Growth in Reading and How Children Spend Their Time Outside of School," *Reading Research Quarterly* 23 (1988): 285–303. Also see W. Nagy and R. C. Anderson, "How Many Words Are There in Printed School English?" *Reading Research Quarterly* 19 (1984): 304–330; R. L. Allington, "Content Coverage and Contextual Reading in Reading Groups," *Journal of Reading Behavior* 16 (1984): 85–96; R. L. Allington, "If They Don't Read Much, How Are They Ever Gonna Get Good?" *Journal of Reading* 21 (1977): 57–61; and

A. E. Cunningham and K. E. Stanovich, "What Reading Does for the Mind," *American Educator* 22 (1998): 8–15.

258 Reading instruction for the dyslexic reader: Joseph K. Torgesen has made eloquent arguments concerning the necessity for instruction that is more intense, explicit, and supportive for children at risk for reading difficulties. These conditions demand teachers who are well trained and highly skilled in teaching reading. See J. K. Torgesen, "The Prevention of Reading Difficulties," *Journal of School Psychology* 40 (2002): 7–26.

258 As my colleague Louisa: L. C. Moats, *Teaching Reading Is Rocket Science* (Washington, D.C.: American Federation of Teachers, 1999).

258 Recent studies highlight: B. Wise and R. K. Olson, "Computer-Based Phonological Awareness and Reading Instruction," *Annals of Dyslexia* 45 (1995): 99–122. This work demonstrates the importance of teachers even in computer-based reading instruction. Also see J. K. Torgesen et al., "Intensive Remedial Instruction for Children with Severe Reading Disabilities: Immediate and Long-term Outcomes from Two Instructional Approaches," *Journal of Learning Disabilities* 34 (2001): 33–58.

258 According to the researcher: J. K. Torgesen, et al., "Intensive Remedial Instruction for Children with Severe Reading Disabilities: Immediate and Long-term Outcomes from Two Instructional Approaches," *Journal of Learning Disabilities* 34 (2001): 33–58, quote on pp. 53. Torgesen attributes the success of experienced teachers to their expertise in interacting with the child, helping him first to identify and then to develop strategies for correcting his reading errors.

259 In another study: B. Wise, J. King, and R. Olson, "Training Phonological Awareness with and Without Explicit Attention to Articulation," *Journal of Experimental Child Psychology* 72 (1999): 271–304.

259 One of the most common: B. Wise, J. King, and R. Olson, "Individual Differences in Gains from Computer-Assisted Remedial Reading," *Journal of Experimental Child Psychology* 77 (2000): 197–235, and J. Torgesen et al., "Intensive Remedial Instruction for Children with Severe Reading Disabilities: Immediate and Long-term Outcomes from Two Instructional Approaches," *Journal of Learning Disabilities* 34 (2001): 33–58. These works emphasize that longer durations of intervention may be necessary in order to provide sufficient opportunities for a child to practice reading and develop fluency.

Chapter 19: Teaching the Dyslexic Child to Read

261 Highly effective prevention and early intervention: See the review by Torgesen: J. K. Torgesen, "The Prevention of Reading Difficulties," *Journal of School Psychology* 40 (2002): 7–26, and also J. K. Toregesen, "Preventing Reading Failure in Young Children with Phonological Processing Disabilities," *Journal of Educational Psychology* 91 (1999): 579–93, and B. Foorman et al., "The Role of Instruction in Learning to Read: Preventing Reading Failure in At-Risk Children," *Journal of Educational Psychology* 90 (1998): 37–55.

261 Reading performance tends to be stable: The stability of reading performance has

been demonstrated many times. See C. Juel, "Learning to Read and Write: A Longitudinal Study of Fifty-four Children from First Through Fourth Grades," *Journal of Educational Psychology* 80 (1988): 437–47; B. Shaywitz et al., "Matthew Effect for IQ but Not for Reading: Results from a Longitudinal Study of Reading, *Reading Research Quarterly* 30 (1995): 894–906.

261 According to G. Reid Lyon: G. Reid Lyon, "Overview of Reading and Literacy Initiatives," testimony on April 28, 1998, before the Committee on Labor and Human Resources, Washington, D.C.

261 In one Tallahassee, Florida: As described by J. K. Torgesen in "The Prevention of Reading Difficulties," *Journal of School Psychology* 40 (2002): 7–26.

262 Common threads run through: See the Report of the National Reading Panel, "Teaching Children to Read: An Evidence-Based Assessment of the Scientific Research Literature and Its Implications for Reading Instruction" (Washington, D.C.: U.S. Department of Health and Human Services, Public Health Service, National Institutes of Health, National Institute of Child Health and Human Development, 2000), and C. E. Snow, M. S. Burns, and P. Griffin (eds.), *Preventing Reading Difficulties*, 1998.

263 The tide has turned: Report of the National Reading Panel, "Teaching Children to Read: An Evidence-Based Assessment of the Scientific Research Literature and Its Implications for Reading Instruction" (Washington, D.C.: U.S. Department of Health and Human Services, Public Health Service, National Institutes of Health, National Institute of Child Health and Human Development, 2000).

263 The Reading First legislation is the No Child Left Behind Act of 2001, Pub. L. No. 107–110, 115 Stat. 1425 (2002).

263 Examples of effective: *Proactive Beginning Reading* is produced by Open SRA/McGraw-Hill, Columbus, Ohio, 2003. *The Optimize Intervention Program* is produced by Scott Foresman, Glenview, Illinois 2002. *The Read, Write & Type! Learning System* is produced by Talking Fingers, San Rafael, California, 2000 (www.Readwritetype.com)

263 *Open Court Reading:* This is produced by SRA/McGraw-Hill, Columbus, Oh., 2002.

265 The programs that follow: Programs for older students meet the rigorous standards set by the State of California for the adoption of reading programs: *Language! A Literacy Intervention Curriculum* is produced by Sopris West, Longmont, Colorado. *READ 180* is produced by Scholastic, New York, New York. Fast Track Reading Program is produced by the Wright Group/McGraw-Hill, Bothell, Washington. *High Point* is produced by Hamptom-Brown, Carmel, California. The *REACH System* including *Corrective Reading, Reasoning and Writing,* and *Spelling Through Morphographs* are produced by SRA/McGraw-Hill, Columbus, Ohio.

266 You may hear reading programs: Orton-Gillingham represents a method for teaching reading that is multisensory, systematic, and structured. Other programs adhering to this approach include *Alphabetic Phonics,* developed at the Scottish Rite Hospital in Dallas, Texas (www.sofdesign.com/dyslexia); *Language!* produced by Sopris West of Longmont, Colorado; *Project Read,* Bloomington, Minnesota (projectread.com); Slingerland Institute for Literacy, Bellevue, Washington

(www.slingerland.com); Spalding Education International, Phoenix, Arizona (www.spalding.org); Wilson Reading System (Millbury, Massachusetts) was originally developed for older primary school children and is now complemented by a new program, *Fundations,* aimed at kindergarten through third grade children.

266 Still another program: *Spell Read P.A.T.* of Charlottetown, Prince Edward Island, Canada and Rockville, Maryland, was found to be highly effective in a study by C. A. Rashotte, K. MacPhee, and J. K. Torgesen, "The Effectiveness of a Group Reading Instruction Program with Poor Readers in Multiple Grades," *Learning Disability Quarterly* 24 (2001): 1–16.

267 Strategies for reading: *Benchmark School Word Identification/Vocabulary Development Program,* Benchmark School, Media, Pennsylvania. *Spelling Through Morphographs,* SRA/McGraw-Hill, Columbus, Ohio. REWARDS, Sopris West, Longmont, Colorado.

267 This method, focusing directly: The *Lindamood Phoneme Sequencing Program* is from Lindamood-Bell of San Luis Obispo, California.

267 You will hear many claims: Different effective reading programs produce similar outcomes. See B. Wise, J. King, and R. Olson, "Training Phonological Awareness with and Without Explicit Attention to Articulation," *Journal of Experimental Child Psychology* 72 (1999): 271–304; B. Wise, J. King, and R. Olson, "Individual Differences in Gains from Computer-Assisted Remedial Reading," *Journal of Experimental Child Psychology* 77 (2000): 197–235; and J. Torgesen et al., "Intensive Remedial Instruction for Children with Severe Reading Disabilities," *Journal of Learning Disabilities* 34 (2001): 33–58.

269 In his study of superior athletes: B. S. Bloom, "Automaticity," *Educational Leadership* 43 (1986): 70–77.

270 Graduated word lists: Oxton House Publishers can be reached at P.O. Box 209, Farmington, Maine 04938, 1-800-539-READ.

270 This accomplishes for dyslexic readers: The "self-teaching" mechanism is discussed in D. L. Share, "Phonological Recoding and Self-Teaching: Sine Qua Non of Reading Acquisition," *Cognition* 55 (1995): 151–218.

270 "Imagine yourself": T. V. Rasinski, "Speed Does Matter in Reading," *The Reading Teacher* 54 (2000): 147.

271 Having a child practice: Ibid., 146–51. Rasinski offers suggestions for practicing fluency, including poetry parties and Readers Theatre.

271 In one recent study: M. Martinez, N. Roser, and S. Strecker, "'I Never Thought I Could Be a Star'": A Readers' Theatre Ticket to Fluency," *The Reading Teacher* 52 (1999): 326–34.

272 Daily fluency practice: C. Mercer et al., "Effects of a Fluency Intervention for Middle Schoolers with Specific Learning Disabilities," *Learning Disabilities Research and Practice* 15 (2000): 179–189. This program is available from K. U. Campbell, *Great Leaps Reading Program,* Gainesville, Fla.: Diarmuid.

272 One, *Read Naturally:* Read Naturally, 750 S. Plaza Drive, St. Paul, Minnesota 55120.

272 An exciting new program: *Readit* is available from Soliloquy Learning, Union City, California.

273 In addition, for those who want: *Practices for Developing Accuracy and Fluency* is available from Neuhaus Education Center, Bellaire, Texas.

274 To address this need: M. E. Curtis and A. M. Longo, *When Adolescents Can't Read: Methods and Materials That Work* (Cambridge, Mass.: Brockline Books, 1999): 29.

277 There are useful guidelines: These ranges are adapted from J. E. Hasbrouck and G. Tindal, "Curriculum-Based Oral Reading Fluency Norms for Students in Grades 2 Through 5," *Teaching Exceptional Children* 24 (1992): 41–44; R. H. Good, D. C. Simmons, and E. J. Kame'enui, "The Importance and Decision-Making Utility of a Continuum of Fluency-Based Indicators of Foundational Reading Skills for Third-Grade High-Stakes Outcomes," *Scientific Studies of Reading* 5 (2001): 257–88; and C. D. Mercer et al., "Effects of Reading Fluency Intervention for Middle Schoolers with Specific Learning Disabilities," *Learning Disabilities Research and Practice* 15 (2000): 179–89.

277 A group of researchers: Rates based on R. H. Good, D. K. Simmons, and E. J. Kame'enui, "The Importance and Decision-Making Utility of a Continuum of Fluency-Based Indicators of Foundational Reading Skills for Third-Grade High Stakes Outcomes," *Scientific Studies of Reading* 5 (2001): 257–88.

277 To measure your child's fluency: Procedures for measuring fluency are based on M. R. Shinn (ed.), *Curriculum-Based Measurement: Assessing Special Children* (New York: Guilford, 1989), pp. 239–40. Additional reading materials for assessing fluency can be found in *Standard Reading Passages,* which includes ninety generic readings for grade levels one to six. It is available from Children's Educational Services, Inc., 16526 W. Seventy-eighth St., Eden Prairie, Minnesota (www.reading-progress.com).

278 One is called curriculum-based measurement: For a helpful review see L. S. Fuchs and D. Fuchs, "Curriculum-Based and Performance Assessments," in E. S. Shapiro and T. R. Kratochwill (eds.), *Behavioral Assessment in Schools: Theory, Research and Clinical Foundations* (New York: Guilford, 2000).

278 A child's *rate* of reading growth: L. S. Fuchs et al., "Formative Evaluation of Academic Progress: How Much Growth Can We Expect?" *School Psychology Review* 22 (1993): 27–48.

279 *DIBELS:* R. A. Kaminski and R. H. Good III, "Assessing Early Literacy Skills," in M. R. Shinn (ed.), *Advanced Applications of Curriculum-Based Measurements* (New York: Guilford Press, 1998), and R. H. Good, D. C. Simmons, and E. J. Kame'enui, "The Importance and Decision-Making Utility of a Continuum of Fluency-Based Indicators of Foundational Reading Skills for Third-Grade High-Stakes Outcomes," *Scientific Studies of Reading* 5 (2001): 239–56.

280 The second approach: R. W. Woodcock, Woodcock Reading Mastery Test, Revised (Circle Pines, Minn.: American Guidance Service, 1987).

281 Fortunately, standardized tests: J. K. Torgesen, R. K. Wagner, and C. Rashotte, Test of Work Reading Efficiency (TOWRE) (Austin, Tex.: PRO-ED, 1999). J. L. Weiderholt and B. R. Bryant, Gray Oral Reading Tests-4 (Austin, Tex.: PRO-ED, 2001).

281 One study that examined: J. D. McKinney, "Longitudinal Research on the Behavioral Characteristics of Children with Learning Disabilities," in J. Torgesen (ed.),

Cognitive and Behavioral Characteristics of Children with Learning Disabilities (Austin, Tex.: PRO-ED, 1990), pp. 115–38.

281 Findings from another study: E. A. Hanushuk, J. F. Kain, and S. G. Rivkin, "Does Special Education Raise Academic Achievement for Students with Disabilities?" *National Bureau of Economic Research,* Working Paper No. 6690, Cambridge, Mass. 1998.

282 It is not surprising: S. Vaughn, S. W. Moody, and J. S. Schumm, "Broken Promises: Reading Instruction in the Resource Room," *Exceptional Children* 64 (1998): 211–25.

282 To make matters worse: R. L. Allington and A. McGill-Franzen, "School Response to Reading Failure: Instruction for Chapter 1 and Special Education Students in Grades Two, Four and Eight," *Elementary School Journal* 89 (1989): 529–42.

282 Studies examining "inclusion classrooms": N. Zigmond and J. Jenkins, "Special Education in Restructured Schools," *Phi Delta Kappan* 76 (1995): 531–35; and N. Zigmond, "Organization and Management of General Education Classrooms," in D. L. Speece and B. K. Keogh (eds.), *Research on Classroom Ecologies* (Mahwah, N.J.: Erlbaum, 1996), pp. 163–90.

282 On the other hand: J. K. Torgesen et al., "Intensive Remedial Instruction for Children with Severe Reading Disabilities," *Journal of Learning Disabilities* 34 (2001): 33–58.

282 *The Read, Write & Type!:* This learning system is produced by Talking Fingers, San Rafael, California. Results are in: J. K. Torgesen et al., "The Effectiveness of Teacher-Supported Computer-Assisted Instruction in Preventing Reading Problems in Young Children: A Comparison of Two Methods," unpublished manuscript (Florida State University: Tallahassee, Fla., 2000).

283 Colorado researchers: R. K. Olson et al., "Computer-Based Remedial Training in Phoneme Awareness and Phonological Decoding: Effects on the Post-Training Development of Word Recognition," *Scientific Studies of Reading* 1 (1997): 235–53.

283 In summing up the evidence: The Report of the National Reading Panel, Teaching Children to Read: An Evidence-Based Assessment of the Scientific Research Literature and Its Implications for Reading Instruction" (Washington, D.C.: U.S. Department of Health and Human Services, Public Health Service, National Institutes of Health, National Institute of Child Health and Human Development, 2000), p. 6–12.

284 Recording for the Blind and Dyslexic (RFB&D): 20 Roszel Road, Princeton, N.J. 08540, 1-866-RFBD-585.

284 *Hey! Listen to This: Stories to Read Aloud* by J. Trelease (New York: Penguin Books, 1992), and J. Trelease, *Read All About It!* (New York: Penguin Books, 1993).

285 While a child's: M. J. Snowling, *Dyslexia* (Oxford, England: Blackwell, 2000); J. K. Torgesen et al., "Intensive Remedial Instruction for Children with Severe Reading Disabilities," *Journal of Learning Disabilities* 34, (2001): 33–58; J. K. Torgesen, C. A. Rashotte, and A. Alexander, "Principles of Fluency Instruction in Reading: Relationships with Established Empirical Outcomes," in M. Wolf (ed.), *Time, Fluency, and Dyslexia* (Parkton, Md.: York Press, 2001); B. Wise, J. Ring, and R.

Olson, "Training Phonological Awareness with and Without Explicit Attention to Articulation," *Journal of Experimental Child Psychology* 72 (1999): 271–304; B. Wise, J. King, and R. Olson, "Individual Differences in Gains from Computer-Assisted Remedial Reading," *Journal of Experimental Child Psychology* 77 (2000): 197–235.

286 Children show impressive growth: J. K. Torgesen et al., "Intensive Remedial Instruction for Children with Severe Reading Disabilities, *Journal of Learning Disabilities* 34 (2001): 33–58.

286 This increase is particularly: A. E. Cunningham and K. E. Stanovich, "What Reading Does for the Mind," *American Educator* 22 (1998): 8–15.

286 They have not yet established: D. P. Hayes and J. Grether, "The School Year and Vacations: When Do Students Learn?" *Cornell Journal of Social Relations* 17 (1983): 56–71; and K. Alexander and D. Entwisle, "Schools and Children at Risk," in A. Booth and J. Dunn (eds.), *Family-School Links: How Do They Affect Educational Outcomes?* (Hillsdale, N.J.: Erlbaum, 1996), pp. 67–88.

Chapter 20: Helping Adults Become Better Readers

288 Research attests to the plasticity: see S. Shaywitz et al., "Estrogen Alters Brain Activation Patterns in Postmenopausal Women During Working Memory Tasks," *Journal of the American Medical Association* 281 (1999): 1197–1202, and E. Taub, G. Uswatte, and T. Elbert, "New Treatments in Neurorehabilitation Founded on Basic Research," *Nature Reviews Neuroscience* 3 (2002): 228–36.

288 There are many dyslexic adults: The General Education Development (GED) diploma was originally developed to allow World War II soldiers to earn a high school equvalency degree. The GED test is designed to assess the components included in a full four-year high school curriculum.

288 Lack of literacy: I. S. Kirsch et al., *Adult Literacy in America* (Washington, D.C.: Educational Testing Service, 1993).

288 This may explain why: R. S. Puglsley, *Vital Statistics: Who Is Served by the Adult Education Program?* (Washington, D.C.: U.S. Department of Education, Division of Adult Education and Literacy, 1990), and R. S. Venezky and D. A. Wagner, "Supply and Demand for Adult Literacy Instruction," *Adult Education Quarterly* 46 (1996): 197–208.

288 In fact in the: A. J. Carnevale and D. M. Desrochers, "Connecting Education Standards and Employment: Course-taking Patterns of Young Workers," American Diploma Project: Workplace Study, ETS. Paper Prepared for the National Alliance of Business, October 1, 2002.

289 Printed materials we read: Personal communication from Elaine Cheesman, director emeritus of the YMCA's Read to Succeed Adult Reading Clinic, Hartford, Connecticut.

289 Happily, highly effective programs: J. F. Greene, "Language! Efforts of an Individualized Structured Language Curriculum for Middle and High School Students," *Annals of Dyslexia* 40 (1990): 97–121.

290 Consistency is critical: L. Candelli, et al. *What Works Study for Adult ESL Literacy Students: Final Report.* Planning and Evaluation Service, U.S. Department of Education, 2000.

290 Adults work during the day: M. B. Young et al., *National Evaluation of Adult Education Programs: Final Report* (Arlington, Va.: Development Associates, 1994).

290 Adult students can expect: F. Tao, B. Gamse, and H. Tarr, *National Evaluation of the Even Start Family Literacy Program: 1994–1997. Final Report* (Arlington, Va.: Fu Associates, Ltd. 1998).

290 For teaching adults: *Language!* Longmont, Col.: Sopris West 2002; the *Wilson Reading System* (Millbury, MA); *Starting Over: A Combined Teaching Manual and Student Workbook for Reading, Writing, Spelling, Vocabulary and Handwriting* by J. Knight is available from Educators Publishing Service, Cambridge, Mass.

290 As you now know: The Degrees of Reading Power (DRP) (Available from TASA, 4 Hardscrabble Heights, Brewster, New York, 10509).

291 In addition: *Lexia Reading SOS* is available from Lexia Learning Sysems, Inc., 2 Lewis Street, P.O. Box 466, Lincoln, Mass., 01773, 800-435-3942.

292 *News for You* is available from New Readers Press, P.O. Box 35888, Syracuse, N.Y., 13235, 800-448-8878.

292 Thumbprint Mysteries are published by McGraw-Hill, 1 Prudential Plaza, 130 East Randolph St., Suite 400, Chicago, Ill. 60601, 800-621-1918.

293 For more information: The GED Testing Service is headquartered in 1 Dupont Circle NW, Suite 250, Washington, D.C. 20036, 202-939-9475.

293 Tom Sticht, who developed: T. G. Sticht et al. *Cast-off Youth: Policy and Training Methods from the Military Experience* (New York: Praeger, 1987).

Chapter 21: Choosing a School

295 Parents and teachers: Report of the National Reading Panel, "Teaching Children to Read: An Evidence-Based Assessment of the Scientific Research Literature and Its Implications for Reading Instruction" (Washington, D.C.: U.S. Department of Health and Human Services, Public Health Service, National Institutes of Health, National Institute of Child Health and Human Development, 2000.

295 Particularly with the impetus: No Child Left Behind Act of 2001.

298 Society tends to view people: According to a Roper-Starch Worldwide survey, *Measuring Progress in Public Schools and Parental Understanding of Learning Disability* (2000), commissioned by the Emily Hall Tremaine Foundation, 65 percent of those surveyed confuse learning disability with mental retardation.

Chapter 23: Accommodations

314 Studies carried out over: For studies demonstrating persistence of phonologic deficit see: S. E. Shaywitz et al., "Persistence of Dyslexia: The Connecticut Longitudinal Study at Adolescence," *Pediatrics* 104 (1999): 1351–59; M. Bruck, "Persis-

tence of Dyslexics' Phonological Awareness Deficits," *Developmental Psychology* 28 (1992): 874–86; M. Bruck, "Word Recognition Skills of Adults with Childhood Diagnoses of Dyslexia," *Developmental Psychology* 26 (1990): 439–54; R. Felton, C. Naylor, and F. Wood, "Neuropsychological Profile of Adult Dyslexics," *Brain and Language* 39 (1990): 485–97; K. Gross-Glenn, "Nonsense Passage Reading as a Diagnostic Aid in the Study of Adult Familial Dyslexia," *Reading and Writing: An Interdisciplinary Journal* 2 (1990): 161–73; and R. Davidson and J. Strucker, "Patterns of Word Recognition Error Among Adult Basic Education Students," *Scientific Studies of Reading* 6 (2002): 299–316. In addition, several studies have now shown that students who are learning-disabled significantly improve their performance with extra time, while nondisabled students do not; see M. K. Runyan, "The Effect of Extra Time on Reading Comprehension Scores for University Students with and Without Learning Disabilities," in S. E. Shaywitz and B. A. Shaywitz (eds.), *Attention Deficit Disorder Comes of Age: Toward the Twenty-first Century* (Austin, Tex.: PRO-ED, 1992): 185–95; and S. M. Weaver, "The Efficacy of Extended Time on Tests for Postsecondary Students with Learning Disabilities," *Learning Disabilities: A Multidisciplinary Journal* 10 (2000): 47–56.

316 Instead of the intense activation: B. Shaywitz et al., "Disruption of Posterior Brain Systems for Reading in Children with Developmental Dyslexia," *Biological Psychiatry* 52 (2002): 101–10.

316 "The patterns of deficits that characterize": M. Bruck, "Outcomes of Adults with Childhood Histories of Dyslexia," in C. Hulme and R. M. Joshi (eds.), *Reading and Spelling: Development and Disorders* (Mahwah, N.J.: Erlbaum, 1998), pp. 179–200; quote, p. 197.

316 Observations in university students: E. Paulesu, et al., "Dyslexia: Cultural Diversity and Biological Unity," *Science* 291 (2001): 2165–67.

319 "I could remember": Essays written by Seth Burstein for the 1999 Marion Huber Learning Through Listening Awards, sponsored by RFB&D.

320 Currently, RFB&D is making: According to John Kelly, senior vice president for Education at Recording for the Blind and Dyslexic, this conversion to digital format is being carried out in cooperation with the publishing industry.

323 This approach is called SQ3R: F. P. Robinson, *Effective Study* (New York: Harper Collins, 1946).

324 Obtain recorded versions: Recordings for the Blind and Dyslexic, 20 Roszel Rd. Princeton, N.J., 08540.

324 As an alternative: The Kurzweil 3000 is available from Kurzweil Educational Systems, Inc., 14 Crosby Drive, Bedford, Massachusetts, 01730. WYNN (What You Need Now) 3.1 is available from Freedom Scientific, 480 S. California Ave., Suite 201, Palo Alto, California 94306.

325 Connectix: 955 Campus Drive, San Mateo, Calif. 94403.

325 Bookshare.org: The Benetech Initiative, 480 S. California Ave., Palo Alto, Calif. 94306.

325 There is a continuing stream: *NaturallySpeaking*, ScanSoft, 9 Centennial Drive, Peabody, Mass.; *ViaVoice*, IBM, 1133 Westchester Ave., White Plains, N.Y. 10604; *iListen*, MacSpeech, 3 Executive Park Dr., Bedford, N.H. 03110. KeyStone *Screen-*

Speaker, Words Worldwide Ltd., Ash House, Bell Villas, Ponteland, Newcastle upon Tyne, England NE209BE.

325 Speech recognition programs: *TextHelp* is available from Wordsmith, 25 Randalstown Road Antrim, Co; Antrim BT 41 41L, Northern Ireland; *Co:Writer 4000,* Don Johnston, 26799 West Commerce Drive, Volo, Illinois 60073.

326 Computer aids are also available: Speaking Spelling Ace, Franklin Electronic Publishers, One Franklin Plaza, Burlington, N.J. 08016; *Home Page Reader,* IBM, 1133 Westchester Ave., White Plains, N.Y. 10604; *eReader,* CAST, 40 Harvard Hills Square, Suite 3, Wakefield, Mass. 01880.

326 Streamlined Shakespeare and Cornerstone classics available from High Noon Books, 20 Commercial Boulevard, Novato, Calif. 94949.

327 A company called Audible: 65 Willowbrook Blvd., Wayne, N.J. 07470.

327 New assistive technology: The Quicktionary Reading Pen II is a product of WizCom Technologies, Jerusalem, Israel; their U.S. office address is 257 Great Road, Acton, Massachusetts 01720.

328 *Inspiration V6:* This is available from Inspiration Software, Inc., 7412 Beaverton Hillsdale #102 of Portland, Oregon 97225.

329 Alphasmart 3000: 973 University Ave., Los Gatos, California 95032.

329 For taking notes: The QuickLink Pen is available from WizCom Technologies of Jerusalem, Israel; their U.S. office is in Acton, Massachusetts.

335 Scientific evidence shows: E. Paulesu et al. *Dyslexia: Cultural Diversity and Biological Unity, Science* 291 (2001): 2165–67.

337 Imaging studies demonstrate: B. Shaywitz et al., "Disruption of Posterior Brain Systems for Reading in Children with Developmental Dyslexia," *Biological Psychiatry* 52 (2002): 101–10.

337 Researchers have compared: M. K. Runyan, "The Effect of Extra Time on Reading Comprehension Scores for University Students with and Without Learning Disabilities," in S. E. Shaywitz and B. A. Shaywitz (eds.), *Attention Deficit Disorder Comes of Age: Toward the Twenty-first Century* (Austin, Tex.: PRO-ED, 1992), pp. 185–95, and S. M. Weaver, "The Efficacy of Extended Time on Tests for Postsecondary Students with Learning Disabilities," *Learning Disabilities: A Multidisciplinary Journal* 10 (2000): 47–56.

338 Recently, a blue-ribbon panel: The findings of the panel are reported in *The Flagging of Test Scores of Individuals Who Are Granted the Accommodation of Extended Time: A Report of the Majority Opinion of the Blue Ribbon Panel on Flagging.* The report is available on the Web site of the nonprofit law firm Disability Rights Advocates, www.dralegal.org. The address is 449 Fifteenth Street, Oakland, California 94612, 510-451-8644.

339 The practice of flagging: Ibid. See also Breimhorst et al., c. Educational Testing Service, Case No. C-99-3387 WHO (N.D. Cal, March 27, 2001). Disability Rights Advocates is located in Oakland, California.

339 He charged that: The quotes are taken from the *New York Times,* February 8, 2001, page A1.

339 "The majority position of the Panel": The full majority position is available at www.dralegal.org.

341 At the next level: Lani Guinier, now a professor at Harvard Law School, reports that differences in scores obtained on the LSAT explain less than 14 percent of the differences in student grades during the first year of law. See L. Guinier, M. Fine, and J. Balin, *Becoming Gentlemen* (Boston: Beacon Press, 1997).

341 One judge proposed: U.S. District Court Judge Bernard A. Friedman as reported in the *Wall Street Journal,* March 29, 2001, page B1.

342 Most recently, Richard C. Atkinson: This was reported in the *New York Times,* February 17, 2001, page A1.

342 As for higher levels: R. C. Davidson and E. Lewis, "Affirmative Action and Other Special Consideration Admissions at the University of California, Davis, School of Medicine," *Journal of the American Medical Association* 278 (1997): 1153–58.

343 "Applicants who qualified for": Editorial, "Medical School Admissions Criteria: The Needs of Patients Matter," *Journal of the American Medical Association* 278 (1997): 1196–97.

Acknowledgments

I am grateful to the community of scientists, educators, policy makers, advocates, and ordinary individuals who inspired me to write this book and provided the expertise and guidance to make it a reality. I have been extraordinarily fortunate to have had wise and generous mentors and colleagues who shared their accumulated wisdom. If I have succeeded in some small way, the credit is theirs. If there are lapses or misunderstandings in this book, the fault is entirely mine.

For the past two decades I have been blessed by having G. Reid Lyon at my side as my guide and companion. His leadership created the modern study of reading and reading disability, and his uncommon vision forged the science and public policy together as a seamless and natural whole. I am grateful most of all for his friendship and unfailing support; he has been like a brother to me.

I am thankful for the personal support, shared expertise, and intellectual stimulation of my colleagues who are or have been part of the Yale Developmental Functional Neuroimaging Group, led by Bennett Shaywitz and including Todd Constable, Robert Fulbright, John Gore, Cheryl Laccadie, Einar Mencl, Ken Pugh, Doug Rothman, and Pawel Skudlarski. I am indebted to my associates at the Yale Center for the Study of Learning and Attention for their commitment and support: John Holahan, Carmel Lepore, Karen Marchione, and Abigail Shneider. I want to especially acknowledge the important contribution of the late Isabel and Alvin Liberman who shared their expertise and love of the study of reading with me and were there to guide me at an early stage of my research in reading. My conceptualization of reading and dyslexia has been informed by discussions with my close collaborators over the years: Stan Dehaene, Jack Fletcher, David Francis, Len Katz, Rafael Klorman, Bruce McCandliss, Robin Morris, Michael Posner, Donald Shankweiler, and Michael Studdert-Kennedy.

I want to express my deep gratitude to the many researchers who through their writings and presentations, their thoughtful comments and exchanges, especially during my service on the Committee for Preventing Reading Difficulties in Young Children and on the National Reading Panel, or their quick response to an urgent e-mail query allowed me to continually refine and perfect this book. The imprint of the greater community of reading scientists is reflected in each of the pages of this book, and I am grateful for that. At the same time I want to single out certain individuals who were always there to offer wise counsel and to respond to my many questions: Marilyn Jager Adams, Isabel Beck, Virginia Berninger, Doug Carnine, Linnea Ehri, Rebecca Felton, Barbara

Acknowledgments

Foorman, Uta Frith, Lynn Fuchs, John Gabrieli, David Gray, Noel Gregg, Ed Kame'enui, Barbara Keogh, Maureen Lorett, Nancy Mather, Louisa Moats, Dennis and Victoria Molfese, Richard Olson, Bruce Pennington, Charles Perfetti, Elaine Silliman, Marcy Stein, Joe Torgesen, Sharon Vaughn, Richard Wagner, and Barbara Wise.

Adults who are dyslexic have a special place in my heart, and I have gained valuable insights into their special circumstance from conversations with researchers Judy Alamparese, Elaine Cheesman, Mary Beth Curtis, Rosalie Fink, Thomas Sticht, and John Strucker.

My comments about effective programs for teaching reading have benefited from my service on the National Reading Panel and from ongoing discussions with colleagues involved in producing reading programs, particularly Nanci Bell, Suzanne Carreker, Nancy Eberhardt, Jane Greene, Jeanne Herron, Pamela Hook, Steve Truch, and Barbara Wilson. I am infinitely wiser about selecting reading programs as a result of conversations with my colleagues in California, Vicki Alterwitz, Alice Furry, Marvilene Hagopian, and, above all, Marion Joseph.

Duane Alexander, director of the National Institute of Child Health and Human Development (NICHD), deserves special mention. Through his efforts as chair of the Interagency Committee on Learning Disabilities, Dr. Alexander opened the field of learning disabilities to a rigorous scientific research agenda, and his unfailing support over the long term is responsible for the depth and elegance of our current knowledge. Working with Peggy McCardle and others at NICHD gave me incredible respect for those who are at the nexus of science and public policy, and I am grateful for their willingness to share their expertise and to illuminate my perspective. I am also indebted to Dan Federman, former dean for medical education at Harvard Medical School; Florence Haseltine, director, Center for Population Research at NICHD; and educator Nancy Nordmann for helping me understand more clearly the impact of dyslexia on different populations and for caring so much about those who are affected by it.

I want to thank many hardworking and tireless advocates—especially William Hamill and the Baldwin Foundation; Susan Hall and the Coordinated Campaign for Learning Disabilities; Will Baker and The Dyslexia Foundation; Cynthia and Bob Haan and Allen Breslau and the Haan Foundation; Bill Cosby and Carolyn Oliver and the Hello Friend/Ennis William Cosby Foundation; Emerson Dickman, Nancy Hennesey, and Tom Viall and the International Dyslexia Association; Harry Sylvester, Larry Silver, and the International Learning Disabilities Association; Ann Ford, Jim Wendorf, Sheldon Horowitz, and the National Center for Learning Disabilities; Alexa Culwell and the Charles and Helen Schwab Foundation—for the support they have always given me, for all they have taught me about dyslexia, and for providing me a frequent platform to present and share the excitement of new scientific discoveries. A very special acknowledgment must go to Shirley Cramer of the Dyslexia Institute in England who has been a wonderful sounding board, steadfast support, and constant friend.

I am grateful to the many teachers throughout Connecticut and New York who have invited me into their classrooms and opened my eyes to the extraordinary challenge of teaching reading. My colleagues on the Reading First review panel, Sharon Kurns, Kelly Mueller, and Lucinda Townsend, have provided me with many valuable insights about teaching reading. Bella Rosenberg of the American Federation of Teachers was helpful in clarifying issues concerning adolescent and adult readers. A heartfelt thanks goes to headmaster Mark Griffin and his dedicated staff at the Eagle Hill School in Greenwich, Connecticut, for enlightening me about the potential and possibilities offered by special schools to dyslexic students. I also extend my appreciation to Judith Hochman of the Windward School and Rosalie Whitlock of the Charles Armstrong School for their helpful insights. My thanks to Yvea Duncan, Carol Griffin, Rosa Hagin, Gail Hirsch, Doric Little, Kay Runyan, Helaine Schupack, Robert Shaw, Susan Vogel, and Claire Wurtzel for sharing their specialized knowledge about college students who are dyslexic.

Sari Feldman, executive director of the Cleveland Public Library, educated me about the expanded role of contemporary librarians in serving the needs of children and adults who are dyslexic. Mary Schumacher and the librarians at the Middle County Public Library in Centerville, Long Island, and Bunny Yesner, former head librarian at the Beecher Road School in Woodbridge, Connecticut, helped put together the reading lists found throughout this book. John Kelly and Peter Smith from Recording for the Blind and Dyslexic provided me with in-depth knowledge of this accommodation and its importance for dyslexic students. Computer consultant Enrico Melchiorri brought to my attention new developments in computer technology to assist dyslexic students, as did David Rose at CAST.

I am grateful for the richness and depth of scholarship at Yale, my academic home, that has allowed me to pursue the science of reading in its many manifestations. I am also indebted to my university for affording me an opportunity to observe firsthand how a demanding and compassionate school responds to its dyslexic students. Beginning with a call almost twenty years ago from the late Dean Martin Griffin, who wanted to share his concern about a possibly dyslexic student, and continuing to the present day, I have been able to examine close-up the place of a dyslexic student in a highly competitive academic environment. And I have come away heartened. It has been my good fortune to work collaboratively with and learn from Sally Esposito and Judy York, the very able directors of the Office for Students with Disabilities at Yale; Joseph Gordon, dean of undergraduate education; Richard Schenker, dean of academic affairs; and Margit Dahl, director of undergraduate admissions.

Needless to say, I am eternally indebted to the many children, parents, young adults, and adults who opened their hearts and souls to me and taught me about the reality of dyslexia. A special thanks goes to the children and families who participated in our research program, especially the Connecticut Longitudinal Study. My goal has been to reward their extraordinary trust with honesty and truth about dyslexia.

Carole Pollard was instrumental in ensuring that I received editorial assistance and Christy Peppard helped collate the information for the notes.

I have been very lucky in pursuing this project, first, in the unwavering support and wise counsel of my agents, Glen Hartley and Lynn Chu. I also thank Katy Sprinkel for her good cheer and helpfulness. Next, I, and ultimately, the reader, have benefited greatly from the uncommon commitment of my editor, Jon Segal, to the message of this book; his devotion and attention allowed me to find my true voice and, in the process, made this a better book. Ida Giragossian has been a true pleasure to work with.

I could not have written this book without my family. My children Adam, Jonathan, David, and his bride-to-be, Diana, have showered me with affection, providing me with

Index

Abler, William, 46
abstract thinking, 141, 355, 366
accommodations, 5, 172, 305, 314–44,
  358; alternate formats for tests, 321,
  328; answers to most frequently asked
  questions about, 335–42; best time to
  start, 338; computer assistance, 321,
  324–7; digitized texts, 320, 324–5;
  evaluation process and, 333–4; extra
  time on tests, 253, 293, 314–18, 320,
  322, 334, 336–7, 338; flagging scores
  of tests taken with, 339–40; foreign
  language requirements and, 318–19,
  321, 328; handwriting difficulties and,
  329; multiple-choice tests and, 317,
  328, 333–4, 340, 341–2, 344; neurologic
  support for, 78, 81, 82, 82, 83, 84, 87,
  154, 155, 314–17, 337; occupational
  success and, 340–1; oral responses in
  class and, 330–1; potential downside of,
  338–40; quiet separate room during
  testing, 116, 318, 320–1, 322; recorded
  vs. written essays, 329–30; sample plan
  for (Andrew, high school student),
  321–32; sample plan for (Gregory,
  medical school student), 332–4; textbooks on tape or CD-ROM, 254,
  319–20, 321, 324; worries about
  "advantage" of, 337
accuracy, in reading, 133, 139, 189, 231,
  335
acquired alexia, 14–17, 18, 67, 140
active reading, 323–4
activist stance, for parents,
  173–4
Adams, Marilyn, 272
Adams, Scott, 310

adult literacy programs, 288–93; consistency and duration in, 290; getting
  information about, 292–3; group setting
  for, 289–90; placement testing and,
  289; readymade programs for, 290–1;
  work-related motivation and, 291–2,
  293
adults, dyslexic, 288–93; clues to dyslexia
  in, 125–7; college and graduate students, 150–65, 335–6; diagnosis of, 130,
  154–65, 335–6; essential facts about,
  162; evaluating cognitive ability of,
  135–6, 139; reading materials for,
  292
age: dyslexics' brain activation and, 81, 82;
  reading gap and, 264–5, 265; specific
  signs of dyslexia related to, 121–7
A.J. (reversals), 101
Alex (gifted dyslexic child), 36, 37–8, 96
Alexander, Duane, 25, 175
alexia, acquired, 14–17, 18, 67, 140
alliteration, 178, 181, 186
alphabet: ABC song and, 98, 188. See also
  letters
alphabet blocks, 190
alphabetic languages, logographic languages vs., 31
Alphabetic Phonics, 386n
alphabetic principle, 44, 45, 102–3, 176–7
AlphaSmart 3000, 254, 329
American Heritage Dictionary, 327
American Speech-Language-Hearing
  Association, 128
American Tragedy, An (Dreiser), 326
animal communication systems, 46
anterior lobes, 75, 76
aphasia, 15, 64–7

Aristotle, 60

Ashley (third grader), 131–2, 135, 136–7, 138–9, 142

Atkinson, Richard C., 342

at-risk children, 142–9; comprehensive evaluation of, 143–9; kindergarten screening and, 142–3, 194–5, 261; prevention and early intervention programs for, 261–4

attention deficit/hyperactivity disorder (ADHD), 141, 336

Audible, 327

AudioPlus, 320

auditory system, 48–9, 141

automaticity, 105, 155, 231, 256, 280, 315–16; overlearning and, 268–9; word form area and, 78, 79–81, 80, 87, 155, 231, 256, 280

autoregulation of cerebral blood flow, 69–70

Baader, Joseph, 62

baby talk, 94, 122

beginning reading program, questions to ask about, 208–11

behavior problems, 33

Bemelmans, Ludwig, 181–2

Benacceraf, Baruj, 117, 118

Benchmark School Word Identification/Vocabulary Development Program, 267

Bennett, Andrew (high school student), 321–32

Berlin, Rudolf, 15

big-picture approach, 125, 127, 283, 284, 366

Binet-Simon Intelligence Scale, 20

blending, 144, 182, 183, 184–5, 206; synthetic phonics and, 202–3

Bloom, B. S., 269

Bloomfield, Leonard, 50

boarding schools, 296–7

"Bob Books" (Maslen), 189, 221

Bohr, Niels, 310

Boies, David, 315, 317–18, 326, 340, 345

books: for children, vocabulary in, 105, 106; decodable texts, 189–90, 221, 271; digitized, 320, 324–5; for dyslexic high school students to read aloud, 274–5;

easy readers, 225–6; gauging level of difficulty of, 222–4; for parent to read to dyslexic child, 284–5; picture books, 224–5, 226–7; poetry, 225, 226; to read aloud to child on cusp of reading, 192–3; on tape or CD-ROM, 254, 282, 284, 319–20, 321, 324, 327; that joyfully play with sounds of language, 179–80; transitional, chapter, 227–8. *See also* textbooks

Bookshare.org, 325

"Books to Remember" (Appleton-Smith), 221

Boston Naming Test, 138, 139

Boston University, 164

Bradley, Lynette, 55

brain: basic landmarks of, 75–6, 76; blood flow in, 69–70; earliest conceptions of, 59–61; localization of function in, 60–7, 66; sex differences in organization of, for language, 77, 77; ventricles of, 61, 61–2. *See also* neural pathways of reading

brain imaging, 4, 40, 59, 68–75, 76–89, 141; computed tomography (CT), 68–9; effects of reading interventions evaluated with, 85–6, 86, 257–8; functional magnetic resonance imaging, 69–89, 72–4, 77, 80, 82, 83, 84, 86, 257–8, 315–16; magnetic resonance imaging (MRI), 69, 71, 76, 80; neural pathways of reading identified with, 78–85, 80, 82, 83, 84, 315–16; positron emission tomography (PET), 69; sex differences in brain organization for language identified with, 77, 77

Branson, Sir Richard, 310, 359, 366

Breimhorst, Mark (plaintiff, flagging suit), 339

Briana (college student), 150–1, 156

British Medical Journal, 13–14

Broadbent, Sir William, 14–15

Broca, Paul, 64–5, 67

Broca's aphasia, 64, 67

Broca's area, 64, 65, 66, 73, 78, 81, 84

Bruck, Maggie, 154, 316

Bruner, W. E., 24

Bryant, Peter, 55

Bulifant, Joyce, 88

Burstein, Seth (college student), 319

Bush, George W., 175
businessmen and businesswomen, renowned dyslexic, 356–9, 364–5

Caitlyn (first grader), 7–9
California, standards for reading programs in, 208–9, 266
Calliope, 229
Cambier, Nicholas, 14
Cannell, Stephen J., 317, 353–6
Caperton, Gaston, 364–5
categorical model of dyslexia, 27–9
Centers for the Study of Learning and Attention, 25–6
cerebellum, 75, *76*
cerebral cortex, 65
Chambers, John, 359
chapter books, transitional, 227–8
Charles Armstrong School, 301
Charles and Helen Schwab Foundation for Learning, 130, 358
Charlotte (law student), 5
Cheever, John, 356
Children's Books in Print, 223–4
China, ancient, 60
China, dyslexia in, 31
Chomsky, Noam, 45
Chugga-Chugga Choo-Choo (Lewis and Kirk), 178
Classic Comics, 326
clumsiness, 101
coarticulation, 48, *48*, 51
cognition, 62
cognitive ability, tests of, 135–7, 139
Coiter, Volcher, 62
college students, dyslexic, 150–65; diagnosis of, 154, 155–65, 335–6; personal history and, 156–7; reading speed of, 154–5
compensatory reading systems, 82–4, *84*
complex words, 113, 267
composition, difficulties with, 254
compound words, 206, 212, 215, 221
comprehension, 52, 53, 54, 57, *58*, 105–6, 115, 120, 123, 125, 148, 262, 281; activities after finishing book and, 241, 244; activities before book is opened and, 241, 242; activities during reading and, 241, 243–4; fluency and, 231, 276;

hyperlexia and, 140; parents' nurturing of, 241–7; phonics and, 203; reading tests and, 133, 134; of spoken language, 40; trouble signs for, 246–7; vocabulary and, 106, 191, 192, 235; worldly knowledge and, 235
Comprehensive Test of Phonological Processing, 137
computed tomography (CT), 68–9
computers, 300–1, 338; accommodations and, 321, 324–6; digitized texts and, 320, 324–5; homonym checkers and, 325, 326; keyboarding skills and, 254, 264, 283; oral presentations and, 300, 331; as practice tool, 276, 282, 283, 291; *ReadIt* and, 273; speech recognition software and, 325, 330; spell checkers and, 114, 326, 330, 334; stimulating phonological awareness and, 187; teaching reading with, 259, 282–3; teaching vocabulary with, 276; as writing aid, 115, 254, 283, 300
concepts, 123, 125, 127, 262, 321; formation of, 57, *58*; learning and, 283–4, 331–2
congenital word-blindness, 16–17, 18–24; appropriate teaching for, 22–3; detection of, 20–2, 23
Congress, U.S., 25, 174, 175
Connecticut Longitudinal Study, 26–35, 378*n*; gender bias in school identification procedures and, 31–3; participants in, 27; persistence of dyslexia and, 33–5, 121; prevalence of dyslexia and, 29–31; relation between good and poor readers and, 27–9
consonants: dividing long words between, 206, 215–17, *216*; phonics and, 200, 201
context, reliance on, 111–12, 114, 118, 124, 315, 316–17, *317*, 322
Cormack, Allan M., 69
Cornerstone Classics, 326–7
corpus callosum, 75, *76*
correct words per minute (CWPM), 277, 278–9
Cosgrove, Delos M. (Toby), 317, 362–4
course load, 322
Co:Writer 4000, 325
creativity, 24, 53, 57, 344

Cricket, 228–9

critical thinking, 57, 58

Cruise, Tom, 310

current events, children's magazines on, 229

curriculum-based measurement (CBM), 278–9

Curtis, Mary E., 274

Cushing, Harvey, 364

DaisyQuest, 187

Daisy's Castle, 187

Daniel (spelling), 114

Davis, Ronald, 117

day schools, private nonspecialized, 295–9, 306

decodable texts, 189–90, 221, 271

decoding, 10, 50–1, 52, 53, 54, 102, 104, 113–14, 177, 231, 262; ability to read nonsense words as measure of, 133–4; brain imaging and, 59, 76–89; deficits in, 52–4, 54, 55, 58; knowledge of word meanings and, 191–2; normal development of phonemic awareness and, 51–2, 54–5. *See also* sounding out

DeFrancis, John, 45–6

Degrees of Reading Power (DRP) system, 222–3, 255, 275, 290

Dejerine, Jules, 79

developmental dyslexia, 14, 140. *See also* dyslexia

diagnosis of dyslexia, 10, 35, 53, 93–165, 135–7; in bright young adults, 154, 155–65, 335–6; as clinical diagnosis, 132, 335; delay in speaking and, 94; at different ages, 121–7; dimensional vs. categorical model and, 27–9; among disadvantaged children, 23, 338; early clues in, 94–8, 122–3; early research and, 20–2, 23; feelings about, 312–13; fluency and, 113, 114, 115–16, 123, 125; functional imaging and, 87–8; function (little) words and, 111–12, 123–4; gender bias and, 31–3, 32; genetic predisposition and, 98–100; getting help and, 127–30; handwriting difficulties and, 114–15, 124; identification of at-risk children and, 142–9, 172, 194–5; later clues in, 102–19, 123–7; myths and misunderstandings and,

100–1; observing your child's progress and, 112–19; optimal age for intervention and, 30–1, 120–1, 257; other disorders that may impact reading and, 140–1; phonological difficulties and, 55, 97–8, 111, 122; potential contributing factors and, 141; pretending to be dyslexic and, 164–5; pronunciation difficulties and, 94–5, 122, 123, 125; reliance on context and, 111–12, 124; retesting later in life and, 164; retrieval difficulties and, 96–7, 111, 123; sea of strenghts model and, 93; sensitivity to rhyme and, 95–6, 122; signs that child should be evaluated and, 120–30; spelling difficulties and, 114, 124, 126; substituted, omitted, or mispoken words and, 114, 124, 126; timed reading tests and, 155–6, 161, 163; underidentification and, 23, 28–9, 30–1, 136–7, 338. *See also* evaluation for dyslexia

DIBELS (Dynamic Indicators of Basic Early Literacy Skills), 194–5, 279

dictionaries, 208, 238

Dictionary.com, 238

digitized texts (e-text), 320, 324–5

digraphs, 201

dimensional model of dyslexia, 27–9

Direct Instruction (DI), 263, 265–6

Disability Rights Advocates (DRA), 339

disadvantaged children, reading difficulties underidentified in, 23, 338

discourse, 53

distractions, 116; minimizing, 322, 323

DNA, particulate principle and, 46, 47

Dreiser, Theodore, 326

DRP-Booklink, 222

Duane, Drake, 68

dyslexia: in adults, 150–65, 288–93, 335–6; basic nature of, 36–89; brain activation patterns in, 78, 81–5, 82, 83, 84, 314–17; children's questions about, 311; concrete evidence of, 87; definition of, 132; diagnosis of (*see* diagnosis of dyslexia; evaluation for dyslexia); doubts about existence of, 4, 87;

etymology of word, 311; explaining to child, 310–11; "faking," 337–8; family history of, 33, 94, 98–100, 122, 127, 132, 148, 261, 374n; future for those with, 340–2, 342–4; gender and, 31–3; hidden nature of, 4, 5, 87; historical roots of, 13–24; impact of, 4, 9, 31, 116–17, 131, 169–71, 291–2, 346, 353, 358, 359, 361–2, 362–3; localized nature of problem in, 40; myths and misunderstandings about, 100–1; neurological origin in, 5, 17, 67–8, 87; occupational prospects and, 340–1; other problems confused with, 336; overcoming (*see* accommodations; overcoming dyslexia; reading intervention; reading programs); persistence of, 33–5, *34*, 82, 121, 154, 160–1, 164, 336–7; phonologic model of, 40–4; prevalence of, 29–31; as problem in language system, 39–44, *41*, *48*, 52–4, *52*, *54*; recent research on, 25–35, 71–89; strengths in other areas and, 24, 36, 37, 57–8, 93, 122–3, 124–5, 126–7, 172, 285–6, 295, 314; successful people with, 117–19, 310–11, 345–66; two major groups of poor readers with, 85; visual acuity and, 15–17, 19, 39–40
"Dyslexia" (S. Shaywitz), 31
dyslexia brain bank, 68

Eagle Hill School, 299–301
ear infections, 141
Earobics, 187
echo reading, 232
Educational Testing Service (ETS), 339
Education Department, U.S., 25, 29
Egypt, ancient, 59–60
Eine besondre Art der Wortblindheit (A Particular Kind of Word-Blindness) (Berlin), 15
Encarta World English Dictionary, 327
encyclopedias, 235
eReader, 326
errors in reading, 103, 122
Esposito, Sally, 164–5
essays, recorded vs. written, 329–30
e-text (digitized texts), 320, 324–5
etymology, 207

evaluation: adult placement testing, 289; alternative modes of (accommodations), 333–4; fluency measurement, 134–5, 269, 277, 278–9; IQ tests, 135–7, 139, 147, 152, 335, 378n; ongoing, of reading skills, 210–11; of phonologic skills, 143–6; of progress in reading intervention program, 252, 255, 278–80
evaluation for dyslexia, 132–41; cognitive ability and, 135–7, 139; comprehensive, for preschool and kindergarten children, 142–9; determining need for, 120–7; getting referral for, 128–30; IQ tests in, 135–7, 139, 378n; kindergarten screening in, 142–3, 194–5, 261; phonologic tests in, 137, 139, 143–6; reading tests in, 133–5, 138; tailored to individual, 132–3; vocabulary tests in, 138, 139
evolution, 48, 50
Excel@High School, 276
Excel@Middle School, 276
expressive language, *66*, 96; loss of, 64, 65
extracurricular activities, 305–6
eye movements, of readers, 105
eye training, 39–40

family history of dyslexia, 33, 94, 98–100, 122, 127, 132, 148, 261, 374n
Fast Track Reading Program, 265
fetal development, 17, 67–8
finger pointing, as aid in reading, 285
Fink, Rosalie, 117–18
first graders, 113, 198–205; clues to dyslexia in, 122–3; early intervention programs for, 257, 261–4; expected fluency rates for oral reading in, 277; guide to development of reading-related skills in, 109–10; magazines for, 228, 229; phonics instruction for, 199–205; practice activities at home for, 211–27; questions to ask about reading programs for, 209–11; remediation for, 257
Fisher, Matt (typing), 115
Flack, Marjorie, 242
Flagg, Fanny, 356
flash cards, for sight words, 190

fluency, 81, 86, 105, 120, 133, 230–5; automatic brain processes and, 79, 104, 105, 231, 256, 268–9, 273–4; brevity of sessions for, 272; comprehension and, 231, 276; description of, 230–1; guided repeated oral reading and, 232–3, 272–3; helping older children with, 274–6; identification of dyslexia and, 113, 114, 115–16, 123, 125; as index of dyslexia in bright adult, 335–6; love of reading and, 230; measurement of, 134–5, 269, 277, 278–9; overlearning and, 268–9; parents' role in building of, 233–5; permanency and, 280; poetry and, 271; reading intervention programs and, 253, 262, 268–77; ready-made programs for, 272–3; repeated practice and, 257, 268–76; room noises and, 116, 318; in speaking, lack of, 123, 125, 276, 330; speeded word training and, 269–70; working at home on, 272–4

Ford, Richard, 356

foreign languages, 116, 124, 360; waiving requirement for, 318–19, 321, 328

fourth graders and above, 113, 205–8; clues to dyslexia in, 123–5; expected fluency rates for oral reading in, 277; fluency among, 231; guide to development of reading-related skills in, 110; magazines for, 228–9, 229; practice activities at home for, 211–24, 230–45

"fourth grade slump," 275

Franklin Electronic Publishers, 326

frontal lobes, 75, 76; dyslexics' activation of, 81–4, 82, 83, 84, 256, 316

Fuchs, Lynn and Douglas, 278

functional magnetic resonance imaging (fMRI), 69–89; effects of reading interventions evaluated with, 85–6, 86, 257–8, 347n; neural pathways of reading identified with, 77–85, 78, 80, 82, 83, 84, 315–16; patient's experience in, 71–5, 72–4; sex differences in brain organization for language identified with, 77, 77; theoretical basis of, 69–70

function words, 111–12, 123–4

Fundations, 386n

Galen, 60

Gall, Franz Joseph, 62–4

Garza, Norma, 173–4

gender: identification of dyslexia and, 31–3, 32; organization of brain for language and, 77, 77

General Education Development (GED) diploma, 288, 289, 293, 318, 390n

genetic factors, 98–100, 141, 374n. See *also* family history of dyslexia

Geschwind, Norman, 68

Gillingham, Anna, 266

Goebel, Timothy, 189

grade point average (GPA), 342, 343

Graduate Management Admissions Test (GMAT), 339

Graduate Record Exam (GRE), 339

graduate students, identification of dyslexia in, 335–6

gray matter, 75

Gray Oral Reading Tests (GORT), 134, 163, 255, 281

Great Leaps Reading, 272

Greece, ancient, 60

Greek roots, 207, 239

Gregory (medical student), 36, 38–9, 53, 57, 58, 96, 153, 332–4

Grisham, John, 356

Griswold, Kettler, 311

Grossman, Paul, 88, 130

guided repeated oral reading, 232–3, 272

Hamlet (Shakespeare), 326

Hammond, Graeme, 317, 342, 359–62

handwriting, legibility of, 38, 114–15, 124, 254, 329, 330

Harvey, William, 66

Haseltine, Florence, 117

hearing, 48, 49, 141

heart, ancients' conceptions of, 59, 60

hemispheres, 75

Hewlett, William, 359

Hey! Listen to This (Trelease), 284

High Noon Books, 327

High Point, 265

high school students, dyslexic, materials to read aloud for, 274–5

Hinshelwood, James, 16–23

hobbies, importance of, 312

Home Page Reader, 326
homework, 124; lack of fluency and,
    115–16; reducing time required for, 338
homonyms, 325, 326, 330
Hounsfield, Sir Godfrey N., 69
hyperlexia, 140–1

iListen, 325
imagination, 60, 62, 123, 191, 193
inclusion classrooms, 282
independent reading level, 233
individualized instruction, 210, 258, 282
inferior frontal gyrus, 77, *78,* 81, *82, 83,*
    84, 84, 86
Inspiration, 328, 331
intelligence, 55, 59, 60; intact in dyslexics,
    15, 19, 24, 40, 53; IQ tests and, 135–7,
    139, 147, 152, 335, 378*n;* phonologic
    abilities and, 56–7
Interagency Committee on Learning
    Disabilities (ICLD), 25
interests, importance of, 312
International Dyslexia Association, 130
International Learning Disabilities
    Association, 130
intervention. *See* overcoming dyslexia;
    reading intervention; reading programs
intuitiveness, 366
invented spelling, 191
IQ tests, 135–7, 139, 147, 152, 335, 378*n*
irregular words. *See* sight words
Irving, John, 312, 315, 317, 345–50

Jackson, Edward, 24
Jackson, John Hughlings, 67
Japan, dyslexia in, 31
Jewel, 310
jingles, 182, 186
Johns Hopkins University, 26
Johnson, Jack, Inez, and Eddie (choosing
    a school), 295–6, 298–9, 301
Jolly Phonics, 204
Joseph, Marion, 208
Journal of Physiology, 69
Journal of the American Medical Associa-
    tion (JAMA), 342–3

Kacie (brain imaging), 71–4, *72, 74*
Kame'enui, Ed, 264
Kamprad, Ingvar, 359

Katz, Robert B., 56
Kendell, R. E., 28
Kent State University, 272
keyboarding, 254, 264, 283
Kilroy, Ken, 173, 359
kindergarten, delaying entry into, 149
kindergarten children, 98, 128, 176–97,
    203; appropriateness of instruction for,
    193–6; checklist for, 196–7; clues to
    dyslexia in, 122–3; developing aware-
    ness of rhyme in, 177, 178–82; drawing
    attention of, to sounds of language,
    177–87; evaluating phonologic skills
    and reading-readiness of, 143–9; guide
    to development of reading-related skills
    in, 108–9; invented spelling and, 191;
    letters linked to sounds by, 176–7, 178,
    188; listening, playing, and imagining as
    activities for, 191–3; practice important
    for, 188–90; prevention measures for,
    257, 261–4; recognition and writing of
    letters by, 190–1; retention of, 195–6;
    screening of, 142–3, 194–5, 261; self-
    confidence of, 193; sight words and,
    190; words pulled apart into sounds by,
    176, 177, 182–7
Kirk, Daniel, 178
Klass, Perri, 380*n*
Knapp, Robert, 117
knowledge: *general,* 57, 58; meaning vs.
    memorization as route to, 283–4;
    worldly, 120–1, 235, 255, 286, 327
Knowledge Adventure, 276
Kurzweil, 324–5, 327
Kussmaul, Adolf, 14, 15

"Ladders to Literacy," 187
Ladybug, 228, 229
Lancet, The, 16
Langenberg, Donald, 175
language: ability to distinguish speech
    sounds from noise and, 48–9; animal
    communication systems vs., 46; general
    skills in, 286; left side of brain associ-
    ated with, 75; open-ended nature of,
    46–7; origins of, 45–6; phonologic
    model of, 40–4; sex differences in
    organization of brain for, 77, *77. See*
    also sounds of language; spoken
    language

Index

Language!, 252–3, 255, 265, 271, 275, 290, 386*n*
language disorders (aphasias), 15, 64–7
language-learning disability, 140
late talking, 94
Latin roots, 207, 239
Law, Sylvia, 118, 317–18
Law School Admissions Tests (LSAT), 341–2
learning: active, 323–4; of content, facilitation of, 283–4, 331–2; evaluating capability for, 133, 135–7, 138–9
learning disabilities: federally funded research on, 25–6; statistics on, 29
learning to read. *See* reading acquisition
Leborgne (Tan), 64, 65
lecture notes, 321, 329
left-handedness, 101
left side of brain, 75, 76
Leno, Jay, 310
Leonardo da Vinci, 62
letter cards, 190
Letterland, 205
letters: difficulties with naming of, 40, 147; learning names of, 97, 98, 122, 147, 148, 188; linking to sounds, 51–2, 97, 102–3, 111, 113, 122, 147, 148, 176–7, 178, 188, 199–205 (*see also* phonics); recognition and writing of, 190–1; reversals of, 100–1
Lewis, Kevin, 178
Lexia Reading SOS (Strategies for the Older Student), 291
Lexile Framework, 223, 275
libraries, 246
life span perspective, 172
limericks, 271
Lindamood Phoneme Sequencing Program (LiPS), 267
listening, 48, 49, 50, 54, 148; active, encouraging in child, 241; for signs of problems in your child, 94, 113; to stories read aloud, 191, 192–3; to your child read aloud, 112–13
Literacy Directory, 292–3
little words, difficulties with, 111–12
logographic languages, dyslexia and, 31
logographic stage, 102
Lombardi, Carmine (adult), 291–2, 293

Longo, Ann Marie, 274
Lordat, Jacques, 65
Lyon, G. Reid, 132*n*, 261

Madeline (Bemelmans), 181–2
magazines: audio, 327; for beginning readers, 228–9; on tape and CD-ROM, 284
magnetic resonance imaging (MRI), 69, 71, *76, 80. See also* functional magnetic resonance imaging
magnetic resonance spectroscopy, 87
Marion Huber Learning Through Listening Award, 319
Maslen, Bobby Lynn, 221
math, 13–14, 38, 329
Matthew effect, 34
Matthews, Talia (reading intervention), 169–71
McCaw, Craig, 359
McCready, E. Bosworth, 24
Medical College Admissions Test (MCAT), 317, 342, 343
medical school admissions, 342–3
memorization: knowledge gained through meaning vs., 283–4, 331–2; of sight (irregular) words, 190, 202, 218–20; in vocabulary bulding, 102, 116, 177, 196
memory, 18, 60, 349; deficits in, 39, 57–8, 123, 125; localization of brain function and, 61, 62, 63; phonologic, 145–6; short-term, phoneme pace and, 48
Mercer, Cecil, 272
mind, earliest conceptions of, 59–62
mirror writing, 100–1
Moats, Louisa, 258
Moose on the Loose (Ochs), 181
Morgan, W. Pringle, 13–14, 16–17, 20
morphemes, 207
motivation, 284
Multigrade Inventory for Teachers (MIT), 147, 378*n*
multiple-choice tests, 126, 317, 328, 333–4, 340, 341–2, 344
museums, 327
Mystery Writers of America, 292

name of child, knowing letters in, 122; counting number of syllables in, 183; writing, 190

naming objects, 14, 56, 138, 139
National Assessment of Educational
    Progress (NAEP), 29–30, 231, 369n
National Board of Medical Examiners
    Licensing Examination, 342, 361
National Center for Learning Disabilities,
    130
National Institute of Child Health and
    Human Development (NICHD), 25
National Institutes of Health (NIH),
    25–6
National Reading Panel (NRP), 174–5,
    200, 203, 204, 208, 209–10, 232, 233,
    263, 266, 267, 268, 283, 295,
    382n–383n
National Research Council, 30
Naturally Speaking, 325
Nelson-Denny Reading Test, 163
Nemesius, 61
Nettleship, E., 23
Neuhaus Education Center, 273
neural pathways of reading, 67–8, 78–81;
    building of, 84–5, 85–6, 104, 105, 177,
    188–9, 220, 256, 257–8, 273–4; in
    dyslexics vs. good readers, 78, 81–4, *82,
    83, 84,* 155, 314–17; mapped through
    brain imaging, 77–85, *78, 80, 82, 83,
    84,* 315–16; in skilled vs. novice read-
    ers, 78, 79–81
New Scoop, 229
News for You, 292
newspapers, audio, 327
Newsweek, 29
Noah (function words), 111–12
No Child Left Behind Act, 175, 264. *See
    also* Reading First
noise: ability to distinguish speech sounds
    from, 48–9; dyslexics' vulnerability to,
    116, 318, 322
nonsense words, 37–8, 133–4
notetaking, 321, 323, 329
novels, alternate versions of, 284,
    326–7
nursery rhymes, 95, 122

occipital lobes, 75, *76*
occipito-temporal region, *78,* 78–9, 80,
    81, *83, 84,* 85–6, *86,* 104. *See also* word
    form area
Ochs, C. P., 181

Olson, Richard, 283
One Fish Two Fish Red Fish Blue Fish
    (Seuss), 181
"On the Regulation of the Blood-Supply
    of the Brain," 69
Open Court Reading, 209, 263–4, 271
opening sentences, 243
Optimize Intervention Program, The, 263,
    264
oral instruction, 18, 19
oral presentations, 300, 331
oral reading. *See* reading aloud by child;
    reading aloud to child
oral responses, 123, 125, 330–1
Oregon, accommodations in, 334
Orfalea, Paul J., 359
Orton, Samuel, 266, 359
Orton Dyslexia Society, 68
Orton-Gillingham approach, 266, 290,
    291, 386n
overcoming dyslexia, 10, 88, 171,
    251–344, 345–66; intrinsic qualities of
    child and, 172–3; life span perspective
    and, 172; optimal age for intervention
    and, 30–1, 257–8, 261; persistence of
    dyslexia and, 34–5; sample program for
    (Sam), 251–6; school choice and,
    294–308; scientifically proven methods
    for, 174–5; significant adults in dyslexic
    child's life and, 172, 173–4. *See also*
    accommodations; reading intervention;
    reading programs
overlearning, 268–9
Owen, Otis R., 25
Oxton House Publishers, 270, 275

paired reading, 272
Palm OS handheld devices, 329
paragraph, analyzing main idea in,
    243–4
parenting of dyslexic children, 7–9, 88,
    169–71, 350, 355–6; activist vs. passive
    stance in, 173–4; nurturing child's
    positive sense of self in, 309–13
parietal lobes, 75, *76*
parieto-temporal region, *78,* 78–9, 81, 256
particulate principle, 46–9, *47*
passive stance, 173
pauses: in eye movements of readers, 105;
    in speech, 97

Peabody Picture Vocabulary Test, 138
pediatricians, 128, 130
perception, 61
Percy F., 13–14, 16–17
perfectionism, 355
permanency, fluency as marker for, 280; lacking in dyslexia, 111
personality traits, localization of brain function and, 62–4
phonemes, *42, 43,* 176; analyzing syllables into, 98, 183–5, 206; coarticulation of, 48–9, *48,* 51; defined, 41–2; dyslexics' difficulty with, 42–4; open-ended nature of language and, 46–7; oral motor characteristics of, 267; pace of, 47–8; particulate principle and, 46–9, *47;* in words, counting, 184, 186, *186*
phonemic awareness, 51–5, 97–8, 144–5, *145,* 147, 177, 262, 263, 285; as predictor of ability to read, 55; developing an awareness of rhyme and, 177, 178–82; drawing child's attention to sounds of language and, 177–87; hints for building success in, 185–7; impairment of, 52–4, 55; linking letters to sounds and, 176, 178, 188; mutual reinforcement of reading and, 55; normal development of, 51–2, 54–5, 108–9; pulling apart words into sounds and, 122, 176, 177, 182–7; ready-made programs for, 187; separating syllables into phonemes and, 183–5; separating words into syllables and, 182–3; spelling and, 202
"Phonemic Awareness in Young Children," 187
phonics, 199–205, 262, 263, 285; complex letter-sound patterns and, 201; defined, 188; essentials of, 200–1; past criticisms of, 199; ready-made programs and, 204–5; patterns and rules taught in, 200, 201–2; simple letter-sound relationships and, 200–1; spelling and, 202, 204; two approaches to identifying words in, 202–3
"phonologic," derivation of word, 40
phonologic access, 146
Phonological Awareness Literacy Screening (PALS), 194
"Phonological Awareness Training for Reading," 187

phonologic awareness, 144, 264
phonologic memory, 145–6
phonologic model of dyslexia, 40–4; reading and, 43–4; speaking and, 42–3, 45
phonologic module: ability to distinguish speech sounds from noise and, 48–9; defined, 40; as genetically determined, 45; phonologic model of dyslexia and, 40–4
phonologic skills: evaluation of, 143–6, 148; importance of, 144–5
phonologic slips, 331
phonologic tests, 137, 139
phrenology, 62–4, *63*
physicians, renowned dyslexic, 117–18, 340–1, 359–64
picture books with rhymes/pattern/repetition, 226–7
picture cards, 183–5
pig latin, 137
Pilkey, Dar, 311
Pinker, Steven, 45
playing, 191
plays, alternative versions of, 284, 326–7
pleasure, reading for, 124, 126, 254, 255
plot summaries, 243, 244
poetry, 182, 225, 226, 271
positron emission tomography (PET), 69
posterior lobes, 75, *76*
posterior reading system, 78–81, *80, 84;* dyslexics' underactivation of, 81–4, *83,* 316; repair of, 85–6, *86,* 256; wiring of, in poor readers, 85
PowerPoint, 300, 331
practice, 254–5, 262; activities at home for, 211–29; choice of reading materials for, 220–9; fluency and, 257, 268–74; importance of, 188–90, 206, 257; reading aloud and, 232–3; during summer vacation, 286–7
Practices for Developing Accuracy and Fluency, 273
Praxis, 339
prefixes, 206–7, 217–18, 239–40, 266
preschool children, 380n; clues to dyslexia in, 122; evaluating phonologic skills and

reading-readiness of, 143–9; getting help for, 128; guide to development of reading-related skills in, 108; training of, to attend to sounds of words, 55

"pretending" to be dyslexic, 164–5

prevention of reading problems, 88, 172, 257, 261–4; two effective approaches for, 263–4

preview reading, 253, 256, 275–6, 327

private schools, nonspecialized, 295–9, 306

Proactive Beginning Reading, 263, 264

problem solving, 57, 58, 141, 366

procrastination, 313

Project Read, 386n

pronunciation, 94–5, 104, 207, 327; difficulties with, 5, 37–8, 39, 122, 123, 363; fluency and, 231, 232, 233; identification of dyslexia and, 94–5, 122, 123, 125; oral motor characteristics of phonemes and, 267; phonics and, 200–2, 203; of unknown words, 206

public radio, 327

public schools, 294–5, 296, 297, 306; benefits of, 294, 306; improvements in, 295; ineffectiveness of special education programs in, 281–2, 294

quadrigraphs, 201

QuickLink Pen, 329

Quicktionary Reading Pen II, 327

quiet, 323; during testing, 318, 320–1, 322

Rachel (adult), 11–12

Ranger Rick, 229

rapid automatic naming test (RAN), 146

Rasinski, Timothy, 270

Reach Out & Read Program, 380n

REACH System, 265–6

READ 180, 265

Read, Write & Type! Learning System, The, 263, 264, 282–3

Readability Reports, 222

Read All About It! (Trelease), 284

Readers' Theatre, 271

reading: as acquired act, 49–50; brain imaging and, 59, 70–5, 76–89; decoding and comprehension as major components of, 52, 53; increase in local blood flow during, 70; localization of brain function and, 65; more difficult than speaking, 49–51; mutual reinforcement of phonemic awareness and, 55; neural pathways of (*see* neural pathways of reading); proficiency in, amount of reading related to, 382n–383n, 384n; purpose of, 242, 244. *See also* comprehension; fluency

reading acquisition, 10, 102–10, 384n; appropriateness of instruction for child's individual needs and, 193–6, 210–11; checklists for, 196–7, 209–11; choice of reading program and, 208–10; comprehension and, 105–6, 241–7; decoding and, 102–3, 104, 177; drawing child's attention to sounds of language and, 177–87; early intervention programs and, 261–4; in first grade, 198–205; fluency and, 105, 230–5; gaining meaning from text and, 235; guide to development of skills related to, 108–10; importance of practice in, 188–90, 206, 257; invented spelling and, 191; judging your child's progress in, 112–15; at kindergarten level, 176–97; linking letters to sounds and, 102–3, 176–7, 178, 188; listening, playing, and imagining in, 191–3; logographic stage of, 102; most effective, scientifically proven methods for, 174–5; neural pathways developed in, 84–5, 85–6, 86, 104, 105, 177, 188–9, 220, 256, 257–8, 274; ongoing assessment of reading skills and, 194–5, 210–11, 277, 278–9; phonemic awareness and, 102–3, 176, 177–87; practice activities at home and, 211–29; recognition and writing of letters and, 190–1; research on normal rate of, 26–7; sight words and, 190, 202; sounding out small words and, 199–205; systematic phonics and, 199–205; taking apart bigger words and, 205–8, 212–13, 215–18; time spent reading each day and, 106, 107; unnaturalness of, 49–50, 203; vocabulary building and, 103–5, 106, 191–2, 236–41 reading aloud by child, 38, 244–5, 287; expected reading growth rates in, 278–9; fear of, 114, 124, 126; fluency and, 231, 232–5, 268–76, 335–6; in front of classmates, 253; guided repeated oral reading and, 232–3, 233–5, 272; identification of dyslexia and, 112–13, 114, 124, 126; materials for dyslexic high school students for, 274–5; observing your child's progress in, 112–13; with parents, 233–5, 272; rhythm of, 114; speeded word training and, 269–70; tests of, 134

reading aloud to child, 191, 192, 221, 380n; books suggested for, 192–3, 284–5; nurturing comprehension in, 241–7

Reading First, 175, 195, 204, 235, 263, 264, 282, 295, 306. *See also* No Child Left Behind

reading intervention, 87, 261–87; for adults, 288–93; after-school support and, 254–6, 272–4; age-related learning leap and, *265*, 265–6; brain imaging and, 85–6, *86*, 257–8; duration of, 259, 281; early identification of problem and, 30–1, 120–1, 257–8, 261; essentials of, 257–60, 262; fluency training and, 253, 262, 268–77; general language skills and, 286; group size in, 258; integration of regular schoolwork and, 252, 253–4, 275–6; intensity of instruction in, 258; in kindergarten and first grade, 261–4; monitoring progress in, 252, 255, 278–80; neural pathways developed in, 256, 257–8, 274; for older children, 264–8; public school programs for, 281–2, 294; quality of instruction in, 258–9; removing child from, 281; in sample comprehensive program (Sam), 252–4; sea of strengths and, 93, 172, 285–6. *See also* overcoming dyslexia; reading programs

Reading/Language Arts Framework for California Public Schools, 208

reading programs, 386n; adult literacy programs, 288–93; evaluation of, 208–10; evidence-based, 174–5, 209, 262–4; for fluency improvement, 272–3; for high-risk younger children, 263–4; for older children, 264–8; systematic phonics, 199–205; total "off-the-shelf" vs. eclectic, 262; whole language, 203, 204

reading tests: decoding and comprehension skills and, 133, 134; in evaluation for dyslexia, 133–5, 138, 148–9; fluency and, 134–5; oral reading and, 134; standardized, 278, 280, 281; timed, 155–6, 161, 163

ReadIt, 272–3

Read Naturally, 272

Read to Succeed, 291–2

reasoning, 36, 55, 57, *58*, 141, 235, 244, 285–6, 316–17, 331–2

receptive language, 66

reciting poems and jingles, 182

Recording for the Blind and Dyslexic (RFB&D), 284, 319–20, 324, 338

remediation, 172, 257. *See also* reading intervention

"Report of the National Reading Panel, Teaching Children to Read," 174–5, 295

Research-Based Framework for Houghton Mifflin Reading, A, 209

resource room instruction, 253

retention, 195–6

retrieval of words, 5, 57, 58, 96–7, 111, 123, 125, 138, 276, 330–1, 333

reversals of letters and words, 100–1

REWARDS (Reading Excellence: Word Attack and Rate Development Strategies), 267

rhymes, 122, 186; developing an awareness of, 177, 178–82; fMRIs and, 72–3, *73,* 76–7; identification of dyslexia and, 95–6; picture books with, 226–7

rhythm of reading, 114

"Road to the Code," 187

Rogers, Brandon (college student), 153–4, 156

Rome, ancient, 65

Romerio, Nicholas (Nikki) (medical student), 157–61, 162

Roy, C. S., 69

Sam (third grader), 251–6

Saris, Judge Patti, 164

SATs, 317, 339–40, 341, 342
saying c's rule, 212, 214–15
Schmidt, Johann, 14
schools: checklist of questions to ask about, 302–6; choosing, 294–308; getting help from, 128–30; priorities and, 302; private, nonspecialized, 295–9, 306; public, 294–5, 296, 297, 306; specialized, 296, 298–301, 307
Schwab, Charles, 317–18, 326, 356–9
Schwalbe, Kerri, 29
Scientific American, 31, 153, 332
scientists, renowned dyslexic, 117–18
ScreenSpeaker, 325
sea of strengths model of dyslexia, 57–8, 58, 93, 172,, 285–6
second graders, 113, 205, 206, 264–5; clues to dyslexia in, 123–5; expected fluency rates for oral reading in, 277; fluency among, 231; guide to development of reading-related skills in, 110; magazines for, 228, 229; practice activities at home for, 211–24; questions to ask about reading program of, 208–11
segmentation, 144, 182–3, 184, 185
self-confidence, 193
self-esteem, 117, 120, 124, 127, 199, 257, 346, 353, 358; interest or hobby and, 312; nurturing of, 309–13; special schools and, 299, 301
semantics, 41
sequence of events, recounting of, 243, 244
Seuss, Dr., 181
Shakespeare, William, 47, 326–7
Shaywitz, Bennett, 26
Sherrington, C. S., 69
shoelace tying, 101
short-term memory, phoneme pace and, 48
sight (irregular) words, 190, 202, 218–20, 262, 275
silent e rule, 212, 213–14, 221
Simmons, Deborah, 264
simplifying, 366
Slingerland Institute for Literacy, 386n
Smith, Stephen, 342
software. *See* computers
Sokoloff, Louis, 69–70

Soliloquy Reading Assistant, 273
songs, 271, 380n
soul, ancients' conceptions of, 59, 60
sound-based confusions, 42–3, 56, 56, 57, 58, 95, 96, 97, 123
sound comparison tests, 144
sounding out, 177, 222, 262; phonologic memory and, 145–6; smaller words, 199–205, 212; unknown or difficult words, 285. *See also* decoding
"Sounds Abound Program, The," 187
sounds of language: books that joyfully play with, 179–80; drawing child's attention to, 177–87; linking letters to, 51–2, 102–3, 111, 113, 122, 147, 148, 176–7, 178, 188, 199–205 (*see also* phonics); nonlanguage sounds vs., 48–9; pulling words apart into, 122, 176, 177, 182–7; rhymes and, 177, 178–82; sound-matching games and, 183–4
Spalding Education International, 386n
sparktop, children's Web site, 311
spatial difficulties, 101
Speaking Spelling Ace, 326
special education programs, 22–3, 33, 294; categorical model of dyslexia and, 27–9; eligibility for, 136; general ineffectiveness of, 281–2, 294; statistics on, 29
specialization: dyslexics' success with, 117–18, 126, 349, 352; word lists and, 276
specialized schools, 296, 298–301, 307; recommended (list), 307
speech: loss of, 65–6. *See also* spoken language
speech and language pathologists, 128, 143
speech recognition software, 325, 330
speeded word training, 269–70
speed-reading classes, 328
spell checkers, 114, 326, 330, 334
spelling, 5, 191, 207, 208, 254, 262, 330, 338; difficulties with, 21, 38, 114, 124, 126, 135, 202; effective instruction in, 202; invented or temporary, 191; learning process for, 182, 189; phonics and, 204
spelling tests, 135

Spelling Through Morphographs, 267
Spell Read P.A.T. (Phonemic Analysis Training), 266–7, 386n
Spider, 228, 229
spoken language, 17, *42;* comprehension of, 40; delay in, 94; difficulties with, 37–8, 39, 42–3; as innate and natural, 45, 49–50, 51; lack of fluency in, 276; listening and, 48, 49, 50; origins of, 45–6; phonemes and, 42; phonemic awareness and, 176, 177–87; printed word related to, 44, 45; pronunciation difficulties and, 37–8, 39; reading more difficult than, 49–51; sound-based confusions and, 42–3, 56, *56, 57,* 58, 95, 96, 97, 123
Sports Illustrated for Kids, 229
Spurzheim, Johann, *63,* 64
SQ3R approach, 323
Stanovich, Keith, 106
Starting Over, 290, 291
Sticht, Tom, 293
"sticky sounds," 310
stories, making up, 193
Story About Ping, The (Flack and Wiese), 242, 243, 244
Streamlined Shakespeare, 326–7
strengths in other areas, 24, 36, 37, 57–8, *58,* 295, 314; identification of dyslexia and, 93; placing emphasis on, 172; reading intervention and, 285–6; at various ages, 122–3, 124–5, 126–7
structural brain MRI, 69, 74–5
study groups, 328
subvocalization, 81
suffixes, 207, 217, 218, 239, 266
summer vacation, reading practice during, 286–7
supplemental programs, 263–4
Swedenborg, Emanuel, 62
Swonk, Diane, 311, 359
syllables: analyzing into phonemes, 98, 183–5, 206; breaking words into, 98, 182–3, 206
syntax, 41, 53
synthetic phonics, 202–3
Syracuse University, 169, 170

talking around a word, 96, 97
Tan (Leborgne), 64, *65*

teachers, 173, 284, 305; assessment by, 378n; classroom observations of, 147, 195, 211; interactions with, 210, 258, 259, 327–8; parents' consultation with, 128–9; reading, training and experience of, 258–9; working in harmony with, 187, 211, 212
temporal lobes, 75, *76*
Test of English as a Foreign Langauge (TOEFL), 339
Test of Word Reading Efficiency (TOWRE), 134, 255, 281
Test of Written Spelling-4, 135
tests: alternate formats for, 321, 328; extra time on, 253, 293, 314–18, 320, 322, 334, 336–7, 338; flagging scores of, taken with accommodations, 339–40; General Education Development (GED), 293; medical boards, 342, 360–1; multiple-choice, 126, 316–17, 328, 333–4, 340, 341–2, 344; quiet separate room for, 116, 318, 320–1, 322. *See also* evaluation; reading tests
Texas Education Agency, 194
Texas Primary Reading Inventory (TPRI), 194
textbooks: digitized, 254–5, 320, 324–5; information on difficulty of, 222, 223–4; previewing reading assignments in, 253, 256, 275–6, 327; on tape or CD-ROM, 254, 319–20, 321, 324
thinking, 115, 191, 235; dyslexics' exceptional skills in, 36, 53, 54, 57–8, 123, 125, 127, 349, 355, 357, 359, 365, 366; localization of brain function and, 61, 62
third graders, 113, 205, 206; clues to dyslexia in, 123–5; expected fluency rates for oral reading in, 277; guide to development of reading-related skills in, 110; magazines for, 228, 229; practice activities at home for, 211–24; questions to ask about reading program of, 208–11
three-phoneme words, 184, 185
Thumbprint Mysteries, 292
time: spent reading each day, 106, *107;* on tests, extra, 253, 293, 314–18, 320, 322, 334, 336–7, 338
Time for Kids, 229

tongue, inability to speak and, 65–6
Torgesen, Joseph K., 121, 384*n*
Treacher Collins, E., 21
Trelease, Jim, 284
trigraphs, 201
Turner, Ted, 359
tutoring, 255–6, 327; by older dyslexic students for younger students, 271–2
twin studies, 99
two-phoneme words, 184, 185

Ultimate Word Attack, 276
United States Medical Licensing Examination, 342, 361
University of California at Davis, 342–3
University of Colorado, 26
University of Oregon, 277
University of Virginia, 194

vague words, tendency to use, 96, 123
ventricles, *61,* 61–2
ViaVoice, 325
videos, of novels or plays, 284, 326–7
Virginia Department of Education, 194
vision, 49, 141
visual acuity, 15–17, 19; dyslexia incorrectly ascribed to defects in, 39–40
visual cues, words associated with, 102
visualization, 321, 323–4, 328, 366
vocabulary, 41, 52, 53, 54, 55, 57, *58,* 123, 198, 210, 262, 274, 286, 316–17, *317,* 320; building of, 103–5, 106, 111, 120, 191–2, 196, 220, 236–41, 276; choosing words for, 237–8; comprehension and, 106, 191, 192, 235; decoding ability and, 104, 111, 191–2; gained through everyday experiences, 240–1; instruction methods for, 236–40; parents' role in development of, 238–41; potentially difficult or unfamiliar words or concepts in, 242; size of, 236–7; specialization and, 118, 125, 276; spoken vs. written, 125, 236
vocabulary tests, 138, 148
vowel sounds, 206; omitted in invented spelling, 191; phonics and, 200–1

wait-and-see approach, 121, 128–30, 195
Wasserstein, Wendy, 310, 351–2

Wechsler Individual Achievement Test-II, 135
Wernicke, Carl, 66–7
Wernicke's aphasia, 67
Wernicke's area, *66*
whole language reading programs, 203, 204
Wide Range Achievement Test, Revised, 135
Wiese, Kurt, 242
Willis, Thomas, 62
Wilson Reading System, 266, 290–1, 386*n*
Windward School, 301
Winsford, Kara (independent school), 297–8
Wise, Barbara, 283
Woodcock-Johnson III, 134, 135
Woodcock Reading Mastery Tests (WRMT), 134, 147, 255, 280
word analysis, *78,* 79, 81
word attack, 133–4
word-blindness, 13–24; acquired alexia and, 14–17, 18; coining of term, 15; congenital, 16–17, 18–24
word derivations, 206–7, 217–18
word form area, *78,* 79–81, *80, 83, 86, 86,* 87, 104, 155, 231, 256, 280
word meaning, 41
word processing, 115, 283, 334
word roots, 206–7, 217–18, 239–40, 266
words: bigger, taking apart, 205–8, 212–13, 215–18; breaking into syllables, 98, 182–3, 206; compound, 206, 212, 215, 221; counting phonemes in, 184, 186, *186;* long, dividing between consonants, 206, 215–17, *216;* nonsense, 37–8, 133–4; pulling apart into sounds of language, 122, 176, 177, 182–7; rapid retrieval of, 5, 57, 58, 96–7, 111, 123, 125, 138, 276, 330–1, 333; reversals of, 100–1; sight (irregular), 190, 202, 218–20, 262, 275; small, sounding out, 199–205, 212; small "function," 111–12, 123; substituted, omitted, or mispoken, 114, 124, 126; unfamiliar, 104, 123, 126
WordSmith, 325
worldly knowledge, 120–1, 235, 255, 286, 327
World Reports, 229

writers, renowned dyslexic, 345–56
writer's block, 355
writing, 189; as acquired act, 49–50; backward, 100–1; composition difficulties and, 254; handwriting legibility and, 38, 114–15, 124, 254, 329, 330; letters, 109, 190–1
WYNN, 324–5, 327

Yale Law School, 339
Yale University, 26, 152, 319
Yale University School of Medicine, 169
Yopp, Hallie Kay, 180

Zang Fu, 60
Zuckerman, Barry, 380*n*

Permissions Acknowledgments

Figures 1, 3, 4, 8a, 8b, 9, 11, 35: © 2002 by S. E. Shaywitz.

Figures 2 and 34: © 2002 by S. E. Shaywitz, after D. J. Francis et al., "The Measurement of Change," in G. R. Lyon, ed., *Frames of Reference for the Assessment of Learning Disabilities* (Baltimore: Paul H. Brookes, 1994).

Figures 5, 7, 10, 31, 32, 33: Drawn by Yan Nascimbene.

Figure 6: Adapted from William Abler, "On the Particulate Principle of Self-Defining Systems," *Journal of Social and Biological Structures* 12 (1989): 1–13.

Figures 12, 15, 17, 19, 20, 21, 22, 24, 25, 27, 28: Drawn by W. Hill (© 2003 by S. E. Shaywitz).

Figure 13: Reproduced from *Origins of Neuroscience,* by Stanley Finger (New York: Oxford University Press, 1994), p. 33. Original produced by Johann Spurzheim in 1825.

Figure 14: Reproduced from *The Enchanted Loom,* edited by Pietro Corsi (New York: Oxford University Press, 1991), p. 217. Original photograph from Musee Dupuytren, Paris, courtesy of Dr. Jean-Louis Signoret.

Figure 16: Photograph by Jerry Domian (© 2003 by S. E. Shaywitz).

Figure 18: Photograph by B. A. Shaywitz (© 2003 by S. E. Shaywitz).

Figures 20, 22: fMRI images B. A. Shaywitz, Yale NMR Research.

Figure 23: Dehaene et al., "Cerebral Mechanisms of Word Masking and Unconscious Repetition Priming," *Nature Neuroscience* 4 (2001): 752–58.

Figure 26: E. Paulesu et al., "Dyslexia: Cultural Diversity and Biological Unity," *Science* 291 (2001) 2165–67.

Figure 29: Drawn by W. Hill, © 2003 by S. E. Shaywitz, based on data from R. O. Anderson, P. T. Wilson, and I. G. Fielding, "Growth in Reading and How Children Spend Their Time Outside of School," *Reading Research Quarterly* 23 (1988): 285–303.

Figure 30: Adapted from J. K. Torgesen, "Assessment and Instruction for Phonemic Awareness and Word Recognition Skills," in H. W. Catts and A. G. Kamhi, eds., *Language and Reading Disabilities* (Boston: Allyn & Bacon, 1999), p. 131.

A NOTE ABOUT THE AUTHOR

Sally Shaywitz, M.D., professor of pediatrics and codirector of the Yale Center for the Study of Learning and Attention, is a member of the Institute of Medicine of the National Academy of Sciences. A neuroscientist and pediatrician, she studies reading and writes frequently for scientific journals. Dr. Shaywitz collaborates closely with her husband, Bennett. They live in Connecticut and Martha's Vineyard.

A NOTE ON THE TYPE

This book was set in Caledonia, a Linotype face designed by W. A. Dwiggins (1880–1956). It belongs to the family of printing types called "modern face" by printers—a term used to mark the change in style of the type letters that occurred around 1800. Caledonia borders on the general design of Scotch Roman but it is more freely drawn than that letter.

Composed by North Market Street Graphics,
Lancaster, Pennsylvania
Printed and bound by Berryville Graphics,
Berryville, Virginia
Designed by Virginia Tan